IN AND OUT
OF OUR RIGHT MINDS

D1553564

(opposite) Lega six-faced pigmented wooden ritual figure, Congo-Kinshasa

IN AND OUT
OF OUR RIGHT MINDS

THE MENTAL HEALTH OF
AFRICAN AMERICAN WOMEN

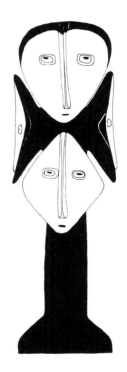

EDITED BY
DIANE R. BROWN
AND VERNA M. KEITH

COLUMBIA UNIVERSITY PRESS
NEW YORK

COLUMBIA UNIVERSITY PRESS

Publishers Since 1893

New York   Chichester, West Sussex

Copyright © 2003 Columbia University Press

Library of Congress Cataloging-in-Publication Data

In and out of our right minds : the mental health of African
    American women / edited by Diane R. Brown and
    Verna M. Keith
        p. cm.
    Includes bibliographical references and index.
    ISBN 0–231–11378–1 (cloth : alk. paper)—
    ISBN 0–231–11379–X (paper : alk. paper)
    1. African American women—Mental health I. Robinson-
Brown, Diane. II. Keith, Verna.

RC451.5.N415 2003
362.2'089'96073—dc21

                                                    2003046005

Printed in the United States of America

Designed by Lisa Hamm

c 10 9 8 7 6 5 4 3 2 1
p 10 9 8 7 6 5 4 3 2 1

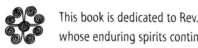 This book is dedicated to Rev. Eugene J. Robinson and Murphy M. Keith, whose enduring spirits continue to guide and inspire.

CONTENTS

ABOUT THE CONTRIBUTORS

EVELYN L. BARBEE, PH.D., is a Black feminist and nurse-anthropologist. She was educated at Teachers College, Columbia University, and the University of Washington. She has served on the faculties of the Massachusetts College of Pharmacy and Health Sciences, University of Wisconsin, and the University of Michigan. She also served as a visiting professor in the Department of Anthropology, Michigan State University, and the Department of Preventive Medicine of the Colorado Health Sciences Center. Dr. Barbee's writings are published in anthropology and nursing journals. Her research interests focus on cultural strategies used by women of color to deal with dysphoria and the impact of violence. Her research on dysphoria and Black women was supported by the National Science Foundation and the Bunting Fellowship Program at Radcliffe College, Harvard University

LULA A. BEATTY, PH.D., has a degree in psychology from Howard University and is chief of the Special Populations Office at the National Institute on Drug Abuse of the National Institutes of Health. Her areas of research expertise and interests are: drug abuse prevention, substance abuse in African American communities, drug abuse and women, health disparities, career development and research training, research infrastructure development, and child abuse and neglect.

DIANE R. BROWN, PH.D., is executive director of the Institute for the Elimination of Health Disparities at the University of Medicine and Dentistry of New Jersey and professor in the School of Public Health. Prior to that she was a professor and director of the Urban Health Program, College of Urban, Labor, and Metropolitan Affairs at Wayne State University. Dr. Brown also served as a health scientist administrator at the National Institutes of Health and as a faculty member at Howard University. She earned her Ph.D. from the University of Maryland, followed by postdoctoral work in psychiatric epidemiology at the Johns Hopkins University School of Public Health. Her research interests focus on health and mental health among African

Americans, women, and the elderly and on understanding how age, race, and gender influence health status, the use of health-care services, and clinical trial participation. She is a Fellow of the Gerontological Society of America.

CLEOPATRA H. CALDWELL, PH.D., earned her Ph.D. in social psychology from the University of Michigan. She is Assistant Professor in the Department of Health Behavior and Health Education in the School of Public Health at the University of Michigan. Dr. Caldwell's research interests include the intergenerational context of early childbearing; risk and protective factors for adolescent well-being; Black churches as community-based institutional support systems; and help-seeking behavior among African American women.

LINDA M. CHATTERS, PH.D., has a degree in psychology from the University of Michigan, with a specialization in gerontology. She holds a joint appointment as an associate professor in the School of Social Work and the Department of Health Behavior and Health Education at the School of Public Health, University of Michigan. She is also a faculty associate with the Program for Research on Black Americans Research Center for Group Dynamics at the Institute for Social Research. Her research interests include religion and health, religious involvement among African Americans, and social support within African American families. Dr. Chatters is principal investigator on a National Institute on Aging grant entitled, "Church-Based Assistance and Older Blacks" (AG18782).

DONNA L. COCHRAN, M.S.W., PH.D., earned her Ph.D. in social work and social psychology from the University of Michigan, followed by postdoctoral studies at Duke University. She has held a joint appointment as assistant professor at the Institute of Gerontology and the School of Social Work at Wayne State University. Her research has focused on older adults, health and intergenerational relationships in the context of African American and minority families, and the recruitment and retention of older African Americans in research.

LAWRENCE E. GARY, M.S.W., PH.D., is a professor in the School of Social Work at Howard University. He earned his doctorate from the University of Michigan and has held endowed chairs at Virginia Commonwealth University (Samuel S. Wertzel) and Hunter College (Henry and Lucy Moses). He has also held distinguished visiting professorships at several other universities. He has a long list of publications, including five books and monographs along with numerous research articles that appear in journals such as the *American Journal of Public Health, American Journal of Psychiatry, Behavioral Medicine, Community Mental Health Journal,* and *Journal of Health and Social Behavior,* among others. With a distinguished track record of research on mental health among African Americans, he is the recipient of numerous awards and citations.

BEVERLY A. GRAY, PH.D., is a professor of psychology in the College of Arts and Sciences and a core member of the Center for Working Class Studies at Youngstown State University, Youngstown, Ohio. She is a consultant with Associates in Counseling Services in Liberty, Ohio, and has conducted numerous workshops on occupational stress, coping, social networks, and diversity for academic, professional, and government organizations. Her publications and research interests include stress management, social support, psychotherapy, class and race issues, diversity, and spirituality, particularly among African Americans and other minorities.

PAMELA BRABOY JACKSON, PH.D., is an associate professor of sociology at Indiana University, Bloomington. She previously served on the faculty at Duke University and as a research fellow at the Center for the Study of Aging and Human Development at that same institution. Her research interests include the effects of social-role occupancy on mental health; stress and social support; and the experience of racism (and sexism among women) among the Black middle class.

VERNA M. KEITH, PH.D., is chair and associate professor of Sociology at Arizona State University. She completed her Ph.D. at the University of Kentucky and did postdoctoral work in the School of Public Health and the Institute of Gerontology at the University of Michigan. She has authored articles and book chapters on racial and gender stratification, life stress and mental health, and minority health care issues. Her work has appeared in the *American Journal of Sociology, Demography, Journal of Marriage and the Family,* and *Research on Aging.* She has served on numerous committees and/or held elective office in the Association of Black Sociologists, the American Sociological Association, and the Southern Sociological Society. Her research interests include the impact of problematic social relations on mental health, drug use among middle and high school students, and gender differences in the mental health of African Americans.

AURORA P. JACKSON, M.S.W., PH.D., is associate professor of social work at the University of Pittsburgh. Her areas of expertise and research interests include the following: maternal employment, sources of income, parenting, psychological well-being, and children's development in poor and near-poor families headed by single Black mothers. She has recent articles in *American Journal of Community Psychology, Child Development, Journal of Family Issues, Journal of Marriage and Family, Social Service Review, Social Work, Social Work Research,* and *Journal of Social Service Research.*

JAMES S. JACKSON, PH.D. is the Daniel Katz Distinguished University Professor of Psychology; professor of health behavior and health education, School of Public Health; and director of the Research Center for Group Dynamics, senior research scientist and director of the Program for Research on Black Americans, Institute for Social Research; and director of the Center for Afro-American and African Studies, all at the University of Michigan. He was elected in 2002 as a member of the Institute of Medicine of the National Academy of Sciences. He has conducted research and published numerous books, scientific articles, and chapters on international, comparative studies on immigration, race and ethnic relations, physical and mental health, adult development and aging, attitudes and attitude change, and African American politics. He is the principal investigator of the most extensive social and health survey conducted on the Black American population ever done, the National Survey of American Life supported by the National Institutes of Health.

KAREN D. LINCOLN, M.S.W., M.A., PH.D. is assistant professor in the School of Social Work at the University of Washington. Dr. Lincoln received her M.S.W., M.A. in sociology and Ph.D. in social work and sociology from the University of Michigan and is a former research assistant at the Institute for Social Research, Program for Research on Black Americans. The primary focus of her research has been the role of informal social support networks in the stress process among African Americans across the life course. Dr. Lincoln has published in the areas of positive and negative interaction and psychological well-being, and religious participation among African Americans. Her most recent work examines racial differences and the influence of personal and sociocultural factors in mental health.

ANNA L. RILEY, PH.D., is a scientific review administrator intern at the Center for Scientific Review, the National Institutes of Health. Prior to that she was a National Institute on Aging research fellow at the University of Michigan. She has also served as an assistant professor of sociology at the University of Missouri-Columbia. Her research examines the importance of employment and job conditions for African American women's mental health and older African Americans' psychological well-being.

MAXINE THOMPSON, PH.D., earned her Ph.D. from the University of Wisconsin-Madison. She is associate professor of sociology at North Carolina State University. Her research interests include networks of social support for adolescent mothers, social networks and supports of family members of persons with severe mental illness, and family structure and psychological well being among African American women.

M. BELINDA TUCKER, PH.D., earned her Ph.D. from the University of Michigan. She is a social psychologist and professor of psychiatry and biobehavioral sciences at the University of California, Los Angeles. Her research interests include the causes and consequences of changing patterns of family formation, cultural and familial contexts for adolescent achievement and transition to adulthood, and interethnic relations. Dr. Tucker is principal investigator on a national survey that examines the social context and social and psychological correlates of family formation behaviors and attitudes.

PREFACE

C ommon portrayals of African American women in the literature and popular media often depict them as "pillars" of the African American community. They are viewed as stalwart and nurturing mothers, sisters, wives, and grandmothers who are resilient in the face of all adversities. By implication, these portrayals suggest that African American women have few mental health–related problems. Yet at the same time the research literature and demographic data present a profile of African American women that by all accounts places them at increased risk for mental illness and psychological distress. Lower incomes, greater poverty and unemployment, unmarried motherhood, and poor physical health are factors that disproportionately affect African American women and that potentially can contribute to mental health problems. Given this demographic and social profile, it is amazing that African American women do not have higher rates of mental illness than those reported in epidemiologic field studies and in hospital admissions for mental illness. Accordingly, one of the objectives of this volume is to explore this apparent contradiction of strength and vulnerability.

No other publication of which we are aware has addressed the mental health of African American women on an empirical basis. Previous works on the health status of this group have covered factors that affect physical health but generally have omitted or have only cursorily dealt with factors associated with mental health. Although many African American literary scholars have written eloquently about the emotional and psychological experiences of African American women, their work has rarely encompassed empirical data. Such information is important, however, for making and changing public policies, as well as for establishing services to meet the mental health needs of African American women. Hence the impetus to pull together this volume.

The factors contributing to mental illness and mental health in general are complex and multifaceted, and this book is an effort to understand the specific issues that are relevant to the mental well-being of African American women in particular. This volume brings together the works of an emerging group of very talented African American women scholars whose research moves us closer to an understanding of the social, psychological, and cultural context of mental well-being for African American women. The analyses are based on scientific data and address issues of relevance to mental health researchers, practitioners and policy makers, and African American women themselves.

Unfortunately, this volume could not cover every aspect of mental health among African American women. Limitations of space and limitations of available data circumscribed our efforts. Thus we focus primarily on adult women, although we realize the importance of life span mental health issues that affect African American girls, as well as those that affect elderly Black women. We would have liked to cover more on Black mothers as well as childless Black women, middle-class Black women, and Black women in particular at-risk situations, such as those who are homeless and those who suffer from chronic illnesses. We also would have liked to expand the discussion on mental health services, diagnosis, and treatment.

In addition to the scholarly and scientific motivation for producing this volume, we have had personal experiences and observations that generated our interest in the mental well-being of African American women. As young girls growing up in Black churches in the South and in the North, we fairly often heard our pastors admonish their Sunday morning congregation to "praise God for allowing us to wake up clothed in our right minds," but it was only as adult women that we truly understood what the phrase "being in our right minds" meant and gained insight about what it meant to be "out of one's right mind." Most African American women can relate to this expression because they probably have wondered at different points in their lives if indeed they have been in their "right mind." Besieged and bombarded with a multitude of demands in our daily lives, at times we may have seen our humanity and sense of self—as women and as African Americans—challenged and shaken. Many among us have been kicked to the curb and disrespected, over and over again. While being out of one's mind may be an unsettling, surreal experience, being in one's right mind is reaffirming, with the clear knowledge that we are sane, that our perceptions and experiences are in sync. It means knowing who we are deep within our innermost being—even when the rest of the world is engaged in confusion and craziness.

While the two of us are trained as medical sociologists with empiricist reductionist perspectives, we serendipitously gained greater depth and insight in our understanding of African American women's mental health as a result of gathering the contributions to this volume. The process was certainly not a straight trajectory from start to finish. At times, in fact, it challenged our own sanity. It was interwoven with the many transitions and life changes that we face as African American women, among them the traumatic loss of loved ones, new jobs, the welcomed but life-altering addition of a new family member, and concerns centering around elder caregiving responsibilities. As a result, the book took much longer than we had anticipated. In the long run, however, these life experiences deepened our understanding and appreciation of the contexts in which African American women strive to maintain their mental well-being.

We want to express our appreciation to our coauthors and our copy editor Jan McInroy and to Columbia University Press for their patience and support throughout this process. Many other persons were also instrumental in helping us with this effort, including Alma Young, dean of the College of Urban, Labor, and Metropolitan Affairs at Wayne State University, who provided financial support; William Eaton and Lawrence Gary, who provided the intellectual foundation; the Urban Health Program staff at Wayne State University—Terrence Crimes, Cheryl Miree, Lari Warren-Jeanpiere, Angela Boyce-Mathis, Krim Lacey, and Ebony Lee—as well as Marcella Jones from Arizona State University's Department of Sociology and Mylka Blascochea from the University of Medicine and Dentistry of New Jersey. Much appreciation also goes to Howard Chilcoat, Amy Pienta, Corey Smith, and Myriam Torres for their help with the data acquisition and analysis, and to Ronald Manderscheid from the Substance Abuse and Mental Health Services Administration (SAMHSA) for his assistance with data on mental health services. Our thanks also are due our colleagues Juan Battle, Velma Ward, and Bette Woody for lending an ear and for being a steady source of encouragement.

Finally, we want to express our appreciation and love to our families—George and Rochelle Blair and L. Ray Carr—for their sacrifices and support so that we could work on this project.

Diane R. Brown
Verna M. Keith

PART I

INTRODUCTION

i am in a box
on a tight string
subject to pop
without notice

everybody says how strong
i am
only black women
and white men
are truly free
they say

its not difficult to see
how stupid they are

—Nikki Giovanni, "Boxes," in
Selected Poems of Nikki Giovanni
(New York: Morrow, 1996)

1 A CONCEPTUAL MODEL OF MENTAL WELL-BEING FOR AFRICAN AMERICAN WOMEN

Diane R. Brown

At the outset it is important to articulate the perspective that guides this book. This volume focuses on the societal factors that affect mental health and mental illness among African American women. Although medical science endeavors to identify biological and genetic bases for mental health and mental illness, we contend that societal factors are the most salient influences on the mental well-being of African American women. The primacy of such societal factors as race, gender, and social class shapes the reality in which African American women experience their lives. Their lives differ from those of African American men and from those of women of other racial and ethnic groups. Given the uniqueness of their social *location* in American society and the experiences that this location engenders, conceptual models of mental well-being that work for Caucasian and other women are not likely to apply to African American women. Accordingly, we need to develop a conceptual model of mental well-being for African American women that is distinct from models for other racial and gender subgroups of the U.S. population.

For the purposes of this discussion, race and gender are viewed primarily as social constructs. In contrast to biological or genetic conceptions of race, the social construction of race embodies perceptions based upon phenotype, specifically skin color, and other physical features, as well as cultural practices by which we ascertain that one is African American or not. Similarly, gender is viewed as a social construct to which we ascribe particular physical traits, social roles, and normative behaviors associated with being feminine or masculine.

Being Black and being female in American society are two social statuses that are derogated and less valued than others; specifically, they are less valued than being Caucasian and being male. Occupying these two disadvantaged social statuses not only influences how African American women see themselves but also shapes the perceptions, expectations, and responses of others toward them, as illustrated by the stereotypical low-status perceptions of African American women as mammies, domestic workers, welfare mothers, domineering matriarchs, and prostitutes (Gilkes 1983; Smith 1988). The responses of others to those who are *African American and female* are evidenced by the racism and sexism that African American women encounter on a daily basis.

A diagram of our conceptual framework is presented in figure 1.1. We use the broad term *mental well-being* to refer to the full spectrum of mental states. The terms *mental health, mental illness,* and *mental disorder* are defined in chapter 2.

By definition, racism is discriminatory treatment based upon a social construction of race. Within the context of African American women's mental well-being, it is most commonly perpetrated by non–African Americans. However, racism internalized by African Americans can also affect their mental well-being (Taylor, Henderson, and Jackson 1991). Sexism consists of discriminatory treatment based upon a social construction of gender. African American women are the targets of sexist behavior from males, irrespective of race, as well as from women who have internalized sexist perspectives. These dually disadvantaged statuses render African American women vulnerable to the conjunctive effects of racism and sexism in ways that no other race and gender subgroup of the U.S. population endures. Whether overt or covert, institutionalized or individualized, experiences of racism and sexism are critical aspects of the social context in which African American women strive to maintain their mental well-being. Neither African American men, with whom they share a racial identity, nor women of other racial or ethnic groups face the same combination of race and gender-based threats to their mental well-being that occur at the macro (societal), meso (community and neighborhood), and micro (individual) levels (Zsembik 1995).

Figure 1.1 also shows that the race and gender statuses occupied by African American women have a direct impact on their socioeconomic status (SES), i.e., their level of economic and material resources and their opportunities for enhancing their material well-being. The racism and sexism associated with being *African American and female* serve to diminish personal and household income, educational attainment, occupational achievements, and overall wealth accumulation. Racism and sexism also limit access to resources and opportunities for socioeconomic advancement such that African American women have far fewer resources than their White counterparts, and thus their ability to achieve economic security and to cope with life's crises and adversities is limited.

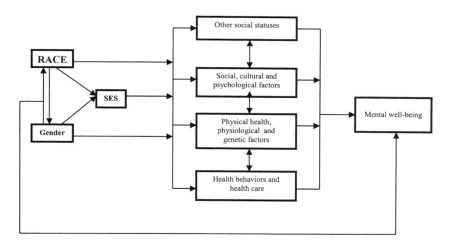

FIGURE 1.1 Conceptual Framework of African American Women's Mental Well-Being

It is fairly well documented that the educational achievement of African American women tends to be lower than that of White women. In 2000, 78.7 percent of African American women twenty-five and and older had four years of high school or more, and 16.8 percent had completed four or more years of college. In comparison, 88.4 percent of White women twenty-five and older had completed at least four years of high school, and 25.5 percent had completed four or more years of college (U.S. Census Bureau 2000a). It is also important to note that while African American women on the whole have less education than Whites, they have higher levels of education than African American men. In 2000 among African Americans fifteen and older, 41.1 percent of African American women had obtained at least some post-secondary education in comparison to 37.4 percent of African American men (U.S. Census Bureau 2000b). The higher level of educational attainment is not without ramifications for the mental well-being of African American women, given that the female/male gap in education may have an effect on the availability of eligible mates and the dynamics of Black male-female relationships, as well as family and marital stability.

As another indicator of socioeconomic status, occupation is important to mental well-being not only because of the monetary resources gained but also because of the opportunity to use one's talents and skills and to take advantage of a source of self-fulfillment. The low-status occupations in which many African American women are employed, however, tend to allow little discretion over work tasks, consist of backbreaking, physically and mentally exhausting work, expose them to occupational hazards, and are characterized by poor social relations (Leigh and Lindquist 1999). Data from March 1999 indicate that only 24 percent of all employed African American women held managerial or professional positions; approximately 38 percent held technical, sales, or administrative positions; and approximately 27 percent held service positions, with many of those still engaged in domestic work. In contrast, 35 percent of White women held managerial and professional specialty positions; 41 percent were in technical, administrative, and sales jobs; and only 15 percent were in service jobs as operators, fabricators, and laborers (McKinnon and Humes 2000).

Racism and sexism play a part not only in the occupations of African American women but also in the income and benefits they receive. According to the U.S. Census Bureau (2001a), the median annual income for African American women in 2000 was $16,081, in comparison to $16,218 for White women, $21,662 for Black men, and $29,696 for White men. With regard to employee benefits, African American women working full-time are less likely to have employer-provided retirement plans than their White counterparts (Herz, Meisenheimer, and Weinstein 2000).

African American women are nearly three times as likely as White women to live in poverty. In 2000, nearly a quarter (22.9 percent) of African American women had incomes that fell below the poverty line, while only 8.3 percent of White women faced similar circumstances (U.S. Census Bureau 2001b). Furthermore, poverty is highest in families headed by African American women. In 2000, 44.9 percent of families headed by Black women lived in poverty, in comparison to 29.0 percent of families headed by White women (U.S. Census Bureau 2001b). Poorer and with fewer economic resources, a substantial proportion of African American women must struggle continually to make ends meet. Poverty and low income, in turn, increase the likelihood that they will be exposed to another form of discrimination, that of *classism,* or prejudice against the poor. In her work with women and psychotherapy, Russell (1996) contends that the devaluation and stigmatization of poor and working-class individuals affect not only their self-concept and self-esteem but also their relationships with others. McDonald (1997) elaborates on the hidden psychosocial costs of classism for Black women, especially African American mothers, resulting in their isolation and lack of cross-class communal support. Altogether, classism combined with racism and sexism can have a devastating impact on the lives of African American women.

Figure 1.1 shows that the triangulation of race, gender, and socioeconomic status is a key factor in African American women's mental well-being. While the singular impacts of race, gender, and socioeconomic status critically affect the mental well-being of African American women, the combined and multiplicative effects have even more powerful consequences. The triangulation of these three factors may also affect mental well-being through its impact on other social statuses; social, cultural, and psychological factors; physical health and biological and genetic factors; and health behaviors and health care. The figure also depicts the complex interrelationships among these factors.

OTHER SOCIAL STATUSES

Among the social statuses associated with mental well-being are being older, married, a mother, head of household, and being employed. The relationship of age to mental well-being may depend on one's stage in the life cycle as well as on the sociocultural context and socioeconomic status. The challenges to mental well-being that younger African American women face typically arise from struggling to define and redefine themselves in terms of intimate and family relationships, childrearing, employment, and economic viability. Older African American women, on the other hand, may have developed resiliency and effective coping strategies with regard to many of the family, economic, and physical health issues, but now must confront ageism (prejudice against older people).

As another important social status that has implications for the mental well-being of African American women, marriage is associated with enhanced emotional, instrumental, and economic support (Brown 1996). African American women are less likely than White women to be married, however, and if married, they more likely to be divorced or widowed. In 2000, only 28.9 percent of African American women fifteen and over were married, in contrast to 54.4 percent of White women (U.S. Census Bureau 2001c). Further, 42.4 percent of African American women had never been married, 9.6 percent were widowed, and 17.5 were separated or divorced. Among White women, 22.1 percent had never been married, 10.2 percent were widowed, and 22.1

percent were separated or divorced (U.S. Census Bureau 2001c). Among the factors contributing to the higher proportions of unmarried African American women are joblessness, incarceration, and economic marginality among Black men (Benin and Keith 1995). It is important to note that even among married African American women, the benefits may not be the same as they are for White women. More likely to be employed than married White women, Black women still perform most of the traditional chores of cooking and cleaning (Broman 1988). Most important, the African American wife must cope with the effects of racism on her husband's earning ability and his mental well-being.

At the same time that African American women are less likely to be married, they are more likely to be mothers, and to be single mothers. In 2000 the birthrate among African American women was 17.6 per 1,000 women aged 15–44 in comparison to 14.1 for White women in the same age group (Martin et al. 2002). Further, the birthrate among unmarried Black women was 71.5 per 1,000, while among similar White women the rate was 27.9 per 1,000 (Ventura et al. 2001). The majority of single mothers are also heads of household and assume the major economic responsibility for housing, food, clothing, transportation, and other necessities for household members, as well as undertaking nurturing and household maintenance tasks. According to the U.S. Census Bureau (2001d), in 2000 African American women headed 29.7 percent of all Black family households. In contrast, White women with no spouse present constituted approximately 9.6 percent of the total White family households. The households headed by Black women are often larger, and frequently multigenerational, including minor children and sometimes adult children, as well as older adults and often nonrelatives or pseudo kin. Among female householders with no spouse present, 62.6 percent of African American women had three or more household members, in comparison to 42.8 percent of Whites (McKinnon and Humes 2000).

Being employed outside the home is another social status that African American women have historically been more likely to hold than White women have. Among people occupying positions of paid employment, 65.6 percent of African American women twenty and older were employed in 2000, in comparison to 60.2 percent of White women in that age group (U.S. Bureau of Labor Statistics 2001). At the same time that employment is greater among African American women than among White women, unemployment is also higher. Specifically, in 2000, 6.3 percent of African American women were unemployed, in comparison to 3.1 percent of White women (U.S. Bureau of Labor Statistics 2001). Being employed in most cases is essential to maintaining the family's quality of life as well as one's own individual mental well-being, particularly because African American women are apt to be the major breadwinners in their households, whether or not there are spouses or partners living with them.

SOCIAL, CULTURAL, AND PSYCHOLOGICAL INFLUENCES

Our conceptual model shows that numerous social, cultural, and psychological factors also influence mental well-being, at times enhancing it, at other times having a negative effect. Among social factors that have a deleterious effect on the mental well-being of African American women are stressors resulting from the triangulation of racism, sexism, and low socioeconomic status (Allen and Britt 1983). In particular, poverty and chronic economic pressure present demands that challenge the adaptive abilities of many African American women. Also, African American women may be exposed to more stressful circumstances than other women because of the particular set of roles that they must fulfill. As noted above, African American women have historically combined employment, childrearing, and family roles, thus increasing the likelihood of role overload and role conflict, particularly in circumstances where coping resources are limited. African American women who hold a demanding job, are single parents raising young children without the support of the father, and engaged in multiple caregiving roles for grandchildren, aging relatives, adult children, and other kin who may be unemployed, ill, or disabled experience acute role overload.

Being upwardly mobile and in the middle class does not necessarily protect African American women from encountering myriad stressors and strains. While having greater economic resources can reduce some stress exposure, strain may still result from the marginality they experience as people who are part of two cultures (African American and Euro-American) but not wholly in either. As further noted by Chisholm (1996), many African American women professionals experience a profound schism between their professional lives and their personal lives. They exist uncomfortably in both worlds and are perceived and treated differently in each.

Additional social influences on the mental well-being of African American women may stem from their residential and physical environment. The combination of race, gender, and low socioeconomic status tends to circumscribe the choice of residential settings available to them, increasing the likelihood that they will live in inner-city, segregated neighborhoods characterized by substandard housing. Both acute and chronic stressors are linked to concerns about inadequate services and safety in their neighborhoods and living environments. African American women and their families may be exposed to environmental hazards such as asbestos insulation, lead poisoning, and pest infestation; they and their families may develop health problems stemming from housing decay, inadequate ventilation, air and noise pollution, or faulty heating, wiring, and plumbing systems (Zsembik 1995). Another persistent concern for many African American women centers on having access to jobs, transportation, grocery stores, health care, and other goods and services, as well as to quality educational institutions for their children and themselves. Those who live in inner-city neighborhoods are also less apt to have access to recreational and cultural amenities such as parks, playgrounds, fountains, jogging and bicycle paths, libraries, museums, and arboretums—resources that are readily available to residents of more affluent neighborhoods (Zsembik 1995). In poorer neighborhoods, the amenities that do exist are often not well maintained or safe, given fewer economic resources and higher rates of crime in inner-city neighborhoods. African American women are more likely than White women to find themselves in life-threatening situations as the victims of sexual harassment (Hine 1995; Wyatt and Riederle 1995), domestic violence, sexual assault, and physical injuries (Marsh 1993; Leigh and Lindquist 1999) and homicide (Stevens et al. 1999).

The cultural values, beliefs, and practices that are promulgated in African American communities can also have important positive and negative ramifications for the mental well-being of African American women. Traditional psychiatry, however, has given insufficient attention to understanding the impact of African American culture on the mental well-being of African Americans, irrespective of gender. Culture influences one's perceptions of the world and shapes interpretations of life experiences. It also provides a sense of identity, along with norms and customs pertaining to social interactions. Contemporary African American culture represents nearly every region of the globe from Africa, Europe, and the Caribbean to South America, as well as varying degrees of urbanicity (urban, small city, rural) and regions within the United States (north, south, east, west). While aspects of culture may at times be a powerful source for promoting mental well-being, at other times and under other circumstances, aspects of culture can be detrimental.

Among the characteristics of African American culture that have positive effects for the mental well-being of African American women are valued relationships with others (Akbar 1991), including involvement in extended family and friendship networks. These connections with kin, friends, and coworkers not only provide a source of social support for African American women but also offer them the opportunity to derive pleasure from giving reciprocal support and care to others (Lawton et al. 1992; Brown and Monye

1995). The importance of the family as an African American sociocultural institution is well documented by Billingsley (1968, 1992) and others.

> My childhood was surrounded by family members who worked extremely hard to rise above prejudicial laws and customs. Expressing racial pride through their values and standard of behavior as good, ambitious people, they benefited and contributed to the growing concern for black civil rights on a personal and local level.
> (GARROD ET AL. 1999:191)

EXTENDED FAMILIES and friends have historically provided African American women with many of the resources needed to cope with family, job, and other demands. Especially those women who are young or poor depend on extended family and pseudo kin to help relieve work and family role strain. It appears, however, that changing demographics and declining economic opportunities in African American communities are severely challenging the African American extended family's ability to fulfill its traditional supportive functions (Benin and Keith 1995). It is not clear that modern African American families, especially those headed by women alone, receive the support from family networks that they need.

Other positive cultural influences on mental well-being may come from Black women's spirituality and social participation in religious and community organizations.

> Members of my church always encouraged my efforts, pushed me to do more, and told me they were proud of me. . . . My personal relationship with God became the most important factor in my success and in the preservation of my sanity and self-esteem.
> (GARROD ET AL. 1999:191)

CHERYL GILKES (2001) has eloquently described the significant roles that African American women have undertaken in their churches and their communities. Gilkes notes that both churched and unchurched Black women persistently attest to the sustaining power of their religious tradition and how it has aided in the survival of Black women, their families, and their communities. She goes on to describe how involvement in the church is linked to social participation in neighborhood, community action, civil rights, and political and economic organizations on the local, regional, and national levels. Overall, the participation of African American women in voluntary organizations has been a source of empowerment that has helped them to combat the oppression associated with race, gender, and poverty (Terborg-Penn 1985; Collins 2000).

Within African American communities, some aspects of the culture do serve as sources of distress for African American women. While on the one hand, family relationships may provide social support, on the other, they can sometimes have a negative impact that is detrimental to mental well-being (Okun and Keith 1998). Involvement with family members can be particularly stressful if they have chronic financial, physical, or emotional problems. Of concern also are family conflicts stemming from parent/child, sibling, and male/female relationships.

Many African American women experience distress because of the continuing social preferences in their communities for lighter skin color, long, straight hair, and Caucasoid features. Despite the increased social value given to the beauty of "Blackness" and the greater presence of African American models in fashion and beauty advertisements, African American women are still confronted with Euro-American standards of beauty (St. Jean and Feagin 1998). For African American women hair and skin color become complex issues not only as social, political, and fashion statements but also in terms of self-perceptions and self-esteem. Particularly among young African American girls, excessive concern about the length and texture of the hair may have negative consequences for social adjustment (Greene, White, and Whitten 2000).

African American cultural stereotypes may also affect African American women's perceptions and expectations of themselves. Socialized differently than White women are (Ladner 1972), they are expected to be mothers, to be independent, to be caregivers, and to assume extended-family obligations. While these subtle cultural expectations may serve as positive influences on the mental well-being of many African American women, they may have deleterious effects for others. According to hooks (1993), as African American women, "we feel it is necessary to keep it all together. Black women are so well socialized to push ourselves past healthy bounds that we often do not know how to set protective boundaries that would eliminate certain forms of stress in our lives."

PHYSICAL HEALTH, BIOLOGICAL AND GENETIC FACTORS

On the basis of the literature, the conceptual framework also contends that substantial interplay exists between mental well-being and physical health. Poor physical health can be distressing, especially if the condition is debilitating, is life-threatening, or requires a drastic change in lifestyle.

Good physical health is an important personal resource, while poor health limits one's ability to deal with the challenges of daily living. It is well documented that African American women tend to have poorer health than their White counterparts, and it is also likely that their mental well-being is more likely to be affected. For example, African American women have disproportionately greater morbidity associated with diabetes, hypertension, HIV, and lupus than do White women (Leigh and Lindquist 1999; National Center for Health Statistics 2000). With regard to mortality, deaths from heart disease, cancer, cerebrovascular disease, AIDS, and diabetes are higher for African American women than for White women (Leigh and Lindquist 1999). Overall, national data indicate a life expectancy at birth for African American women that is 5.2 years shorter than that for White women (Andersen 2001).

Although poor physical health may have a detrimental effect on mental well-being for many African American women, it is only one of many challenges that they face. Despite physical illness and disability, African American women are much more likely than White women to continue working and fulfilling household responsibilities (Brown 1988). The multiple demands that many African American women must face even when confronted with a life-threatening illness are illustrated by a comment from one participant in a focus group of women recently diagnosed with breast cancer: "Could not even think about it [breast cancer] because of taking care of my mother. . . . There was just too much happening. It was a shock when I found out. . . . I was in denial. I can't believe this is happening. I'm taking care of too many people, you know . . . the grandkids . . . my mother, and I don't really even have the time."

Finally, the conceptual framework shows that biological and genetic factors have potential implications for the mental well-being of African American women. In recent years scientists have increasingly focused on examining associations between biological factors and mental well-being (Goodman 2000; Conrad 2001). For example, specific studies have linked genetics to antisocial behavior among women (Goldstein, Prescott, and Kendler 2001), while other research has found that the genetic epidemiology of Alzheimer's dementia appears to differ between African Americans and Whites (Froehlich, Bogardus, and Inouye 2001). Nonetheless, there is no scientific evidence to date that identifies any biological or genetic factor uniquely associated with the mental well-being of African American women. Further exploration is clearly needed to determine the extent to which biological and genetic factors affect any race differences in mental well-being.

Most important, it would be essential for such research to control for the effects of social and physical environment factors on biology.

HEALTH BEHAVIORS AND HEALTH CARE

The conceptual framework also posits that health behaviors have implications for the mental well-being of African American women. The general assumption is that specific health-promoting behaviors such as getting regular exercise and eating a balanced, nutritious diet can positively affect mental well-being (Fox 1999). Current research is documenting a negative association between obesity and mental well-being (Carpenter et al. 2000; Siegel, Yancey, and McCarthy 2000). This is a particularly important indicator for African American women, given their greater prevalence of obesity. According to the National Center for Health Statistics (2000), 37.7 percent of Black women were reported to be obese, compared with 23.5 percent of White women. Thompson (1996) contends that eating problems begin as survival strategies to cope with traumas stemming from sexual abuse, racism, classism, sexism, and poverty. It is likely that other lifestyle behaviors, such as cigarette smoking, use of alcohol and illicit drugs, and engaging in risky sexual behaviors, also impinge on the mental well-being of African American women. Although they are less likely to use cigarettes and alcohol and have a lower lifetime use of illicit drugs (Wiemann, Berenson, and San Miguel 1994), their use of these substances may help to anesthetize them and alleviate the distress of the racism, gender oppression, and economic strain that they endure (Leigh and Lindquist 1999; Hummer 1996; Thompson 1996). It is important to note that health behaviors are not just individual preferences but are influenced by social forces such as racism, sexism, socioeconomic instability, targeted marketing, education, and cultural values (Hummer 1996; Cooper and Simmons 1985; Ahmed et al. 1994).

Health care is another dimension of the conceptual framework that is related to mental well-being. Access to quality health care is critical for mental well-being—better health care translates to healthier, longer lives (Hummer 1996). Ideally, quality health care for African American women includes access to and utilization of mental health services that are culturally appropriate and sensitive to the social context of their lives (Chisholm 1996). In fact, primary care physicians often serve as gatekeepers for referrals to mental health or behavioral health services, particularly in managed-care organizations. Furthermore, the nature and duration of mental health services may be restricted, and clients—even those who are insured—may incur out-of-pocket costs. Access to mental health services is also very much related to socio-economic status and the ability to acquire adequate health insurance coverage. For African American women, however, other factors such as cultural beliefs, stigma, and lack of understanding of the nature and treatability of mental illness also influence the use of mental health services (U.S. Department of Health and Human Services 2001).

IN SUMMARY, the conceptual framework provides a basis for understanding those factors that affect the mental well-being of African American women. It links what we know about the lives of African American women with the research on mental well-being. The model emphasizes the social factors that impinge on the mental well-being of African American women. The impact of race, gender, and socioeconomic status and the associated macro social forces of racism, sexism, and classism are fundamental. For African American women, the convergence of these factors in their lives is extremely powerful, for they affect and transform other social statuses, social, cultural, and psychological resources, physical health, health behaviors, and health care—all of which further affect mental well-being.

It is important to note that the conceptual framework is not socially deterministic. The major components of the model combine in different ways for different African American women, encompassing the vast heterogeneity of this population. Not all African American women are poor single mothers living in the inner city. Many are married, highly accomplished professional women. Others are homemakers, retirees, bus drivers, community organizers, and volunteers. Nonetheless, no matter where they fall on the spectrum of social statuses, the reality of their race, gender, and socioeconomic status has implications for their mental well-being. As Collins (2000) noted, being Black and female in the United States continues to expose African American women to certain common experiences. The relationships among the components in the model are complex, and much remains to be learned about how they operate. Building upon this conceptual framework, the chapters in this volume go on to address in more detail some of the factors that influence the mental well-being of African American women.

ORGANIZATION OF THE BOOK

The book is divided into six parts. This first part has articulated the conceptual framework and discussed the salient social factors that permeate the lives of African American women. Part 2 provides definitions of *mental health* and *mental illness,* along with epidemiological data on mental illness and mental health among African American women and data on the prevalence of the major disorders identified in the fourth edition of the American Psychiatric Association's *Diagnostic and Statistical Manual of Mental Disorders (DSM-IV).* This section also highlights those segments of the population of African American women who are most at risk for poor mental health. Lula Beatty (chapter 3) presents a demographic and psychological profile of African American women who abuse drugs and discusses the consequences, along with approaches for prevention and treatment.

Part 3 focuses on race, gender, and aspects of African American culture that affect the mental well-being of African American women. In chapter 4, Diane Brown, Verna Keith, James Jackson, and Lawrence Gary analyze the impact of both chronic and acute experiences of racial discrimination on psychological well-being. Evelyn Barbee, writing on violence and rape against African American women, uses a qualitative case study approach to describe the relationships between violence and depression (chapter 5). Verna Keith and Maxine Thompson (chapter 6) examine the importance of skin color for self-concept and mental well-being among African American women.

Part 4 examines the mental well-being of African American women in terms of the particular social statuses and roles they occupy, specifically focusing on marriage, employment, socioeconomic status, and family caregiving roles. The section begins with Belinda Tucker's investigation of the impact of male/female relationships on mental well-being, which analyzes data from a twenty-one-city study (chapter 7). In contrast, Aurora Jackson, in chapter 8, focuses on low-income, non-married Black mothers and how the involvement of their children's fathers affects the mothers' mental well-being. In chapter 9, Pamela Jackson explores the importance of income and socioeconomic status to the mental well-being of married African American women. In chapter 10, Anna Riley and Verna Keith take an in-depth look at the association between employment and job conditions and the expressed life satisfaction of African American women. Chapter 11 concludes the section with Diane Brown and Donna Cochran's analysis of the experiences of midlife and older African American women in managing the multiple role responsibilities associated with being wife, mother, volunteer, and caregiver.

Part 5 explores cultural factors and other strategies used to protect against poor mental health and to enhance mental well-being. Karen Lincoln and Linda Chatters (chapter 12) present empirical findings on the role of religion in maintaining the mental well-being of African American women. Beverly Gray and Verna Keith (chapter 13) review research findings on the critical contribution to mental well-being of social support from family members and friends, and Cleopatra Caldwell (chapter 14) covers the use of formal and informal mental health services by African American women. Finally, Verna Keith's concluding commentary in part 6 presents a critical summary of the major mental health issues pertaining to African American women, identifying remaining gaps in the literature and offering recommendations for future research.

REFERENCES

Ahmed, F., D. R. Brown, L. E. Gary, and F. Saadatmand. 1994. Religiosity as a predictor of cigarette smoking among women of childbearing age. *Journal of Behavioral Medicine* 20 (1): 34–43.

Akbar, N. 1991. The Evolution of Human Psychology for African Americans. In R. L. Jones, ed., *Black Psychology,* 99–123. Berkeley, Calif.: Cobb and Henry.

Allen, L. and D. W. Britt. 1983. Black women in American society: A resource development perspective. *Issues in Mental Health Nursing* 5 (1–4): 61–79.

Andersen, R. N. 2001. United States life tables. *National Vital Statistics Reports* 48 (18): 1–35. Hyattsville, Md.: National Center for Health Statistics.

Benin, M. and V. M. Keith. 1995. The social support of employed African American and Anglo mothers. *Journal of Family Issues* 16 (3): 275–297.

Billingsley, A. 1968. *Black Families in White America.* Englewood Cliffs, N.J.: Prentice Hall.

———. 1992. *Climbing Jacob's Ladder: The Enduring Legacy of Black Families.* New York: Simon and Schuster.

Broman, C. 1988. Household work and family life satisfaction among Blacks. *Journal of Marriage and the Family* 50:743–748.

Brown, D. R. 1988. *Employment and Health Among Older Black Women: Implications for Their Economic Status.* Wellesley College Center for Research on Women. Working Paper Series.

———. 1996. Marital status and mental health. In J. S. Jackson and H. W. Neighbors, eds., *Mental Health in Black America,* 77–94. Thousand Oaks, Calif.: Sage.

Brown, D. R. and D. B. Monye. 1995. *Midlife and Older Caregivers of Urban School-Aged Children.* Final Report to the AARP Andrus Foundation. Washington, D.C.

Carpenter, K. M., D. S. Hasin, D. B. Allison, and M. S. Faith. 2000. Relationships between obesity and DSM-IV major depressive disorder, ideation. and suicide attempts: Results from a general population study. *American Journal of Public Health* 90 (2): 251–257.

Chisholm, J. F. 1996. Mental health issues in African-American women. *Annals of the New York Academy of Sciences* 789:161–179.

Collins, P. H. 2000. *Black Feminist Thought: Knowledge, Consciousness, and the Politics of Empowerment.* 2d ed. New York: Routledge.

Conrad, P. 2001. Genetic optimism: Framing genes and mental illness in the news. *Culture, Medicine, and Psychiatry* 25 (2): 225–247.

Cooper, R. and B. Simmons. 1985. Cigarette smoking and ill health among Black Americans. *New York State Journal of Medicine* 85 (7): 344–349.

Fox, K. R. 1999. The influence of physical activity on mental well-being. *Public Health Nutrition* 2 (3A): 411–418.

Froehlich, T. E., S. T. Bogardus, Jr., and S. K. Inouye. 2001. Dementia and race: Are there differences between African Americans and Caucasians? *Journal of the American Geriatric Society* 49 (4): 477–484.

Garrod, A., J. V. Ward, T. Robinson, and R. Kilkenny. 1999. *Souls Looking Back: Life Stories of Growing Up Black*. New York: Routledge.

Gibbs, J. T. and D. Fuery. 1994. Mental health and well-being of black women: Toward strategies of empowerment. *American Journal of Community Psychology* 22 (4): 559–582.

Giddings, P. 1984. *Where and When I Enter: The Impact of Black Women on Race and Sex in America*. New York: William Morrow.

Gilkes, C. T. 1983. Going up for the oppressed. The career mobility of Black women community workers. *Journal of Social Issues* 39:115–139.

———. 2001. *If It Wasn't for the Women*. New York: Orbis Books.

Goldstein, R. B., C. A. Prescott, and K. S. Kendler. 2001. Genetic and environmental factors in conduct problems and adult antisocial behavior among adult female twins. *Journal of Nervous and Mental Disease* 189 (4): 201–209.

Goodman, A. H. 2000. Why genes don't count for racial differences in health. *American Journal of Public Health* 90 (11): 1699–1702.

Green, V. 1978. The Black Extended Family in the United States: Some Research Suggestions. In D. B. Shimkin, E. M. Shimkin, and D. A. Frate, eds., *The Extended Family in Black Societies*. The Hague, The Netherlands: DeGruyter.

Greene, B., J. C. White, and L. Whitten. 2000. Hair Texture, Length, and Style as a Metaphor in the African American Mother-Daughter Relationship. In L. C. Jackson and B. Greene, eds., *Psychotherapy with African American Women*, 166–193. New York: Guilford.

Harris, J., and P. Johnson. 2001. *Tenderheaded: A Comb-Bending Collection of Hair Stories*. New York: Pocket Books.

Herz, D. E., J. R. Meisenheimer, and H. G. Weinstein. 2000. Health and retirement benefits: Data from two BLS surveys. *Monthly Labor Review* 123 (3): 3–20.

Hine, D. C. 1995. For Pleasure, Profit, and Power: The Sexual Exploitation of Black Women. In G. Smitherman, ed. *African American Women Speak Out on Anita Hill–Clarence Thomas*, 168–177. Detroit: Wayne State University Press.

hooks, b. 1993. *Sisters of the Yam: Black Women and Self Recovery*. Boston: South End Press.

Hummer, R. A. 1996. Black-White differences in health and mortality: A review and conceptual model. *Sociological Quarterly* 37 (1): 105–125.

Keith, V. M. 1997. Life Stress and Psychological Well-being Among Married and Unmarried Blacks. In R. J. Taylor, J. S. Jackson, and L. M. Chatters, eds., *Family Life in Black America,* 95–116. Thousand Oaks, Calif.: Sage.

Ladner, J. 1972. *Tomorrow's Tomorrow.* Garden City, N.Y.: Anchor Books.

Lawton, M. P., D. Rajagopal, E. Brody, and M. H. Kleban. 1992. The dynamics of caregiving for a demented elder among black and white families. *Journal of Gerontology: Social Sciences* 47 (4): S156–S164.

Leigh, W. and M. Lindquist. 1999. *Women of Color Health Data Book.* Washington, D.C.: Office on Women's Health, National Institutes of Health, U.S. Department of Health and Human Services.

Marsh, C. E. 1993. Sexual assault and domestic violence in the African American community. *Western Journal of Black Studies* 17 (3): 149–155.

Martin, J. A., B. E. Hamilton, S. J. Ventura, F. Menacker, and M. M. Park. 2000. Births: Final data for 2000. *National Vital Statistics Reports* 50 (5). Hyattsville, Md.: National Center for Health Statistics.

McDonald, K. B. 1997. The Psychosocial Dimension of Black Maternal Health: An Intersection of Race, Gender, and Class. In C. Herring, ed., *African Americans and the Public Agenda: The Paradoxes of Public Policy,* 68–84. New York: Russell Sage Foundation.

McKinnon, J. and K. Humes. 2000. U.S. Census Bureau. Current Population Reports, Series P20–530. Washington, D.C.: U.S. Government Printing Office.

Moss, B. 1995. Ambiguity, Autonomy, and Empowerment. In K. M. Vaz, ed., *Black Women in America,* 19–27. Thousand Oaks, Calif.: Sage.

National Center for Health Statistics. 2000. *Health, United States, with Adolescent Health Chartbook.* Hyattsville, Md.: U.S. Public Health Service.

Nobles, W. 1991. African Philosophy: Foundations for Black Psychology. In R. L. Jones, ed., *Black Psychology,* 47–63. Berkeley, Calif.: Cobb and Henry.

Okun, M. A. and V. M. Keith. 1998. Effects of positive and negative social exchanges with various sources on depressive symptoms in younger and older adults. *Journal of Gerontology: Psychological Sciences* 53 (1): P4–20.

Robins, L. N. and D. A. Regier. 1991. *Psychiatric Disorders in America.* New York: Free Press.

Russell, G. 1996. Internalized classism: The role of class in the development of self. *Women and Therapy* 18 (3–4): 59–71.

St. Jean, Y. and J. R. Feagin. 1998. *Double Burden: Black Women and Everyday Racism.* New York: M. E. Sharpe.

Siegel, J. M., A. K. Yancey, and W. J. McCarthy. 2000. Overweight and depressive symptoms among African American women. *Preventive Medicine* 31 (3): 232–240.

Smith, J. C. 1988. *Images of Blacks in American Culture.* New York: Greenwood.

Stevens, J. A., L. M. Hasbrouck, T. M. Durant, A. M. Dellinger, and P. K. Batabyal. 1999. Surveillance for injuries and violence among older adults. *Morbidity and Mortality Weekly: Reports of the Centers for Disease Control Summary* 48 (8): 27–50.

Taylor, J., D. Henderson, and B. B. Jackson. 1991. A holistic model for understanding and predicting depressive symptoms in African American women. *Journal of Community Psychology* 19 (4): 306–320.

Terborg-Penn, R. 1985. Survival Strategies among African American Women Workers: Continuing Process. In R. Milkman, ed., *Women, Work, and Protest: A Century of U.S. Women's Labor History*, 139–155. Boston: Routledge and Kegan Paul.

Thompson, B. W. 1996. "A way outa no way": Eating Problems Among African American, Latina, and White Women. In E. N. Chow, D. Y. Wilkinson, and M. Baca-Zinn, eds., *Race, Class, and Gender: Common Bonds, Different Voices*, 52–69. Thousand Oaks, Calif.: Sage.

U.S. Bureau of Labor Statistics. 2001. Current Population Survey. Civilian Labor Force. http://data.bls.gov/servlet/SurveyOutputServlet.

U.S. Census Bureau. 2000a. Current Population Reports, P20-536. Table 10. Educational Attainment of People 25 Years of Age and Over by Nativity, and Period of Entry, Age, Sex, Race and Hispanic Origin, March 2000. http://www.census.gov/population/socdemo/education/p20-536/tab10.pdf.

———. 2000b. Current Population Reports, P20-536. Educational attainment of people 15 years of age and over by age, sex, race, and Hispanic origin, March 2000. http://www.census.gov/population/socdemo/education/p20-536/tab01.pdf.

———. 2001a. Current Population Reports, March 2000. Table 7. Median Income of People by Selected Characteristics in 2000, 1999, and 1998. http://www.census.gov/hhes/income/income00/inctab7.html.

———. 2001b. Current Population Reports, March 2000. Table 1. People and Families in Poverty by Selected Characteristics: 1999 and 2000. http://www.census.gov/hhes/poverty/poverty02/table2.pdf.

———. 2001c. Current Population Reports, P20-537. Table A1. Marital Status of People 15 Years and Over, by Age, Sex, Personal Earnings, Race, and Hispanic Origin, March 2000. http://www.census.gov/population/www/socdem/hh-fam/p20-537-00html.

———. 2001d. Current Population Reports, P20-537. Table H1. Households by Type, Tenure, and Race, and Hispanic Origin of Householder: March 2000. http://www.census.gov/population/socdemo/hh-fam/p20-537/2000/tabH1.txt.

U.S. Department of Health and Human Services. 2001. *Mental Health: Culture, Race, and Ethnicity. A Supplement to Mental Health: A Report of the Surgeon General.* Washington, D.C.: Government Printing Office.

Ventura, S. J., J. A. Martin, S. C. Curtin, F. Menacker, B. E. Hamilton. 2001. *National Vital Statistics Reports Births: Final Data for 1999.* Vol. 49(1). Hyattsville, Md.: National Center for Health Statistics.

Wiemann, C. M., A. B. Berenson, and V. V. San Miguel. 1994. Tobacco, alcohol and illicit drug use among pregnant women: Age and racial/ethnic differences. *Journal of Reproductive Medicine* 39 (10): 769–776.

Williams, D. R. 1990. Socioeconomic differentials in health: A review and redirection. *Social Psychology Quarterly* 53: 81–99.

———. 1997. Race and health: Basic questions, emerging directions. *Annals of Epidemiology* 7 (5): 322–333.

Williams, D. R., R. Lavizzo-Mourey, and R. Warren. 1994. The concept of race and health status in America. *Public Health Reports* 109 (1): 26–42.

Wyatt, G. E. and M. H. Riederle. 1995. The prevalence and context of sexual harassment among African American and White American women. *Journal of Interpersonal Violence* 10 (3): 309–321.

Zsembik, Barbara A. 1995. Issues for women of racial and ethnic groups. *Research in Human Social Conflict* 1:257–273.

PART II
MENTAL HEALTH AND MENTAL ILLNESS AMONG AFRICAN AMERICAN WOMEN

All day long I am worried;
All day long I am blue;
I'm so awfully lonesome,
I doan know what to do.
So I ask yo' Doctor,
See if you can fin'
Somethin' in yo satchel
To pacify my min.'
Doctor! Doctor!
Write me a prescription fo' dih blues.
De mean ole blues.

—Clara Smith

2 THE EPIDEMIOLOGY OF MENTAL DISORDERS AND MENTAL HEALTH AMONG AFRICAN AMERICAN WOMEN

Diane R. Brown and Verna M. Keith

What did I do
To be so Black
And Blue?
—ANDY RAZAF

INTRODUCTION

The purpose of this chapter is to examine current scientific data on the distribution of mental disorders and mental health among African American women. A review of the epidemiological data facilitates an understanding of the extent to which African American women experience mental illness, the types of mental disorders that are most prevalent in this population, and who is most (and least) at risk. In addition, the chapter examines subclinical psychiatric symptomatology, including experiences of psychological distress and minor depression. The importance of subclinical psychiatric symptoms is reviewed in light of the sociocultural and historical context of the lives of African American women, comparing data on African American women to findings for other segments of the U.S. population.

DEFINITIONS OF MENTAL DISORDERS AND MENTAL HEALTH

Definitions of mental health and mental illness are influenced as much by social factors, cultural values, and normative expectations regarding deviant behavior as by scientific knowledge. For the purposes of this discussion, the term *mental illness* refers collectively to diagnosable mental disorders as defined by the *Diagnostic and Statistical Manual of Mental Disorders* of the American Psychiatric Association. The term *mental disorder* generally refers to health conditions that are characterized by alterations in thinking, mood, or behavior (or some combination thereof). They are conceptualized as a clinically significant behavioral or psychological syndrome or pattern that occurs in an individual and that is associated with distress, impaired functioning, significantly heightened risk of suffering, death, pain, disability, or an important loss of freedom (American Psychiatric Association 1994).

The term *mental health* is more difficult to define. There is no universally accepted conceptualization of mental health, although most researchers and practitioners in the field would agree that it is not simply the absence of mental disorder. Some earlier definitions characterize mentally healthy people as those who are able to adjust to new situations and to handle personal problems without marked distress (Fromm 1947; Allardt 1976). Expanding the definition, Kolb (1968) posits that a mentally healthy adult exhibits behavior that confirms an awareness of self or personal identity, coupled with a life purpose and a willingness to perceive reality and cope with its vicissitudes; to be active and productive; to respond flexibly to stress; to receive pleasure from a variety of sources; and to accept limitations realistically. Finally, a recently articulated definition states that mental health is a state of successful performance of mental function, resulting in productive activities, fulfilling relationships with other people, and the ability to adapt to change and to cope with adversity (Surgeon General 1999).

Although these definitions may be useful for the general population, they are based upon normative parameters that exclude consideration of race and gender. For African American women, the intersection of race and gender, as well as their experiences of racism and sexism, are integral to definitions of their mental health. Speaking primarily to the issue of racism, Thomas and Comer (1973) contend that mental health for Blacks must encompass feelings of self-worth within the total context of society as well as within one's identifiable subgroup. According to Wilcox (1973), mental health is the foundation of survival in a racist society. Among Blacks, mental health necessarily comprises an awareness and adaptation to an often racially hostile environment. Wilcox notes that mentally healthy behavior for Blacks may sometimes seem to be deviant to normative society, perhaps manifested in what appears to be paranoid behavior. However, Grier and Cobbs (1968) point out that it is essential that Blacks develop a level of vigilance about racism or "cultural paranoia" in order to survive and maintain some degree of mental equilibrium. For African American women, the cultural paranoia goes beyond issues of race to include those related to gender as well.

The humanistic literature on African American women provides a basis for defining mental health. Given the impact of both racism and sexism on their lives, attainment and maintenance of mental health for African American women means rejecting distorted, false, denigrating, anti-self, anti-African messages that they have internalized, such as negative images related to skin color and physical appearance as well as stereotypes of sexual promiscuity, domestic servitude, welfare dependency, and many, many others. At the same time, achieving mental health involves a process of accepting, empowering, and positively embracing all aspects of themselves, as well as finding ways of engaging in self-validation and development of their capabilities regardless of racist and sexist assaults. It means living with hope, despite obstacles that often seem beyond their control (Franklin and Jackson 1990; hooks 1993; Manuel 2000).

PREVALENCE OF MAJOR MENTAL DISORDERS

Historically, only limited data on the epidemiology of major mental disorders in the African American population have been available. For many years, epidemiological data on major mental disorders among African Americans were gathered primarily from people receiving clinical treatment and from small, unrepresentative samples (Brown 1990). It is well documented that data based on people receiving psychiatric treatment do not accurately reflect prevalence in community-based populations (Adebimpe 1994; Brown 1990). Because these early data could not be generalized to non-institutionalized community-based populations of African Americans, prevalence estimates of mental disorders among African Americans were not reliable. Needless to say, data on African American women were virtually nonexistent because gender differences in mental disorders in the African American population were rarely the focus of analysis.

In recent years, a number of field investigations have addressed some of the methodological concerns of earlier studies and have included larger, more representative samples of African Americans. The Epidemiologic Catchment Area (ECA) Study sponsored by the National Institute of Mental Health represented a major effort to obtain better epidemiological data on psychiatric illnesses in community-based populations (Robins et al. 1981). The ECA Study included a large sample aggregated across five sites ($N = 18{,}572$), with a subsample of 4,287 African American adults, and collected data using the Diagnostic Interview Schedule (DIS), which was designed to provide case identification of psychiatric disorders based upon the criteria of the revised third edition of the *Diagnostic and Statistical Manual* (*DSM-III-R*) of the American Psychiatric Association (1987).

Data on the one-year prevalence of mental disorders from the ECA study are presented in table 2.1 by race and gender. When compared to African American men and Whites, African American women had the highest rates of schizophrenia, generalized anxiety disorder, somatization, and phobia during a one-year period. Phobia was the most frequently occurring mental disorder among African American women. The one-year prevalence of 18.2

per 100 African American women was significantly higher than that for White women at 10.9, African American men at 10.2, and White men at 5.1. With regard to alcohol and drug abuse disorders, the ECA data show that African American women had higher one-year prevalences than White women, but their prevalence rates were lower than rates for men. Rates for major depression and obsessive-compulsive disorders for African American women were similar to those for White women but higher than the rates for men. However, African American women had lower rates of dysthymia than White women. The prevalence of cognitive impairment was 2.3 for African American women; this was similar to that for African American men (2.4) but was considerably higher than the prevalence for White men (0.9) and White women (0.9). Finally, the one-year prevalence of mania among African American women differed only slightly from that for African American males and White females, but was higher than that for White males. Overall, the ECA data suggest that the greatest disparities in mental disorders between African American women and other segments of the population occur with regard to phobia, generalized anxiety disorder, schizophrenia, and somatization. Cognitive impairment is also of concern, because of its higher prevalence in Blacks than in Whites.

Another landmark psychiatric epidemiologic study with a sizable African American sample was the National Comorbidity Survey (NCS) (Kessler et al. 1994). Also funded by the National Institute of Mental Health, the NCS had as its primary purpose to study the comorbidity of substance use disorders and non–substance use disorders in the United States population. Using a population that differed somewhat from that of the ECA study, the NCS included a national probability sample of 8,098 people, 15 to 54 years of age, residing in the noninstitutionalized civilian population in the forty-eight contiguous states. African Americans accounted for 12.5 percent of the respondents. The psychiatric diagnoses were based on the *DSM-III-R* (American Psychiatric Association 1987). A modified version of the Composite International Diagnostic Interview (CIDI) was administered by trained nonclinician interviewers.

The one-year prevalences of major mental disorders from the NCS are given in table 2.2. Generally, findings from the NCS differ somewhat from those of the ECA Study, with NCS prevalence estimates tending to be higher than those reported in the ECA. While Kessler et al. (1994) report that there were no disorders where prevalence was greater for Blacks and Whites, their analyses were not disaggregated by both gender and race as shown in table 2.2. Further analyses of NCS data show that African American women have the highest one-year prevalence of dysthymia of any of the race/gender

TABLE 2.1 One-Year Prevalence of Major Mental Disorders by Race and Gender: ECA Data

MENTAL DISORDER	AFRICAN AMERICAN %	WHITE %
Mania	0.8	0.6
	1.0	0.5
Major depression (no grief)	4.9	4.6
	1.0	2.1
Major depression (grief)	5.1	5.0
	1.1	2.3
Dysthymia[a]	3.6	4.2
	1.2	2.3
Alcohol abuse	2.3	1.9
	10.2	10.0
Drug abuse	2.1	1.4
	3.8	3.2
Schizophrenia	1.6	0.9
	1.2	0.7
Obsessive-compulsive disorder	1.9	1.9
	1.3	1.4
Cognitive impairment[a]	2.3	0.9
	2.4	0.9
Generalized anxiety disorder	6.6	4.7
	5.5	2.1
Phobia	18.2	10.9
	10.2	5.1
Somatization[a]	0.8	0.2
	0.1	0
Panic	1.4	1.2
	0.5	0.6
Antisocial personality	0.6	0.3
	1.5	2.0

Source: Epidemiologic Catchment Area Study, weighted data across five sites.

Note: For each row, the top numbers are for females, the bottom numbers are for males.
[a] Current prevalence, not one-year, is reported for dysthymia, cognitive impairment, and somatization.

subgroups—a finding that differs from the ECA Study. African American women also have the highest one-year prevalences for mania, simple phobia, agoraphobia, post-traumatic stress disorder (PTSD) and nonaffective psychosis (schizophrenia). Post-traumatic stress disorder was not reported in the ECA Study. In contrast to the ECA data, the NCS data indicate that African American women have the lowest one-year prevalences of alcohol dependence, alcohol abuse, drug abuse, and drug dependence in comparison with African American men and Whites. Other differences occur with regard to affective disorders. The one-year prevalence of major depression (10.99) for African American women is lower than that of White women (12.68) but higher than the rates for African American men (4.99) and for White men (7.62). It should be noted that findings from the two studies differ considerably with regard to the one-year prevalence of generalized anxiety disorder among African American women. Although this group has the highest prevalence of generalized anxiety disorder in the ECA Study, the one-year prevalence from the NCS (2.73) is lower than that for White women (4.50). Because of differing methods, differing diagnostic criteria, and differing sampling strategies, the consistencies across studies pertaining to African American women are few. However, data from both studies appear to indicate that African American women are at greater risk than Whites and African American men for phobia, specifically agoraphobia and simple phobia, along with schizophrenia. PTSD and dysthymia are additional disorders whose higher prevalence among African American women in the NCS warrant further attention.

Table 2.3 shows the lifetime prevalence of major mental disorders from the NCS. The race and gender comparisons are similar to those for the one-year prevalences. The data show that among African American women, the most commonly experienced disorders over the lifetime are major depression, simple phobia, agoraphobia, social phobia, and PTSD. Also over the lifetime, African American women are more likely to have agoraphobia, mania, post-traumatic stress disorder, and nonaffective psychoses than are other race/gender subgroups. However, they have the lowest lifetime rates of alcohol dependence, alcohol abuse, drug abuse, and drug dependence. Overall, given the absence of racial differences in the NCS, the lifetime prevalence of any disorder is 47.3 per 100 females (Kessler et al. 1994).

RISK FACTORS FOR MAJOR MENTAL DISORDERS

While risk factors do not necessarily represent causes of mental disorder, they provide an understanding of who is most likely to experience a

TABLE 2.2 One-Year Prevalence of Major Mental Disorders: National Comorbidity Study

MENTAL DISORDER	AFRICAN AMERICAN		WHITE	
	FEMALE % (SE)	MALE % (SE)	FEMALE % (SE)	MALE % (SE)
Alcohol dependence	1.28 (0.42)	5.47 (1.36)	4.31 (0.50)	10.88 (0.93)
Alcohol abuse	1.42 (0.53)	2.25 (0.98)	1.83 (0.27)	3.71 (0.47)
Agoraphobia	8.56 (2.35)	1.18 (0.56)	4.68 (0.57)	2.35 (0.46)
Major depression w/o hierarchy	10.99 (2.02)	4.99 (1.41)	12.68 (0.88)	7.62 (0.79)
Drug abuse w/o dependence	0.15 (0.12)	0.70 (0.38)	0.35 (0.10)	1.53 (0.35)
Drug dependence	1.58 (0.71)	3.43 (1.13)	1.89 (0.32)	3.89 (0.40)
Dysthymia w/o hierarchy	3.82 (1.27)	2.26 (1.22)	2.83 (0.43)	1.69 (0.29)
Generalized anxiety disorder w/o hierarchy	2.73 (1.29)	1.74 (1.16)	4.50 (0.60)	2.04 (0.32)
New mania w/o hierarchy	1.08 (1.07)	0.15 (0.15)	0.27 (0.19)	0.29 (0.14)
Panic disorder	1.98 (1.40)	0.46 (0.34)	3.49 (0.57)	1.40 (0.32)
Simple phobia	14.85 (2.59)	3.56 (1.15)	12.10 (0.89)	4.11 (0.53)
Social phobia	8.97 (2.22)	2.92 (0.83)	9.09 (0.82)	7.12 (0.52)
Posttraumatic stress disorder	6.96 (1.90)	1.68 (0.67)	4.41 (0.37)	2.13 (0.40)
Nonaffective psychosis	0.87 (0.54)	0.07 (0.07)	0.21 (0.10)	0.13 (0.07)

mental disorder and who is not. Current scientific knowledge suggests a complex combination of biological, psychological, and social factors that underlie the onset of major mental disorders. The various disorders have different risk factors, symptomatology, etiology, and treatment. Biological and genetic factors play a prominent role, since some disorders (such as schizophrenia) may be inherited. Biochemical factors associated with alcohol and drugs may precipitate the onset of some mental disorders, while social, cultural, and environmental factors may play a larger part with others. Risk factors vary from disorder to disorder, as the following discussion of two of the most commonly occurring disorders among African American women, anxiety disorders and major depression, will show.

ANXIETY DISORDERS. Anxiety disorders, the most common psychiatric disorders in the community, include phobia, panic disorder, PTSD, generalized

TABLE 2.3 Lifetime Prevalence of Major Mental Disorders: National Comorbidity Study

	AFRICAN AMERICAN		WHITE	
MENTAL DISORDER	FEMALE % (SE)	MALE % (SE)	FEMALE % (SE)	MALE % (SE)
Alcohol dependence	3.56 (1.17)	9.11 (1.75)	9.53 (0.79)	21.19 (1.10)
Alcohol abuse	2.55 (0.82)	7.17 (1.79)	7.26 (0.60)	14.10 (0.94)
Agoraphobia	13.08 (2.33)	2.27 (0.85)	8.20 (0.72)	4.48 (0.59)
Antisocial personality disorder	1.41 (0.45)	4.37 (1.46)	0.94 (0.27)	5.29 (0.50)
Major depression w/o hierarchy	15.53 (2.16)	7.25 (1.89)	22.26 (0.98)	13.51 (0.97)
Drug abuse w/o dependence	1.33 (0.62)	3.45 (1.25)	3.97 (0.50)	5.93 (0.56)
Drug dependence	4.01 (1.38)	5.28 (1.22)	6.34 (0.59)	9.94 (0.76)
Dysthymia w/o hierarchy	5.95 (1.65)	3.97 (1.42)	8.43 (0.70)	4.54 (0.40)
Generalized anxiety disorder w/o hierarchy	3.25 (1.30)	2.64 (1.63)	7.38 (0.65)	3.89 (0.52)
New mania w/o hierarchy	1.08 (1.07)	0.15 (0.15)	0.41 (0.22)	0.32 (0.14)
Panic attack	5.55 (1.67)	1.13 (0.57)	11.00 (0.73)	5.38 (0.50)
Simple phobia	16.80 (2.59)	4.92 (1.30)	14.86 (1.08)	6.81 (0.60)
Social phobia	12.46 (2.47)	5.17 (1.20)	15.60 (1.09)	12.22 (0.93)
Post-traumatic stress disorder	10.99 (2.15)	2.08 (0.77)	8.53 (0.54)	4.42 (0.67)
Non-affective psychosis	1.48 (0.66)	0.46 (0.35)	0.62 (0.17)	0.48 (0.11)

anxiety disorder, and obsessive-compulsive disorder. Symptoms may include feelings of fear or dread, trembling, rapid heart rate, perspiration, shortness of breath, and cold hands or feet. Symptoms of anxiety are aroused most intensely by immediate threats to one's safety, but may also occur in response to dangers that are relatively remote or abstract (Surgeon General 1999). Anxiety disorders pose increased risk for depression and alcohol use disorder (Breslau et al. 1997). Psychiatric researchers have, however, given little attention to understanding anxiety disorders and their risk factors among African Americans in general (Neal and Turner 1991; Paradis, Friedman, and Hatch 1997) or for African American women in particular (Neal-Barnett and Crowther 2000).

Phobia appears to be the most frequently occurring anxiety disorder among African American women. Phobia can be chronic and tends to occur in the presence of other psychiatric disorders such as substance abuse or depression (Pavkov, McGovern, and Geffner 1993; Ziedonis et al. 1994). However, fewer than 25 percent of those with symptoms constituting a phobic disorder actually receive treatment (Boyd et al. 1990). Furthermore, Neal and Turner (1991) contend that African Americans are less likely to receive appropriate treatment for anxiety disorder because symptoms of anxiety may be manifested differently in African Americans than in Whites.

With an average onset in childhood or teenage years, phobic disorders are of three major types: agoraphobia, social phobia, and simple phobia. Agoraphobia is the most severe and pervasive; it is also the most common among people seeking treatment. It is generally denoted by a fear of being alone in public places from which it would be difficult to escape or where help would not be available in the event of sudden incapacitation. Less severe, social phobia encompasses a compelling desire to avoid a situation in which the individual is exposed to possible scrutiny by others and where she may act in a way that would be humiliating or embarrassing (American Psychiatric Association 1994). Examples include speaking or eating in front of others. The third category, simple phobias, involves fear of specific objects or situations, such as spiders, snakes, or thunderstorms.

An analysis of data from the ECA Study (table 2.4) indicates that African American women have higher one-year and lifetime rates of phobias than any other race/gender subgroup of the population (Eaton, Dryman, and Weissman 1991). The one-month rates are also the highest (Brown, Eaton, and Sussman 1990). Results of a multivariate analysis show that those at greatest risk for recent phobia are young female African Americans with low educational attainment who have been previously married. With regard to types of phobia, NCS data in tables 2.2 and 2.3 show that African American women have the highest rates of agoraphobia and simple phobia, but not social phobia. For example, the one-year prevalence of agoraphobia is 8.56 for African American women and 4.68 for White women. Similarly, the one-year prevalence of simple phobia is 14.85 for African American women but only 12.10 for White women. On the other hand, social phobia is higher among White women. The one-year prevalence of social phobia is 9.09 for White women and slightly lower for African American women, at 8.97. In an analysis of risk factors for social phobia, Heimberg et al. (2000) conclude that social phobia is higher among White, well-educated, married people.

The research literature offers little explanation for the higher rates of phobic disorders among African American women. There appear to be few

TABLE 2.4 Prevalence of Phobic Disorder by Age, Sex, and Ethnicity

| | | MEN | | WOMEN | |
ETHNICITY	SAMPLE SIZE	ONE-YEAR % (SE)	LIFETIME % (SE)	ONE-YEAR % (SE)	LIFETIME % (SE)
Whites					
18–29	2,020	5.84 (0.83)	10.65 (1.09)	12.24 (1.18)	14.84 (1.28)
30–44	1,997	5.82 (0.90)	10.27 (1.17)	16.35 (1.40)	22.33 (1.56)
45–64	2,146	6.23 (0.91)	9.93 (1.12)	10.49 (1.11)	15.56 (1.30)
65+	2,244	4.20 (1.10)	7.18 (1.41)	8.45 (1.27)	13.01 (1.53)
Blacks					
18–29	1,285	11.46 (3.00)	16.18 (3.46)	22.99 (3.81)	27.23 (4.00)
30–44	1,156	10.48 (3.35)	14.29 (3.81)	18.04 (3.83)	24.60 (4.26)
45–64	851	12.71 (4.01)	20.26 (4.78)	21.03 (4.40)	30.63 (4.90)
65+	822	12.04 (5.96)	15.30 (6.58)	14.80 (5.37)	24.17 (6.42)

Note: Four sites' combined respondents (Baltimore, St. Louis, Durham, Los Angeles) weighted to the United States by age, sex, and ethnicity.

Source: Eaton, Dryman, and Weissman 1991

biological bases for it (American Psychiatric Association 1994). An examination of the impact of race, gender, and social class on the lives of African American women may yield some insight, however, given that phobia in particular reflects fear about situations in which one has little control. Race and gender discrimination engender circumstances of poverty and uncertainty that African American women may feel powerless to change. Many of them reside in inner-city neighborhoods where they live in fear of crime and violence over which they have little control. For African American women in these and other potentially threatening circumstances, anxiety arises from not knowing exactly what dangers they will face in their daily lives and from not knowing how they will deal with them.

Elements of African American culture may also promote anxiety and phobia among African American women. As a result of historical experiences of racial violence and racial discrimination, anxiety has become a functional aspect of the culture. From generation to generation, African American families have socialized their children to be extremely cautious and apprehensive of situations that might involve race-based attacks to their safety and well-being. Although racial segregation and discrimination against Blacks are no longer public policy, African American women continue to face subtle and overt threats that contribute to anxiety. Future research needs to investigate the relationships between anxiety disorders and the circumstances that lead to high levels of psychological stress among African American women. Research is also warranted on the etiology and risk factors related to other anxiety disorders, including post-traumatic stress disorder (especially stemming from rape and partner violence), panic disorder, generalized anxiety disorder, and isolated sleep paralysis disorder, which has a higher prevalence among African Americans (Paradis, Friedman, and Hatch 1997).

MAJOR DEPRESSION. Major depressive disorder (MDD) is one of the most commonly occurring affective or mood disorders in the general population and among African American women. The causes of MDD appear to be multiple. For some individuals, social and environmental factors such as major stressful events may precipitate MDD (American Psychiatric Association 1987). For others, MDD may have a larger genetic component, or it may be the result of a medical illness or changes in the central nervous system, often as a consequence of substance use or medication (Weissman et al. 1991).

A diagnosis of MDD, which is also known as clinical depression, requires at least five specific symptoms during a two-week period, one of which must be a depressed mood or loss of interest or pleasure in the usual activities of life, and the presence of these symptoms must represent a change from previous functioning. Other symptoms may include significant weight loss or gain, insomnia or hypersomnia, fatigue or loss of energy, psychomotor retardation, diminished ability to concentrate or think, and recurrent thoughts of death or suicide. Without treatment, MDD can be disabling, making it difficult to engage in self-care or to maintain normal social roles, such as those of parent, worker, spouse, or friend.

The ECA Study shows a one-year MDD prevalence of 4.9 per 100 for African American women, while the NCS data report a one-year prevalence of 10.99. The lifetime prevalence for any affective disorder varies from 8.7 per 100 for African American females in the ECA Study to 15.5 for major depression for African American females and 23.9 for all females for any affective disorder in the NCS data (Kessler et al. 1994; Kessler and Zhao 1999). Although these studies differ in their reported prevalences, the rates of MDD among African American women are similar or lower than rates for White women. Somervell et al. (1989) note an exception in the ECA Study, finding that African American women 18 to 24 years of age had higher rates than similar White women. In addition to the ECA and NCS data, the Norfolk Area Health Study (NAHS) (Gary et al. 1989) offers additional epidemiologic data on the prevalence of MDD in an African American population. The study consisted of a field survey of African American adults in which a multi-stage cluster probability sampling procedure was used to sample 444 females and 421 males. Similar to the ECA Study, data for this analysis were gathered using the Diagnostic Interview Schedule. The NAHS, however, expanded the traditional demographic risk factors to include sociocultural and familial characteristics that may particularly reflect the experiences of African Americans. Results from the NAHS show a one-year prevalence of MDD of 3.2 for African American women, with the average age of onset being 26.1 years.

Another source of data on MDD among African Americans is the National Survey of Midlife Development in the United States (MIDUS) (Wang, Berglund, and Kessler 2000). The MIDUS study used an initial telephone survey and follow-up mail questionnaire to gather data from a nationally representative sample of 3,485 noninstitutionalized English-speaking adults, 25–74 years of age. The weighted sample includes 214 African American women. MDD was based upon meeting the *DSM* criteria for a diagnosis. The results show that 13.1 percent of African American women met the criteria for MDD, in contrast to 17.1 percent of White women, 10.0 percent of White men, and 8.0 percent of African American men. The MIDUS, ECA, and NCS studies all show that African American women had higher rates of MDD than did African American men, indicating that female gender is a risk factor for MDD. In the NAHS, however, gender difference was not statistically significant.

Data from the studies described above provide insight into various demographic, socioeconomic, cultural, and other risk factors for MDD among African American women. Data from the MIDUS study, shown in table 2.5, indicate that with regard to age, MDD occurs more frequently among younger (18.9%) than among older African American women (3.8%). Similarly, findings from the NAHS indicate that there is a higher lifetime and one-year prevalence of MDD among 18- to 44-year-olds than among older women. The highest rates occur among those 20 to 29 years of age. Marital status also appears to be a significant risk factor for MDD. In the MIDUS study, MDD is significantly lower among married African American women than among those who are not married (i.e., separated, widowed, divorced, or never married). The NAHS data confirm lower rates among married African Americans in contrast to those who are not married.

The findings pertaining to MDD and socioeconomic status are not consistent across studies. Data from the ECA and the NAHS indicate that neither

TABLE 2.5 Social and Demographic Correlates of Depression: National Survey of Midlife Development in the United States (MIDUS), 1995–1996

	%	ODDS RATIO	95% CI
Age			
25–44	18.9	6.00*	1.75–20.58
45 and older	3.8	1.00[a]	
Marital status			
Married	4.2	0.18*	0.16–0.85
Not married	19.5	1.00[a]	
Parental status			
No children under 18	13.8	1.17	0.52–2.63
One child or more under 18	12.1	1.00[a]	
Education			
High school or <	8.2	0.37*	0.16–0.85
Some college or more	19.0	1.00[a]	
Median household income			
$24,000 or <	15.4	1.46	0.61–3.47
> $24,000	11.1	1.00[a]	
Median personal income			
$13,500 or <	7.5	0.35*	0.14–0.84
> $13,500	17.9	1.00[a]	
Employment status			
Working or self-employed	18.0	7.90*	1.82–34.34
Not working	2.7	1.00[a]	
Chronic conditions			
One or more	16.4	5.81*	1.33–25.33
None	3.3	1.00[a]	
How religious			
Very	17.1	1.62	0.73–3.62
Some, not very, not at all	11.3	1.00[a]	
How spiritual			
Very	15.2	1.31	0.69–2.90
Some, not very, not at all	12.0	1.00[a]	

Note: Respondents met criteria for depression diagnosis.

[a] Odds ratio of 1.00 indicates the reference category.

* $p \leq .05$

low income nor little education is a significant risk factor for one-year major depression (Weissman et al. 1991; Brown et al. 1995). However, other studies (Kessler et al. 1994; Bruce and Hoff 1994; Turner and Lloyd 1999) find that low income is a risk factor for affective disorders. The MIDUS survey also provides evidence for an association between socioeconomic status and MDD, particularly among African American women. The results with regard to education are somewhat surprising; they indicate that African American women with at least some college education (19.0%) have a higher risk of MDD than do those with less education (8.2%). While there was no significant relationship between MDD and median household income, lower personal income was associated with greater risk for MDD for African American women. This is understandable, since personal income most often stems from one's employment. Women with the lowest personal incomes are less likely to be employed or, if employed, are more likely to hold low-paying or part-time positions. Consequently, it is not surprising that employment status is also a significant risk factor for MDD among African American women, as shown in the MIDUS survey and NAHS data (Brown et al. 1995). Unemployed African American women are more likely to have MDD than are those who are in the paid labor force. However, the direction of the association is not evident in these cross-sectional data, since having a major mental disorder such as MDD could have contributed to being unemployed.

According to the NAHS findings, physical illness is a significant risk factor for MDD. African Americans in good to excellent health had the lowest rate of MDD, at 2.2 percent, while those in poor health experienced a significantly higher rate of 6.9 percent. Data from MIDUS support similar conclusions: MDD was significantly higher among African American women with one or more chronic illnesses (16.4%) in comparison to those who had none (3.3%). Few sociocultural factors examined in earlier studies tend to be significant predictors of MDD among African Americans. Neither religiosity nor spirituality among African American women in the MIDUS analyses produced significant associations with MDD. In the NAHS, although African Americans with a religious preference had a lower one-year prevalence (2.8%) of MDD than those who expressed no preference (6.4%), this was not significant. Similarly, the NAHS reported no statistically significant findings pertaining to MDD and perceptions of family closeness, having lived with both parents until the age of sixteen, or having a family member with a mental problem. However, changing residences during the past five years was significantly associated with the one-year prevalence of MDD in the NAHS; those who had moved at least once had a higher rate of MDD than did those who had not moved. While MDD may have precipitated greater residential mobility, it is also likely that frequent moves may reflect lack of stability in economic and social support resources, as well as major changes in life circumstances.

Increased risk for MDD among African Americans was also associated with severe psychosocial stressors such as death of a family member, divorce, or loss of employment. African Americans experiencing the greatest number of acute stressful events during the past year had the highest one-year prevalence of MDD. Specifically, those with MDD reported a mean of 13.10 events ($SD = 7.61$), in comparison to people who were not depressed with an average of 9.23 ($SD = 2.82$); t = 2.55, df = 28, $p = 0.016$. As Keith (1997) pointed out, stressful life problems appear to be major risk factors for African American women, particularly those who are separated, divorced, or never married. Further analyses from the MIDUS study indicate that the greatest sources of stress for African American women stemmed from financial problems, familial relationships (spouse/partner, children, parents), emotional problems, work, or school. It is not surprising that familial relations are a major stress factor for African American women, since personal relationships appear to be an important cultural value among African Americans (Akbar 1991; Nobles 1991).

MDD also appears to have a significant biological component. Researchers have identified genetic factors that predispose individuals to MDD (Malhi, Moore, and McGuffin 2000; American Psychiatric Association 1994), along with changes in the central nervous system and biochemical factors such as prescription medication, alcohol, and illicit drugs (Weissman et al. 1991; American Psychiatric Association 1994). Although substance use diagnoses are fairly low among women, especially African American women, the comorbidity of depression and substance abuse is high (Mowbray et al. 1998). An extended discussion of the biological risk factors for MDD is beyond the scope of this chapter, but the available knowledge regarding these issues among African Americans in general and African American women in particular is meager. There is a need to investigate familial patterns of MDD among African Americans and to ascertain the extent to which social and biological factors affect the onset and course of MDD.

CONSEQUENCES OF MAJOR DEPRESSION. Major depression in itself may be a risk factor for physical health morbidity and mortality, particularly for conditions that African American women encounter (American Psychiatric Association 1994). Specifically, MDD may predispose African American women to alcoholism (Brown, Schulberg, and Madonia 1996) and possibly to changes in the immune system, as noted in a study of the general population (Tilders et al. 1999). More important, MDD has been linked to excess mortality from heart disease (Frasure-Smith et al. 2000) and breast cancer (Gallo et al. 2000), conditions for which African American women have higher rates of mortality than do White women. In studies of the general population, MDD appears to be a risk factor for Type II diabetes (Eaton et al. 1996; Talbot and Nouwen 2000) and osteoarthritis (Martin 1996). However, no research on the consequences of MDD has specifically focused on African American populations or on African American women.

MDD is also a risk factor for suicide, an important one among African American women (Frierson and Lippmann 1990). Up to 15 percent of individuals with severe MDD commit suicide (American Psychiatric Association 1994). Rates of suicide among African American women have generally been lower than those for White women, African American men, and White men, remaining at approximately 2 per 100,000 for the past twenty years (National Vital Statistics Report 2000). Age-specific rates of suicide tend to be highest for African American women 25 to 44 years of age, the age at which depression is also the highest. Suicide is lowest among African American women who are 65 years of age and older, at 1.6 per 100,000 people. Cultural values appear to mitigate against suicide among African American women. In exploring reasons for the low rate of suicide among older African American women in comparison to similar White women, Bender (2000) found that attitudes toward suicide were more negative among older African American women. Specifically, they were less apt to agree that suicide was acceptable, even in circumstances of incurable illness or when suffering from a terminal illness. Stack (1998) notes that while religiosity lowers suicide acceptability for Black women, level of education is the stronger correlate.

Despite the documented low rate of suicide among African American women, reason for concern arises when research examining attempted suicide is reviewed. In a study of medically treated attempts of suicide, the highest rate was among young African American females (Spicer and Miller 2000). Further, in a case control study of low-income African American women 18–64 years of age who attempted suicide, Kaslow and colleagues (2000) found that psychological distress, hopelessness, drug use, and relationship discord were the strongest predictors of attempted suicide. Those who attempted suicide were also more likely to have low levels of social support, to have experienced physical and nonphysical partner abuse, to have a history of childhood maltreatment, and to have less education; they were more likely to be unemployed, and they had more children living with them than did those women who did not try to kill themselves. Kaslow and colleagues point out that the demographic characteristics of African American women who attempt suicide reflect the high-risk social context in which they are trying to cope.

SUMMARY OF MAJOR MENTAL DISORDERS

Overall, the epidemiologic data suggest that fewer than half of African American women will experience a major mental disorder at some point in their lives. Further, significant race differences are few, even though the lives of African American women may differ considerably from those of White women. Race differences occur primarily with regard to the higher prevalence of phobia and schizophrenia among African American women than among White women. The lack of race differences may in part reflect shortcomings in methods for ascertaining the epidemiology of mental disorders among African Americans. A number of researchers have noted differences in the expressions of psychiatric symptomatology between African Americans and Whites (Neighbors and Lumpkin 1990; Baker et al. 1995; Gallo, Cooper-Patrick, and Lesikar 1998). Although Brown, Schulberg, and Madonia (1996) found similarities in core mood symptoms between African Americans and Whites diagnosed with MDD, African Americans differed in terms of somatic symptom severity, psychiatric and physical comorbidities, physical functioning, health perceptions, and psychological distress. Psychiatric symptoms among African Americans may not be recognized or interpreted correctly, given that the clinical expression of psychiatric symptoms tends to be evaluated within the context of Eurocentric perspectives and diagnostic norms (Neighbors and Lumpkin 1990; Wohi, Lesser, and Smith 1997; Adebimpe 1994; Brown, Schulberg, and Madonia 1996). Historically, clinicians have tended to overdiagnose schizophrenia in African Americans and underdiagnose affective disorders such as depression. With regard to the appropriate interpretation of paranoid symptoms previously classified as schizophrenia, Blazer, Hays, and Salive (1996) suggest that these symptoms in African Americans may represent an appropriate response to a hostile environment rather than a psychopathic trait. According to Neighbors and colleagues (Neighbors and Lumpkin 1990; Neighbors et al. 1999), it is conceivable that the degree to which African Americans and Whites differ in the presentation of psychopathological symptoms is conditional upon social class, gender, the specific disorder, or some other factor.

Other methodological concerns also arise with regard to the available epidemiologic data on African American women. While sample sizes of African

American women have increased, data are not always reported out by gender and race. Furthermore, given the difficulties of recruiting minorities into clinical studies (Adebimpe 1994; Brown et al. 2000), it is not clear to what extent the women participating in these studies are representative of the sociodemographic and cultural diversity in the population of African American women. With few exceptions, most major epidemiologic studies exclude factors that may be particularly salient for understanding psychiatric morbidity among African Americans in general or for understanding how the combination of race, gender, and social class affects risk factors for mental disorders.

Numerous issues remain unanswered with regard to the distribution of mental disorders among African American women. Research is warranted on those disorders (simple phobia and agoraphobia) for which there is a clear disparity between African American women and other race/gender segments of the U.S. population, as well as on disorders for which there are possible disparities, including schizophrenia, generalized anxiety disorder, and post-traumatic stress disorder (PTSD). Research specifically is needed on PTSD related to violence and partner abuse as well as on the association between anxiety disorders and MDD. Eating disorders are another focus for future investigation with African American women, as emerging research points to comparative levels of eating disturbances among African American and White females (Wilfley et al. 1996). Further work is needed on understanding differences in the risk factors and etiology of the subtypes of clinical depression among African American women, including dysthymia and bipolar disorder.

PSYCHOLOGICAL DISTRESS AND DEPRESSIVE SYMPTOMS

In contrast to diagnosable mental disorders, most of the mental health research on African American women has focused on forms of psychological distress or mental health problems, which generally exhibit subclinical psychiatric symptoms that do not meet the *DSM* threshold or criteria for a diagnosis of mental disorder. Even though symptoms of psychological distress may range in severity from low to high, they may still have insufficient intensity or duration for a diagnosis of mental disorder. The presence of depressive symptoms is the most commonly used indicator of psychological distress.

Over the past two decades, a preponderance of studies have shown that African American women have higher rates of depressive symptoms than do Whites and African American men (Warheit, Holzer, and Schwab 1973; Eaton and Kessler 1981; Roberts, Stevenson, and Breslow 1981; Murrell, Himmelfarb, and Wright 1983; Jones-Webb and Snowden 1993; Cochran, Brown, and McGregor 1999). Table 2.6 compares findings for African American women with those for other race/gender segments of the population. With a few exceptions, African American women express the highest levels of psychological distress. Even with different measures and different methods, the empirical research generally points out that African American women are more likely than African American men and Whites to have levels of depressive symptoms sufficiently high for a clinical diagnosis of depression (Eaton and Kessler 1981; Roberts, Stevenson, and Breslow 1981; Brown and Gary 1987; Brown, Milburn, and Gary 1992; Gazmararian, James, and Lepkowski 1995; Rickert, Wiemann, and Berenson 2000; Jonas and Wilson 1997). It is noteworthy that the NCS data did not reflect higher minor depression among Blacks, although the findings were not analyzed by gender and race (Kessler et al. 1997).

RISK AND PROTECTIVE FACTORS

The past decade has seen expanded research on the social, psychological, and cultural factors that exacerbate as well as diminish psychological distress among African American women. NAHS data illustrate some of the risk factors associated with psychological distress, specifically depressive symptoms as measured by the Center for Epidemiologic Studies Depression Scale (CES-D) (Radloff 1977). Table 2.7 presents findings for African American women in comparison to those for African American men. Depressive symptoms vary significantly by age, with higher levels of depressive symptoms for African American women 18 to 44 years of age. Rickert, Wiemann, and Berenson (2000) also find younger African American women to be at greater risk for depressive symptoms than older women. Marital status is also associated with depressive symptoms, with marriage constituting a protective mechanism against psychological distress. Specifically, unmarried African American women are at greatest risk (Gazmararian, James, and Lepkowski 1995), while married African American women have the lowest symptoms (Eaton and Kessler 1981; Brown 1988; Brown 1990; Jones-Webb and Snowden 1993). Data from NAHS show never-married women to have the highest levels of depressive symptoms (Brown 1990). Analysis of data from the National Survey of Black Americans, however, indicates no significant marital status differences in perceived stress when women are faced with a personal problem (Brown 1996).

TABLE 2.6 Psychological Distress Among Race and Gender Groups

	ACL—AMERICANS' CHANGING LIVES, WAVE I, 1986[a]				NATIONAL SURVEY OF FAMILIES AND HOUSEHOLDS, 1987[b]			
	N	MEAN	F-RATIO	P-VALUE	N	MEAN	F-RATIO	P-VALUE
African American females	232	1.54			791	1.64		
African American males	174	1.43			624	1.42		
White females	1,619	1.41			5,391	1.29		
White males	1,469	1.33			4,900	1.04		
Total	3,494		28.55	.000	11,706		20.45	.000

	CMHS—COMMONWEALTH FUND MINORITY HEALTH SURVEY, 1994[c]				SURVEY OF MIDLIFE DEVELOPMENT IN THE UNITED STATES, 1995–1996[d]			
	N	MEAN	F-RATIO	P-VALUE	N	MEAN	F-RATIO	P-VALUE
African American females	243	2.43			212	1.68		
African American males	202	2.22			125	1.39		
White females	1,465	2.37			1,393	1.64		
White males	1,356	2.14			1,083	1.52		
Latino females	91	2.47				na		
Latino males	81	2.25				na		
Total	3,445		11.54	.000	2,813		12.76	.000

[a] African American females significantly higher than African American males and Whites
[b] African American females significantly higher than all Whites
[c] African American females significantly higher than White males
[d] African American females significantly higher than African American and White males

The relationship between socioeconomic status and depressive symptoms is also significant. African American women of the lowest incomes report the highest levels of depressive symptoms (Gazmararian, James, and Lepkowski 1995; Taylor, Henderson, and Jackson 1991). However, poor African American women were similar to poor White women in their reports of depressive symptoms, while African American women of higher incomes had significantly more depressive symptoms than did similar White women. As another measure of socioeconomic status, educational attainment is inversely related to depressive symptoms. As illustrated in table 2.7, college-educated African American women tend to report fewer depressive symptoms than do women with less education. African American women with less than twelve years of education have the highest rates of negative affect (Jonas and Wilson 1997).

Both stressful life events and chronic stressors are associated with higher levels of psychological distress in the general population (Chen et al. 2000), although chronic stressors contribute more to psychological distress than do acute stressful life events (McGonagle and Kessler 1990). Data in table 2.7 show that economic strain, as a chronic stressor, is a significant risk factor for depressive symptoms. African American women experiencing the highest level of economic strain report the most depressive symptoms. Other sources of chronic stress contributing to higher levels of depressive symptoms for this population include job stress (Snapp 1992; Mays, Coleman, and Jackson 1996); unemployment, especially for single mothers (McLoyd et al. 1994); having minor children in the household (Brown 1988; Brown and Gary 1988); partner violence and sexual assault (Van Hook 1999; Rickert, Wiemann, and Berenson 2000); living in an urban environment (Baker et al. 1996); living in a multigenerational household where adult children are in and out of the household because of drug abuse, incarceration, and so on (Hirshorn, Van Meter, and Brown 1999); and social stresses stemming from poverty (Bennett 1987) and multiple caregivers (Brown and Mars 1999; Wallsten 2000).

A strong association exists between stressful life events and elevated depressive symptoms for African American women (Brown and Gary 1987; Keith 1997). For three of the most frequently occurring stressful life events (financial problems, family members fighting among themselves, and personal injury) cited in a community-based study of African Americans, findings indicate that African American women had CES-D scores that approximated those of clinical depression (Brown, Ndubuisi, and Gary 1990). Further, in a sample of one hundred middle-class African American women, Warren (1997) found that stressful life events, particularly having more responsibility at work and changes in church activities contributed significantly to increases in psychological distress.

TABLE 2.7 Distribution of CES-D Scores for Demographic, Socioeconomic, Sociocultural, and Economic Strain Variables for African Americans

	FEMALE			MALE		
	MEAN	SD	p	MEAN	SD	p
Age			.001			.024
18–29	16.67	9.91		13.83	8.53	
30–34	14.69	10.40		12.75	9.30	
45–64	11.99	10.54		11.76	8.29	
65+	11.09	8.25		10.09	7.97	
Marital status			.005			.001
Married	11.97	9.75		10.43	7.60	
Previously married	14.25	10.38		15.10	10.03	
Never married	15.92	9.59		13.54	8.71	
Income			.005			.001
Under $6,000	15.57	9.65		15.94	9.20	
$6,000–$11,999	14.79	10.38		15.43	8.66	
$12,000–$24,999	13.01	10.49		11.64	8.76	
$25,000+	10.25	9.76		9.84	7.66	
Education			.024			.048
Less than high school	14.93	9.97		12.89	8.56	
High school	14.24	9.61		13.43	8.83	
Some college+	11.86	10.28		10.91	8.90	
Social participation			.001			.002
No organization	16.69	10.91		13.23	8.34	
One organization	13.52	9.36		13.76	9.74	
Two organizations	12.51	9.62		11.54	8.24	
Three or more organizations	9.45	8.56		9.31	7.77	
Religiosity			.001			.081
Low	16.94	10.77		13.49	8.49	
Medium	14.28	10.17		12.51	8.65	
High	11.15	8.80		10.18	9.52	
Economic Strain			.001			.001
None	8.13	7.35		8.71	8.30	
Low	12.62	9.00		11.08	7.81	
Medium	16.43	9.71		14.31	7.85	
High	20.89	10.83		18.20	8.57	

Note: The significance levels are based upon one-way analysis of variance performed separately by gender. The Ns vary because of missing data.

Source: *Norfolk Area Health Study*, Gary et al. 1989.

Similar to findings related to MDD, poor health is often a risk factor for depressive symptoms and psychological distress. In a study of African American elderly people, Okwumabua and colleagues (1997) found that medical illness, including hypertension, arteriosclerosis, and circulatory problems, as well as taking prescription medication, were associated with increased depressive symptoms. African American women with HIV reported higher levels of depressive symptoms (Moneyham et al. 2000). Diabetes also appears to increase the risk for depressive symptoms, especially for those with more diabetes-related complications (Peyrot and Rubin 1997). Although this study did not focus specifically on African American women, the findings are potentially applicable, given the high morbidity and mortality related to diabetes among African American women.

Beyond factors that increase risk for psychological distress, a number of studies have examined protective aspects of African American culture associated with lowering levels of psychological distress. Table 2.7 presents an analysis of the relationships between depressive symptoms and two sociocultural factors that are particularly relevant to the lives of African American women. Inversely related to depressive symptoms, religious involvement in particular appears to be important to reducing the level of psychological distress among African American women when they are faced with various stressful life events (Bourjolly 1998; McIntosh and Danigelis 1995; Brown, Ndubuisi, and Gary 1990). Religious involvement is high among African American women, irrespective of socioeconomic status (Gilkes 1998; Lincoln and Mamiya 1990). Across different measures, religious involvement appears inversely related to psychological distress. Having a denominational affiliation was associated with fewer depressive symptoms among African Americans (Ellison 1995). Similarly, greater social participation is related to fewer depressive symptoms. African American women who are involved in organizations in their community, neighborhood, and place of employment report fewer depressive symptoms than do women without such involvement. It is likely that the fellowship with others as well as the resources stemming from social participation help to offset the stressors they face in their lives.

Another protective factor against psychological distress is the social support derived from interpersonal relationships with family members and friends. Research has shown that greater satisfaction with perceived social support from relatives and friends is important in reducing levels of depressive symptoms. For example, social support was a significant predictor of lower psychological distress in a sample of African American males and females with disabilities (Zea et al. 1996). Social support reduced depressive symptoms among unemployed African American women (Brown and Gary 1988), employed mothers (Benin and Keith 1995), and older Black women (Ulbrich and Bradsher 1993). At the same time, it is not clear that all social support has positive impact on psychological distress. Future research is needed to explore the complexity of social support in the African American communities as well as to examine the impact of negative support on psychological distress and mental health (Okun and Keith 1998).

In summary, current evidence indicates that African American women experience the highest levels of psychological distress; their reported distress tends to be higher than that of White women, African American men, and White men. At any given time, from 16 percent to 28 percent of the women in this group have psychological distress that is indicative of clinical depression. Thus, while current data do not point to race differences among women in MDD, research does show significant race differences among women with regard to subclinical depressive symptomatology.

The high levels of subclinical or subthreshold depression among African American women should be of concern to policy makers and mental health practitioners because the consequences of subclinical depression may be just as debilitating as those of MDD (Hybels, Pieper, and Blazer 2002; Coulehan et al. 1990). Subclinical depression may contribute to other health issues and other social morbidity and may affect health services utilization. Although the consequences of subclinical or minor depression for African American women are not fully understood, future investigations need to ascertain the extent to which subclinical depression among African American women contributes to greater mortality from heart disease, diabetes, cancer, and other conditions that disproportionately affect this population. While some contend that minor depression is a variant of MDD (Kessler, Zhao, and Swartz 1997; Beekman et al. 1995), it may be time to reassess the nature of subclinical depressive symptomatology for the purposes of establishing criteria for a specific diagnostic category and assessment. In particular, diagnostic criteria for subclinical depression need to recognize the detrimental mental health effects of racism and sexism. There is clearly a basis in DSM for doing so. In addition to its specific disorders, the appendix of DSM-IV includes a range of other conditions that may be the focus of clinical attention, such as bereavement, academic, occupational, phase-of-life, religious or spiritual problems. No mention is made of conditions or symptoms stemming from racist or sexist assaults or experiences. The closest category is "acculturation problem." Long overdue is consideration of an "oppression-reaction disorder due to race and/or gender discrimination." Such recognition would facilitate diagnosis and treatment.

The review of research in this chapter indicates that disparities in mental disorders and mental health exist for African American women with regard to their greater prevalence of anxiety disorders and greater psychological distress. The conjoint effects of racism and sexism contribute directly and indirectly to the diminished mental health status of African American women, although more research is clearly needed to examine factors of particular salience to their lives. Given that racism and sexism place African American women in positions of increased risk for mental disorder and psychological distress, it is amazing that psychiatric morbidity is not greater among them. The research also suggests, however, that cultural factors such as perceived social support, deep religiosity and spirituality, extended families, personal relationships, positive self-perception, and other coping strategies serve to soften the assaults on their mental well-being.

REFERENCES

Adebimpe, V. R. 1994. Race, racism, and epidemiological surveys. *Hospital and Community Psychiatry* 45 (1): 27–31.

Akbar, N. 1991. The Evolution of Human Psychology for African Americans. In R. L. Jones, ed., *Black Psychology*, 99–123. Berkeley, Calif.: Cobb and Henry.

Aldous, J. and R. F. Ganey. 1999. Family life and the pursuit of happiness: The influence of gender and race. *Journal of Family Issues* 20 (2): 155–180.

Allardt, E. 1976. *On the Relationship Between Objective and Subjective Predicaments.* Research Group for Comparative Sociology, Helinski, No. 16.

Alston, M. and S. Anderson. 1995. Suicidal Behavior in African American Women. In S. Canetto and D. Lester, eds., *Women and Suicidal Behavior*, 133–143. New York: Springer.

Alvidrez, J. 1999. Ethnic variations in mental health attitudes and service use among low-income African American, Latina, and European American young women. *Community Mental Health Journal* 35 (6): 515–530.

American Psychiatric Association. 1980. *Diagnostic and Statistical Manual of Mental Disorders–III.* Washington, D.C.

———. 1987. *Diagnostic and Statistical Manual of Mental Disorders—III.* Revised. Washington, D.C.

———. 1994. *Diagnostic and Statistical Manual of Mental Disorders—IV.* Washington, D.C.

Baker, F. M. 1984. Black suicide attempters in 1980: A preventive focus. *General Hospital Psychiatry* 6 (2): 131–137.

Baker, F. M., J. O. Okwumabua, V. Philipose, and S. Wong. 1996. Screening African-American elderly for the presence of depressive symptoms: A preliminary investigation. *Journal of Geriatric Psychiatry and Neurology* 9 (3): 127–132.

Baker, F. M., D. A. Parker, C. Wiley, S. A. Velli, and J. T. Johnson. 1995. Depressive symptoms in African-American medical patients. *International Journal of Geriatric Psychiatry* 10 (1): 9–14.

Ball, R. E. 1993. Children and marital happiness of Black-Americans. *Journal of Comparative Family Studies* 24 (2): 203–218.

Ball, R. E. and L. Robbins. 1986. Marital status and life satisfaction among Black Americans. *Journal of Marriage and the Family* 48 (2): 389–394.

Barzargan, M. 1996. Self-reported sleep disturbance among African American elderly: The effects of depression, health status, exercise, and social support. *International Journal of Aging* 42 (2): 143–160.

Beatty, P. and S. A. Tuch. 1997. Race and life satisfaction in the middle class. *Sociological Spectrum* 17 (1): 71–90.

Beck, A. T. 1972. *Depression: Causes and Treatment*. Philadelphia: University of Pennsylvania Press.

Beekman, A. T., D. J. Deeg, T. van Tilburg, J. H. Smit, C. Hooijer, and W. van Tilburg. 1995. Major and minor depression in later life: A study of prevalence and risk factors. *Journal of Affective Disorders* 36 (1–2): 65–75.

Bender, M. L. 2000. Suicide and older African American women. *Mortality* 5 (2): 158–170.

Benin, M. and V. M. Keith. 1995. The social support of employed African American and Anglo mothers. *Journal of Family Issues* 16 (3): 275–297.

Bennett, M. B. 1987. Afro-American women, poverty, and mental health: A social essay. *Women and Health* 12 (3–4): 213–228.

Blazer, D. G., J. C. Hays, and M. E. Salive. 1996. Factors associated with paranoid symptoms in a community sample of older adults. *Gerontologist* 36 (1): 70–75.

Blazer, D. G., R. C. Kessler, K. A. McGonagle, and M. S. Swartz. 1994. The prevalence and distribution of major depression in a national community sample: The National Comorbidity Survey. *American Journal of Psychiatry* 151 (7): 979–986.

Bosworth, H. B., K. S. Parsey, M. I. Butterfield, L. M. McIntyre, E. Z. Oddone, K. M. Stechuchak, and L. A. Bastian. 2000. Racial variation in wanting and obtaining mental health services among women veterans in a primary care clinic. *Journal of the National Medical Association* 92 (5): 231–236.

Bourjolly, J. N. 1998. Differences in religiousness among black and white women with breast cancer. *Social Work in Health Care* 28 (1): 21–39.

Boyd, J. H., D. S. Rae, J. W. Thompson, B. J. Burns, K. Bourdon, B. Z. Locke, and D. A. Regier. 1990. Phobia: Prevalence and risk factors. *Social Psychiatry and Psychiatric Epidemiology* 25 (6): 314–323.

Breslau, N., G. C. Davis, E. L. Peterson, and L. Schultz. 1997. Psychiatric sequelae of posttraumatic stress disorder in women. *Archives of General Psychiatry* 54 (1): 81–87.

Brim, O. G., P. B. Baltes, L. L. Bumpass, P. D. Cleary, D. L. Featherman, W. R. Hazzard, R. C. Kessler, M. Marmot, A. S. Rossi, C. D. Ryff, and R. A. Shweder. 2000. *National Survey of Midlife Development in the United States (MIDUS), 1995–1996*. Ann Arbor: DataStat, Inc./Boston: Harvard Medical School, Department of Health

Care Policy [producer], 1996. Ann Arbor: Inter-University Consortium for Political and Social Science Research [distributor].

Broman, C. L. 1987. Race differences in professional help seeking. *American Journal of Community Psychology* 15 (4): 473–489.

———. 1988. Satisfaction among Blacks: The significance of marriage and parenthood. *Journal of Marriage and the Family* 50 (1): 45–51.

———. 1997a. Families, Unemployment, and Well-being. In R. J. Taylor, J. S. Jackson, and L. M. Chatters, eds., *Family Life in Black America*, 157–166. Beverly Hills: Sage.

———. 1997b. Race-related factors and life satisfaction among African Americans. *Journal of Black Psychology* 23 (1): 36–49.

Brown, C., H. Schulberg, and M. Madonia. 1996. Clinical presentations of major depression by African Americans and Whites in primary medical care practice. *Journal of Affective Disorders* 41 (3): 181–191.

Brown, D. R. 1988. Socio-demographic vs. domain predictors of perceived stress: Racial differences among American women. *Social Indicators Research* 20:517–532.

———. 1990. Depression: An Epidemiologic Perspective. In D. Smith-Ruiz, ed., *Handbook of Mental Health and Mental Disorder Among Black Americans*, 71–93. New York: Greenwood.

———. 1996. Marital Status and Mental Health. In H. W. Neighbors and J. S. Jackson, eds., *Mental Health in Black America*, 77–94. Thousand Oaks, Calif.: Sage.

Brown, D. R., F. Ahmed, L. E. Gary, and N. G. Milburn. 1995. Major depression in a community sample of African Americans. *American Journal of Psychiatry* 152 (3): 373–378.

Brown, D. R., W. W. Eaton, and L. Sussman. 1990. Racial differences in prevalence of phobic disorders. *Journal of Nervous and Mental Disease* 178 (7): 434–441.

Brown, D. R., M. Fouad, K. Basen-Enquist, and G. Tortolero-Luna. 2000. Recruitment and retention of ethnic minority women to cancer clinical trials. *Annals of Epidemiology* 10 (8 Supplement): S13–S21.

Brown, D. R. and L. E. Gary. 1987. Stressful life events, social support networks, and the physical and mental health of urban Black adults. *Journal of Human Stress* 13 (4): 165–174.

———. 1988. Unemployment and psychological distress among Black American women. *Sociological Focus* 21 (3): 209–221.

Brown, D. R. and J. Mars. 1999. Intergenerational Caregiving Among African Americans: Strengths and Stresses. In C. Cox, ed., *To Grandmother's House We Go and Stay: The Issues, Needs, and Policies Affecting Grandparents Raising Grandchildren*. 203–217. New York: Springer.

Brown, D. R., N. G. Milburn, and L. E. Gary. 1992. Symptoms of depression among older African-Americans: An analysis of gender differences. *Gerontologist* 32 (6): 789–795.

Brown, D. R., S. C. Ndubuisi, and L. E. Gary. 1990. Religiosity and psychological distress among Blacks. *Journal of Religion and Health* 29 (1): 55–68.

Brown, D. R. and A. Sankar. 1998. HIV and older minorities. *Research on Aging* 20 (6): 865–884.

Bruce, M. L. and R. A. Hoff. 1994. Social and physical health risk factors for first-onset major depressive disorder in a community sample. *Social Psychiatry and Psychiatric Epidemiology* 29 (4): 165–171.

Chen, L. S., W. W. Eaton, J. J. Gallo, G. Nestadt, and R. M. Crum. 2000. Empirical examination of current depression categories in a population-based study: Symptoms, course, and risk factors. *American Journal of Psychiatry* 157 (4): 573–580.

Chisholm, J. F. 1996. Mental health issues in African-American women. *Annals of the New York Academy of Sciences* 789:161–179.

Chung, H., J. C. Mahler, and T. Kakuma. 1995. Racial differences in treatment of psychiatric inpatients. *Psychiatric Services* 46 (6): 586–591.

Ciechanowski, P. S., W. J. Katon, and J. E. Russo. 2000. Depression and diabetes: Impact of depressive symptoms on adherence, function, and costs. *Archives of Internal Medicine* 160 (21): 3278–3285.

Clark, L. S. 1993. The role of social support in mediating depressive symptomatology in African American women. *DAI* 54–04B:2190.

Cochran, D., D. R. Brown, and K. McGregor. 1999. Racial differences in the multiple social roles of midlife women: Implications for their mental well-being. *Gerontologist* 39 (4): 465–472.

Coulehan, J. L., H. C. Schulberg, M. R. Block, J. E. Janosky, and V. C. Arena. 1990. Depressive symptomatology and medical co-morbidity in a primary care clinic. *International Journal of Psychiatric Medicine* 20 (4): 335–347.

Davidson, J. R., D. L. Hughes, L. K. George, and D. G. Blazer. 1993. The epidemiology of social phobia: Findings from the Duke Epidemiological Catchment Area Study. *Psychological Medicine* 23 (3): 709–718.

Derogatis, L. R., R. S. Lipman, K. Rickels, E. H. Uhlenhuth, and L. Covi. 1974. The Hopkins Symptom Checklist (HSCL): A self-report symptom inventory. *Behavioral Science* 19 (1): 1–15.

Dimsdale, J. E. 2000. Stalked by the past: The influence of ethnicity on health. *Psychosomatic Medicine* 62 (2): 161–170.

Eaton, W. W., H. Armenian, J. Gallo, L. Pratt, and D. E. Ford. 1996. Depression and risk for onset of type II diabetes: A prospective population-based study. *Diabetes Care* 19 (10): 1097–1102.

Eaton, W. W., A. Dryman, and M. M. Weissman. 1991. Panic and Phobia. In L. N. Robins and D. A. Regier, eds., *Psychiatric Disorders in America: The Epidemiologic Catchment Area Study*, 155–179. New York: Free Press.

Eaton, W. W. and L. G. Kessler. 1981. Rates of symptoms of depression in a national sample. *American Journal of Epidemiology* 114 (4): 528–538.

Eisenberg, D. M., R. B. Davis, S. L. Ettner, S. Appel, S. Wilkey, M. Van Rompay, and R. C. Kessler. 1998. Trends in alternative medicine use in the United States, 1990–1997: Results of a follow-up national survey. *Journal of the American Medical Association* 280 (18): 1569–1575.

Ellison, C. G. 1995. Race, religious involvement, and depressive symptomatology in a southeastern U.S. community. *Social Science and Medicine* 40 (11): 1561–1572.

Franklin, A. J. and J. S. Jackson 1990. Factors Contributing to Positive Mental Health. In D. S. Ruiz, ed., *Handbook of Mental Health and Mental Disorder Among Black Americans*, 291–307. New York: Greenwood Press.

Frasure-Smith, N., F. Lesperance, G. Gravel, A. Masson, M. Juneau, M. Talajic, and M. G. Bourassa. 2000. Social support, depression, and mortality during the first year after myocardial infarction. *Circulation* 101 (16): 1919–1924.

Frerichs, R. R., C. S. Aneshensel, and V. A. Clark. 1981. Prevalence of depression in Los Angeles County. *American Journal of Epidemiology* 113 (6): 691–699.

Friedman, S., C. M. Paradis, and M. Hatch. 1994. Characteristics of African-American and white patients with panic disorder and agoraphobia. *Hospital and Community Psychiatry* 45 (8): 798–803.

Frierson, R. L., and S. B. Lippmann. 1990. Attempted suicide by black men and women: An 11 year study. *Journal of the Kentucky Medical Association* 88 (6): 287–292.

Fromm, E. 1947. *Man for Himself.* New York: Rinehart.

Gallo, J. J., H. K. Armenian, D. E. Ford, W. W. Eaton, and A. S. Khachaturian. 2000. Major depression and cancer: The 13-year follow-up of the Baltimore epidemiologic catchment area sample (United States). *Cancer Causes and Control* 11 (8): 751–758.

Gallo, J. J., L. Cooper-Patrick, and S. Lesikar. 1998. Depressive symptoms of whites and African Americans aged 60 years and older. *Journals of Gerontology Series B Psychological Sciences* 53 (5): P277–P286.

Gary, L. E., D. R. Brown, N. G. Milburn, F. Ahmed, and J. A. Booth. 1989. *Depressive Symptoms Among Urban Black Adults: The Norfolk Area Health Study Final Report.* Washington, D.C.: Howard University.

Gazmararian, J. A., S. A. James, and J. M. Lepkowski. 1995. Depression in Black and White women. *Annals of Epidemiology* 5 (6): 455–463.

Giblin, P. T., M. L. Poland, and J. W. Ager. 1990. Effects of social supports on attitudes, health behaviors, and obtaining prenatal care. *Journal of Community Health* 15 (6): 357–368.

Gilkes, C. T. 1998. Plenty good room: Adaptation in a changing Black church. *Annals of the Academy of Political and Social Science* 558:101–121.

Goodman, S. H., E. L. Cooley, D. R. Sewell, and N. Leavitt. 1994. Locus of control and self-esteem in depressed, low-income African-American women. *Community Mental Health Journal* 30 (3): 259–269.

Grier, W. H. and P. M. Cobbs. 1968. *Black Rage.* New York: Basic Books.

Haley, W. E., C. A. West, V. G. Wadley, G. R. Ford, F. A. White, J. J. Barrett, L. E. Harrell, and D. L. Roth. 1995. Psychological, social, and health impact of caregiving: A comparison of black and white dementia family caregivers and noncaregivers. *Psychology and Aging* 10 (4): 540–552.

Hebl, M. R. and T. F. Heatherton. 1998. The stigma of obesity in women: The difference is Black and White. *Personality and Social Psychology Bulletin* 24 (4): 417–426.

Heimberg, R. G., M. B. Stein, E. Hiripi, and R. C. Kessler. 2000. Trends in the prevalence of social phobia in the United States: A synthetic cohort analysis of changes over four decades. *European Psychiatry* 15 (1): 29–37.

Hemmings, M., J. O. Reimann, D. Madrigal, and R. J. Velasquez. 1998. Predictors of scores on the Brief Symptom Inventory for ethnically diverse female clients. *Psychological Reports* 83 (3, Part 1): 800–802.

Henderson, C. 2000. Hypertension: People with symptoms of depression or anxiety at higher risk, especially Black women. *Medical Letter on the CDC and FDA.* NewsRx.com:N/A.

Hirshorn, B., M. J. Van Meter, and D. R. Brown. 1999. Strengthening Parenting Across Generations: A Self-Management Learning Program for Grandparents Raising Grandchildren. In B. Hayslip and R. Goldberg-Glen, eds., *Grandparents Raising Grandchildren: Theoretical, Empirical, and Clinical Perspectives,* 269–287. New York: Springer.

Hogue, C., M. A. Hargraves, and K. S. Collins. 2000. *Minority Health in America: Findings and Policy Implications from Commonwealth Fund Minority Health Survey.* Baltimore: Johns Hopkins University Press.

hooks, b. 1993. *Sisters of the Yam: Black Women and Self Recovery.* Boston: South End Press.

Horwath, E., J. Johnson, G. L. Klerman, and M. M. Weissman. 1994. What are the public health implications of subclinical depressive symptoms? *Psychiatric Quarterly* 65 (4): 323–337.

House, J. S. 1986. *Americans' Changing Lives: Wave I.* Ann Arbor: Survey Research Center [producer]. Ann Arbor: Inter-University Consortium for Political and Social Science Research [distributor].

Hybels, C. F., C. F. Pieper, and D. G. Blazer. 2002. Sex differences in the relationship between subthreshold depression and mortality in a community sample of older adults. *American Journal of Geriatric Psychiatry* 10 (3): 283–291.

Jonas, B. S., P. Franks, and D. D. Ingram. 1997. Are symptoms of anxiety and depression risk factors for hypertension? Longitudinal evidence from the National Health and Nutrition Examination Survey I epidemiologic follow-up study. *Archives of Family Medicine* 6 (1): 43–49.

Jonas, B. S., and R. W. Wilson. 1997. Negative Mood and Urban Versus Rural Residence: Using Proximity to Metropolitan Statistical Areas as an Alternative Measure of Residence. In *Advance Data from Vital and Health Statistics,* no. 281. Hyattsville, Md.: National Center for Health Statistics.

Jones-Webb, R. J., D. R. Jacobs, Jr., J. M. Flack, and K. Liu. 1996. Relationships between depressive symptoms, anxiety, alcohol consumption, and blood pressure: Results from the CARDIA Study. Coronary Artery Risk Development in Young Adults Study. *Alcoholism, Clinical, and Experimental Research* 20 (3): 420–427.

Jones-Webb, R. J. and L. R. Snowden. 1993. Symptoms of depression among Blacks and Whites. *American Journal of Public Health* 83 (2): 240–244.

Kachur, S. P., L. B. Potter, S. P. James, and K. E. Powell. 1995. *Suicide in the United*

States: 1980–1992. Violence Surveillance Summary Series, no. 1. Atlanta: National Center for Injury Prevention and Control, Centers for Disease Control.

Kaslow, N. J., M. P. Thompson, A. E. Brooks, and H. B. Twomey. 2000. Ratings of family functioning of suicidal and nonsuicidal African American women. *Journal of Family Psychology* 14 (4): 585–599.

Keith, V. M. 1997. Life Stress and Psychological Well-being Among Married and Unmarried Blacks. In R. J. Taylor, L. M. Chatters, and J. S. Jackson, eds., *Family Life in Black America,* 95–116. Newbury Park, Calif.: Sage.

Kendler, K. S., T. J. Gallagher, J. M. Abelson, and R. C. Kessler. 1996. Lifetime prevalence, demographic risk factors, and diagnostic validity of nonaffective psychosis as assessed in a U.S. community sample: The National Comorbidity Survey. *Archives of General Psychiatry* 53 (11): 1022–1031.

Kessler, R. C., G. Borges, and E. E. Walters. 1999. Prevalence of and risk factors for lifetime suicide attempts in the National Comorbidity Survey. *Archives of General Psychiatry* 56 (7): 617–626.

Kessler, R. C., K. A. McGonagle, S. Zhao, C. B. Neson, M. Hughes, S. Eshleman, H. U. Wittchen, and K. S. Kendler. 1994. Lifetime and 12-month prevalence of DSM-III-R psychiatric disorders in the United States: Results from the National Comorbidity Survey. *Archives of General Psychiatry* 51 (1): 8–19.

Kessler, R. C., K. D. Mickelson, and D. R. Williams. 1999. The prevalence, distribution, and mental health correlates of perceived discrimination in the United States. *Journal of Health and Social Behavior* 40 (3): 208–230.

Kessler, R. C., A. Sonnega, E. Bromet, M. Hughes, and C. B. Nelson. 1995. Posttraumatic stress disorder in the National Comorbidity Survey. *Archives of General Psychiatry* 52 (12): 1048–1060.

Kessler, R. C., P. Stang, H. U. Wittchen, M. Stein, and E. E. Walters. 1999. Lifetime co-morbidities between social phobia and mood disorders in the U.S. National Comorbidity Survey. *Psychological Medicine* 29 (3): 555–567.

Kessler, R. C. and S. Zhao. 1999. The Prevalence of Mental Illness. In A. W. Horwitz and T. L. Scheid, eds., *A Handbook for the Study of Mental Health,* 58–78. Cambridge, Eng.: Cambridge University Press.

Kessler, R. C., S. Zhao, D. G. Blazer, and M. Swartz. 1997. Prevalence, correlates, and course of minor depression and major depression in the National Comorbidity Survey. *Journal of Affective Disorders* 45 (1–2): 19–30.

Kolb, L. C. 1968. *Noyes' Modern Clinical Psychiatry.* Philadelphia: Saunders.

Lawton, M. P., D. Rajagopal, E. Brody, and M. H. Kleban. 1992. The dynamics of caregiving for a demented elder among Black and White families. *Journal of Gerontology: Social Sciences* 47 (4): S156–S164.

Lincoln, C. E. and L. H. Mamiya. 1990. *The Black Church in the African American Experience.* Durham: Duke University Press.

Magee, W. J., W. W. Eaton, H. U. Wittchen, K. A. McGonagle, and R. C. Kessler. 1996. Agoraphobia, simple phobia, and social phobia in the National Comorbidity Survey. *Archives of General Psychiatry* 53 (2): 159–168.

Malhi, G. S., J. Moore, and P. McGuffin. 2000. The genetics of major depressive disorder. *Current Psychiatry Reports* 2 (2): 165–169.

Manuel, E. 2000. Seeking enchantment in the midst of oppression. *Journal of Women and Religion* 18:17–20.

Martin, J. C. 1996. Determinants of functional health of low-income black women with osteoarthritis. *American Journal of Preventive Medicine* 12 (5): 430–436.

Mayberry, R. M., F. Mili, and E. Ofili. 2000. Racial and ethnic differences in access to medical care. *Medical Care Research* 57 (Supplement 1): 108–145.

Mays, V. M., L. M. Coleman, and J. S. Jackson. 1996. Perceived race-based discrimination, employment status, and job stress in a national sample of black women: Implications for health outcomes. *Journal of Occupational Health Psychology* 1 (3): 319–329.

McGonagle, K. A., and R. C. Kessler. 1990. Chronic stress, acute stress, and depressive symptoms. *American Journal of Community Psychology* 18 (5): 681–706.

McIntosh, B. R. and N. L. Danigelis. 1995. Race, gender, and the relevance of productive activity for elders' affect. *Journals of Gerontology: Series B Psychological Sciences and Social Sciences* 50 (4): S229–S239.

McLoyd, V. C., T. E. Jayaratne, R. Ceballo, and J. Borquez. 1994. Unemployment and work interruption among African American single mothers: Effects on parenting and adolescent socioemotional functioning. *Child Development* 65 (2 Spec No): 562–589.

Moneyham, L., R. Sowell, B. Seals, and A. Demi. 2000. Depressive symptoms among African American women with HIV disease. *Scholarly Inquiry for Nursing Practice* 14 (1): 9–39, 41–46.

Mowbray, C. T., D. Oyserman, D. Saunders, and A. Rueda-Riedle. 1998. Women with Severe Mental Disorders: Issues and Service Needs. In Bruce Luborsky Levin, Andrea K. Blanch, and Ann Jennings, eds., *Women's Mental Health Services,* 175–200. Thousand Oaks, Calif.: Sage.

Murrell, S. A., S. Himmelfarb, and K. Wright. 1983. Prevalence of depression and its correlates in older adults. *American Journal of Epidemiology* 117 (2): 173–185.

National Vital Statistics Report. 2000 (July). Table 8. Deaths and Death Rates for the Ten Leading Causes of Death in Specified Age Groups, by Race and Sex, United States, 1998 National Vital Statistics Report 48 (11): 26–36.

Neal, A. M. and S. M. Turner. 1991. Anxiety disorders research with African Americans: Current status. *Psychological Bulletin* 109 (3): 400–410.

Neal-Barnett, A. M. and J. H. Crowther. 2000. To be female, middle class, anxious, and Black. *Psychology of Women Quarterly* 24: 129–136.

Neighbors, H. W. and S. Lumpkin. 1990. The epidemiology of mental disorder among Black Americans. In D. S. Ruiz, ed., *Handbook of Mental Health and Mental Disorder Among Black Americans,* 55–70. New York: Greenwood.

Neighbors, H. W., M. A. Musick, and D. R. Williams. 1998. The African American minister as a source of help for serious personal crises: Bridge or barrier to mental health care? *Health Education and Behavior* 25 (6): 759–777.

Neighbors, H. W., S. J. Trierweiler, C. Munday, E. E. Thompson, J. S. Jackson, V. J. Binion, and J. Gomez. 1999. Psychiatric diagnosis of African Americans: Diagnostic divergence in clinical structured and semistructured interviewing conditions. *Journal of the National Medical Association* 91 (11): 601–612.

Nobles, W. 1991. African Psychology: Toward Its Reclamation, Reascension, Revitalization. In R. L. Jones, ed., *Black Psychology,* 47–63. Berkeley, Calif.: Cobb and Henry.

Okun, M. A. and V. M. Keith. 1998. Effects of positive and negative social exchanges with various sources on depressive symptoms in younger and older adults. *Journal of Gerontology: Psychological Sciences* 53 (1): P4–P20.

Okwumabua, J. O., F. M. Baker, S. P. Wong, and B. O. Pilgram. 1997. Characteristics of depressive symptoms in elderly urban and rural African Americans. *Journal of Gerontology: Medical Sciences* 52 (4): M241–M246.

Orr, S. T., D. D. Celantano, J. Santelli, and L. Burwell. 1994. Depressive symptoms and risk factors for HIV acquisition among black women attending urban health centers in Baltimore. *AIDS Education Prevention* 6 (3): 230–236.

Paradis, C. M., S. Friedman, and M. Hatch. 1997. Isolated sleep paralysis in African Americans with panic disorder. *Cultural Diversity and Mental Health* 3 (1): 69–76.

Parker, K. D. 1996. Predictors of life satisfaction among Black Americans. *Western Journal of Black Studies* 20 (3): 134–139.

Parker, K. D., and T. Calhoun. 1996. Gender differences in global life satisfaction among African Americans. *National Journal of Sociology* 10 (1): 1–13.

Pavkov, T. W., M. P. McGovern, and E. S. Geffner. 1993. Problem severity and symptomatology among substance misusers: Differences between African-Americans and Caucasians. *International Journal of Addictions* 28 (9): 909–922.

Peek, M. K. and G. S. O'Neill. 2001. Networks in later life: An examination of race differences in social support networks. *International Journal of Aging and Human Development* 52:207–229.

Peyrot, M. and R. R. Rubin. 1997. Levels and risks of depression and anxiety symptomatology among diabetic adults. *Diabetes Care* 20 (4): 585–590.

Radloff, L. S. 1977. The CES-D: A self-report depression scale for research in the general population. *Journal of Applied Psychological Measurement* 1:385–401.

Rickert, V. I., C. M. Wiemann, and A. B. Berenson. 2000. Ethnic differences in depressive symptomatology among young women. *Obstetrics and Gynecology* 95 (1): 55–60.

Roberts, R. E., M. A. Stevenson, and L. Breslow. 1981. Symptoms of depression among blacks and whites in an urban community. *Journal of Nervous and Mental Disease* 169 (12): 774–779.

Robins, L. N., J. E. Helzer, J. Croughan, and K. Ratcliff. 1981. National Institute of Mental Health Diagnostic Interview Schedule: Its history, characteristics, and validity. *Archives of General Psychiatry* 38 (4): 381–389.

Roxburgh, S., A. S. London, and J. Ali. 2000. *Gender Differences in Depression: Can We Generalize Across Race?* Washington, D.C.: American Sociological Association.

Russo, N. F., J. E. Denious, G. P. Keita, and M. P. Koss. 1997. Intimate violence and Black women's health. *Women's Health* 3 (3–4): 315–348.

Schnittker, J., J. Freese, and B. Powell. 2000. Nature, nurture, neither, nor: Black-white differences in beliefs about the causes and appropriate treatment of mental illness. *Social Forces* 78 (3): 1101–1132.

Snapp, M. B. 1992. Occupational stress, social support, and depression among black and white professional-managerial women. *Women and Health* 18 (1): 41–79.

Snowden, L. and F. Cheung. 1990. Use of inpatient mental health services by members of ethnic minority groups. *American Psychologist* 45:347–355.

Somervell, P. D., P. J. Leaf, M. M. Weissman, D. G. Blazer, and M. L. Bruce. 1989. The prevalence of major depression in black and white adults in five United States communities. *American Journal of Epidemiology* 130 (4): 725–735.

Son, B. K., J. H. Markovitz, S. Winders, and D. Smith. 1997. Smoking, nicotine dependence, and depressive symptoms in the CARDIA Study: Effects of education status. *American Journal of Epidemiology* 145 (2): 110–116.

Spicer, R. S. and T. R. Miller. 2000. Suicide acts in eight states: Incidence and case fatality rates by demographics and method. *American Journal of Public Health* 90 (12): 1885–1891.

Stack, S. 1998. The relationship between culture and suicide: An analysis of African Americans. *Transcultural-Psychiatry* 35 (2): 253–269.

Stevens, J. W. 1997. African American female adolescent identity development: A three-dimensional perspective. *Child Welfare* 76 (1): 145–172.

Surgeon General. 1999. *Mental Health: A Report of the Surgeon General.* Washington, D.C.: U.S. Government Printing Office.

Sweet, J., L. Bumpass, and V. Call. 1988. The design and content of the National Survey of Families and Households. NSFH Working Paper #1. Center for Demography and Ecology, University of Wisconsin-Madison.

Talbot, F. and A. Nouwen. 2000. A review of the relationship between depression and diabetes in adults: Is there a link? *Diabetes Care* 23 (10): 1556–1562.

Taylor, J., D. Henderson, and B. Jackson. 1991. A holistic model for understanding and predicting depressive symptoms in African American women. *Journal of Community Psychology* 19 (4): 306–320.

Thomas, C. and J. P. Comer. 1973. Racism and Mental Health. In C. V. Willie, M. Kramer, and B. Brown, eds., *Racism and Mental Health: Essays.* Pittsburgh: University of Pittsburgh Press.

Thomas, M. E. and B. J. Holmes. 1992. Determinants of satisfaction for Blacks and Whites. *Sociological Quarterly* 33 (3): 459–472.

Thompson, C. L. 2000. African American Women and Moral Masochism. In L. Jackson and B. Greene, eds., *Psychotherapy with African American Women,* 239–250. New York: Guilford Press.

Tilders, F. J., E. D. Schmidt, W. J. Hoogedijk, and D. F. Swaab. 1999. Delayed effects of stress and immune activation. *Baillieres Best Practice and Research Clinical Endocrinology and Metabolism* 13 (4): 523–540.

Turner, R. J. and D. A. Lloyd. 1999. The stress process and the social distribution of depression. *Journal of Health and Social Behavior* 40 (4): 374–404.

Ulbrich, P. M. and J. E. Bradsher. 1993. Perceived support, help seeking and adaptation to stress among older Black and White women living alone. *Journal of Aging and Health* 5 (3): 365–386.

Van Hook, M. P. 1999. Women's help-seeking patterns for depression. *Social Work in Health Care* 29 (1): 15–34.

Wallsten, S. S. 2000. Effects of caregiving, gender, and race on the health, mutuality, and social supports of older couples. *Journal of Aging and Health* 12 (1): 90–111.

Wang, P. S., P. Berglund, and R. C. Kessler. 2000. Recent care of common mental disorders in the United States. *Journal of General Internal Medicine* 15 (5): 284–292.

Warheit, G. J., C. E. Holzer, and J. J. Schwab. 1973. An analysis of social class and racial differences in depressive symptomatology. *Journal of Health and Social Behavior* 14 (4): 291–299.

Warren, B. J. 1994. Depression in African-American women. *Journal of Psychosocial Nursing* 32 (3): 29–33.

———. 1997. Depression, stressful life events, social support, and self-esteem in middle class African American women. *Archives of Psychiatric Nursing* 11 (3): 107–117.

Weissman, M. M., R. C. Bland, G. J. Canino, S. Greenwald, C. K. Lee, S. C. Newman, M. Rubio-Stipec, and P. J. Wickramaratne. 1996. The cross-national epidemiology of social phobia: A preliminary report. *International Clinical Psychopharmacology* 11 (Supplement 3): 9–14.

Weissman, M. M., M. L. Bruce, P. J. Leaf, L. P. Florio, and C, Holzer. 1991. Affective Disorders. In L. N. Robins and D. A. Regier, eds., *Psychiatric Disorders in America: The Epidemiologic Catchment Area Study.* New York: Free Press.

Wilcox, P. 1973. Positive Mental Health in the Black Community: The Black Liberation Movement. In C. Willie, B. Kramer, and B. Brown, eds., *Racism and Mental Health,* 463–524. Pittsburgh: University of Pittsburgh Press.

Wilfley, D. E., G. B. Schreiber, K. M. Pike, R. H. Striegel-Moore, D. J. Wright, and J. Rodin. 1996. Eating disturbance and body image: A comparison of a community sample of adult black and white women. *International Journal of Eating Disorders* 20 (4): 377–387.

Williams, D. 1999. Race, socioeconomic status, and health: The added effects of racism and discrimination. *Annals of the New York Academy of Science* 896: 173–188.

Wohi, M., I. Lesser, and M. Smith. 1997. Clinical presentations of depression in African American and white outpatients. *Cultural Diversity in Mental Health* 3 (4): 279–284.

Zea, M. C., F. Z. Belgrave, T. G. Townsend, S. L. Jarama, and S. R. Banks. 1996. The influence of social support and active coping on depression among African Americans and Latinos with disabilities. *Rehabilitation Psychology* 41 (3): 225–242.

Ziedonis, D. M., B. S. Rayford, K. J. Bryant, and B. J. Rounsaville. 1994. Psychiatric comorbidity in white and African-American cocaine addicts seeking substance abuse treatment. *Hospital and Community Psychiatry* 45 (1): 43–49.

Zollar, A. C. and J. S. Williams. 1987. The contribution of marriage to the life satisfaction of Black adults. *Journal of Marriage and the Family* 49:87–92.
Zung, W. W., C. B. Richards, and M. J. Short. 1965. Self-rating depression scale in an
outpatient clinic: Further validation of the SDS. *Archives of General Psychiatry* 13
(6): 508–515.

3 CHANGING THEIR MINDS: DRUG ABUSE AND ADDICTION IN BLACK WOMEN

Lula A. Beatty

Substance abuse has had a devastating effect on Black communities. It is causally linked to serious health problems, violence and crime, neighborhood deterioration, and family disruption (Pinn 1998; Nobles and Goddard 1989). It has robbed families and communities of income, resources, and dignity. Traditionally women have been a stalwart, stabilizing force in Black communities, providing financial, emotional, spiritual, and social support to kin and friends and to community organizations such as the church (Billingsley 1992). What makes a Black woman—mama, sister, daughter, friend, wife—voluntarily take a substance into her body that alters her perceptions and feelings of well-being? Why does she seek to literally change her mind, change the way she sees, thinks, and behaves? What effect does this have on her life, the lives of her children and family, and the vitality of her community? How many and how frequently do Black women use drugs?

The goals of this chapter are to: (1) provide an overview of Black women's use of drugs, including a demographic and psychological profile of Black female drug abusers; (2) discuss the major problems they are likely to experience as a result of their drug use; (3) explore reasons offered to explain drug abuse by Black females; (4) present approaches to prevention and treatment; and (5) identify issues and problems related to substance use by Black women that are in need of further study.

SUBSTANCE ABUSE IN BLACK WOMEN

One in three alcoholics and two in five illicit drug abusers in the United States are estimated to be women (Russac and Weaver 1995; Reed 1987). In comparison to men, the number of women using illicit drugs has increased (Leshner 1995), from a ratio of 1:5 in the 1960s to 1:2 in the 1990s (Anthony and Helzer 1991).

The National Household Survey on Drug Abuse (NHSDA) (SAMHSA 1999), which reports annually on drug-using behavior of people 12 and older living in households in the general population, provides perhaps the best data on Black adults who are not institutionalized, although analyses by gender and ethnicity are sometimes limited by sample size and biases. I use this data source to present an overview of drug use among Black women. Since data are not routinely or uniformly reported by gender and ethnicity, a special analysis was run on the prevalence of drug use for specific substances (i.e., marijuana, cocaine, and cigarettes) for Black women for the years 1994–1998 (table 3.1). Past-month data are used for cigarettes and marijuana and, because of its infrequent use in the population, past-year data are used for cocaine. The great majority of Black females do not use drugs. When they do use drugs, they are more likely to report using cigarettes, with the two oldest age groups (26–34 and 35 and over) reporting more smoking. Of the two illicit drugs reported, marijuana is the more frequently used, with the highest use reported by the two youngest age groups (12–17 and 18–25); however, the largest percentage reporting use is 11.3 percent of 18-to-25-year-olds in 1997. Cocaine is more likely to be used by women in the 26–34 age group, nearly 4 percent of whom reported using cocaine in 1997, the highest number of any age group in the five years reported. A disturbing trend came to light in the use of marijuana by young girls: Since 1995 marijuana use in the 12–17 age group has steadily increased.

SAMHSA (1999) reports that in 1997, 34.3 percent of Black females reported using alcohol in the past month, 48.1 percent reported using alcohol in the past year, and 66.7 percent reported that they had used alcohol in their lifetime. More drinking was reported by women in the age groups 18–25 and 26–34 than in others. Nearly a third of those in the 12–17 age group, however, reported that they had used alcohol in their lifetime, a percentage point lower than White and Hispanic girls of the same age (43.8% and 35.8%, respectively) but higher than Black males of the same age (29.9%). Fewer than one percent of Black women report lifetime use of heroin, the only drug they use more than White women do (SAMHSA 1997a).

Another important measure of drug use is the number of people who experience drug use as a problem—those for whom substance use has led to social or physical health problems, including dependence. This measure includes those who needed or received drug treatment in the past year, were dependent on illicit drugs in the past year, were frequent drug users (e.g., used marijuana daily or more often, or used psychotherapeutics, hallucinogens, inhalants, or cocaine weekly or more often), were injection drug users in the

TABLE 3.1 Prevalence of Substance Use Among Black Women by Age and Substance, 1994–1998

(REPORTED IN PERCENTAGES)

	1994	1995	1996	1997	1998
Marijuana use past month					
12–17	6.4	4.8	6.3	7.0	7.6
18–25	7.4	6.6	8.1	11.3	9.5
26–34	4.9	4.7	5.7	5.2	4.6
35+	2.9	1.5	2.7	2.6	1.2
Total	4.4	3.3	4.5	4.9	3.8
Cocaine use past year					
12–17	0.4	*	*	0.3	*
18–25	0.5	0.9	1.0	0.9	0.9
26–34	3.5	3.0	1.9	3.9	3.3
35+	1.5	0.7	2.4	1.9	1.1
Total	1.6	1.1	2.1	1.9	1.3
Cigarette use past month					
12–17	11.9	10.3	8.7	12.8	10.6
18–25	22.2	19.7	23.1	22.8	25.0
26–34	30.0	33.3	30.0	28.1	27.6
35+	28.8	28.6	28.8	29.8	28.9
Total	26.1	25.8	25.7	26.4	25.9

* Low precision

Source: SAMHSA, National Household Survey on Drug Abuse, 1994–1998. Special analysis run by Andrea Kopstein, Ph.D., SAMHSA

past year, or used heroin in the past year. Heavy cigarette use was defined as smoking one pack or more per day, and heavy alcohol use was defined as having had five or more drinks per occasion on five or more days in the past month. Among Black females age 12 and over, 6 percent reported heavy cigarette smoking for the past month, 2.2 percent reported past month heavy alcohol use, 4.1 percent reported past year substance dependence, and 2.1 percent reported past year problem drug abuse (SAMHSA 1997a). These categories are not mutually exclusive; women may have problems with multiple substances. Except in the case of cigarette smoking, there appears to be little difference in the degree to which Black and White women experienced substances as problems. Even though Black women reported more drinking (from

1984 to 1992), it was not followed by increased consequences or dependence (Jones-Webb et al. 1997). It has been suggested also that the age at onset for problem substance use is later for Black people (Herd 1989), with problem use more likely to occur in early or middle adulthood than in adolescence.

Sociodemographic variables, particularly marital status, educational level, and employment, are thought to be associated with drug use. To determine if cigarette, marijuana, and any illicit drug use among Black women is related to these variables, a special analysis was run on the NHSDA for the years 1997 and 1998, using past-month data (table 3.2). Employment and marital status appear to have substantial effects. Unemployed women are more likely to smoke (49.77% versus 27.15%) and are five times more likely to use marijuana or any illicit drug (11.92% versus 2.68% and 15.12% versus 3.31%, respectively). Educational attainment presents a more complex picture. More education seems to predict less illicit drug use, but the differences are not remarkable. High school graduates report more smoking than women who did not finish high school and women with some college.

CONSEQUENCES OF SUBSTANCE USE

The epidemiologic data clearly show that, overall, Black women do not use substances any more frequently than other groups of women do. However, research indicates that sex and race/ethnicity lead to disparate experiences in the consequences of drug use, with women and Blacks showing more serious consequences in comparison to men and Whites, respectively (Gordis 1990; Brunswick and Messeri 1999).

VIOLENCE AND SUBSTANCE USE

Women who are the victims of violence are often substance abusers or are in relationships with substance abusers. Drinking by either the man or the woman or both is related to violence between spouses (Kantor and Straus 1989), and higher levels of severe violence inflicted by males on their female partners were found among women participating in alcohol treatment programs than among women in the general population (Downs, Miller, and Panek 1993). Miller (1998) interviewed more than six hundred women from three groups (an outpatient drug treatment program, shelters for partner violence, and the general community) to determine if drug use increased the risk of partner violence and/or if partner violence increased the risk of drug

TABLE 3.2 Prevalence of Substance Use Among Black Women by Marital Status, Educational Attainment, and Employment Status, 1997 and 1998

	CIGARETTE USE PAST MONTH	MARIJUANA USE PAST MONTH	ANY ILLICIT DRUG USE PAST MONTH
	%	%	%
Marital status			
Married	21.43	2.35	2.89
Not married	30.20	5.50	6.96
Educational attainment			
Not high school graduate	25.22	4.99	6.90
High school graduate	30.60	4.88	5.79
Some college	22.18	3.46	4.37
College/graduate degree	23.59	*	*
Employment status			
Full-time	27.15	2.68	3.31
Part-time	26.42	*	*
Unemployed	49.77	11.92	15.12

* Low precision

Source: SAMHSA, National Household Survey on Drug Abuse, 1997 and 1998 combined. Special analysis run by Andrea Kopstein, Ph.D., SAMHSA

use. As expected, women in the shelters experienced high levels of severe violence, but surprisingly, women in the drug treatment group reported equally high levels of severe violence (e.g., hit with fist or object, beat up, threatened with gun or knife, forced to have sex). Moreover, women in the community who had alcohol and drug problems were two to four times more likely to experience severe violence than community women without such problems were. Using drugs frequently at a young age leads to illegal and violent behavior later for Black women (Friedman et al. 1996). Women under the influence of drugs also appear to be more likely to abuse or neglect their children (Walker, Zangrollo, and Smith 1991) and more likely to be involved in situations that lead to partner violence (Gilbert et al. 2001). Black women have slightly higher death rates resulting from alcohol- and drug-induced causes in comparison to White women, and they are more likely than White women to be murdered.

HIV INFECTION AND AIDS

About 60 percent of AIDS cases among females are drug-related (Centers for Disease Control and Prevention 1998). Of all women, Black women have been most severely affected by HIV/AIDS (Hobfoll et al. 1993). Black and Latina women represented 86 percent of the AIDS cases in women in 1991, and non-Hispanic Black women accounted for more than 50 percent of the documented AIDS cases in 1993. AIDS is currently the leading cause of death for Black women in the 25–44 age group, the prime years for family and work obligations (Centers for Disease Control and Prevention 1993, 1994).

Poor Black women using crack cocaine, the "hard drug" of choice of Black women, may be the most vulnerable group for HIV/AIDS infection (Sikkema, Heckman, and Kelly 1997). Black women who use crack are more likely to engage in risky sexual behavior such as not using condoms and exchanging sex for drugs to support and/or maintain drug-using habits, which leads to their increased likelihood of contracting the HIV virus and other sexually transmitted diseases (Logan and Leukefeld 2000). Moreover, Black women who inject drugs may be more likely to share needles (Singer 1991).

HEALTH CARE ACCESS

Access to care and the quality of treatment provided is worse for drug-using and HIV-infected women. Women with HIV infection appear to have poorer access to care than HIV-positive men do (Selwyn and Gourevitch 1998), but people of color and injecting drug users with HIV/AIDS receive poorer care than any other group (Moore et al. 1991). Black substance-abusing women may be less likely to seek prenatal care because they fear that staff will find out about their substance use problem (Mikhail 1999). Drug-injecting women and women who have been incarcerated and who are seeking care for their HIV-infected babies have also been found to be less likely to receive care (Butz et al. 1993).

PREGNANCY AND CHILD OUTCOMES

The use of licit and illicit drugs is associated with a number of conditions that affect Black women during pregnancy and the health of their children (Hanna, Faden, and Dufour 1997; Oyemade et al. 1994). Maternal cigarette smoking is associated with low birth weight and premature births, and maternal drinking is associated with the incidence of Fetal Alcohol Syndrome, the leading cause of mental retardation (Blumenthal 1998). The drug prevalence studies of perinatal drug use, given some problems with sample methodology (Vega et al. 1997), report higher levels of drug use in Black women tested at delivery (Berenson et al. 1991). Newborns testing positive for cocaine were more likely to be discharged to nonmaternal care if their mothers were Black (Neuspiel 1996). Examining age trajectories for perinatal use of cocaine, marijuana, and alcohol, Vega and colleagues (1997) concluded that Black women experienced a disproportionate burden of risk factors. Unmarried Black women on public assistance were at greatest risk of perinatal cocaine use, a risk that increased with age. Warner, Flores, and Robinson (1995), in a review of hospital records, found that 41 percent of the admissions were directly related to cocaine use, with pregnant women accounting for about a third of the patients with a positive screen. The pregnant women were more likely to be nonwhite (usually Black). The majority of pediatric AIDS cases are drug-related (Centers for Disease Control and Prevention 1998), with most of the cases being children born to Black women.

EMOTIONAL HEALTH AND PSYCHIATRIC DISORDERS

The comorbidity of psychiatric disorders and drug addiction is well established (Cottler, Abdallah, and Compton 1998), and the relationship appears to be stronger among women than men (Lex 1991). Rates of psychiatric disorders are higher among substance users than nonusers for every *DSM-III* substance use or dependence category as assessed in the Epidemiologic Catchment Area Study (Regier et al. 1990) and the National Comorbidity Survey (Kessler et al. 1994). Depression, affective disorders, anxiety disorders, and PTSD are the most commonly seen mental health problems in the substance-abusing population. Marital conflict and depression are associated with higher levels of drinking and smoking in women (Lex 1991), and nicotine dependence is associated with major depression (Covey 1998). Post-traumatic stress disorder, which often occurs in women as a result of early trauma such as childhood sexual abuse and rape, is associated with substance abuse later in life (McCauley et al. 1997), and data from a large community epidemiologic survey indicate that 70 percent of those who have PTSD are women (Helzer, Robins, and McEvoy 1987). Two studies of illicit drug users, 67 percent of whom were Black women, found that a substantial proportion of the women met the criteria for a psychiatric disorder, with the most common disorders being phobia, major depression, antisocial personality disorder, and PTSD; early users were more likely to meet the diagnostic criteria for these disorders (Cottler, Abdallah, and Compton 1998). Drug use has been found to be a risk factor for suicide ideation and attempts among Black women (Kaslow et al. 2000; Hill, Boyd, and Kortge 2000).

Self-esteem also has been indicated as a factor in drinking (Yanish and Battle 1985) and other substance use in women, although the relationship, some argue, is not a straightforward one (McNair, Carter, and Williams 1998). Although there is little research on the issue of stigma and shame associated with drug use by women within the Black community, it is thought to be severe, considering the high cultural norms regarding the social behavior of women. Treatment providers have commented that the extent of support and tolerance for relapse extended by family and friends to Black women appears to be low. Women in treatment express a profound sense of guilt and shame (Corse, McHugh, and Gordon 1995) and suffer a great loss of self-esteem, which can interfere with their motivation and ability to respond to treatment. Black women in treatment report unresolved feelings of guilt and shame concerning their perceived failure as mothers (Ehrmin 2001). Children and parents of Black female addicts may themselves feel particularly stigmatized by the woman's drug use, sharing some of the blame for the addiction. Findings that Black youths are sometimes introduced to drugs by parents suggest there may be some legitimacy to a perception of blame (Moon et al. 1999).

EXPLANATIONS FOR DRUG ABUSE
IN BLACK WOMEN

The last thirty years of the twentieth century saw a proliferation of theoretical models that seek to explain and predict drug use, e.g., the stress-vulnerability model (Pearlin et al. 1981), problem behavior (Jessor and Jessor 1980), the gateway theory (Kandel 1985), relative deviance (Dembo et al. 1979), the ecological model (Brunswick and Messeri 1984; Sanders-Phillips 1998), and the dispositional model (Brook et al. 1997). As research identifies a large range of variables and conditions (e.g., gender, environment, personality) that contribute to drug use etiology, it becomes increasingly unlikely that any one theory is sufficient to explain drug use behavior for all people. For women and Blacks, factors related to the interaction of stress and trauma and family and interpersonal relationships appear to be the most predictive for drug abuse (Alegria et al. 1998; King 1982; Russac and Weaver 1995).

Russac and Weaver (1995), in a review of data and theories, found six predisposing factors that were of special significance in understanding female adolescent substance use: sex role conflict, parents, relationships, personality traits, social networks, and biological factors. Certain parent behaviors are particularly influential for understanding female drug use, e.g., parental abuse of alcohol or other drugs, child abuse, sexual abuse, and violence. Other parent behaviors associated with substance use in women include lack of proper supervision (Dishion, Patterson, and Reid 1988) and parental absence and family conflict (McCarthy and Anglin 1990). A study with a majority Black (80%), female (79%) sample of narcotic addicts supported the importance of parental influences (Nurco et al. 1998). Few (less than 2 percent) of the addicts' parents had problems with illicit drugs, but 47 percent of the respondents reported that parental alcohol abuse caused problems in the family. Fathers of the addicts tended to be emotionally distant, less involved, and had weaker relationship bonds with their children than did mothers of addicts. Few gender differences were found; however, female addicts rated their fathers as less dysfunctional than their mothers on punitive actions and female addicts with alcohol-abusing mothers rated their mothers as extremely dysfunctional in terms of parent responsibility. A prospective study of Black women who were sexually abused as children found that multiple incidents of child sexual abuse predicted heavy alcohol use (Jasinski, Williams, and Siegel 2000). In a retrospective study of Black women who smoked crack, the majority of the women reported that family members used alcohol and drugs, and they had experienced sexual trauma and some other stress (Boyd et al. 1998). Among Black women, experiences such as the loss of child custody or the death of a child or desertion or rejection by a significant person led to increased drug use (Roberts 1999).

Men play pivotal roles in women's substance use. Women are more likely to be introduced to drug use by their sexual partners (Henderson, Boyd, and Mieczkowski 1994; Bresnahan, Zuckerman, and Cabral 1992; Stenbacka, Allebeck, and Romelsjo 1992) and to have histories of sexual (Inciardi, Lockwood, and Pottegier 1993) or physical abuse (Robles et al. 1998). Marital conflict has been associated with higher levels of drinking and smoking in women (Lex 1991). Windle (1997), however, found that the prevalence of spousal problem drinking was lower for Black women whether they had drinking problems themselves or not.

Women often use drugs as a coping mechanism when confronted with high levels of stress (Hser, Anglin, and McGlothlin 1987). The association between stressful life events and substance use may be intensified in poor and minority women (Sanders-Phillips 1998) because they face unique stressors that are not commonly experienced by White women. For example, Taylor, Henderson, and Jackson (1991) report that internalized racism in addition to exposure to violence and other stressful life events is related to alcohol use in Black women. Similarly, Singleton, Harrell, and Kelley (1986) found stress and racism experiences to be related to cigarette smoking in Black women.

Black women are poorer, and poverty and related socioeconomic indicators are purportedly associated with drug use (SAMHSA 1999), although some argue that no clear pattern of relationships between sociodemographic variables and drug use emerges from the data (Knupfer 1989; Kopstein and Gfrorerer 1990). Marital status can be a proxy for exposure to stress for women in that it is an indicator of economic and social well-being, with married women having the advantage of generally being more affluent and having more resources. It is not surprising, then, to find that married women are less likely to use illicit drugs, be heavy drinkers, or have problems with drugs in comparison to women who have never married or are divorced or separated (SAMHSA 1997b, 1999). Moreover, divorced or separated women, followed by married women, are more likely to be heavy smokers (SAMHSA 1997b, 1999). Black women are much less likely than White women or men to be married or to ever marry (Rodgers and Thornton 1985; Norton and Moorman 1987; Bennett, Bloom, and Craig 1989) although they desire marriage (Billingsley 1992). They may experience stress related to unfulfilled personal and cultural marital expectations, at least during the years when marriage is normally expected (and the years of highest substance use in this group), in addition to the economic and social stressors associated with being single or a single mother.

Other factors specific to Black women in understanding drug use and abuse have not been well explored. For example, Gottfredson and Koper (1996) found that risk factors were less predictive of drug use among Black female adolescents in comparison to White females. The investigators attributed this result to the low frequency of drug use by Black females generally, but it may indicate that there are other, uninvestigated factors that better explain drug use by Black females.

PREVENTION AND TREATMENT

Effective prevention programs for women and minorities must address the gender- and culture-specific needs of these target groups as guided by both risk and protective factors important to them. Key risk factors for drug abuse in women were identified earlier. Less is known about protective factors, but the most promising ones for Black people appear to be religiosity or spirituality (Wallace et al. 1995), supportive mentors and parents (Rhodes, Gingiss, and Smith 1994), and Africentric values (Belgrave et al. 1994; Goddard 1993).

Women do better in drug treatment programs designed specifically for them (Dahlgren and Willander 1989; Center for Substance Abuse Treatment 1994), comprehensive programs that address all of their needs, providing parenting skills, child care, and residential care for both mother and child (Luthar and Walsh 1995), vocational training (Marr and Wenner 1996), and all the ancillary services, including the involvement of family and significant others (Marsh and Miller 1985). Moreover, women substance abusers often need treatment for sexual abuse and emotional distress (Wallen 1992), rape and incest (Stevens, Arbiter, and Glider 1989), depression, low self-esteem, and feelings of shame (Reed 1985; Uziel-Miller et al. 1998), as well as programs that increase their confidence about their ability to change (Audrain et al. 1997).

Women experience more stigmatization and community barriers to recovery (Turner et al. 1998; Turnbull 1989), and they may not respond as well to the confrontational style used in many drug treatment programs designed for men (Hall 1993). Women may be more reluctant to seek drug abuse treatment because of negative expectations (Kline 1996) and fear of losing custody of their children to the child welfare system (Corse, McHugh, and Gordon 1995), a fear that may be accentuated for Black women, who are more likely to be single, poor, and reported to authorities (Primm 1992). Black women report child care responsibility and lack of insurance or money as barriers to treatment (Allen 1995).

Ethnicity and culture influence treatment needs and effectiveness. Blacks entering substance abuse treatment programs were found to have more severe problems with employment and higher primary use of alcohol and other drugs than whites (Lee, Mavis, and Stoffelmayr 1991). Woll (1996) observes that "women who attempt to recover from alcohol and other drug abuse in a culture and/or community different from the one in which they grew up must learn new modes of communication, new beliefs and new styles of courtship, parenthood, marriage, maturation, aging, and dying for which they have had no preparation."

Some argue that Black women will do better in treatment programs that are African-centered (Rowe and Grills 1993; Poitier, Niliwaambieni, and Rowe 1997). Treatment programs that are successful with Whites may be effective with Black women, but the data are not clear. Black women are accepting of treatment (Messer, Clark, and Martin 1996), however, Black women in an outpatient treatment program had a lower retention/treatment completion rate than other women (Mertens and Weisner 2000). On the other hand, Black women with children in foster care were more likely to complete treatment (Scott-Lennox et al. 2000). Saulnier (1996) questions the suitability of Alcoholics Anonymous for Black women, arguing that it denies differences, is not culturally sensitive, and promotes powerlessness, especially among marginalized people. However, Blacks who attended 12-step programs after treatment showed greater reductions in their use of alcohol and other drugs than Blacks who did not (Humphreys, Mavis, and Stoffelmayr 1994), and Blacks in AA reported more affiliation and service with the organization (Kaskutas et al. 1999). Moreover, women may be particularly receptive to 12-step programs because they encourage discussion of feelings, provide a social support system, and rely on a spiritual base.

Promising new interventions have been shown to be successful in changing behaviors of Blacks. A church-based program to reduce smoking among rural African Americans was successful for both women and men (Schorling et al. 1997), and a "women-based, culturally influenced, multifaceted residential treatment program for women and their children" designed by and for Black women reported a low relapse rate (12.5% relapsed during treatment) and employment or job training at discharge (Uziel-Miller et al. 1998).

Community-level interventions are frequently touted as the best way to reach Black and other minority women (Sanders-Phillips 1998), but community organizations are not always available to assist in recovery. In an exploratory study of sixty-three women (twenty-one Black) in recovery, six community institutions (i.e., home, church, workplace, school, law enforcement, and medical care system) were found to have played very minor roles in the women's recovery and relapse prevention (Turner et al. 1998). Minority women (mostly Black), however, were more likely than Anglo women to be members of a church and to attend religious services, suggesting that church involvement in recovery may be more viable and salient for them.

LIMITATIONS OF EXISTING DATA AND RESEARCH

The research literature on drug abuse in Black women and men has been seriously hindered by a number of persistent limitations, including the scarcity of sound data, inappropriate conceptual frameworks, methodological flaws such as the use of the comparative paradigm, and the lack of analyses by gender and race/ethnicity (Harper 1991; Sanders-Phillips 1998; Beatty 1994). Although some fairly good data on Black women and substance use from rigorous, well-controlled studies are available, significant gaps and under-explored areas about Black women and substance abuse still exist.

ISSUES AND PROBLEMS IN NEED OF FURTHER STUDY

In order to better serve Black women, we need more information on those factors that are indicated to be most significant in preventing and treating substance abuse with them. Black people, particularly Black women, start using drugs at a later age, yet little is known about the late-onset phenomenon or about prevention with Black adult populations. We need to examine how peer and family relationships affect etiology, prevention, and treatment and assess how relationships with men and beliefs and expectations about intimate relationships affect Black women's involvement in risky behaviors across the life span. We need to know more about the experience of trauma and stress, including racism and sexism. Protective factors specific to Black females across the life span need to be identified. They are likely to include the role of spirituality and the church, as well as instrumental and emotional support from family, intimate partners, and friends. We need to know how to engage community institutions, particularly faith-based organizations, to become more involved in programs that support recovery. We need research to determine how to reestablish ties with children (including adult children) and families. We need to know how to make prevention and treatment more culturally appropriate and effective, to know what aspects of culture to emphasize and how to present them for the particular audience. Research is needed on drug abuse in the Black lesbian community. In addition, we need to examine the effect of public and health care policy on access to and quality of service for Black substance-abusing women. The diversity of experience—that is, age, family configuration, income, country of origin, cultural identification, geographic region—within the Black female population needs to be represented in the research.

REFERENCES

Alegria, M., M. Vera, G. Negron, M. Burgus, C. Albizo, and G. Canino. 1998. Methodological and Conceptual Issues in Understanding Female Hispanic Drug

Users. In C. L. Wetherington and A. B. Roman, eds., *Drug Addiction Research and the Health of Women*, 21. NIH Publication 98-4290. Rockville, Md.: National Institute on Drug Abuse.

Allen, K. 1995. Barriers to treatment for addicted African-American women. *Journal of the National Medical Association* 87 (10): 751–756.

Anthony, J. C. and J. E. Helzer. 1991. Syndromes of Drug Abuse and Dependence. In L. Robins and D. Regier, eds., *Psychiatric Disorders in America*, 116–154. New York: Free Press.

Audrain, J., A. Gomez-Caminero, A. R. Robertson, R. Boyd, C. T. Orleans, and C. Lerman. 1997. Gender and ethnic differences in readiness to change smoking behavior. *Women's Health: Research on Gender, Behavior, and Policy* 3 (2): 139–150.

Beatty, L. A. 1994. Issues in Drug Abuse Prevention Intervention Research with African Americans. In A. Cazares and L. A. Beatty, eds., *Scientific Methods for Prevention Intervention Research*. NIDA Research Monograph No. 139. Rockville, Md.: National Institute on Drug Abuse.

Belgrave, F. Z., V. R. Cherry, D. Cunningham, S. Walwyn, K. Letlaka-Rennert, and F. Phillips. 1994. Influence of Africentric values, self-esteem, and Black identity on drug attitudes among African American fifth graders: Preliminary study. *Journal of Black Psychology* 20 (2): 143–156.

Bennett, N. G., D. E. Bloom, and P. H. Craig. 1989. The divergence of black and white marriage patterns. *American Journal of Sociology* 95 (3): 692–722.

Berenson, A. B., N. J. Stiglich, G. S. Wilkinson, and G. D. Anderson. 1991. Drug abuse and other risk factors for physical abuse in pregnancy among white non-Hispanic, Black, and Hispanic women. *American Journal of Obstetrics and Gynecology* 164 (6, part 1): 1491–1499.

Billingsley, A. 1992. *Climbing Jacob's Ladder: The Enduring Legacy of African-American Families*. New York: Simon and Schuster.

Blumenthal, S. J. 1998. Women and Substance Abuse: A New National Focus. In C. L. Wetherington and A. B. Roman, eds., *Drug Addiction Research and the Health of Women*, 13–32. NIH Publication No. 98-4290. Rockville, Md.: National Institute on Drug Abuse.

Boyd, C. J., E. Hill, C. Holmes, and R. Purnell. 1998. Putting drug use in context. Lifelines of African American women who smoke crack. *Journal of Substance Abuse Treatment* 15 (3): 235–249.

Bresnahan, K., B. Zuckerman, and H. Cabral. 1992. Psychosocial correlates of drug and heavy alcohol use among pregnant women at risk for drug use. *Obstetrics and Gynecology* 80 (6): 976–980.

Brook, S. S., M. Whiteman, E. B. Balka, and P. Cohen. 1997. Drug use and delinquency: Shared and unshared risk factors in African American and Puerto Rican adolescents. *Journal of Genetic Psychology* 158 (1): 25–39.

Brunswick, A. F. and P. Messeri. 1983–1984. Causal factors in onset of adolescents' cigarette smoking: A prospective study of urban Black youth. *Advances in Alcohol and Substance Abuse* 3 (Fall–Winter, 1–2): 35–52.

————. 1999. Life stage, substance use, and health decline in a community cohort of urban African Americans. *Journal of Addictive Diseases* 18 (1): 53–71.

Butz, A. M., H. Hutton, M. Joyner, J. Vogelhut, D. Greenberg-Friedman, D. Schreibeis, and J. R. Anderson. 1993. HIV-infected women and infants: Social and health factors impeding utilization of health care. *Journal of Nurse Midwifery* 28 (2): 103–109.

Centers for Disease Control and Prevention. 1993. *HIV/AIDS Surveillance Reports* 5 (1, April).

————. 1994. *HIV/AIDS Surveillance Report* 6 (5–10, Mid-year edition).

————. 1998. *HIV/AIDS Surveillance Report* 10 (1).

Center for Substance Abuse Treatment. 1994. *Practical Approaches in the Treatment of Women Who Abuse Alcohol and Other Drugs.* Rockville, Md.: Department of Health and Human Services, Public Health Services.

Corse, S. J., M. K. McHugh, and S. M. Gordon. 1995. Enhancing provider effectiveness in treating pregnant women with addictions. *Journal of Substance Abuse Treatment* 12 (1): 3–12.

Cottler, L. B., A. B. Abdallah, and W. M. Compton. 1998. Association Between Early or Later Onset of Substance Use and Psychiatric Disorders in Women. In C. L. Wetherington and A. B. Roman, eds., *Drug Addiction Research and the Health of Women.* NIH Publication 98-4290. Rockville, Md.: National Institute on Drug Abuse.

Covey, L. S., A. H. Glassman, and F. Steiner. 1998. Cigarette smoking and major depression. *Journal of Addictive Diseases* 17 (1): 35–46.

Dahlgren, L. and A. Willander. 1989. Are special treatment facilities for women alcoholics needed? A controlled two-year study from a specialized female unit (EWA) versus a mixed male/female treatment facility. *Alcoholism: Clinical Experimental Research* 13 (4): 499–504.

Dembo, R., D. Farrow, J. Scmeidler, and W. Burgos. 1979. Testing a casual model of early drug movement of inner city junior high school youths. *American Journal of Drug and Alcohol Abuse* 6 (3): 313–336.

Dishion, T. J., G. R. Patterson, and J. G. Reid. 1988. Parent and Peer Factors Associated with Drug Sampling in Early Adolescence: Implications for Treatment. In E. R. Rahdert and J. Grabowski, eds., *Adolescent Drug Abuse: Analyses of Treatment Research,* 69–93. Rockville, Md.: National Institute on Drug Abuse.

Downs, W. R., B. A. Miller, and D. D. Panek. 1993. Differential patterns of partner-to-woman violence: A comparison of samples of community, alcohol-abusing, and battered women. *Journal of Family Violence* 8 (2): 113–135.

Ehrmin, J. T. 2001. Unresolved feelings of guilt and shame in the maternal role with substance-dependent African American women. *Journal of Nursing Scholarship* 33 (1): 47–52.

Friedman, A. S., S. Kramer, C. Kreisher, and S. Granick. 1996. The relationships of substance abuse to illegal and violent behavior, in a community sample of young adult African American men and women (gender differences). *Journal of Substance Abuse* 8 (4): 379–402.

Gilbert, L., N. El-Bassel, V. Rajah, A. Foleno, and V. Frye. 2001. Linking drug-related activities with experiences of partner violence: A focus group study of women in methadone treatment. *Violence and Victims* 16 (5): 517–536.

Goddard, L. L. 1993. Natural Resistors in AOD Abuse Prevention in the African-American Family. In L. L. Goddard, ed., *An African-Centered Model of Prevention for African-American Youth at High Risk*. CSAP Technical Report 6. Rockville, Md.: U.S. Department of Health and Human Services.

Gordis, E. 1990. Alcohol and women: A commentary by NIAAA. *Alcohol Alert* 10:1–3.

Gottfredson, D. C. and C. S. Koper. 1996. Race and sex differences in the prediction of drug use. *Journal of Consulting and Clinical Psychology* 64 (2): 305–313.

Hall, J. M. 1993. What really worked? A case analysis and discussion of confrontational intervention for substance abuse in marginalized women. *Archives of Psychiatric Nursing* 7 (6): 322–327.

Hanna, E. Z., V. B. Faden, and M. C. Dufour. 1997. The effects of substance use during gestation on birth outcome, infant and maternal health. *Journal of Substance Abuse* 9:111–125.

Harper, F. D. 1991. Substance abuse and the Black American family. *Urban Research Review* 13 (1): 1–5.

Helzer, J. E., L. N. Robins, and L. McEvoy. 1987. Post-traumatic stress disorder in the general population. Findings of the Epidemiologic Catchment Area survey. *New England Journal of Medicine* 317 (26): 1630–1634.

Henderson, D. J., C. Boyd, and T. Mieczkowski. 1994. Gender, relationships, and crack cocaine: A content analysis. *Research in Nursing and Health* 17 (4): 265–272.

Herd, D. 1989. The Epidemiology of Drinking Patterns and Alcohol-Related Problems Among U.S. Blacks. In D. Spiegler, D. Tate, S. Aitken, and C. Christian, eds., *Alcohol Use Among U.S. Ethnic Minorities*, 3–50. NIAAA Research Monograph No. 18. DHHS, Publication No. (ADM) 89-1435. Washington, D.C.: U.S. Government Printing Office.

Hill, E. M., C. J. Boyd, and J. F. Kortge. 2000. Variation in suicidality among substance-abusing women: The role of childhood adversity. *Journal of Substance Abuse Treatment* 19 (4): 339–345.

Hobfoll, S., A. Jackson, J. Lavin, P. J. Britton, and J. B. Shepherd. 1993. Safer sex knowledge, behavior, and attitudes of inner-city women. *Health Psychology* 12 (6): 481–488.

Hser, Y., D. Anglin, and W. McGlothlin. 1987. Sex differences in addict careers. I. Initiation of use. *American Journal of Drug and Alcohol Abuse* 13 (1–2): 33–57.

Humphreys, K., B. E. Mavis, and B. E. Stoffelmayr. 1994. Are Twelve-Step Programs Appropriate for Disenfranchised Groups? Evidence from a Study of Posttreatment Mutual Help Involvement. In F. Lavoie, T. Borkman, and B. Gidron, eds., *Self-Help and Mutual Aid Groups: International and Multicultural Perspectives*, 165–180. New York: Haworth.

Inciardi, J. A., P. Lockwood, and A. E. Pottegier. 1993. *Women and Crack Cocaine*. New York: Macmillan.

Jasinski, J. L., L. M. Williams, and J. Siegel. 2000. Childhood physical and sexual abuse as risk factors for heavy drinking among African-American women: A prospective study. *Child Abuse and Neglect* 24 (8): 1061–1071.

Jessor, R. and S. L. Jessor. 1980. *Problem Behavior and Psychosocial Development: A Longitudinal Study of Youth.* San Diego: Academic Press.

Jones-Webb, R., C. Y. Hsiao, P. Hannan, and R. Caetano. 1997. Predictors of increases in alcohol-related problems among black and white adults: Results from the 1984 and 1992 National Alcohol Surveys. *American Journal of Drug and Alcohol Abuse* 23 (2): 281–289.

Kandel, D. 1985. Stages in adolescent involvement in drug use: A developmental perspective. *Advances in Alcohol and Substance Abuse* 4 (3–4): 139–163.

Kantor, G. K. and M. A. Straus. 1989. Substance abuse as a precipitant of wife abuse victimizations. *American Journal of Drug and Alcohol Abuse* 15 (2): 173–189.

Kaskutas, L. A., C. Weisner, M. Lee, and K. Humphreys. 1999. Alcoholics Anonymous affiliation at treatment intake among white and black Americans. *Journal of Studies on Alcohol* 60 (6): 810–816.

Kaslow, N., M. Thompson, L. Meadows, S. Chance, R. Puett, L. Hollins, S. Jessee, and A. Kellermann. 2000. Risk factors for suicide attempts among African American women. *Depression and Anxiety* 12 (1): 13–20.

Kessler, R. C., K. A. McGonagle, S. Zhao, L. B. Nelson, M. Hughes, S. Eshleman, H. U. Wittchen, and K. S. Kendler. 1994. Lifetime and twelve-month prevalence of DSM-III-R psychiatric disorders in the United States. *Archives of General Psychiatry* 51 (1): 8–19.

King, L. M. 1982. Alcoholism: Studies Regarding Black Americans. In National Institute on Alcohol Abuse and Alcoholism, ed., *Special Population Issues,* 385–407. Alcohol and Health Monograph No. 4. Rockville, Md.: National Institute on Alcohol Abuse and Alcoholism.

Kline, A. 1996. Pathways into drug user treatment: The influence of gender and racial/ethnic identity. *Substance Use and Misuse* 31 (3): 323–342.

Knupfer, G. 1989. The prevalence in various social groups of eight different drinking patterns, from abstaining to frequent drunkenness: Analysis of 10 U.S. surveys combined. *British Journal of Addiction* 84 (11): 1305–1318.

Kopstein, A. and J. Gfrorerer. 1990. Drug Use Patterns and Demographics of Employed Drug Users. Data from the 1988 Household Survey. In S. Gust, J. M. Walsh, L. B. Thomas, and D. J. Crouch, eds., *Drugs in the Workplace: Research and Evaluation Data,* 2:11–24. NIDA Research Monograph No. 100. Rockville, Md.: National Institute on Drug Abuse.

Lee, J. A., B. E. Mavis, and B. E. Stoffelmayr. 1991. A comparison of problems-of-life for Blacks and Whites entering substance abuse treatment programs. *Journal of Psychoactive Drugs* 23 (3): 233–239.

Leshner, A. I. 1995. Filling the gender gap in drug abuse research. *NIDA Notes* 10 (1): 3, 7.

Lex, B. W. 1991. Some gender differences in alcohol and polysubstance users. *Health Psychology* 10 (2): 121–132.

Logan, T. K. and C. Leukefeld. 2000. Sexual and drug use behaviors among female crack users: A multi-site sample. *Drug and Alcohol Dependence* 58 (3): 237–245.

Luthar, S. S. and K. G. Walsh. 1995. Treatment needs of drug-addicted mothers: Integrated parenting psychotherapy interventions. *Journal of Substance Abuse Treatment* 12 (5): 341–348.

Marr, D. D. and A. Wenner. 1996. Gender-specific treatment for chemically dependent women: A rationale for inclusion of vocational services. *Alcohol Treatment Quarterly* 14 (1): 21–30.

Marsh, J. C. and N. A. Miller. 1985. Female clients in substance abuse treatment. *International Journal of the Addictions* 20 (6–7): 995–1019.

McCarthy, W. J. and M. D. Anglin. 1990. Narcotic addicts: Effects of family and parental risk factors on timing of emancipation, drug use onset, pre-addiction incarcerations, and educational achievement. *Journal of Drug Issues* 20 (1): 99–123.

McCauley, J., D. E. Kern, K. Kolodner, L. Dill, A. F. Schroeder, H. R. DeChant, J. Ryden, L. R. Derogatis, and E. B. Bass. 1997. Clinical characteristics of women with a history of childhood abuse: Unhealed wounds. *Journal of the American Medical Association* 277 (17): 1362–1368.

McNair, L. D., J. A. Carter, and M. K. Williams. 1998. Self-esteem, gender, and alcohol use: Relationships with HIV risk perception and behaviors on college students. *Journal of Sex and Marital Therapy* 24 (1): 29–36.

Mertens, J. R. and C. M. Weisner. 2000. Predictors of substance abuse treatment retention among women and men in an HMO. *Alcoholism, Clinical, and Experimental Research* 24 (10): 1525–1533.

Messer, K., K. A. Clark, and S. L. Martin. 1996. Characteristics associated with pregnant women's utilization of substance abuse treatment services. *American Journal of Drug and Alcohol Abuse* 22 (3): 403–422.

Mikhail, B. I. 1999. Perceived impediments to prenatal care among low-income women. *Western Journal of Nursing Research* 21 (3): 335–350.

Miller, B. A. 1998. Partner Violence Experiences and Women's Drug Use: Exploring the Connections. In C. L. Wetherington and A. B. Roman, eds., *Drug Addiction Research and the Health of Women*, 407–416. NIH Publication No. 98-4290. Rockville, Md.: National Institute on Drug Abuse.

Moon, D. G., M. L. Hecht, K. M. Jackson, and R. E. Spellers. 1999. Ethnic and gender differences and similarities in adolescent drug use and refusals of drug offers. *Substance Use and Misuse* 34 (8): 1059–1083.

Moore, R. D., J. Hidalgo, B. W. Sugland, and R. E. Chaisson. 1991. Zidovudine and the natural history of the acquired immunodeficiency syndrome. *New England Journal of Medicine* 324 (20): 1412–1416.

Neuspiel, D. R. 1996. Racism and perinatal addiction. *Ethnicity and Disease* 6 (1–2): 47–55.

Nobles, W. W. and L. L. Goddard. 1989. Drugs in the African American Community: A Clear and Present Danger. In J. Dewart, ed., *The State of Black America*, 161–182. New York: National Urban League.

Nolen-Hoeksema, S. 1987. Sex differences in unipolar depression: Evidence and theory. *Psychological Bulletin* 101 (2): 259–282.

Norton, A. J. and J. E. Moorman. 1987. Current trends in marriage and divorce among American women. *Journal of Marriage and the Family* 49 (1): 3–14.

Nurco, D. N., R. J. Blatchley, T. E. Hanlon, K. E. O'Grady, and M. McCarren. 1998. The family experience of narcotic addicts and their subsequent parenting practices. *American Journal of Drug and Alcohol Abuse* 24 (11): 37–59.

Oyemade, U. J., O. J. Cole, A. A. Johnson, E. M. Knight, O. E. Westney, H. Laryea, G. Hill, E. Cannon, A. Fomufod, L. S. Westney et al. 1994. Prenatal substance abuse and pregnancy outcomes among African American women. *Journal of Nutrition* 124 (6, Supplement): 994S–999S.

Pearlin, L. I., M. A. Lieberman, E. C. Menaghan, and J. T. Mullan. 1981. The stress process. *Journal of Health and Social Behavior* 22 (4): 331–356.

Pinn, V. 1998. Role of the Office of Research on Women's Health. In C. L. Wetherington and A. B. Roman, eds., *Drug Addiction Research and the Health of Women*, 5–12. NIH Publication No. 98-4290. Rockville, Md.: National Institute on Drug Abuse.

Poitier, V. L., M. Niliwaambieni, and C. L. Rowe. 1997. A rite of passage approach designed to preserve the families of substance-abusing African American women. *Child Welfare* 76 (1): 173–195.

Primm, B. J. 1992. Future outlook: Treatment improvement. In J. H. Lowinson, P. Ruiz, and R. B. Millman, eds. and J. G. Langood, associate ed., *Substance Abuse: A Comprehensive Textbook.* 2d ed. 612–626. Baltimore: Williams & Wilkins.

Reed, B. G. 1985. Drug misuse and dependency in women: The meaning and implications of being considered a special population or minority group. *International Journal of the Addictions* 20:13–62.

———. 1987. Developing women-sensitive drug dependence treatment services: Why so difficult? *Journal of Psychoactive Drugs* 19 (2): 151–164.

Regier, D. A., M. E. Farmer, D. S. Rae, B. Z. Locke, S. J. Keith, L. L. Judd, and F. K. Goodwin. 1990. Comorbidity of mental disorders with alcohol and other drug abuse: Results from the Epidemiologic Catchment Area Study. *Journal of the American Medical Association* 264 (19): 2511–2518.

Rhodes, J. E., P. L. Gingiss, and P. B. Smith. 1994. Risk and protective factors for alcohol use among pregnant African-American, Hispanic, and White adolescents: The influence of peers, sexual partners, family members, and mentors. *Addictive Behaviors* 19 (5): 555–564.

Roberts, C. A. 1999. Drug use among inner-city African American women: The process of managing loss. *Qualitative Health Research* 9 (5): 620–638.

Robles, R. R., C. A. Marreo, T. D. Matos, H. M. Colon, L. I. Cancel, and J. C. Reyes. 1998. Social and Behavioral Consequences of Chemical Dependence. In C. L. Wetherington and A. B. Roman, eds., *Drug Addiction Research and the Health of Women*, 355–364. NIH Publication No. 98-4290. Rockville, Md.: National Institute on Drug Abuse.

Rodgers, W. L. and A. Thornton. 1985. Changing patterns of first marriage in the United States. *Demography* 22 (2): 265–279.

Rowe, D. and C. Grills. 1993. African-centered drug treatment: Alternative conceptual paradigm for drug counseling with African-American clients. *Journal of Psychoactive Drugs* 25 (1): 21–33.

Russac, R. J. and S. T. Weaver. 1995. Trends and Theories Concerning Alcohol and Other Drug Use Among Adolescent Females. In R. R. Watson, ed., *Drug and Alcohol Abuse Reviews*. Vol. 8, *Drug and Alcohol Abuse During Pregnancy and Childhood*, 77–123. Totowa, N.J.: Human Press.

Sanders-Phillips, K. 1998. Factors Influencing Health Behaviors and Drug Abuse Among Low-Income Black and Latino Women. In C. L. Wetherington and A. B. Roman, eds., *Drug Addiction Research and the Health of Women*, 439–466. NIH Publication No. 98-4290. Rockville, Md.: National Institute on Drug Abuse.

Saulnier, D. F. 1996. African-American women in an alcohol intervention group: Addressing personal and political problems. *Substance Use and Misuse* 31 (10): 1259–1278.

Schorling, J. B., J. Roach, M. Siegel, N. Baturka, D. E. Hunt, T. M. Guterbock, and H. L. Stewart. 1997. A trial of church-based smoking cessation interventions for rural African-Americans. *Preventive Medicine* 26 (1): 92–101.

Scott-Lennox, J., R. Rose, A. Bohlig, and R. Lennox. 2000. The impact of women's family status on completion of substance abuse treatment. *Journal of Behavioral Health Services and Research* 27 (4): 366–379.

Selwyn, P. A. and M. N. Gourevitch. 1998. HIV infection in women: Implications for Drug Abuse Treatment and Research. In C. L. Wetherington and A. B. Roman, eds., *Drug Addiction Research and the Health of Women*, 339–354. NIH Publication No. 98-4290. Rockville, Md.: National Institute on Drug Abuse.

Sikkema, K. J., T. G. Heckman, and J. A. Kelly. 1997. HIV risk behaviors among inner-city African American women. The Community Housing AIDS Prevention Study Group. *Womens Health* 3 (3–4): 349–366.

Singer, M. 1991. Confronting the AIDS epidemic among IV drug users: Does ethnic culture matter? *AIDS Education and Prevention* 3 (3): 258–283.

Singleton, E. G., J. P. Harrell, and L. M. Kelley. 1986. Racial differentials in the impact of maternal cigarette smoking during pregnancy on fetal development and mortality: Concerns for Black psychologists. *Journal of Black Psychology* 12 (2): 71–83.

Stenbacka, M., P. Allebeck, and A. Romelsjo. 1993. Initiation into drug abuse: The pathway from being offered drugs to trying cannabis and progression to intravenous drug abuse. *Scandinavian Journal of Sociological Medicine* 21 (1): 31–39.

Stevens, S., N. Arbiter, and P. Glider. 1989. Women residents: Expanding their role to increase treatment effectiveness in substance abuse programs. *International Journal of the Addictions* 24 (5): 425–434.

Substance Abuse and Mental Health Services Administration (SAMHSA). (1997a). *National Household Survey on Drug Abuse, Main Findings*. Rockville, Md.: Office of Applied Studies, SAMHSA.

———. (1997b). *Substance Use Among Women in the United States*. Analytic Series A-3. Rockville, Md.: Office of Applied Studies, SAMHSA.

————. (1999). *National household survey on drug abuse, main findings 1997.* Rockville, Md.: Office of Applied Studies, SAMHSA.

Taylor, J., D. Henderson, and B. B. Jackson. 1991. A holistic model for understanding and predicting depressive symptoms in African-American women. *Journal of Community Psychology* 19 (4): 306–320.

Turnbull, J. E. 1989. Treatment issues for alcoholic women: Social casework. *Journal of Contemporary Social Work* 21 (2): 364–369.

Turner, N. H., K. J. O'Dell, G. D. Weaver, G. Y. Ramirez, and G. Turner. 1998. The community's role in the promotion of recovery from addiction and prevention of relapse among women: An exploratory study. *Ethnicity and Disease* 8 (1): 26–35.

Uziel-Miller, N. D., J. S. Lyons, C. Kissiel, and S. Love. 1998. Treatment needs and initial outcomes of a residential recovery program for African-American women and their children. *American Journal on Addictions* 7 (1): 43–50.

Vega, W. A., B. Kolody, P. Porter, and A. Noble. 1997. Effects of age on perinatal substance abuse among Whites and African Americans. *American Journal of Drug and Alcohol Abuse* 23 (3): 431–451.

Walker, C., P. Zangrollo, and J. Smith. 1991. *Parental Drug Abuse and African American Children in Foster Care.* Report available from the National Clearinghouse for Alcohol and Drug Information.

Wallace, Jr., J. M., J. G. Bachman, P. M. O'Malley, and L. D. Johnston. 1995. Racial/Ethnic Differences in Adolescent Drug Use. In G. J. Botvin, S. Schinke, and M. A. Orlandi, eds., *Drug Use Prevention with Multi-ethnic Youth.* Thousand Oaks, Calif.: Sage.

Wallen, J. 1992. A comparison of male and female clients in substance abuse treatment. *Journal of Substance Abuse Treatment* 9 (3): 243–248.

Warner, E. A., R. M. Flores, and B. E. Robinson. 1995. A profile of hospitalized cocaine users: Patient characteristics, diagnoses, and physician responses. *Substance Abuse* 16 (4): 205–212.

Windle, M. 1997. Mate similarity, heavy substance use, and family history of problem drinking among young adult women. *Journal of Studies in Alcohol* 58 (6): 573–580.

Woll, C. H. 1996. What difference does culture make? Providing treatment to women different from you. *Journal of Chemical Dependency Treatment* 6 (1/2): 67–85.

Yanish, D. L. and J. Battle. 1985. Relationship between self-esteem, depression, and alcohol consumption among adolescents. *Psychological Reports* 57 (1): 331–334.

PART III
RACE, GENDER, AND CULTURAL INFLUENCES ON THE MENTAL WELL-BEING OF AFRICAN AMERICAN WOMEN

It's like race is an issue all the time. I've always believed that if you work hard enough, then you are supposed to be able to overcome or work your way through certain things. But people break the rules all the time. And I'm wondering why they aren't playing fair. That kind of feeling contributed to my depression.

—Angela Mitchell, "What the Blues Is All About."

4 (DIS)RESPECTED AND (DIS)REGARDED: EXPERIENCES OF RACISM AND PSYCHOLOGICAL DISTRESS

Diane R. Brown, Verna M. Keith, James S. Jackson, and Lawrence E. Gary

Racism is so universal in this country, so widespread and so deep-seated, that it is invisible because it is so normal.

—SHIRLEY CHISHOLM, 1970, IN MAZEL 1998

I suppose it was naive of me to think . . . that if one only searched one's heart one would know that none of us is responsible for the complexion of his skin, and that we could not change it if we wished to, and many of us don't wish to, and that this fact of nature offers no clue to the character or quality of the person underneath.

—MARIAN ANDERSON, 1956, IN MAZEL 1998

For women of color in America, racism is a reality of everyday existence. From day to day, African American women are potential targets of race-based discriminatory treatment. Experiencing racism as well as perpetuating racism shape how African American women perceive, interpret, behave, and live. The purpose of this chapter is to examine the extent of exposure of African American women to racial discrimination and to investigate its impact on their mental health.

Racism is the belief that race is the primary determinant of human traits and capacities and that racial differences produce an inherent superiority of a particular race. *Racial discrimination* refers to intentional acts that draw unfair or injurious distinctions, that are judged solely on an ethnic or racial basis, and that have effects that are favorable to *in-groups* and negative to *out-groups* (Jackson, Brown, and Kirby 1998). It can encompass direct and overt personal assaults, denials and exclusions of opportunities, or it can consist of subtle and elusive personal injuries, slights, or rude behaviors. That racism is a fundamental part of the lives of African Americans is well documented (Feagin 1991; Ren, Amic, and Levine 1997). It affects all phases of life, from employment to education, housing, transportation, and acquisition of goods and services (Feagin and Vera 1995). Occupying a devalued status in American society, African American women in particular face racism in many ways. Not only is it manifested as disrespect, being ignored, and discourteous responses from others, but it also limits access to better education, higher incomes, improved health care, and adequate housing—all of which are necessary to achieve a reasonable quality of life in American society.

RESEARCH ON RACISM AND MENTAL HEALTH

Research on racial discrimination and mental health has generally used the concept of *perceived discrimination* because objective circumstances of racial discrimination are often difficult to ascertain and measure by using traditional social science research methods. Thus, for research purposes, racial discrimination is relegated to a subjective, perceptive reality. Perceived racial discrimination is defined as a minority group member's subjective perception of unfair treatment based upon racial prejudice and ethnocentrism, even though it may be manifested at an individual, cultural, or institutional level (Jackson, Brown, and Kirby 1998). Visible minorities (that is, those with identifiable physical features such as skin color) tend to perceive more discrimination than do other groups (Dion and Kerry 1996). Specifically with regard to African Americans, Williams and colleagues (1997b) document that compared to Whites, African Americans experience higher levels of unfair treatment and discrimination. In addition, there is evidence that African American women encounter more unfair treatment and acute life events than do White women (Schulz et al. 2000).

Conceptually, the stress process is a theoretical framework that is applicable to examining the impact of racist experiences on mental health. According to the stress process, life events (e.g., being fired or having a relative die) and ongoing chronic strains (e.g., marital problems or economic hardship) place demands on an individual that may challenge his/her adaptive capabilities. When stressful events accumulate within a fairly short time period or when chronic life problems continue unabated over an extended time period, the demands may exceed one's ability to cope, resulting in damage to psychological and physical well-being. Discrimination can be viewed as an acute life event as well as a persistent and chronic daily stressor. Using data from a national study of three thousand adults 25 to 74 years of age, Kessler, Michelson, and Williams (1999) found that almost half (48.9%) of non-Hispanic Blacks reported an occurrence over their lifetimes of at least one of eleven major experiences of discrimination, such as not being hired for a job, being denied a promotion, being prevented from buying a home, and others. The comparable percentage for non-Hispanic Whites was 30.9 percent. With regard to perceptions of day-to-day discrimination, such as being treated with less courtesy and less respect, nearly three-fourths (71.3%) of non-Hispanic Blacks indicated that they "often" or "sometimes" had experiences of perceived discrimination. Only 23.7 percent of non-Hispanic Whites responded similarly. Unfortunately, data were not reported specifically for African American women.

The salience of racial discrimination as a risk factor for detrimental effects on mental health has long been recognized (Kardiner and Ovesey 1951). However, renewed attention to this topic has served to expand the body of empirical research on the mental health consequences of racial discrimination for African Americans (Willie et al. 1995). A recent study by Williams and colleagues (1997b) indicates that African Americans who reported experiences of racial discrimination also reported lower levels of psychological well-being than those who did not experience discrimination. Using data from the National Survey of Black Americans, Jackson and colleagues (1996) not only found that a significant relationship existed between racial discrimination and poorer mental health, but also that subjective perceptions of racial discrimination were cumulative and resulted in poorer mental health for Blacks over time. Similarly, Sanders-Thompson (1996) reports that moderate or severe racism experiences within the past six months were associated with psychological symptoms such as troubling dreams and intrusive thoughts and images. Further, in examining the relationship between various mental health measures and types of discrimination, Kessler, Mickelson, and Williams (1999) report that major experiences of discrimination have a stronger relationship to the measures of mental health for African Americans than do everyday types of discrimination. However, day-to-day discrimination is more strongly linked to psychological distress than is lifetime major discrimination. Similar findings were noted by Brown and colleagues (1999) in their longitudinal analysis. They found that experiences of racial discrimination were linked to psychological distress and only marginally related to a diagnosable mental disorder such as depression. Using the Schedule of Racist Events (SRE) to measure racial discrimination, Landrine and Klonoff (1996) report strong correlations between indicators of racist events (the frequency of racist events in the past year, the lifetime frequency of racist events, and the appraisal of racist events) and five subscales of the Hopkins Symptom Checklist (anxiety, depression, obsessive-compulsive symptoms, interpersonal sensitivity, and somatization). Indeed, only 3 of their 153 subjects reported experiencing no racial discrimination in the past year, and 100 percent reported having encounters of discrimination in their lifetime. None of these studies, however, analyzed data specifically for African American women.

In addition to psychological distress and symptoms of depression, the ubiquitous threat of racial discrimination may lead many African Americans to maintain a heightened state of anxiety and vigilance that has implications for mental health. This hypervigilance is often characterized as mild paranoia or extreme suspiciousness, in which African Americans appear quick to attribute unfair treatment or slights to racial discrimination. As psychiatrist Alvin Poussaint (1999) notes, "When we go into a store and encounter a sales clerk who is nasty, we don't have all day to stand there and determine if she's a nasty person to everyone or just a racist. So we go away not knowing if we've just been insulted by a racist or not." The behavioral and cognitive skills used by African Americans to assess nonsupportive and potentially hostile situations and to decrease their vulnerability to racist encounters has been labeled "armoring" (Faulkner 1983). This heightened guardedness and vigilance may actually be an adaptive coping mechanism in light of the long history of racial discrimination experienced by African Americans (Brown, Schulberg, and Madonia 1996).

RESEARCH ON BLACK WOMEN, RACIAL DISCRIMINATION, AND MENTAL HEALTH

Empirical research is meager on the experiences of racial discrimination among African American women and the consequences for their health and well-being. Investigating gender differences in race and gender discrimination, Mays and Cochran (1998) found that racial and ethnic discrimination occurred more often than did gender-based discrimination for African American women. Also, African American women perceived more race- *and* gender-based discrimination than did African American men. Further, racial discrimination appeared to be more upsetting for African American women than for men. However, this study focused only on African American men and women who were college students. Other studies examining the impact of racial discrimination on health and well-being have found that higher rates of hypertension exist among African American women in comparison to White women (Krieger 1990) and that the chronic stress of everyday discrimination is more detrimental to the mental and physical health of African American women than are more-blatant incidents (Sanders-Thompson 1996). Tomes and colleagues (1990), in their research on low-income African

American women, found a positive relationship between internalized racism and symptoms of depression. Using data collected from 323 African American women, Lawson, Rodgers-Rose, and Rajaram (1999) found that 70 percent of the women reported that they experienced racism all of the time. They encountered racism in medical visits, bank transactions, hotel accommodations, and shopping in retail stores, as well as in other settings. This resulted in depression, anxiety, mental fatigue, and eating and sleeping disorders. However, Williams, Yu, and Jackson (1997a) in their analysis of both men and women found that African Americans who get upset or angry in response to experiences of unfair treatment sometimes do worse than do those who do not get angry.

PURPOSE OF ANALYSIS

Overall, the limited literature on racial discrimination and its impact on the mental health of African American women suggests that racial discrimination does have an impact on their psychological well-being and that day-to-day discrimination is more detrimental to their mental health than are more major discriminatory events. However, the literature does not reveal the extent to which African American women experience racial discrimination, nor does it provide an understanding of how it affects their mental health. Accordingly, the purposes of this analysis are (1) to examine the extent to which African American women experience or perceive racial discrimination and (2) to examine the relationships between experiences of racial discrimination and various indicators of mental health.

METHOD

DATA AND SAMPLING STRATEGY

The data for this analysis come from two urban community-based surveys: the Norfolk Area Health Study (NAHS) and the Detroit Area Study (DAS). The advantages of using these two data sets are that (1) they have different measures of racial discrimination that vary according to different time intervals and (2) they have different measures of mental health, so it is possible to examine psychiatric morbidity as well as less severe measures of mental health. The first survey, the Norfolk Area Health Study (Gary et al. 1989), included 481 African American women, 18 years of age and older, who participated in personal interviews. Participants were selected through a multistage cluster sampling strategy. The response rate was 81 percent. The second data source comes from a sample of 331 African American women who were interviewed as part of the Detroit Area Study (Schulz et al. 2000). The DAS data consist of a multistage probability sample of adult respondents 18 years of age and older. The response rate for this survey was 70 percent. The sociodemographic characteristics of both samples are given in table 4.1.

MEASURES OF DISCRIMINATION

In the NAHS, two approaches were used to assess experiences of racial discrimination as sources of stress; one focused on six-month prevalence of a major stressor and the second on the experience of daily hassles over the past month. For the first approach, participants in the NAHS were queried "During the last six months did you experience unfair treatment because of your race?" Respondents were given a list of specific settings such as: where you work, from the police, from a waiter, etc. Responses consisted of "yes" or "no." In the second approach, the NAHS asked participants three specific questions as part of an assessment of daily hassles. Respondents were asked "Tell me how much of a hassle each item was for you during the past month using 'none,' 'somewhat,' 'quite a bit,' or a 'great deal.'" The three specific hassles pertained to experiencing prejudice and discrimination from others, problems on the job due to being a woman, or problems on the job due to being Black. Responses ranged from "none" to a "great deal."

The DAS specifically also included measures of chronic and acute experiences of racial discrimination. For this analysis, acute stressors were assessed by three specific circumstances of racial discrimination *ever* experienced, identified as unfair treatment associated with being fired or denied a promotion, being hired for a job, or being harassed by the police. These items were combined to provide an overall indicator of acute stress associated with racial discrimination. With regard to the measure of chronic daily experiences of discrimination, participants were asked, "In your daily life, how often have any of the following things happened to you?" Given a list of nine possible experiences ranging from being treated with less courtesy, treated with disrespect, to having received poor service, survey participants were asked to respond on a scale of from 1 (*very often*) to 5 (*never*). Responses to these nine items were converted to an overall score reflective of experiences of everyday discrimination; the Cronbach alpha was .85.

TABLE 4.1 Sociodemographic Characteristics of African American Women in Two Community Surveys: Norfolk Area Health Study (NAHS) and Detroit Area Study (DAS)

	NAHS (N = 481)		DAS (N = 331)	
	N	(%)	N	(%)
Age				
18–29	130	(28.4)	83	(25.2)
30–44	136	(29.6)	96	(29.1)
45–64	114	(24.8)	100	(30.3)
65+	79	(17.2)	51	(15.4)
Marital Status				
Married	148	(31.5)	124	(37.5)
Previously married	204	(43.4)	117	(35.5)
Never married	118	(25.1)	89	(27.0)
Education				
0–11 years	220	(46.5)	99	(30.3)
12 years	130	(27.5)	102	(31.2)
13+ years	123	(26.0)	126	(38.5)
Employment Status				
Employed	219	(47.1)	166	(50.2)
Not employed	246	(52.9)	165	(49.8)

MEASURES OF MENTAL HEALTH

For the analysis of data from the NAHS, the measure of mental health used was the Center for Epidemiologic Studies Depression Scale (CES-D) (Radloff 1977). The Cronbach alpha for the CES-D was .85. The DAS included two measures of mental health: life satisfaction and psychological distress. Life satisfaction was measured by a single-item measure: "Thinking about your life as a whole, how satisfied are you with it?" Responses ranged from *completely satisfied* to *not at all satisfied* on a five-point Likert-type scale. Psychological distress was based upon a six-item scale: "couldn't cheer up," "felt nervous," "felt restless," "felt hopeless," "everything was an effort," "felt worthless." Participants indicated the frequency of such feelings by responding from 1 (*very often*) to 5 (*never*). The Cronbach alpha was .86.

RESULTS

EXPERIENCES OF DISCRIMINATION

The first objective of the analysis was to assess the extent to which African American women reported experiences of discrimination or unfair treatment. When asked if they had experienced unfair treatment during the last six months because of race, fewer than 10 percent of the women in the NAHS responded affirmatively. However, data from the NAHS indicate that responses varied with the specific setting. Although these results are not shown, the highest frequency pertained to unfair treatment occurring at the workplace during the last six months, with 8.7 percent of respondents stating *yes*. Another 6.6 percent encountered racial discrimination from the police and 5.0 percent from a waiter in a restaurant. In contrast, when the women were asked about major occurrences of discrimination ever experienced, data from the DAS show a higher percentage of African American women reporting affirmatively. About half of African American women (52.0%) indicated that they had had one or more of the three events of unfair treatment happen to them in their lifetime. In particular, 31.4 percent of women indicated that they felt that they were unfairly fired or denied a promotion, while another 31.4 percent reported that they were unfairly not hired for a job. Nearly a quarter (23.3%) believed that they had been unfairly stopped or searched by the police.

With regard to chronic or daily experiences of unfair treatment, findings from the NAHS report the frequency at which African American women reported discriminatory experiences. Although the data are not shown, the findings indicate that almost 20 percent (19.9%) of African American women felt hassled during the past month by prejudice and discrimination in their day-to-day lives. In response to questions specifically about daily problems on their job due to gender or race, 11.2 percent reported problems attributable to gender, while 16.2 percent believed day-to-day problems on the job were associated with their race. Not surprisingly, a greater percentage of African American women reported a greater number of job problems related to race than to gender.

Data from the DAS on experiences of everyday discrimination provide additional insight by focusing on more insidious, less overt types of unfair treatment. Overall, DAS data indicate that the majority (81.2%) of African American women report experiencing everyday types of discrimination at some time in their lives. In fact, the majority (61.7%) reported moderate to high levels of everyday experiences of discrimination. As shown in table 4.2,

TABLE 4.2 Everyday Experiences of Discrimination Very Often or Fairly Often Experienced (DAS)

N = 331		
	N	PERCENT
Treated with less courtesy than other people	33	10.0
Treated with less respect than other people	37	11.2
Received poorer service than other people at restaurants or stores	38	11.4
Had people act as if they think you are not smart	56	17.0
Had people act as if they are afraid of you	29	8.5
Had people act as if they think you are dishonest	14	4.3
Had people act as if they were better than you are	80	24.3
Called names or insulted	25	7.5
Threatened or harassed	13	3.8

the most frequently cited experiences were those pertaining to "other people acting as if they were better than you are" for 24.3 percent of African American women, followed by "other people acting as if they think you are not smart" at 17.0 percent. Another 11.4 percent felt that they received poorer service than other people at restaurants and stores, while another 11.2 percent believed that they were treated with less respect than other people.

RACIAL DISCRIMINATION AND MENTAL HEALTH

While occurrences of unfair treatment vary by type of setting and time frame, the second objective of this analysis was to examine the relationship between experiences of racial discrimination and mental health. Using data from the NAHS, table 4.3 presents bivariate analyses examining experiences of racial discrimination and the presence of depressive symptomatology. With regard to occurrences of racial discrimination within the last six months, several significant findings emerge. Specifically, a greater number of depressive symptoms was associated with experience of racial discrimination from a waiter in a restaurant ($p < .001$), and from "elsewhere" ($p < .005$). Other experiences, however, are marginally significant to the presence of depressive symptoms—specifically, experiencing discrimination at work ($p = .07$) and at the beach ($p = .08$). Depressive symptoms were also examined in light of daily hassles associated with unfair treatment. As shown in table 4.4, depressive symptoms were lowest (mean = 12.85; SD = 9.90) for African American women reporting no daily hassles associated with prejudice or discrimination from others. Depressive symptoms significantly increased for African American women who felt hassled "somewhat" to "a great deal" by prejudice or discrimination from others. It is interesting to note, however, that there was no statistically significant relationship between depressive symptoms and being hassled on the job because of gender. On the other hand, the relationship between depressive symptoms and being hassled on the job because of race was significant ($p < .01$). However, some caution must be expressed regarding these findings, as they are based solely on bivariate analyses and do not control for factors such as age, health status, education, or other sources of stress.

The analysis of DAS data provides another perspective on the relationship between experiences of racial discrimination and mental health, since the DAS included measures of life satisfaction and psychological distress. Multiple regression analyses were performed to assess the extent to which experiences of racial discrimination, both acute and chronic, were associated with life satisfaction and psychological distress while controlling for other factors. The other factors included in the regression model were age, education, family income, employment status, marital status, and other acute and chronic stressors. The measure of acute stress included four life events reported by the respondents in the past twelve months, such as being the victim of a serious physical attack or assault, being robbed, having a home burglarized, or moving to a worse residence or neighborhood. Chronic stressors were measured by yes or no responses to five statements ascertaining problems experienced with children, aging parents, spouse, balancing work and family, and hassles at work. The scores were summed to obtain an overall measure of chronic stress.

The results of the multiple regression analyses are shown in table 4.5. With regard to life satisfaction, none of the measures of discrimination were significant. Only other acute and life event stressors were significant predictors of life satisfaction. On the other hand, with regard to psychological distress experiencing everyday discrimination ($beta$ = .475, $p < .001$) was significantly related to an increase in psychological distress while controlling for other factors. To be noted, experiencing a discriminatory event was marginally significant ($beta$ = -.083, p = .07). However, the sign of the coefficient was surprisingly negative, indicating a possible inverse relationship between experiencing a discriminatory event and psychological distress. It is important to point out that the measure of discriminatory events pertained to having

TABLE 4.3 Mean CES-D Scores by Experiences of Racial Discrimination in Different Settings (NAHS)

| | CES-D SCORES | | |
	N	MEAN	SD	SIGNIFICANCE
At work				.070
Yes	34	17.56	11.69	
No	363	13.35	10.13	
From waiter				.000
Yes	22	21.95	11.21	
No	417	13.41	10.01	
From police				.331
Yes	29	15.00	9.83	
No	410	13.75	10.26	
From government agency				.145
Yes	16	17.69	8.11	
No	423	13.68	10.28	
From a bank				.294
Yes	5	19.20	13.54	
No	431	13.76	10.21	
At the beach				.081
Yes	13	20.62	11.03	
No	420	13.63	10.16	
Elsewhere				.005
Yes	7	21.86	9.44	
No	424	13.59	10.07	

"ever" experienced any of three specific events, while the measure of psychological distress pertained to feelings reported over the recent month. It is possible that the discriminatory event might have occurred so far in the past that the long-term effects on current psychological distress were minimal. Another possible explanation is that experiencing such a major discriminatory event in the past may in some circumstances have contributed to resiliency with regard to current reports of psychological distress. Overall, however,

TABLE 4.4 Racial Hassles by Mean CES-D Scores for African American Women (NAHS)

		CES-D SCORES		
	N	MEAN	SD	SIGNIFICANCE
Prejudice/discrimination from others?				.000
None	355	12.85	9.90	
Somewhat	57	18.65	10.35	
Quite a bit	20	19.90	8.63	
A great deal	9	18.89	13.07	
Problems on job due to being a woman?				.558
None	389	13.75	10.14	
Somewhat	34	15.59	10.74	
Quite a bit	13	13.23	8.58	
A great deal	2	26.00	18.38	
Problems on job due to being black?				.012
None	367	13.24	9.94	
Somewhat	47	18.45	11.44	
Quite a bit	16	14.50	7.44	
A great deal	8	20.25	11.95	

these findings suggest that experiences of racial discrimination, particularly everyday discrimination, have an impact on psychological distress but not on life satisfaction.

SUMMARY AND DISCUSSION

The findings from this analysis indicate that racial discrimination is a part of the everyday existence of African American women. However, the prevalence varies by type of perceived discrimination. Slightly more than half of African American women report having experienced a major discriminatory event such as rejection for a job or denial of promotion in their lifetime. Far fewer, approximately one in ten, had experienced such a major discriminatory event within the past month. The prevalence of mundane types of

TABLE 4.5 Regression of Discrimination on Life Satisfaction and Psychological Distress (DAS)

	LIFE SATISFACTION		PSYCHOLOGICAL DISTRESS	
	BETA	SE	BETA	SE
Age	.001	(.003)	−.002	(.003)
Education	−.018	(.022)	−.047*	(.019)
Family income	.001	(.000)	−.001	(.000)
Employment status	.001	(.112)	−.307**	(.102)
Marital status	.104	(.111)	.076	(.100)
Everyday discrimination	−.003	(.072)	.475***	(.065)
Major discrimination	−.002	(.051)	−.083+	(.046)
Chronic stress	−.109*	(.046)	.142***	(.041)
Life events	−.128***	(.046)	.089**	(.033)
Constant	3.736	(.367)	1.827	(.331)
Adjusted R^2	.125		.339	

$* p < .05$ $** p < .01$ $*** p < .001$ $+ p = .07$

discriminatory experiences is much higher than the prevalence of major types of discriminatory experiences. The overwhelming majority of African American women report having experiences of everyday discrimination at some point in their lifetime. About one in five reports experiences of race-based daily hassles within the past month. It is important to note that many of the discriminatory experiences, whether major events or everyday hassles, appear to occur in the workplace. However, African American women also perceived unfair race-based encounters with the police. These findings pertaining to the settings in which perceived discrimination occurred should be accepted with some caution. The data collection methodology specified settings such as the "workplace" rather than allowing respondents to offer the settings in which the racial discrimination occurred. The results might have been different if other settings had been included or if the question had been open-ended.

With regard to the impact of perceived racial discrimination on mental health, the findings vary according to the measure of racial discrimination and the measure of mental health. While perceptions of racial discrimination do not appear to affect how satisfied African American women are with their lives, they are significantly related to psychological distress. In particular, everyday types of discriminatory experiences are associated with higher levels of psychological distress among African American women. The mundane experiences of verbal insults, disrespect, discourteousness, or poor service are distressing. Further, in circumstances where the intensity or exposure to these experiences is high, African American women are also apt to report high levels of depressive symptoms, in some instances, sufficiently high to have the potential of a clinically diagnosed disorder. Again, the findings must be tempered with a note of caution, because further comprehensive multivariate analyses are needed to examine these issues.

Overall, although these analyses point to an association between perceptions of racial discrimination and mental health among African American women, much work remains to be done. A better understanding is needed of the context or circumstances in which the perceptions of racial discrimination occur. Additional qualitative studies would be helpful in addressing these issues as well as providing conceptual and methodological insight. Investigation is also needed to substantiate the relationship between racial discrimination and diagnosable mental disorders, especially depression and anxiety. Future empirical research needs to examine the indirect as well as direct ways in which racial discrimination affects mental health and quality of life for African American women. Racial discrimination is not only perceived, it is also objective, and can be manifested through such conditions as poverty, lower incomes, lower levels of education, and poor housing. Finally, additional research needs to examine the coping responses to racism among those who experience discrimination to discern those that are most effective for maintaining mental health for African American women and under what circumstances.

REFERENCES

Brown, C., H. Schulberg, and M. Madonia. 1996. Clinical presentations of major depression by African Americans and whites in primary medical care practice. *Journal of Affective Disorders* 41 (3): 181–191.

Brown, T. N., D. R. Williams, J. S. Jackson, S. Sellers, K. T. Brown, H. W. Neighbors, and M. Torres. 1999. Being Black and feeling blue: The mental health consequences of racial discrimination. *Race and Society* 2:117–133.

Carroll, G. 1998. *Environmental Stress and African Americans.* Westport, Conn.: Praeger.

Carter, J. H. 1974. Recognizing psychiatric symptoms in Black Americans. *Geriatrics* 29:95–99.

———. 1995. Racism's impact on mental health. *Journal of the National Medical Association* 86 (7): 543–547.

Dion, K. and K. Kerry. 1996. Ethnicity and perceived discrimination in Toronto:

Another look at the personal/group discrimination discrepancy. *Canadian Journal of Behavioral Science* 28:203–213.

Faulkner, J. 1983. Women in interracial relationships. *Women and Therapy* 2:193–203.

Feagin, J. R. 1991. The continuing significance of race: Antiblack discrimination in public places. *American Sociological Review* 56:101–116.

Feagin, J. R. and H. Vera. 1998. *White Racism: The Basics.* New York: Routledge.

Gary, L. E., D. R. Brown, N. G. Milburn, F. Ahmed, and J. A. Booth. 1989. *Depressive Symptoms Among Urban Black Adults: The Norfolk Area Health Study Final Report.* Washington, D.C.: Howard University.

Jackson, J. S., K. T. Brown, and D. Kirby. 1998. International Perspectives on Prejudice and Racism. In J. Eberhardt and S. Fiske, eds., *Confronting Racism: The Problem and the Response,* 101–135. Thousand Oaks, Calif.: Sage.

Jackson, J. S., T. Brown, D. R. Williams, M. Torres, S. Sellers, and K. Brown. 1996. Racism and the physical and mental health of African Americans: A thirteen year national panel study. *Ethnicity and Disease* 6 (1–2): 132–147.

Kardiner, A. and L. Ovesey. 1951. *The Mark of Oppression.* New York: Norton.

Kessler, R. C., K. D. Mickelson, and D. R. Williams. 1999. The prevalence, distribution, and mental health correlates of perceived discrimination in the United States. *Journal of Health and Social Behavior* 40:208–230.

Krieger, N. 1990. Race and gender discrimination: Risk factors for high blood pressure. *Social Science and Medicine* 30:1273–1281.

Landrine, H. and E. A. Klonoff. 1996. The Schedule of Racist Events: A measure of racial discrimination and a study of its negative physical and mental health consequences. *Journal of Black Psychology* 22 (2): 144–168.

Lawson, E., L. Rodgers-Rose, and S. Rajaram. 1999. The psychosocial context of Black women's health. *Health Care for Women International* 20:279–289.

Mays, V. M. and S. D. Cochran. 1998. Racial Discrimination and Health Outcomes in African Americans. In *Proceedings of the 27th Public Health Conference on Records and Statistics and the National Committee on Vital and Health Statistics 47th Annual Symposium.* Washington, D.C.: USDHHS.

Mays, V. M., L. M. Coleman, and J. S. Jackson. 1996. Perceived race-based discrimination, employment status, and job stress in a national sample of Black women: Implications for health outcomes. *Journal of Occupational Health Psychology* 1 (3): 319–329.

Mazel, E. 1998. *And Don't Call Me a Racist.* Lexington, Mass.: Argonaut Press.

Noh, S., M. Beiser, V. Kaspar, F. Hou, and J. Rummens. 1999. Perceived racial discrimination, depression, and coping: A study of Southeast Asian Refugees in Canada. *Journal of Health and Social Behavior* 40:193–207.

Poussaint, A. 1999. America in Black and White. *Woman's Day,* February 1, 59.

Radloff, L. 1977. The CES-D Scale: A self-report depression scale for research in the general population. *Journal of Applied Psychological Measurement* 1:385–401.

Ren, X., B. Amic, and S. Levine. 1997. "Racial Discrimination and Self-Perceived Health." Paper presented at the annual meeting of the American Sociological Association, Toronto, August.

Sanders-Thompson, V. 1996. Perceived experiences of racism as stressful life events. *Community Mental Health Journal* 32:223–233.

Schulz, A., B. Israel, D. R. Williams, E. Parker, A. Becker, and S. James. 2000. Social inequalities, stressors, and self-reported health status among African American and White women in the Detroit metropolitan area. *Social Science and Medicine* 51:1639–1653.

Tomes, E., A. Brown, K. Semenya, and J. Simpson. 1990. Depression in black women of low socioeconomic status: Psychological factors and nursing diagnosis. *Journal of the National Black Nurses Association* 4:37–46.

Turner, C. B. and B. M. Kramer. 1995. Connections Between Racism and Mental Health. In C. V. Willie, P. P. Rieker, B. M. Kramer, and B. S. Brown, eds., *Mental Health, Racism, and Sexism.* Pittsburgh: University of Pittsburgh Press.

Williams, D. R. and R. Williams. 2000. Racism and mental health: The African American experience. *Ethnicity and Health* 5:243–268.

Williams, D. R., Y. Yu, and J. S. Jackson. 1997a. "Discrimination, Race, and Health." Paper delivered at the Joint Meeting of the Public Health Conference on Records and Statistics and Data Users Conference, Washington, D.C., July 28–31.

Williams, D. R., Y. Yu, J. S. Jackson, and N. B. Anderson. 1997b. Racial differences in physical and mental health. *Journal of Health Psychology* 2:335–351.

Willie, C. V., P. P. Rieker, B. M. Kramer, and B. S. Brown, eds. 1995. *Mental Health, Racism, and Sexism.* Pittsburgh: University of Pittsburgh Press.

5 VIOLENCE AND MENTAL HEALTH
Evelyn L. Barbee

The high rates of violence to which African American women are subjected are not well publicized. Compared with other groups of women, African American women are exposed to a disproportionate amount of violence (Tjaden and Thoennes 2000). This violence runs the gamut from unwelcome sexual advances to homicide. The response to violence perpetrated against African American women, like the treatment of their physical health problems, is influenced by the constant circumscribing effect of being African American and female in a White, patriarchal, racist society (Barbee 1992b; Barbee and Little 1993; Crenshaw 1991).

Because of the African American community's patriarchal ideas about gender and power, the community usually limits discussions about violence to the male homicide rate and gang violence (Barbee 1992b; Crenshaw 1991). As a result, violence against African American women is either trivialized or ignored and the connection between violence and African American women's mental health is seldom articulated. In commenting on the omitted history on violence against Black women, historian Elsa Barkley Brown (1995:102) asks:

Why is it that lynching (and the notion of it as a masculine experience) is not just remembered but is in fact central to how we understand the history of Black men, and indeed the Black experience in general? But violence against women—lynching, rape and other forms of violence—is not?

Portions of this chapter were presented at the 97th annual meeting of the American Anthropological Association, Philadelphia, December 2, 1998. Portions were published in 1999 as "Black Women and Mental Health" in *Abafazi* 9 (2): 52–65. The research presented was supported by National Science Foundation grant #BNS 9116735.

The purposes of this chapter are to explore the major types of violence that affect the lives of African American women and to examine the influence of violence on the mental health of African American women, most specifically their experience with depression. The types of violence dealt with are sexual violence, domestic violence, and the more subtle violence of rap lyrics. Research data on low-income African American women's experiences with dysphoria and depression are used to further illustrate points made in the literature.

MYTHS AND AFRICAN AMERICAN WOMEN

African American women are viewed from two opposing perspectives. On the one hand, they are viewed as subordinate to all other women and men in this society. On the other hand, they are viewed as strong and adaptive. These two perspectives reflect the experience of African American women in the United States (Gibbs and Fuery 1994) and in particular their physical and cultural marginalization. To better understand these oppositional views of Black women and their marginalization, we need to understand the role of slavery in the creation and maintenance of historical myths about Black women.

During slavery, African American women performed a dual production role: They provided forced labor and they produced slaves (Giddings 1984). Enslaved Black women were often sexually abused by their White masters as well as by enslaved Black males (Giddings 1984). This abuse and exploitation of Black women was rationalized by White males through the creation of myths about Black womanhood (Collins 1990; hooks 1981; Morton 1991). Thus, slave women were viewed as unrestrained, promiscuous creatures who avidly sought sex with their masters and anyone else (Clinton 1982). Clinton (1982:204) concluded that women were divided into two classes: "Ladies, always White and chaste; and whores comprising all Black women (except for the saintly Mammy) and any White woman who defied the established social constraints on her sexual behavior." In contemporary times, the myth of the sexualized Black women is reified in the Jezebel image (Collins 1990).

Slavery-based myths also provided the roots for contemporary, externally imposed, controlling images of mammy, matriarch, Jezebel, and welfare mother (Collins 1990). The mammy image—the faithful, obedient servant—was created to justify the economic exploitation of Black women during slavery (Collins 1990). Although Collins views mammies and matriarchs as two different images, Morton (1991) suggests that mammy and matriarch are flip sides of the same coin. When meeting the needs of Whites, Black women are considered mammies; when fulfilling similar needs for Blacks, they are called matriarchs. A danger of this image in relation to violence is that Black women who internalize the mammy image may either consciously or unconsciously sustain gender exploitation in a number of ways. For example, in terms of domestic violence they may sometimes excuse their partner's violence through reasoning such as "life is hard for Black men." On the other hand, matriarchs are considered to be overaggressive, emasculating, strong, independent, unfeminine women (Collins 2000). One influence of this image in relation to violence is that it allows "helping" professionals to ignore Black women when they need assistance. Further, the Jezebel image is used both as a reason for the sexual denigration of Black women and as a reason for ignoring or minimizing such sexual abuse.

Morton (1991:154) eloquently summarizes the long-term consequences of these persistent images for Black women:

In almost a century of American historiography the Afro-American woman largely emerged in image only, and in the representations revealing much about what, from patriarchal perspectives, women ought to be and ought not to be. . . . The result for Afro-American women is that they have long continued to be portrayed from the outside, with little attention to their inner lives.

TYPES OF VIOLENCE

Many Black women, particularly poor Black women, are under siege from violence in their communities. Two areas of assault on Black women that emanate from but are seldom mentioned in the Black community are graffiti and rap lyrics. In an analysis of Black graffiti in the Watts area of Los Angeles, Jefferson (1976) identifies a sexual preoccupation with Black women that placed them in devalued positions. Furthermore, the invectives directed against Black women were more profane than invectives directed against Whites or the police. In addition to the covert assault from graffiti, Black women are also psychologically battered through music. Defense of the often violent and misogynistic rap lyrics ranges from upholding sexism to "cultural assaults." One hip-hop expert writes:

As I once told a sister, hip hop lyrics are, among other things what a lot of Black men say about Black women when Black women aren't around. In this sense the music is no more or less sexist than your fathers, brothers, husbands, friends and lovers, and, in many cases, more up front. As an unerringly precise reflection of the community, hip hop's sexist thinking will change when the community changes. Because women are the ones best able to define sexism, they will have to challenge the music—tell it how to change and make it change—if change is to come.   (ALLEN 1989:117)

In an analysis of the obscenity prosecution of the rap group 2 Live Crew, Crenshaw (1991) points out that prosecutions of rap artists, while presumably directed toward the lyrics' assaults on Black women, are actually irrelevant to the protection of Black women. As she further notes, the political and cultural defenses of the group as offered by Henry L. Gates require Black women to "accept misogyny and its attendant disrespect and exploitation in the service of some broader group objective, whether it be pursuing an antiracist political agenda or maintaining the cultural integrity of the Black community" (Crenshaw 1991:1294). Gates's stance is yet another example of the subtle violence directed toward Black women. It would be naive to suggest that there is no connection between the negative images of Black women in both graffiti and rap music and the tolerance for violence against them (Barbee 1992b; Crenshaw 1991; Smith and Boyson 2002).

SEXUAL VIOLENCE

Rape as a crime of violence and control has a higher prevalence among Black women than among other groups of women in the United States (Barbee and Little 1993; National Center for Victims of Crime 1992; Rennison 2001b; Tjaden and Thoennes 2000). The reported rape rate among Black women is almost three times that among White women (Rennison 2001a; U.S. Department of Justice 1991). Estimates of reported rapes range from 12 percent to 23 percent (Koss 1993; Wyatt 1992; National Center for Victims of Crime 1992). Given the range of these reports and the fact that only a small percentage of rapes are reported, the rape rate among Black women is staggering. Although most rapes are perpetrated by persons known to the victim, a comparison study of Black and White women found that Black women reported a higher proportion of attempted rape and more incidents of rape by strangers than White women did (Wyatt 1992).

Too often, in the popular Black press, rape as a crime of violence overwhelmingly perpetrated against women is explained by Black male authorities either as an act caused by male frustration or as an act caused by the victim's behavior. For example, in a article about rape in *Ebony* magazine, Alvin Poussaint, a Black male psychiatrist, is presented as concluding that the high rate of rape of Black women was attributable to the "feelings of rejection" and a need for Black males to bolster their self-esteem (Norment 1991:96). Poussaint's position differs little from the historical rationale used by White males to justify their sexual abuse of Black women. Like many Black males and some Black females, he apparently does not believe that Black males should be held responsible for their violence against Black women (Lorde 1990). Basically, his stance is one that blames the victim. Given the increased awareness of the trauma suffered by rape victims, one would expect that Black male physicians, particularly psychiatrists, might bring more sensitivity and awareness to the problem of rape among Black women.

One result of vulnerability and a lack of empathy toward Black women is that they are less likely to report their rape incidents to either the police or a rape center (Neville and Pugh 1997; Wyatt 1992). Neville and Pugh (1997), in a study of rape reporting patterns, found that of their sample of twenty-nine African American college women, only 14 percent sought medical assistance after the assault and 83 percent did not report their assault to the police. Although reasons for not reporting the assault varied, the majority response pertained to police insensitivity to Black women. Another reason why women of color are reluctant to call the police is they do not wish to subject their private lives to the scrutiny of a police force that is frequently hostile (Moss et al. 1997; Crenshaw 1991). Even when they do report assaults to the police, reporting does not usually mean justice for them.

Although 80 percent of the women in the Neville and Pugh study (1997) immediately disclosed the assault to a significant person, only one third of their sample participated in rape counseling. Given Neville and Pugh's results and the fact that depression is both a short- and long-term effect of rape (Resick 1993; Wyatt 1992), we need to be concerned about Black women's recovery process after sexual assault. In particular, there is a need for awareness of how the common images of Black women may affect their treatment. For example, at a rape workshop that I conducted, a White woman reported that a White emergency room nurse had told her that she didn't counsel Black women rape victims because "Black women didn't feel rape as much as White women." It is obvious that this nurse had difficulty acknowledging that a "strong" Black woman would be traumatized by being raped.

Rape victims have higher rates of suicidal ideation (33% versus 8%) and suicide attempts (13% versus 1%) than nonvictims (Kilpatrick, Edmunds, and Seymour 1992). In addition to the psychological aspects of rape, evidence suggests that rape exposes women to sexually transmitted diseases and the human immunodeficiency virus (HIV). Wingood and DiClemente (1998) compared low-income Black adult women rape survivors with women who did not report a history of rape. They found that rape survivors most frequently named their boyfriends (48%) or a male friend (22%) as the perpetrator. Furthermore, rape survivors, because they may be hesitant to negotiate safer sex owing to fears that assertiveness might provoke a violent attack, were more likely to report not using condoms (Wingood and DiClemente 1998).

CHILDHOOD SEXUAL ABUSE

In addition to their high rape rate, Black women have a high prevalence of childhood sexual abuse. Across all age groups, Black women are at high risk for rape and sexual abuse (Amir 1971; Peters 1976; Kercher and McShane 1984). In a study that examined sexual harassment as part of the sexual abuse continuum in a sample of Black and White women, Wyatt and Riederle (1994) found that 22 percent of their sample of 248 women met the criteria for rape or attempted rape in childhood. Of this group, more than half (56%) were Black women. Wyatt (1985) found that Black preteens who had been abused were most likely to experience abuse in their homes from male nuclear- or extended-family members. Black women reported more incidents of sexual abuse involving stepfathers, mothers' boyfriends, foster fathers, male cousins, and other relatives than did White women (Wyatt 1985). Other studies have found that childhood sexual abuse is associated with increased risk of depression in adults (Fox and Gilbert 1994), high rates of depressive symptoms (Hall et al. 1993), post-traumatic stress disorder (Thompson et al. 1999), and suicidal behavior (Kaslow et al. 2000). Moreover, for African American women, a history of childhood sexual abuse is associated with higher rates of later adult rape (Urquiza and Goodlin-Jones 1994).

DOMESTIC VIOLENCE

Although the literature on battering and Black women has increased, the topic of battering remains a hidden source of major contention in the Black community. Fishbach and Herbert (1997), in a review of data on the prevalence of domestic violence in low-income countries, point out that most battering remains hidden because of differing cultural constructs about its importance as well as individual shame, guilt, fear of recrimination, and social taboos associated with victimization. Within the Black community, woman battering and intimate-partner violence are intertwined with cultural constructs of gender and power. Thus the belief exists that woman battering is a divisive subject that should not be discussed in public (Moss et al. 1997; Barbee 1992b; Richie 1985) and a general community ethos against public intervention (Crenshaw 1991). However, as Crenshaw reminds us, patriarchal ideas about gender and power preclude the recognition of domestic violence as another compelling incidence of Black-on-Black crime. Moreover, suppression of the discussion of woman battering because of concerns about White racism imposes real costs (Crenshaw 1991). One cost is that partner homicide is one of the leading causes of death for Black women (Stark 1990). Another is that where information about violence in the minority community is not available, domestic violence is unlikely to be addressed as a serious issue (Crenshaw 1991), and this lack contributes to the trivialization of violence against Black women.

Some evidence suggests that wife battering may be more prevalent among Blacks than it is among Whites. Hampton and Gelles (1994) found that Black women, when compared with White women, were more than twice as likely to experience severe violence and that in families with incomes greater than $10,000, wife battering was twice as common among Blacks as among Whites. Factors significantly associated with violence are age, socioeconomic status, length of time in the community, and husband's employment status (Hampton and Gelles 1994). Lockhart and White (1989) in a study of husband-to-wife violence among 155 Black women from varied social classes found that 35 percent of the women were victims of violence. The groups with the highest reported incidence of husband-to-wife violence were the middle class and the lower class. The former reported more mild abuse, specifically grabbing, pushing, and shoving. The latter reported more severe violence. Middle-class subjects, because they tended to keep their violence hidden from both formal and informal sources, were at risk for greater isolation than were lower-class women, who sought help from family and friends rather than formal sources. One reason why Black women do not use formal sources such as the police is that they do not trust the system (Taylor 1998). For Black women, factors that serve to protect them from violence are a greater number of years in the neighborhood, a greater number of children, and a greater number of nonnuclear family members in the household (Cazenave and Straus 1979).

VIOLENCE AND MENTAL HEALTH

According to Fishbach and Herbert (1997), a significant portion of the mental distress or disorder observed in women is directly related to their experiences as victims of domestic violence. Gleason (1993) compared the prevalence of mental disorders among three groups of women 25–44 years of age. Two of the groups were battered women—some in a shelter, some living at home—and the third was a random sample from the Epidemiologic Catchment Area (ECA) Study. The respective rates of major depression among the shelter, home, and ECA groups were 63 percent, 81 percent, and 7 percent, respectively. Furthermore, the lifetime prevalence rate for depression was significantly higher for the groups of battered women than for those in the ECA sample at the lifetime, six-month, and one-month periods of time after the battering (Gleason 1993). In a study that examined the association between abuse and attempted suicide, Stark and Flitcraft (1995) found that Black women who attempted suicide were more likely to have a history of battering than White women. Campbell et al. (1997), in an examination of the correlates of depression in battered women, concluded that abuse was both an independent stressor and also interrelated with other stressors in women's lives. Unfortunately, despite the evidence linking violence and women's mental health, the recent federal guidelines on depression in primary care do not mention battering (Campbell et al. 1997). Furthermore, as Fishbach and Herbert (1997) point out, the list of social stresses linked to depression does not include any specific references to the stressors of domestic violence or abuse. As the single most prevalent serious mental health problem for women, depression is also the primary mental health response to battering (Campbell et al. 1997; Gleason 1993; Stark and Flitcraft 1995) and a major short- and long-term response to rape and childhood sexual abuse. As Desjarlais et al. (1995: 50) remind us: "Violence and trauma, particularly when suffered by people who are relatively powerless and have few social and personal resources, are important triggers of depression." The women in my research on depression illustrated this pattern.

METHODS

The research reported here is part of a larger study that explored Black women's experiences with dysphoria and depression, their perceptions of the causes of dysphoria and depression, and the strategies that they used to relieve these mood states. It was theoretically guided by an anthropological theory of emotions and Black feminist thought. It sought to give voice to a group of marginalized women who are routinely vilified in the media and often in the literature as "welfare mothers." Three general questions guided the research: What are the women's experiences with dysphoria and depression? What causes dysphoria and depression? How do they deal with dysphoria and depression? Only some of the data from their experiences with depression and violence are reported here. Fliers placed in community organization offices and a church were used to recruit African American women who were willing to share their experiences of dysphoria. The complete sample characteristics and recruitment procedures are reported in Barbee (1994a).

FOCUS GROUP PARTICIPANTS

The twenty-nine women participating in the focus groups were all from Midwestern communities that ranged in population from 80,000 to 630,000. The mean age of the group was 31 years (range 20–42). Their education ranged from eighth grade to two years of college; more than half had not completed high school. Seventy percent were never married; 10 percent, divorced; 10 percent, separated; 7 percent, married; and 3 percent, widowed. Their approximate annual family income ranged from $5,280 to $18,000. They had a mean of 3.1 children (range 1–7), with a mean of 2.4 children living at home. The mean age of the children living at home was 9.7 years of age.

FOCUS GROUP ILLUSTRATIONS

All of the women reported experiences with depression. They also reported that violent partners or spouses were a cause of depression. Of the twenty-nine women, the majority (76%) moved because of violence. This violence usually involved a physically or emotionally abusive relationship, and the women moved to start a new life for themselves and their children. Although these abusive relationships were usually with a male partner, sometimes they involved a troubled family, the woman's mother, or violent communities. One woman reported a graphic situation of childhood sexual abuse. In addition to domestic violence and childhood sexual abuse, the women cited other sources of violence in their lives, such as being verbally assaulted by men on the street and their fear of general violence in their neighborhoods. One woman related the following:

You know. It's like, OK, now, you know it's like when somebody say "Hi baby," or something and I don't say nothing and they go "Bitch this or ho this."

SEVERAL RESEARCHERS (Stark 1992; Stark and Flitcraft 1988; Stark, Flitcraft, and Frazier 1979) have commented that a pattern of neglectful, improper treatment and punitive intervention by health, mental health, and social service providers erodes women's abilities to cope with domestic conflict and often leads to self-medication with drugs and alcohol, attempted suicide, or abuse of their children. The following excerpts from the focus groups for this study exemplify these points. In the first excerpt, the group members counsel one woman on how to deal with a partner who is abusive to her and her son and also how to deal with the punitive social service agencies. The second example deals with self-medication with alcohol, and the third example addresses fears of child abuse.

Speaker 3 My problem is my boyfriend. He beat my son and Teddy told them at school and the school called.

Speaker 9 Teddy's school called?

Speaker 3 Yeah, you know, and I tell him [her boyfriend] to leave him alone, leave him alone . . .

Speaker 6 Say that child go to school bruised or something they going to . . .

Speaker 3 And he got to sneak in a whupping and . . .

Speaker 5 I'm going tell you something.

Speaker 3 Uh huh.

Speaker 5 It's better for you to leave him! Than for you to come home and find your son dead or hurt.

Speaker 2 Or abused really bad.

Speaker 7 Really hurt. He attend school and the teachers going to see it.

Speaker 5 Cause I whupped my daughter myself and child protective services got in and they talked about giving me ten years.

Speaker 7 For real!

Speaker 5 And, honey, when other people hurt . . .

Speaker 7 Oh, the law done changed.

Speaker 5 . . . your children they give you all kind of hell.

Speaker 7 I didn't know that.

They pointed out the long-term consequences for her and her children if she stayed with this abusive man. They continued to give her advice.

Speaker 9 You don't want him in your life. That's all I got to say.

Speaker 6 You don't want nothing to do with him.

Speaker 8 Right.

Speaker 3 The law don't have nothing to do with it, right.

Speaker 2 You don't want them to get involved. You don't want them involved.

Speaker 5 Yeah. They going to say you an unfit mother. It's best for you to put this man out!

Speaker 2 I got another solution for that. And if he is going through that, to protect herself.

Speaker 4 If they take one child, they going to take all of them.

Speaker 2 Get you a social worker to come in, you know. To see what kind of mother you are. What kind of mother, you know, what kind of environment you raising . . . you don't want them get involved. But to protect your self if you going to stay with this man. 'Cause one day he might do something to hurt that child and at least you got somebody on your side to say that you are not . . .

Speaker 5 That's still not gonna help her . . .

Speaker 2 No?

Speaker 5 . . . because they gone say she's an unfit mother for having him there. And that she allowed him in her home to do that.

Speaker 9 Her love, her love is more important than her children. That's what they gonna say.

Speaker 5 That's what they gonna say.

Speaker 2 Yeah. That's true.

Speaker 5 They gonna cover all the bases.

Speaker 9 That's the system again.

A woman who self-medicated with alcohol related the following:

> I was so depressed that my son, at the age of six, was like doing every-
> thing. He was doin the cookin, the cleanin. Uh. I'd be so high I wouldn't
> know nothing from nothing. . . . And it's like I feel like a lot of times my
> depression robbed my kids of they childhood. You know. Because I was
> depressed, I went out and drank, I mean I just didn't drink. A big purse
> was my home cause I had my fifth in it. And I didn't care where I would
> go. I'd be walking down the street with the purse up to my mouth, you
> know. . . . And my depression . . . what I was feeling rubbed off on my
> kids, you know. All my hurt and my pain went off to them, and when, you
> know, it wasn't intentional, for me to do that, but I feel like I damaged
> them when they should have been out playing and being happy, they trying
> to cheer me up.

In their narratives, the women described symptoms of severe depression
that were consistent with the clinical descriptions of major depressive episodes.
These symptoms of severe depression were: decreased appetite, headache,
extreme sadness, extreme tiredness, and disruption of personal relationships.
Their definition of severe depression, although tautological, was that it was a
condition that needed professional intervention and anyone who needed
professional intervention was severely depressed. And the need for professional intervention also meant that a person had lost control of her life.

Although all of the women related experiences with severe depression,
perhaps because they defined "severe" depression as one requiring professional intervention, only 37 percent of the women either had received or
were currently receiving treatment for depression. Sixty-three percent had
never received such treatment. In the group who had not received professional treatment, eight women described times when they felt so bad that they
wanted to kill themselves. Despite their high number of experiences with
severe depression, the group remained reluctant to seek help for themselves.
The major reasons for their reluctance were (1) an inability to recognize
depression until they were either having suicidal ideation or were actively
suicidal; (2) distrust of White professionals that was based on personal experience; and (3) a lack of Black mental health professionals. This inability to
recognize depression is consistent with the findings of Barbee (1992a) and

Warren (1995). The women in the focus groups used terms like *tiredness, laziness,* and *sadness* to describe their feelings of depression.

DISCUSSION AND SUMMARY

The current emphasis on biochemical explanations of depression ignores the role of social environment in the production of depressed moods. As a result, sociocultural influences on health behaviors are often not acknowledged. As Christensen (1988:191) points out: "No other woman has suffered physical and mental abuse, degradation, and exploitation on North American shores comparable to that experienced by the Black female." When researchers assume that the needs and realities of Black women are identical to those of Black men and White women, they ignore the ways in which race and class influence Black women's experience with violence and hence depression.

In a critique of Western psychiatric epidemiology, Obeyesekere (1985) points out that depressive symptoms are often treated in isolation from their cultural context. Part of the context for poor Black women is the role of violence in the production of their depression. Both the literature and the author's research on depression raise critical questions about the effect of violence on the mental health of Black women. Black women's structural position—poor, Black, and female in a White, racist, patriarchal society—combined with cultural proscriptions about disclosure makes it very difficult for them to break the silence about their abuse and for them to seek professional help when they are severely depressed. There is a need in Black communities to break the silence about violence against Black girls and women. In order to do so, we must identify both short- and long-term goals.

It is imperative that we begin to reconceptualize what is "private" and what is public. As a long-term goal, violent acts perpetrated against girls and women, because of the short- and long-term results, need to be viewed not only as crimes against individuals but also as crimes against the community. A need also exists to help Black women understand that keeping silent about rape, childhood sexual abuse, and domestic violence is not a sign of strength. One way to facilitate their "breaking the silence" is through community-based support groups. Groups help depressed women in two ways. First, groups help to decrease their sense of isolation. Second, groups help Black women in maintaining the sense of community that is necessary for their healing (Taylor 1998). As Taylor (1998:111) found, the recovery process for battered women began "with the process of speaking and sharing the secret of abuse." To facilitate healing, it is important that we encourage all sectors of the community to decry violence against Black women.

REFERENCES

Allen, H. 1989. "Hip Hop Madness!" *Essence* 19 (12): 78–80, 114, 117, 119.

Amir, M. 1971. *Patterns of Forcible Rape.* Chicago: University of Chicago Press.

Barbee, E. L. 1992a. "Dimensions of Depression in African American Women." Paper presented at the Midwest Nursing Research Society meetings, Chicago.

———. 1992b. Ethnicity and Woman Abuse in the United States. In C. Sampselle, ed., *Violence Against Women: Nursing Research, Practice, and Education Issues,* 153–166. New York: Hemisphere Publishing.

———. 1994a. A Black feminist approach to nursing research. *Western Journal of Nursing Research* 16 (5): 495–506.

———. 1994b. Healing time: The blues and African American women. *Health Care for Women International* 15:53–60.

Barbee, E. L. and M. Little. 1993. Health, Social Class, and Black Women. In S. M. James and A. P. A. Busia, eds., *Theorizing Black Feminisms: The Visionary Pragmatism of Black Women,* 182–199. London: Routledge.

Brown, D. R. 1990. Depression Among Blacks. In D. S. Ruiz, ed., *Handbook of Mental Health and Mental Disorder Among Black Americans,* 71–93. New York: Greenwood.

Brown, E. B. 1995. Imaging Lynching: African American Women, Communities of Struggle, and Collective Memory. In G. Smitherman, ed., *Black Women Speak Out on Anita Hill–Clarence Thomas,* 100–124. Detroit: Wayne State University Press.

Campbell, J., J. Kub, R. A. Belknap, and T. N. Templin. 1997. Predictors of depression in battered women. *Violence Against Women* 3:271–293.

Carrington, C. H. 1980. Depression in Black Women: A Theoretical Appraisal. In L. F. Rodgers-Rose, ed., *The Black Woman,* 265–271. Beverly Hills, Calif.: Sage.

Cazenave, N. and M. Straus. 1979. Race, class, network embeddedness, and family violence. *Journal of Comparative Family Studies* 10:281–299.

Christensen, C. P. 1988. Issues in sex therapy with ethnic and racial minority women. *Women and Therapy* 7:187–205.

Clinton, C. 1982. *The Plantation Mistress: Women's World in the Old South.* New York: Pantheon.

Coley, S. M. and J. O. Beckett. 1988. Black battered women: A review of the literature. *Journal of Counseling and Development* 66:266–270.

Collins, P. H. 1990. *Black Feminist Thought: Knowledge, Consciousness, and the Politics of Empowerment.* 2d ed. New York: Routledge.

Crenshaw, K. 1991. Mapping the margins: Intersectionality, identity politics, and violence against women of color. *Stanford Law Review* 43:1241–1299.

Desjarlais, R., L. Eisenberg, B. Good, and A. Kleinman. 1995. *World Mental Health: Problems and Priorities in Low-Income Countries*. New York: Oxford University Press.

Fishbach, R. L. and B. Herbert. 1997. Domestic violence and mental health: Correlates and conundrums within and across cultures. *Social Science and Medicine* 45: 1161–1176.

Fox, K. M. and B. O. Gilbert. 1994. The interpersonal and psychological functioning of women who experienced childhood physical abuse, incest, and parental alcoholism. *Child Abuse and Neglect* 18:849–858.

Gibbs, J. T. and D. Fuery. 1994. Mental health and well-being of Black women: Toward strategies of empowerment. *American Journal of Community Psychology* 22:559–582.

Giddings, P. 1984. *When and Where I Enter: The Impact of Black Women on Race and Sex in America*. New York: Bantam.

Gleason, W. J. 1993. Mental disorders in battered women: An empirical study. *Violence and Victims* 8:53–68.

Hall, A. L., B. Sachs, M. K. Rayens, and M. Lutenbacher. 1993. Childhood physical and sexual abuse: Their relationship with depressive symptoms in adulthood. *Image* 25:37–323.

Hampton, R. L. and R. J. Gelles. 1994. Violence toward Black women in a nationally representative sample of Black families. *Journal of Comparative Family Studies* 24:105–119.

hooks, bell. 1981. *Ain't I a Woman*. Boston: South End Press.

Jefferson, R. S. 1976. Black graffiti: Image and implications. *Black Scholar* 7 (5): 11–19.

Kaslow, N. J., M. P. Thompson, A. E. Brooks, and H. B. Twomey. 2000. Ratings of family functioning of suicidal and nonsuicidal African American women. *Journal of Family Psychology* 14 (4): 585–599.

Kercher, G. and M. McShane. 1984. The prevalence of child sexual abuse victimization in an adult sample of Texas residents. *Child Abuse and Neglect* 8:495–502.

Kilpatrick, D. G., C. N. Edmunds, and A. K. Seymour. 1992. *Rape in America: A Report to the Nation*. Arlington, Va.: National Victim Center.

Koss, M. P. 1993. Rape: Scope, impact, interventions, and public policy responses. *American Psychologist* 48:1062–1069.

Lockhart, L. and B. W. White. 1989. Understanding marital violence in the Black community. *Journal of Interpersonal Violence* 4:421–436.

Lorde, A. 1990. *Need: A Chorale for Black Woman Voices*. Latham, N.Y.: Kitchen Table Press.

Morton, P. 1991. *Disfigured Images: The Historical Assault on Afro-American Women*. New York: Praeger.

Moss, V. A., C. R. Pitula, J. C. Campbell, and L. Halstead. 1997. The experience of terminating an abusive relationship from an Anglo and African American perspective: A qualitative descriptive study. *Issues in Mental Health Nursing* 18:433–454.

National Center for Victims of Crime. 1992. *Rape in America: A Report to the Nation*. Report prepared by the Crime Victims Research and Treatment Center. Charleston, S.C.: Medical University of South Carolina.

Neville, H. and A. O. Pugh. 1997. General and culture-specific factors influencing African American women's reporting patterns and perceived social support following sexual assault. *Violence Against Women* 3:361–381.

Norment, L. 1991. What's behind the dramatic rise in rapes?" *Ebony* 46 (11, September): 92, 94, 96–98.

Obeyesekere, G. 1985. Depression, Buddhism, and the Work of Culture in Sri Lanka. In A. Kleinman and B. Good, eds., *Culture and Depression*, 134–152. Berkeley: University of California Press.

Peters, J. J. 1976. Children who are victims of sexual assault and the psychology of offenders. *American Journal of Psychotherapy* 30:393–421.

Rennison, C. 2001a. Criminal Victimization 2000. Changes 1999–2000 with Trends, 1993–2000. Washington, D.C.: Bureau of Justice Statistics, U.S. Department of Justice.

———. 2001b. Violent Victimization and Race, 1993–1998. Washington, D.C.: Bureau of Justice Statistics, U.S. Department of Justice.

Resick, P. A. 1993. The psychological impact of rape. *Journal of Interpersonal Violence* 8:223–255.

Richie, B. 1985. Battered Black women: A challenge for the Black community. *Black Scholar* 16 (2): 40–44.

Smith, S. L. and A. R. Boyson. 2002. Violence in music videos: Examining the prevalence and context of physical aggressions. *Journal of Communication* 52 (1): 61–83.

Stark, E. 1990. Rethinking homicide: Violence, race, and the politics of gender. *International Journal of Health Services* 20:3–27.

———. 1992. Framing and Reframing Battered Women. In E. Buzawa, ed., *Domestic Violence: The Criminal Justice Response*, 271–289. New York: Auburn House.

Stark, E. and A. Flitcraft. 1988. Women and children at risk: A feminist perspective on child abuse. *International Journal of Health Services* 18:97–118.

———. (1995). Killing the beast within: Woman battering and female suicidality. *International Journal of Health Services* 25:43–64.

Stark, E., A. Flitcraft, and W. Frazier. 1979. Medicine and patriarchal violence: The social construction of a "private" event. *International Journal of Social Science* 9: 461–493.

Taylor, J. Y. 1998. "Resilience and Recovering Among African American Woman Survivors of Domestic Violence." Ph.D. diss., University of Washington, Seattle.

Thompson, M. P., N. J. Kaslow, J. B. Kingree, R. Puett, N. J. Thompson, and L. Meadows. 1999. Partner abuse and posttraumatic stress disorder in a sample of low-income, inner-city women. *Journal of Trauma Stress* 12 (1): 59–72.

Tjaden, P. and N. Thoennes. 2000. Extent, nature, and consequences of intimate partner violence: Findings from the National Violence Against Women Survey. Washington, D.C.: U.S. Department of Justice.

Urquiza, A. J. and B. L. Goodlin-Jones. 1994. Child sexual abuse and adult revictimization with women of color. *Violence and Victims* 9:223–232.

U.S. Department of Justice. Office of Justice Programs. Bureau of Justice Statistics. 1991 (July). *Criminal Victimization in the United States: 1973–88 Trends*. Washington, D.C.: U.S. Government Printing Office.

Warren, B. J. 1995. The Experience of Depression in African American Women. In B. J. McElmurry and R. S. Parker, eds., *Annual Review of Women's Health,* 267–283. New York: National League for Nursing.

Wingood, G. M. and R. J. DiClemente. 1998. Rape among African American women: Sexual, psychological, and social correlates predisposing survivors to risk of STD/HIV. *Journal of Women's Health* 7:77–84.

Wyatt, G. E. 1985. The sexual abuse of Afro-American and White women in childhood. *Child Abuse and Neglect* 9:507–519.

———. 1992. The sociocultural context of Black and White American women's rape. *Journal of Social Issues* 48:77–91.

Wyatt, G. E. and M. Riederle. 1994. Sexual harassment and prior sexual trauma among African American and White women. *Violence and Victims* 9:233–247.

6 COLOR MATTERS: THE IMPORTANCE OF SKIN TONE FOR AFRICAN AMERICAN WOMEN'S SELF-CONCEPT IN BLACK AND WHITE AMERICA

Verna M. Keith and Maxine S. Thompson

> I took color from my mother's side of the family, 'cept I've got a lot of red in my skin. . . . Mama says that she wishes I'd gotten more of Daddy's lighter color and especially his curly hair. . . . Anyway, Mama says she doesn't know where I was when they were handing out color and hair. She says I let my nine-year-old brother David get ahead of me in the hair line and my six-year-old brother Kevin get ahead of me in the color line. But at least I've got nice features, she's thankful for that, Mama always says. In other words, she's glad I don't have a wide nose and big lips like Grandma and some other colored people. And Mama likes that I have high cheekbones, of course.
>
> —SINCLAIR 1994:7–8

Making social comparisons of body images such as those engaged in by Jean Eloise, the central character in April Sinclair's *Coffee Will Make You Black*, occurs early in the process of our coming to know who we are. According to Festinger (1954), we generally compare ourselves to others, and how we stand relative to similar people influences our feelings of personal value or sense of worth. We begin by comparing ourselves to our immediate family members, then to our peers, and later to people in the larger community and media personalities.

Some features and traits are more central than others to one's sense of self-worth. In the African American community, as illustrated by Jean Eloise's statement, skin color is a central trait for determining one's self-image. And darker skin tones are least desirable, particularly for Black females. Sinclair's comments underscore earlier research findings that position dark-skinned women at the bottom of the social ladder, as least marriageable and with few options for higher education and career advancement (Bond and Cash 1992; Chambers et al. 1994). As a consequence, Black women report lower levels of self-esteem and self-efficacy than do Black men (Kiecolt and Acock 1990; Tashakkori and Thompson 1991). Being Black and female carries negative stereotypes, and some researchers refer to the intersection of race and gender as a double burden or double negative (Etter 1994; Gooley 1990; Henriques 1995; Smith and Stewart 1983). Yet, despite recognition of the social influence of colorism, sexism, and racism in the lives of African American women, research studies have not evaluated the relationship between skin tone and psychological functioning for Black women who are immersed in White as opposed to Black communities. Do African American women of different skin tones have similar experiences in White and Black communities? In this paper, we examine the role of skin tone and racial context for self-concept development among African American women.

Social context is one of the most important aspects of a person's social and psychological functioning. The logic of the connection between the social environment and one's self-concept has to do with the fit between the individual's characteristics and the social characteristics of the collective (Rosenberg 1975). Situations in which the individual differs from the group or those in which one's physical or social characteristics are devalued do not affirm one's sense of self and may have a negative impact on the self. That is, low-status individuals may internalize the negative evaluations of society, resulting in low self-esteem. The literature on race and self-esteem finds that this is not the case with regard to Black self-esteem. African Americans have higher self-esteem but lower levels of self-efficacy than do White adults (Hughes and Demo 1989; Porter and Washington 1989:346; Rosenberg and Simmons 1971; Tashakkori and Thompson 1991). Rosenberg (1975) argued that Black self-esteem is affected more by the attitudes of significant others—parents, peers, and teachers—and less by the attitudes of Whites (Hoelter 1982; Rosenberg and Simmons 1971). In contrast, within-group analysis finds that immersion in White-dominant settings does lower the self-esteem of Blacks compared to that of their counterparts who are immersed in Black-dominant settings. Research on prejudice and discrimination supports this pattern, suggesting that interactions with Whites, particularly in environments that are hostile and discriminatory, carry a high psychological cost for Blacks (Feagin and Vera 1995; St. Jean and Feagin 1998). These two literatures mesh to describe the importance of social context in shaping the unique experiences of Black females. In both Black and White communities, physical features are probably more central than abilities are for evaluating a woman's worth. And in both communities, but for different reasons, dark skin tones are devalued. In the African American community skin tone is an indicator of attractiveness and social esteem, whereas in the White community skin tone is probably an indicator of group marginality and discrimination.

There is ample research to document the influence of skin tone bias on life experiences within the African American community. At the structural level, studies have noted that complexion is an important determinant of educational and occupational attainment: lighter-skinned Blacks complete more years of schooling, have more prestigious jobs, and earn more than darker-skinned Blacks (Keith and Herring 1991; Hughes and Hertel 1990). In fact, one study notes that the effect of skin tone on earnings is as great as the effect of race on earnings (Hughes and Hertel 1990). At the social-psychological level, studies find that complexion is related to feelings of self-worth and attractiveness, self-control, satisfaction, and quality of life (Bond and Cash 1992; Boyd-Franklin 1991; Cash and Duncan 1984; Chambers et al. 1994; Neal and Wilson 1989; Okazawa-Rey, Robinson, and Ward 1987).

While there is some evidence that skin tone variations elicit discriminatory responses within the African American community, there is little empirical evidence that the reactions of White America to African Americans are conditioned by skin tone variations or that these reactions have implications for Black self-concept. That is, do lighter-skinned African Americans face less discrimination and prejudice in White America and thus feel more confident than darker-skinned Blacks? Anecdotal and historical evidence on skin tone stratification during slavery suggests that this might be so. Also, current research on employers' preferences shows that most employers feel more comfortable with African Americans who are physically similar to the White European phenotype (Kirschenman and Neckerman 1998). To date, research has not addressed the contextual influence of skin tone effects on self-evaluations. Here, we focus on whether or not skin tone, an ascribed status attribute, influences African American women's self-concept development when considered in concert with the racial composition of their communities. The following section outlines the conceptual argument in greater detail and presents empirical evidence for our consideration of a contextualized relationship between skin tone and self-concept development.

CONCEPTUAL ARGUMENT

THE SELF AND THE SOCIAL CONTEXT

Self-evaluations have two dimensions, one reflecting the person's moral worth and the other reflecting the individual's competency or agency

(Gecas 1989). The former refers to self-esteem, and the latter refers to self-efficacy. Self-esteem, the evaluative dimension of the self, consists of feeling good, liking yourself, and perceiving that you are liked and treated well. Self-esteem consists of two components: racial self-esteem and personal self-esteem. Racial self-esteem refers to the evaluation of Blacks as a group, while personal self-esteem refers to a general evaluative view of the self (Porter and Washington 1989). In our discussion and analyses, self-esteem is conceptualized as personal self-esteem, defined as "feelings of intrinsic worth, competence, and self approval rather than self-rejection and self-contempt" (Porter and Washington 1989:344). Self-efficacy, as defined by Bandura (1977, 1982), refers to a person's belief that he or she can influence events in his or her life or can master situations and control events. Self-esteem and self-efficacy are influenced by both the social comparisons we make of ourselves with others and the reactions that other people have toward us (i.e., reflected appraisals). Social comparisons usually involve such salient characteristics as race, gender, competencies, or identities.

Social comparisons are shaped by the fit between the contextual characteristics of environments and those of the individual—that is, whether we are immersed in environments of similar others versus those of dissimilar others. Rosenberg (1975) employs the term *consonant environmental context* to refer to the match, or symmetry, between contextual and individual characteristics. For example, a consonant racial environment for an African American is one in which the dominant group is African American; for Jews it is one in which the dominant group is Jewish. A dissonant environmental context is one in which a salient characteristic of the individual (e.g., social status or race) is at variance with that of the predominant group in that given social context (e.g., school, work). Thus, a female in an all-male school, an African American in a predominantly White community, and a Jewish person in a predominantly Gentile community are examples of a dissonant environmental context. Rosenberg argues that "the environment is not seen as dissonant or consonant in itself; it is only dissonant or consonant for a given individual" (Rosenberg 1975:98). Therefore, for darker-skinned African Americans a dissonant social context might be one in which both the culture and the majority of people support the belief that lighter skin tone is preferred and held in high social esteem whereas darker skin tones carry low social esteem.

Consonant and dissonant environments affect self-evaluations. In a consonant environmental context significant others will provide affirmation of one's identity, and the similarity between one's self and others shapes evaluations of self. Thus, harmony and homogeneity of social characteristics within a racial environment are most important for fostering and reinforcing positive self-evaluations. In contrast, a person in a dissonant environmental context is, through circumstances beyond his/her control, sociologically deviant.

There is research evidence that dissonant environments have negative effects on self-esteem, especially for individuals from less socially valued groups (Porter and Washington 1989; Verna and Runion 1985). For example, Rosenberg (1975) reported that youth from one race who were enrolled in schools predominantly of another race manifested lower self-esteem than did their counterparts who attended school in a consonant social context (Powell and Fuller 1970; Bachman 1970). Lower self-perceptions of Blacks were related to having directly experienced teasing or name calling, and the incidence of both was greater in the dissonant context (predominantly White school). Further evidence of dissonance effects on self-esteem is reported from studies on individuals in dissonant religious, socioeconomic, and coed environments. The findings consistently show that these individuals have lower self-esteem than their counterparts in consonant environments (Rosenberg 1975).

Although Rosenberg (1975) reported findings consistent with social comparison theory across a number of diverse social contexts, some important gaps remain. While contextual influences on self-concept development are central, variations within the lower-status group have been neglected in this literature. That is, the literature assumes that all individuals within the lower-status group respond to the dissonant context in a similar manner. Contextual dissonance theory, for example, has not addressed the possible influence of colorism on self-esteem within Black and White communities. The heterogeneity of skin tone hues and colorism creates a dissonant racial environment even within the Black community and might be a source of negative self-evaluation. Therefore, in this study we consider status attributes that are known to be related to differences in self-concept development and that may identify differential responses to contextual dissonance, including social class, age, and especially skin tone.

SKIN COLOR AND SELF-EVALUATIONS

On the basis of our argument thus far, it is clear that lighter-skinned people receive high marks on many socially desirable traits and, as a result, have high social exchange value. But do they have more positive feelings about themselves and believe that they can make things happen? Studies of school-age children (Porter 1991), adolescents (Robinson and Ward 1995), and adults (Foster and Perry 1982) have examined the relationship between skin tone and the self by using direct measures of self-evaluation. A study of an Arizona sample examined children's skin color selections and feelings of happiness. Using a skin tone connotation scale to measure preferences, the researchers found that a range of light brown to yellow was the most preferred choice, while dark brown and very dark brown were the least preferred tones (Porter 1991). The latter selections were also associated with negative emotional experiences. Porter (1991:152) concluded that complexion is a very important symbol of attractiveness for middle school children and preferences are motivated by a desire "to be liked" and "to be like others." Robinson and Ward (1995) also report an association between negative self-evaluation, color satisfaction, and skin color among Black adolescents. Self-esteem and skin color satisfaction scores for darker adolescents were lower than those for lighter adolescents.

Among adults, however, there is no evidence of a relationship between skin tone and self-esteem (Foster and Perry 1982). In one study, Foster and Perry (1982) analyzed a subsample of Black respondents in the Detroit Area Study and reported findings showing that "blacks who were either very dark or very light tended to have slightly lower levels of self-valuation than other respondents. The only exception was among people with college training. In this case, darker-skinned blacks had higher valuations of themselves than other blacks" (1982:64). These findings were not statistically significant when satisfaction with family, job, and income was taken into account. The authors did not examine the possibility that dimensions of satisfaction conditioned the effects of complexion on self-esteem.

Other research challenges the notion that skin tone is related to self-evaluation. Ransford (1970) found that skin tone positively influenced income and occupational status, but not feelings of self-worth and confidence. Given the strong evidence of the association between skin tone and education and income (Hughes and Hertel 1990; Keith and Herring 1991), however, research must consider the moderating effect of education and income on the relationship between skin tone and self-esteem. That is, it may be that skin tone interacts with socioeconomic status in its effect on self-concept development, an issue that is addressed in our analyses.

THE IMPORTANCE OF SKIN TONE AND SELF-EVALUATIONS FOR AFRICAN AMERICAN WOMEN

Issues of skin tone and physical attractiveness are closely linked, and because expectations of physical attractiveness are applied more heavily to women across all cultures, stereotypes of attractiveness and color preference are more profound for Black women. Studies show that both African American men and women rate lighter skin tones as more physically attractive (Bond and Cash 1992; Cash and Duncan 1984) and prefer dating and marital partners with lighter skin tones (Freeman et al. 1966; Udry, Bauman, and Chase 1969; Robinson and Ward 1995). One study concluded that light skin tone had social exchange value for women in that upwardly mobile males of darker complexion were married to lighter-skinned females from lower social classes (Udry, Bauman, and Chase 1969). Although Udry and colleagues' study of social status, class mobility, and skin color is dated, a recent study of dating and attitudes about skin color suggests that this pattern has not changed. For example, Black adolescent males believe that lighter skin tones make a female physically attractive (Robinson and Ward 1995), and in another study college women believed that lighter skin was perceived as more attractive by their Black male peers (Bond and Cash 1992).

In the clinical literature (Boyd-Franklin 1991; Okazawa-Rey, Robinson, and Ward 1987; Neal and Wilson 1989) issues of racial identity, skin color, and attractiveness are central concerns of Black women. The "what is beautiful is good" stereotype creates a "halo" effect for light-skinned persons. The positive glow generated by physical attractiveness includes a host of desirable personality traits. Included in these positive judgments are beliefs that attractive people are significantly more intelligent, kind, confident, interesting, sexy, assertive, poised, modest, and successful, and that they appear to have higher self-esteem and self-worth (Dion, Berscheid, and Walster 1972). When complexion is the indicator of attractiveness, similar stereotypic attributes are found. In a study of facial features, skin tone, and attractiveness, Neal (1988, cited in Neal and Wilson 1989) found that "unattractive women were perceived as having darker skin than attractive women and that women with more Caucasoid features were perceived as more attractive to the opposite sex and more successful in their love lives and careers than women with Negroid features" (328). There is evidence that gender differences in the link between skin tone and attractiveness emerge during childhood. Black girls as young as six are twice as likely as Black boys to be sensitive to the social importance of complexion (Russell, Wilson, and Hall 1992:68). Frequent exposure to such negative evaluations beginning in childhood can undermine a woman's self-esteem and self-efficacy.

Several explanations are proffered for skin tone effects on self-esteem among Black women. One is that females are socialized to attend to evaluations of others and are vulnerable to negative appraisals. And the media have encouraged greater negative self-appraisals for dark-skinned females.

A second explanation is that, although colorism and its associated stressors affect Black women of all complexions, the effect is not the same for dark and light-skinned women. Because of racism and its divisive nature in American culture, both dark- and light-skinned women experience some negative reactions in their everyday lives. The drawbacks of light skin tone may come from interacting with those who hold biases toward biracial relationships in the case of biracial children and from those who reject or deny the history of interracial mixing in American society. The uncertainty about relationships and identity that comes from preferential treatment associated with color bias and the lack of recognition of their status as victims of color bias by other Blacks might also be sources of stress for light-skinned women (Brown 1998). Thus the stress of colorism is not as directly negative for light-skinned women. In comparison, for darker-skinned Black women, colorism has a direct impact via negative treatment and expectations regarding attractiveness and attainment. This suggests a triple jeopardy situation: Black women face problems of racism and sexism, and the combination of these two negative-status positions—being Black and being female—with colorism lowers self-esteem and feelings of competence among dark Black women.

HYPOTHESES

Following the literature, we predict that the effect of skin tone on self-efficacy will be primarily mediated by occupation and income, because self-efficacy results from undertaking challenges and succeeding or not succeeding. African American women, regardless of complexion, who experience success in their everyday world will feel more empowered. In contrast, we expect the direct relationship between skin tone and self-esteem to be more robust and only partially moderated by socioeconomic status and body image. Further, we posit that the relationship between skin tone and self-esteem will be stronger for Black females from lower social classes and for Black females who are judged as unattractive. Similar to our reasoning for self-efficacy, we argue that Black women who are successful will have higher levels of self-esteem regardless of complexion and attractiveness. Finally, we expect that African American women who are immersed in predominantly White environments during childhood, the formative years for self-concept development, will have lower self-esteem than those raised in the African American community, and that this relationship will be stronger among darker-skinned women.

DATA AND METHODS

THE SAMPLE

Data for this study come from the National Survey of Black Americans (NSBA) (Jackson and Gurin 1987). The sample for the survey was drawn according to a multistage area probability procedure that was designed to ensure that every Black household in the United States had an equal probability of being selected for the study. Within each household in the sample, one person age 18 or older was randomly selected to be interviewed from among those eligible for the study. Only self-identified Black American citizens were eligible for the study. Face-to-face interviews were carried out by trained Black interviewers, yielding a sample of 2,107 respondents, 1,310 (61.6%) of whom were female. The response rate was approximately 69 percent. For the most part, the NSBA is representative of the national Black population enumerated in the 1980 census with the exception of a slight overrepresentation of females and older Blacks and a small underrepresentation of Southerners (see Jackson 1991; Jackson, Tucker, and Gurin 1987).

MEASURES

DEPENDENT VARIABLES. The self-esteem scale (alpha = .66) consists of six items: (1) I feel that I am a person of worth, (2) I feel I do not have much to be proud of, (3) I feel that I can't do anything right, (4) I feel that my life is not very useful, (5) I am a useful person to have around, and (6) as a person I do a good job these days. Responses range on a five-point scale from (1) *never true* to (4) *almost always true,* with negatively worded items reverse coded so that high values represent positive self-esteem. The four questions asked in the NSBA to measure self-efficacy are the most highly correlated (Wright 1976:107) in a commonly used scale of personal efficacy (see Robinson and Shaver 1969:102 for validity of the scale). The four items are (1) Do you think it's better to plan your life a good ways ahead, or would you say life is too much a matter of luck to plan ahead very far? (2) When you do make plans ahead, do you usually get to carry out things the way you expected or do things come up to make you change your plans? (3) Have you usually felt pretty sure your life would work out the way you want it to, or have there been times when you haven't been sure about it? and (4) Some people feel they can run their lives pretty much the way they want to, others feel the problems of life are sometimes too big for them. Which one are you most like? The positive responses were coded 3, those indicating agreement with both positive and negative responses were coded 2, and negative responses were coded 1. Hughes and Demo's (1989:140) analysis of these data show that the measure of self-efficacy is empirically distinct from the measure of self-esteem. The items were summed to form a scale on which high values represent a high sense of personal efficacy (alpha = .57).

MAJOR INDEPENDENT VARIABLES. Skin tone was measured by asking interviewers to classify respondents as: (1) very dark brown ($N = 87$; 7.4%); (2) dark brown ($N = 330$; 28%); (3) medium brown ($N = 543$; 46.1%); (4) light brown—light-skinned ($N = 182$; 15.5%); and (5) very light brown—very light-skinned ($N = 35$; 3.0%). This measurement scheme is similar to other studies that used objective ratings of skin color (Freeman et al. 1966; Udry, Bauman, and Chase 1969). Interracial contact during childhood was measured by asking respondents to judge the racial composition of two settings: (1) their grammar or elementary school (i.e., grade school contact) and (2) their neighborhood while growing up (i.e., neighborhood contact). Responses were coded as: 1 = all Black, 2 = mostly Black, 3 = about half Black, 4 = mostly White, and 5 = almost all White.

BODY IMAGE VARIABLES.   Interviewers were asked to indicate where the respondent fell on a semantic scale from 1 = unattractive to 7 = attractive and where the respondent fell on a scale from 1 = underweight to 7 = overweight. The correlation between attractiveness and complexion is .19, suggesting that the two variables operate somewhat independently. Disabled is measured as follows: for each of thirteen medical conditions, respondents were asked: "How much does this health problem keep you from working or carrying out your daily tasks?" with responses classified as *a great deal* (2), *only a little* (1), or *not at all* (0). The third set of independent variables included (1) education, years of completed schooling, with eighteen categories ranging from 0 for *none* to 17 for *four or more years of college;* (2) employment status, coded 1 for *working for pay* and 0 for *laid off or not working for pay;* and (3) personal income, with respondents assigned the midpoint of seventeen categories, ranging from 1 for *no income* to 17 for income of *$30,000 or more.* A Pareto curve estimate was used to derive a midpoint for the open-ended categories (see Miller 1964).

CONTROL VARIABLES. Age of the respondent is self-reported age in years. Marital status is dummy coded 1 for currently married, and not married is the comparison category, coded 0. Region of current residence is collapsed into two categories: South, which is coded 1, and non-South, coded 0. For the urbanicity variable, respondents were categorized as urban (1) if they lived in an urban area.

RESULTS

SKIN TONE AND SELF-EFFICACY

Table 6.1 shows the regression of self-efficacy on measures of skin tone, sociodemographic, socioeconomic, and body image variables using a hierarchical multiple regression data analytic strategy. The first equation looks at the bivariate relationship between skin tone and each dependent variable, with subsequent equations adding sociodemographic, socioeconomic status, body image, and interracial contact variables, in that order. Looking at column 1, we see that skin tone has a significant positive effect on self-efficacy. Lighter complexion is associated with higher levels of perceived mastery. Each incremental change in skin color from dark to light is associated with a .06 increment in self-efficacy.

The effect of skin tone on self-efficacy is reduced and no longer statistically significant when the sociodemographic variables are added in the second equation. Of the sociodemographic variables, age and urban residence have significant positive effects on self-efficacy. Each incremental change in age is associated with a .09 increase in self-efficacy. Women who live in urban communities have a higher sense of self-efficacy than those who live in rural communities. Adding the socioeconomic variables to the equation (column 3), we see that education and income have statistically significant effects on self-efficacy. Note that the standardized coefficient for education is not quite twice as large as that of income, suggesting that education has a stronger effect in determining self-efficacy for women. Body image, represented by attractiveness and weight (column 4), is not statistically associated with self-efficacy. Disabling health conditions, however, have a significant negative effect on self-efficacy. Each additional disabling health condition decreases feelings of self efficacy by .10 points. In the final equation, we add the interracial contact variables. Only grade school environment has a significant negative impact on self-efficacy. As the percentage of Whites in one's elementary school increases, feelings of self-efficacy decrease. When all the independent variables are accounted for (column 5), the determinants of self-efficacy for females in this study are age, education, income, disability,

TABLE 6.1 Regression Coefficients for the Relationship Between Skin Tone and Self-Efficacy

	(N = 1,010)				
	(1)	(2)	(3)	(4)	(5)
Skin tone	.057+	.049	.016	.004	.007
	(.165)	(.140)	(.045)	(.012)	(.020)
Age		.093**	.185***	.216***	.208***
		(.013)	(.028)	(.032)	(.030)
Urban		.119***	.070*	.070*	.069*
		(.744)	(.439)	(.438)	(.430)
South		−.055	−.029	−.032	−.051
		(−.287)	(−.151)	(−.170)	(−.266)
Married		.031	.008	.006	.001
		(.167)	(.044)	(.031)	(.006)
Personal income			.117**	.113**	.112**
			(.056)	(.053)	(.053)
Education			.194***	.171***	.176***
			(.157)	(.138)	(.143)
Employed			−.003	−.026	−.031
			(−.014)	(−.135)	(−.162)
Attractiveness				.045	.044
				(.080)	(.078)
Weight				−.011	−.014
				(−.026)	(−.032)
Disabled				−.108**	−.111**
				(−0.76)	(−.078)
Race-school					−.062+
					(−.156)
Race-neighborhood					.004
					(.010)
Constant	7.741	6.738	6.323	6.138	6.256
R^2	.003	.032	.087	.098	.101
Adjusted R^2	.002	.027	.079	.088	.090

Source: National Survey of Black Americans, 1979–1980

Note: Unstandardized coefficients in parentheses
+$p \leq .10$ *$p \leq .05$ **$p \leq .01$ ***$p \leq .001$

urban residence, and grade school contact, although the last is marginal. Age (*beta* = .21) and education (*beta* = .17) have the stronger effects, and both are highly significant. The effect of skin tone is reduced by 87 percent and is no longer statistically significant after all variables are controlled. In additional analyses (data not shown), skin tone has significant direct effects on both education and income. For African American women the skin tone effect on self-efficacy is therefore largely indirect, via its consequence for income and education.

SKIN TONE AND SELF-ESTEEM

A similar analysis for the self-esteem measure is displayed in table 6.2, but skin tone has a very different influence on self-esteem than it has on self-efficacy. Skin tone has a significant positive association with self-esteem, even after all other variables are controlled in the final equation. These findings show that each incremental change in skin tone from darker to lighter shades is associated with a .10 increment in self-esteem. The effect of skin tone on self-esteem is slightly enhanced when the sociodemographic controls are added to the equation (column 2) and is slightly reduced in the face of a strong pattern of socioeconomic effects (column 3). Education, income, and employment have positive effects on self-esteem for African American women. Two indicators for body image have significant positive effects on self-esteem—attractiveness and weight. Disabled condition (column 4) has a significant negative association with self-esteem. None of the socioeconomic effects remains statistically significant when body image variables are controlled, but the skin tone effect does remain statistically significant. The body image variables have a moderate impact on the relationship between skin tone and self-esteem, reducing it by 20 percent. Females who are rated physically attractive have higher self-esteem scores, but attractiveness is at least in part related to skin tone.

Only one of the interracial context variables, racial composition of elementary school, has a significant negative effect on self-esteem. The results show that the higher the percent of Whites in the elementary school, the lower the self-esteem. Note here that the coefficient for the skin tone effect on self-esteem is slightly enhanced when the interracial context variables are added, suggesting that the relationship between skin tone and self-esteem might be in part conditioned by racial context. The strength of the effects for both skin tone and interracial context on self-esteem is modest. Age and disabling health conditions have stronger effects.

TABLE 6.2 Regression Coefficients for the Relationship Between Skin Tone and Self-Esteem

	(N = 1,010)				
	(1)	(2)	(3)	(4)	(5)
Skin tone	.098**	.107***	.085**	.068*	.072*
	(.276)	(.299)	(.239)	(.191)	(.202)
Age		.181***	.189***	.242	.233***
		(.019)	(.028)	(.035)	(.034)
Urban		.023	−.004	−.004	−.005
		(.142)	(−.026)	(−.023)	(−.033)
South		.026	.038	.035	.011
		(.130)	(.195)	(.179)	(.057)
Married		.000	−.019	−.024	−.030
		(−.002)	(−.102)	(−.126)	(−.158)
Personal income			.064+	.057	.056
			(.030)	(.027)	(.026)
Education			.088*	.051	.058
			(.069)	(.040)	(.046)
Employed			.088*	.043	.036
			(.443)	(.218)	(.184)
Attractiveness				.067*	.066*
				(.115)	(.113)
Weight				.055+	.051+
				(.122)	(.115)
Disabled				−.197***	−.201**
				(−.135)	(−.137)
Race-school					−.079*
					(−.194)
Race-neighborhood					.004
					(.009)
Constant	21.067	20.077	19.819	19.498	19.635
R2	.010	.027	.056	.091	.096
Adjusted R2	.009	.023	.048	.081	.085

Source: National Survey of Black Americans, 1979–1980

Note: Unstandardized coefficients in parentheses
+$p \leq .10$ *$p \leq .05$ **$p \leq .01$ ***$p \leq .001$

Although the amount of variance explained in the analyses of self-efficacy and self-esteem are modest, they compare favorably to sociological models predicting self-esteem and self-efficacy. More informative is the size of the coefficient for skin tone compared to other variables in the model, and that the skin tone effect remains significant across all equations. Note that the set of determinants for self-esteem and self-efficacy also differs in that socio-economic factors are important for self-efficacy, whereas body image variables emerge as important determinants for self-esteem.

DO ACHIEVEMENT AND BODY IMAGE CONDITION THE EFFECTS OF SKIN TONE ON SELF-CONCEPT?

The literature suggests that it is reasonable to expect that skin tone may interact with socioeconomic status and body image to affect self-concept, especially among women. We expect that among females the relationships between skin tone and self-esteem and skin tone and self-efficacy will be moderated by socioeconomic status and body image. That is, the relationships will be stronger for Black females from lower social classes, for Black females who are judged as unattractive or overweight, and for Black females who experience disabling medical conditions. To test for these possibilities, we created interaction terms for skin tone and each of the socioeconomic status variables and for skin tone and each of the body image variables. As suggested by Aiken and West (1991), all variables used to compute interaction terms were centered. Each interaction term was entered into the regression equation separately. Simple slope regression analyses were then used to probe significant interactions (Aiken and West 1991).

In the analyses of self-efficacy, there were no significant interaction effects among women. However, in the analyses of women's self-esteem, two signifi-cant interaction effects emerged—skin tone and personal income ($beta = -.031$) and skin tone and interviewer-rated attractiveness ($beta = -.120$). The results from the simple slope analyses indicate that the relationship between skin tone and personal income is positive and significant among women with the lowest incomes. In other words, among women with the lowest levels of income (i.e., 1 SD below the mean) self-esteem increases as color lightens ($beta = .366$, $p \leq .01$). The relationship is also positive and significant for women with average levels of income, although the relationship is not as strong ($beta = .198$, $p \leq .05$). Among women with the highest incomes (i.e., 1 SD above the mean), there is no significant relationship between skin tone and self-esteem ($beta = .030$). Thus, women who are dark and successful evaluate themselves just as positively as women who are lighter and success-ful. Similar to the findings for income, skin tone has a significant positive effect on self-esteem among women evaluated as having low and average levels of attractiveness, although the effect is stronger for the former. Self-esteem increases as skin color becomes lighter among women judged unat-tractive (*beta* = .375, $p \leq$ .001) or average (*beta* = .199, $p \leq$ .05). There is no relationship between skin tone and self esteem for women who are judged highly attractive (*beta* = .023). In other words, skin tone does not have much relevance for self-esteem among women who have higher levels of income and who are attractive.

DISCUSSION

In this essay we argue that social context is one of the important influences in shaping who we are and in determining the role of status attrib-utes in shaping the self. We focus on the importance of skin tone for self-concept development when combined with the racial context of one's early formative environment. Several patterns emerge from the data. First, the process by which skin tone affects self-evaluations differs according to the dimension of the self under consideration. Skin tone has a direct effect on self-esteem, but the effect on self-efficacy is probably indirect via its influence on educational attainment and income. The negative association between skin tone and self-esteem remains even when considered in concert with sociodemographic and socioeconomic variables and with the competing effects of body image and racial context. As most of the ethnographic and clinical literature predicts, as complexion goes from light to dark, feelings of self-worth decrease.

Second, we examine the influence of social context on self-evaluations. Our analyses show that childhood interracial contact, particularly the school environment, is especially important. African American women who attend predominantly White grade schools have lower self-esteem. Interracial neighborhood contacts appear less important. Our explanation for this dif-ference in effects is that school environments involve more intense interac-tions with peers and teachers and provide direct feedback on competence and social esteem via teacher evaluations and peer popularity reports. And when these interactions are mainly with persons who are racially different, the comparisons become a source of stress and negative evaluation. As Rosenberg (1975) found, contextual dissonant environments have deleteri-ous effects on the self-esteem of the lower-status member. But do African

American women of different skin tones have different experiences in White and Black America? The answer to this question is no. There is no evidence that social context conditions the influence of skin tone on self-evaluations. It appears that Whites do not respond differently to dark- and light-skinned Black women, and that light skin tone confers no status advantage in predominantly White school settings, at least as it pertains to self-concept formation. This finding is striking in that early childhood experience has consequences for adult identity. Overall, our findings add to the literature on the importance of early childhood socialization experiences, and these results are consistent with inferences that were drawn from early doll preference studies on the detrimental effects that these experiences can have on self-esteem. Our childhood interracial contact findings also confirm the research on the impact of hostile racial environments for social functioning among African Americans. In sum, the findings suggest that racism is an "equal opportunity operator" in that Black women of all skin tones are equally likely to be deleteriously influenced by these White environments.

The truly disadvantaged by skin tone, however, are Black women with low incomes. Darker skin complexion is associated with low self-worth for women with low incomes. Why does skin color have such importance for self-regard in the context of low income and poverty? Low income shapes self-esteem because it provides fewer opportunities for rewarding experiences or affirming relationships. In addition, there are more negative trait attributes associated with behaviors of persons from lower social-class groups than for persons from higher classes. For example, the derisive comment "ghetto chick" is often used to describe the behaviors, dress, communication, and interaction styles of women from low-income groups. Combine stereotypes of classism and colorism and you have a mixture that fosters an undesirable, if not malignant, context for self-esteem development. An important finding of this research is that not only do skin color and income determine self-worth for Black women, but these factors can work together. Dark skin and low income produce Black women with very low self-esteem.

Physical attractiveness influenced feelings of self-worth for Black women as well. Females have traditionally been concerned with appearance, regardless of ethnicity. Indeed, pursuit of and preoccupation with beauty are central features of female sex-role stereotypes. The literature on attraction also shows that physical attractiveness has psychological benefits. Persons who are judged as attractive have more positive self-concepts and better social skills than less attractive women. Our findings suggest that unattractive women are more vulnerable to color bias than attractive women. Self-esteem increases as skin color becomes lighter among women who are judged unattractive. Thus, skin color is more critical for feelings of self-worth among women judged unattractive than among those judged attractive.

In contrast to feelings of self-worth, neither skin color nor attractiveness appears to be an important predictor of self-efficacy for Black women. Perhaps it is that, as St. Jean and Feagin (1998) argue, Black women have learned that their appearance will not lead to success and therefore they have learned to draw on other aspects of their identity for competence. According to St. Jean and Feagin (1998:91–92), a consequence of Black women's learning that beauty will not be their ticket to success is that they have learned to focus on a wide range of talents for confirmation of their competencies, including educational accomplishments. In our society educational attainment is valued as a vehicle for success. The importance of education and income as predictors of self-efficacy for women in this study underscores how Black women cope with their status in society.

REFERENCES

Aiken, L. S. and S. G. West. 1991. *Multiple Regression: Testing and Interpreting Interactions.* Thousand Oaks, Calif.: Sage.

Bachman, J. G. 1970. *The Impact of Family Background and Intelligence on Tenth-Grade Boys.* Vol. 2 of *Youth in Transition.* Ann Arbor: Survey Research Center, Institute for Social Research.

Bandura, A. 1977. Self-efficacy: Towards a unifying theory of behavioral change. *Psychological Review* 84:191–215.

———. 1982. Self-efficacy mechanism in human agency. *American Psychologist* 37: 122–147.

Bond, S. and T. F. Cash. 1992. Black beauty: Skin color and body images among African-American college women. *Journal of Applied Social Psychology* 22 (11): 874–888.

Boyd-Franklin, N. 1991. Recurrent themes in the treatment of African-American women in group psychotherapy. *Women and Therapy* 11 (2): 25–40.

Brown, K. T. 1998. Consequences of skin tone bias for African Americans: Resource attainment and psychological/social functioning. *African American Research Perspectives* 4 (1): 55–60.

Cash, T. S. and N. C. Duncan. 1984. Physical attractiveness stereotyping among Black American college students. *Journal of Social Psychology* 1:71–77.

Chambers, J. W., T. Clark, L. Dantzler, and J. A. Baldwin. 1994. Perceived attractiveness, facial features, and African self-consciousness. *Journal of Black Psychology* 20 (3): 305–324.

Dion, K., E. Berscheid, and E. Walster. 1972. What is beautiful is good. *Journal of Personality and Social Psychology* 24:285–290.

Etter, G. L. 1994. African American Women in the Workplace: Double Standards/ Double Lives. In Vasilikie Demos and Marcia Texler Seagal, eds., *Ethnic Women: A Multiple Status Reality*, 155–168. Dix Hills, N.Y.: General Hall.

Feagin, J. R. and H. Vera. 1995. *White Racism: The Basics.* New York: Basic.

Festinger, L. 1954. A Theory of Social Comparison Processes. *Human Relations* 7:117–140.

Foster, M. and L. R. Perry. 1982. Self-evaluation among Blacks. *Social Work* (January): 60–66.

Freeman, H. E., J. M. Ross, S. Armor, and T. F. Pettigrew. 1966. Color gradation and attitudes among middle-class income Negroes. *American Sociological Review* 31: 365–374.

Gecas, V. 1989. The social psychology of self-efficacy. *Annual Review of Sociology* 15: 291–316.

Gooley, R. L. 1990. A conceptual model for examining the unique status of Black women. *National Journal of Sociology* 4:231–249.

Henriques, Z. W. 1995. African-American women: The oppressive intersection of gender, race, and class. *Women and Criminal Justice* 7:67–80.

Hoelter, J. W. 1982. Race differences in selective credulity and self-esteem. *Sociological Quarterly* 23:527–537.

Hughes, M. and D. H. Demo. 1989. Self-perceptions of Black Americans: Self-esteem and personal efficacy. *American Journal of Sociology* 95:132–159.

Hughes, M. and B. R. Hertel. 1990. The significance of color remains: A study of life chances, mate selection, and ethnic consciousness among Black Americans. *Social Forces* 68 (4): 1105–1120.

Jackson, J. S. 1991. Methodological Approaches. In J. S. Jackson, ed., *Life in Black America*, 13–30. Thousand Oaks, Calif.: Sage.

Jackson, J. S. and G. Gurin. 1987. *National Survey of Black Americans, 1979–1980* (machine readable codebook). Inter-University Consortium for Political and Social Research, University of Michigan.

Jackson, J. S., B. Tucker, and G. Gurin. 1987. *National Survey of Black Americans, 1979–1980* (MRDF). Ann Arbor: Institute for Social Research.

Keith, V. M. and C. Herring. 1991. Skin tone and stratification in the Black community. *American Journal of Sociology* 97 (3): 760–778.

Kiecolt, K. J. and A. C. Acock. 1990. Childhood family structure and adult psychological well-being of Black Americans. *Sociological Spectrum* 10:169–186.

Kirschenman, J. and K. M. Neckerman. 1998. "We'd Love to Hire Them, But." In A. S. Wharton, ed., *The Meaning of Race for Employers in Working in America: Continuity, Conflict, and Change*, 241–249. Mountain View, Calif.: Mayfield.

Miller, H. P. 1964. *Rich Man, Poor Man.* New York: Cromwell.

Neal, A. and M. Wilson. 1989. The role of skin color and features in the Black community: Implications for Black women in therapy. *Clinical Psychology Review* 9 (3): 323–333.

Okazawa-Rey, M., T. Robinson, and J. V. Ward. 1987. Black women and the politics of skin color and hair. *Women and Therapy* 6:89–102.

Porter, C. P. 1991. Social reasons for skin tone preferences of Black school-age children. *American Journal of Orthopsychiatry* 61 (1): 149–154.

Porter, J. R. and R. E. Washington. 1979. Black identity and self-esteem: A review of studies of Black self-concept, 1968–1978. *Annual Review of Sociology* 5:53–74.

———. 1989. Developments in research on Black identity and self-esteem: 1979–88. *Review of International Psychology and Sociology* 2:341–353.

Powell, G. J. and M. Fuller. 1970. "School Desegregation and Self-concept." Paper presented at the 47th annual meeting of the American Orthopsychiatric Association, San Francisco.

Ransford, H. E. 1970. Skin color, life chances, and anti-White attitudes. *Social Problems* 18:164–179.

Robinson, J. P. and P. R. Shaver. 1969. *Measures of Social Psychological Attitudes.* Ann Arbor: University of Michigan, Institute of Social Research.

Robinson, T. L. and J. V. Ward. 1995. African American adolescents and skin color. *Journal of Black Psychology* 21 (3): 256–274.

Rosenberg, M. 1975. The Dissonant Context and the Adolescent Self-Concept. In E. S. Bragastin and G. H. Elder, eds., *Adolescence in the Life Cycle,* 97–116. Washington, D.C.: Hemisphere.

Rosenberg, M. and R. Simmons. 1971. *Black and White Self-Esteem: The Urban School Child.* Washington, D.C.: American Sociological Association.

Russell, K., M. Wilson, and R. Hall. 1992. *The Color Complex: The Politics of Skin Color Among African Americans.* New York: Harcourt Brace Jovanovich.

Sinclair, A. 1994. *Coffee Will Make You Black.* New York: Avon Books.

Smith, A. and A. J. Stewart. 1983. Approaches to studying racism and sexism in Black women's lives. *Journal of Social Issues* 39:1–15.

St. Jean, Y. and J. R. Feagin. 1998. *Double Burden: Black Women and Everyday Racism.* New York: M. E. Sharpe.

Tashakkori, A. and V. D. Thompson. 1991. Race differences in self-perception and locus of control during adolescence and early adulthood: Methodological implications. *Genetic, Social, and General Psychology Monographs* 117:133–152.

Udry, J. R., K. E. Bauman, and C. Chase. 1969. Skin color, status, and mate selection. *American Journal of Sociology* 76:722–733.

Verna, G. and K. Runion. 1985. The effects of contextual dissonance on the self-concept of youth from high vs. low socially valued group. *Journal of Social Psychology* 125: 449–458.

Wright, B. 1976. *The Dissent of the Governed: Alienation and Democracy in America.* New York: Academic.

PART IV

SOCIAL ROLES, SOCIAL STATUSES, AND THE MENTAL WELL-BEING OF AFRICAN AMERICAN WOMEN

Our mothers bear us into a hostile world that they know cares little about our existence. Our mothers whisper, shout, signal and symbolize what we as women of our race must do: fight, survive, grow, excel! Throughout our childhood they guide and teach us how to adapt and adopt in order to accomplish. Their prayers ask God to bless, punish, and protect us.

—Garrod et al.

7 INTIMATE RELATIONSHIPS AND PSYCHOLOGICAL WELL-BEING
M. Belinda Tucker

There has been relatively little empirical research on the role of marriage and other intimate relationships in the mental health of African American women. Although the sexual and child-bearing behavior of Black women has, in some respects, been unduly scrutinized, psychologists have largely failed to examine in depth the socioemotional content and impact of close personal relationships involving African American women. Despite a high level of concern in the community at large (as demonstrated through popular music, magazine articles, and movies), there is also a noticeable void in clinical writings. In the classic 1960s book *Black Rage,* psychiatrists William Grier and Price Cobbs (1968) placed particular emphasis on the physicality of Blackness (skin color, hair texture, features) and the manner in which unfavorable comparisons to a European ideal hampered the achievement of healthy womanhood and healthy relationships. Although their analysis seems somewhat anachronistic by today's standards of gender sensitivity, they also cited the strains on Black marriage resulting from the inability of the family (as a result of racism) to provide adequate economic, political, and physical protection for its members.

Although one could argue that there has been some (though not nearly sufficient) broadening of the standards by which physical attractiveness in this society is judged, it seems likely that a number of the concerns cited by Grier and Cobbs continue to affect the psychological well-being of Black women. Boyd-Franklin (1989), in her analyses of therapeutic models and functions for Black women, highlights a series of issues that commonly emerge

This investigation was supported by two grants from the National Institute of Mental Health: research grant no. R01 MH 47434 to M. B. Tucker and C. Mitchell-Kernan and Independent Scientist Award no. K02 MH 01278 to Tucker.

in group therapy—a general pessimism about relationships, with the expectation that one will be disappointed or abused by men; the pressures and competing demands faced by Black couples that serve to compromise relationships; the perceived shortage of Black men and its impact on the family and childbearing goals of women; and the effect on current relationships of unresolved issues from previous partnerships. And, although the limited literature on Black women's close relationships focuses primarily on heterosexual partnerships, writing and research on psychological issues in Black lesbian and bisexual relationships has increased quite substantially in recent years (Greene 1994).

Relationship formation and maintenance for African American women are undertaken within an extraordinary context. With respect to female-male relationships, the enduring legacy of the destructive impact of slavery on family and other interpersonal relationships, coupled with continuing economic and social discrimination in the United States, have taken their toll on marriage and family. Since the 1960s, divorce ratios (the number of divorces per 1,000 marriages) have quadrupled, and African Americans are presently more likely to divorce than any other major ethnic group, with a divorce ratio approximately double that of Whites (282 to 133) (Farley 1995). By 1990, more than one-third of Black women in their late thirties and 45 percent of those age 40–44 had their first marriages end in divorce (U.S. Bureau of the Census 1992), and they are now less likely to marry than any other racial group of U.S. women. It has also been estimated that as few as 70 percent of Black women born in the 1950s will marry, compared to more than 90 percent of those born in the 1930s (Rodgers and Thornton 1985). Among the causative factors cited are declining sex ratios (Guttentag and Secord 1983); deteriorating economic fortunes of African American men (Wilson 1996; Darity and Myers 1995); increasing conflicts between the sex role orientations of Black men and women (Taylor 1998); and larger changing societal mores (Thornton 1989). All of these factors seem to have played some role in the changing family formation attitudes and behaviors of Black women, yet the effect on their psychological well-being is not well understood.

My aim in this chapter is to describe what is known about African American women's intimate relationships and mental health and to explore ways in which a better understanding of these issues might be facilitated. The material is organized as follows: First, I will examine the particular features of environmental context that operate to constrain African American women's romantic involvements. Second, I will describe research that has addressed associations between Black women's intimate involvements and mental health. Third, I will present results from my own program of research that address this issue. Fourth, I will offer recommendations for future research on these questions.

CONTEXTUAL BARRIERS TO AFRICAN AMERICAN WOMEN'S RELATIONSHIP FORMATION AND MAINTENANCE

Features of the environment and perceptual problems related to African American womanhood in the United States present formidable barriers to both the formation of relationships and their maintenance. Several issues are of particular concern in this regard: the values of the larger society with respect to mate selection priorities, the mating opportunity structure, external race- and race-gender-related strains on relationships, and gender role conflicts.

MATE SELECTION PRIORITIES

African American women live within a larger society that greatly values the economic role of men. Studies have shown that heterosexual mate selection for women in most industrial societies prioritizes the ability of a potential husband to support a family economically (Buss and Barnes 1986). Though African American men have always fared poorly in the U.S. labor market because of racism, inadequate training, and limited opportunity, in recent decades the virtual collapse of the industrial sector in central cities has further compromised the wage-earning and wealth-development potential of Black men (Oliver and Shapiro 1995). Indeed, research has shown that compared to White women, African American women have broader mate selection standards and are more likely to marry men who are older, less educated, and previously married (Spanier and Glick 1980). At the same time, the gap between salaries of Black women and men is smaller than the gap between what White women and men earn, median income ratios of .71 and .52, respectively, in 1996 (U.S. Bureau of the Census 1997). Therefore the economic gains of marriage are substantially lower for Black women than for other groups of women in the United States. These situations can complicate relationship formation and maintenance by diminishing the pool of eligible mates, affecting the power in relationships, which is often determined by who is providing the most financial support. These situations can also compromise relationship satisfaction owing to an inability to achieve the societal standard in the male provider role, and by lowering the perceived cost of divorce.

Our work has also consistently shown that African American men and women believe more strongly than other ethnic groups that adequate finances are critical for marital success (Tucker and Mitchell-Kernan 1995b; Tucker 2000). Although the development of such a value system is understandable given the persistent trying economic circumstances for African Americans as a whole, this does present a dilemma for heterosexual African American women in relationship formation. That is, if the economic standard is applied, the likelihood of a successful and satisfying mate search is not great.

On the other side of the coin, the same studies that show a continuing emphasis among women on financial prospects in mates show that men nearly universally prioritize attractiveness in women (Buss and Barnes 1986). There is little research determining the standard by which attractiveness is judged among African American men, but the images of Black women projected in music videos and magazines directed toward Black men suggest that though definitions of beauty are broader than they were in the pre—"Black Is Beautiful" days, a preference for long, straight, or wavy hair and lighter skin still exists. Such preferences continue to plague Black women's self-perceptions and their ability to form healthy relationships (Boyd-Franklin 1989; Neal and Wilson 1989; Okazawa-Rey, Robinson, and Ward 1987).

THE MATING OPPORTUNITY STRUCTURE

Sex ratios (i.e., the number of men per 100 women) vary widely by geographical location, but many of the larger cities in the Northeast, South, and Midwest display rather dramatic Black sex ratio imbalances. For example, according to the 1990 Census, the sex ratios for New York City, Milwaukee, Dayton, and New Orleans were 80, 74, 76, and 79, respectively. The extraordinary increase in the imprisonment of African American men has amplified the problem of higher male mortality, especially among lower-income groups. Though studies have not shown that declining sex ratios are the primary cause of the recent Black marital decline, there is evidence that they have contributed to lower marriage rates, higher marital dissolution, and nonmarital births (Kiecolt and Fossett 1995; Sampson 1995).

There has been surprisingly little study of the psychological consequences of constrained mate availability. In a study of 1,100 Southern Californians interviewed in 1989 (Tucker and Mitchell-Kernan 1998), we found that although single White women, and to a somewhat lesser extent Latinas, who believed that there were relatively few mating opportunities for them were more likely to have lower psychological well-being, there was no such association for Black women. We suggest that Black women see male shortages as a systemic condition over which they have no control, while Whites and Latinas may believe that the failure to find a mate is their own fault (resulting in compromised well-being). These data suggest a psychologically adaptive response among Black women to an otherwise disturbing social reality.

EXTERNAL RACE- AND GENDER-RELATED STRAINS ON RELATIONSHIPS

There is a growing body of work on how difficulties in fulfilling the provider role requirement compromises the ability of African American men to perform as husbands (Bowman and Forman 1997; Chadiha 1992; Hatchett, Veroff, and Douvan 1995). But there is a striking absence of similar empirical work on how the external context of racism and sexism affects Black women's relationships and consequent mental health. One question that has often been raised, but not explored empirically, is what the psychological consequences are for African American women of coping with the provider role issues and more general race-related difficulties confronting Black men. There is an implicit expectation that Black women in relationships with men will identify most strongly with the racial demands of the situation and be appropriately protective of the egos of Black men who face these problems. Yet such behavior can cause women to suppress their own socioemotional needs, which over time may compromise both relationships and individual well-being.

One area of growing significance, because of the dramatic increase in the incarceration of Blacks, most particularly men, is the psychological impact of imprisonment on personal relationships. King (1993) reported psychological and interpersonal difficulties, as well as financial problems when family members were jailed. Lidell (1998) specifically examined the mental health correlates and adaptive behavior of women whose husbands and partners were imprisoned. The women reported high levels of stress, as indicated by a range of physical symptoms and difficulty dealing with transportation issues, finances, and the reactions of children to their father's absence. Because of the pervasiveness of imprisoned Black men, a very significant proportion of the African American population, especially women, is at risk for these kinds of problems. Of course, not addressed by these studies are the relationship issues raised when women are imprisoned—a much more likely situation today than in previous times.

GENDER ROLE

Until recently, Black women (including wives) had higher labor force participation rates than the general U.S. population of women (Bureau of Labor Statistics and the Bureau of the Census 1997; U.S. Bureau of the Census 1979), and Black men were more likely to carry out household tasks, including childrearing, and to endorse such behavior (John, Shelton, and Luschen 1995). Other research has shown, however, that now African Americans are more likely than Whites to support male dominance in the home (Kane 1992; Staples and Johnson 1993) and that Black women as well as men believe that providing economic support for the family is primarily the responsibility of men (Taylor, Tucker, and Mitchell-Kernan 1999). The effect of an increasing divergence in the gender role views of African American women and men has significant implications for psychological well-being. Hatchett, Veroff, and Douvan (1995) found that Black marital instability was greater for women who were less "flexible" in the assignment of household tasks and for men who reported more equitable decision making. If relationship preservation requires that women adopt a particular set of values concerning male-female relationships—values that may not ultimately be in an individual woman's best interest—it could eventually take a psychological toll. Furthermore, since African American women have been stereotypically portrayed as emasculating and controlling, many Black women take great pains to avoid behaviors that may be construed in those terms.

EMPIRICAL RESEARCH ON ROMANTIC RELATIONSHIPS AND MENTAL HEALTH

MARITAL STATUS AND MENTAL HEALTH

Although earlier research demonstrated a positive relationship between being married and psychological well-being, though stronger for men (Coombs 1991), more recent studies suggest that the association is less clear-cut (Umberson and Williams 1999). Although there is less research on African American populations, the results overall suggest that gender is key. Broman (1988) found that separated and divorced African Americans, compared to those who were married, displayed lower individual and family life satisfaction. Among elderly Blacks, Chatters (1988) found that widowed and separated persons were less happy than those who were married. Yet the association does not always hold up in some populations of Black women. Using psychiatric assessment, Williams, Takeuchi, and Adair (1992) found that widowed, separated, and divorced Blacks and never married Black men had higher rates of mental disorder. This was not true for never married Black women. Commenting on the range of findings regarding the relative psychological costs/ benefits of the various nonmarital states (i.e., widowed, single, divorced, never married), Keith (1997) examined data from the National Survey of Black Americans (NSBA) and found that married and widowed persons had higher levels of happiness and life satisfaction, while separated and divorced persons had lower levels. This mirrored the level of stressful life problems reported, which in turn was the key predictor of both life satisfaction and happiness. Furthermore, stress exposure was a function, in part, of key status and resource variables. Although proportions of total variance explained remained low, this study does provide some evidence that mental health derives not from marital status per se but from the fact that certain categories of singles are subjected to greater amounts of stress and have fewer resources with which to effectively address such strains. Adding another twist, Brown (1996), using the same NSBA data set, found that previously married Black women had the highest levels of distress, but also discovered that they preferred their present situation over being married.

BATTERED WIVES/DYSFUNCTIONAL RELATIONSHIPS

Abuse is clearly an area of significant concern in any discussion of relationships and psychological well-being. Using a random sample of the Second National Family Violence Survey (Straus and Gelles 1990), Hampton and Gelles (1994) augmented the original sample with an oversample of 508 Black households. After controlling for socioeconomic variables, they found that Black wives compared to White wives were 1.23 times more likely to have experienced minor violence and 2.36 time more likely to have experienced severe violence. A recent study by Joseph (1997) of women who were battered by husbands or partners, however, found no racial difference in the extent of violence experienced, but found that Black women in the study were more reluctant to use social services to address the problem. Coley and Beckett (1988a), however, cautioned that a reliance on biased samples of African American women and anecdotal reports has limited the usefulness of most studies.

Coley and Beckett (1988b) also report that Black women interpret the battering experience differently than White women do, tending to view battering within the overall context of socioeconomic oppression and racism. They suggest that this makes it less likely that Black women will disclose the abuse to White therapists or to a predominantly White therapeutic group. Murray and Stahly (1987) report findings that suggest another motivation for Black women's reluctance to report abuse. From questionnaire responses of college students shown videotaped interviews of purported victims of domestic abuse, they found that Black victims were more likely to be derogated than White victims.

SAME-SEX RELATIONSHIPS AND MENTAL HEALTH

Greene (1994) has described the situation of lesbians as one of "triple jeopardy" from the effects of racism, sexism, and "heterocentric" bias. In a rare national study of African American same-sex relationships, Peplau, Cochran, and Mays (1997) examined 723 coupled Black women and men. They found that African Americans in their sample were more likely to have a partner of another race than the level reported for Blacks who marry and, in contrast to findings with heterosexual samples (including our own), that neither men nor women prioritized either financial wherewithal or attractiveness in mate selection. Although no findings were reported on psychological well-being, they did examine relationship satisfaction and commitment, finding that most women in their sample expressed love for their partners and found their relationships highly satisfying, with the expectation that the unions would last. This study suggests that in many ways, women in same-sex unions are likely to face many of the same problems that women in heterosexual couples face, though they may be less likely to have to contend with problems brought about by socioeconomic status differences. Still, a number of distinctive problems remain that would likely have an impact on well-being, including the greater likelihood of having to deal with racial difference in relationships and the risk of negative responses of family and community to same-sex relationships.

INTERRACIAL RELATIONSHIPS

The number of marriages involving Blacks and persons of other races has increased more than sevenfold since 1960—from 58,000 couples to 404,000 (U.S. Bureau of the Census 1996). Though African American men are still about twice as likely to outmarry as Black women, the rate of increase in interracial marriages has gone up substantially for Black women since 1993, resulting in a doubling of Black female–White male marriages between 1993 and 1995. The tendency for Blacks to outmarry varies greatly by geographic location, with significantly higher rates in the western states (Tucker and Mitchell-Kernan 1990; Tucker and Mitchell-Kernan 1995a). Conclusive evidence on whether interracial unions are more or less stable does not exist, though divorce data from the National Center for Health Statistics show that interracial marriages of all combinations end earlier than same-race marriages and Black women with non-Black husbands had the shortest marriages (Clarke 1995).

FINDINGS FROM A 21-CITY SURVEY

Findings from our program of research that have been presented in other papers and are relevant to the issue at hand have been noted above as appropriate. One aim of our research is to explore the association between individual- and contextual-level factors in family formation attitudes and behaviors and individual well-being. Toward that end, we examine not only characteristics of individuals and their relationships that may be related to well-being but features of the environment as well. The analyses presented here address two questions. First, are differences in psychological well-being as a function of marital status evident in this sample? And second, what contextual variables are related to the psychological well-being of African American women when controlling for marital status? These analyses make another distinction. The category of persons living with an intimate companion, but not married, has increased in recent years. We therefore treat this group as distinct from either married or single respondents.

METHOD

SAMPLE AND PROCEDURES

From August 1995 through January 1996, we conducted telephone interviews with a representative sample of 3,407 residents of 21 U.S. cities. The cities, with populations of at least 100,000, were selected to represent a range of specific community-level variables, including population characteristics such as size, ethnic proportions, and sex ratio, as well as indicators of economic climate. The cities were Albany, Atlanta, Baltimore, Birmingham (Alabama),

Chicago, Dayton (Ohio), Denver, Fort Lauderdale, Greensboro (North Carolina), Houston, Indianapolis, Los Angeles, Milwaukee, Minneapolis, New Orleans, New York City, Norfolk (Virginia), Oklahoma City, Providence (Rhode Island), Sacramento, and Seattle. Respondents were limited to persons 18–55 years of age. African Americans and Whites were interviewed in all 21 cities, and Mexican Americans were interviewed in Denver, Sacramento, and Houston. The analyses presented here are based on the 864 women who identified themselves as being of African ancestry and who had lived in the United States for at least six of the first twelve years of their lives. Since there were so few widowed women in this sample, they were not included in the analyses presented here.

Field activities, including sampling and interviewing, were carried out by the University of Michigan Survey Research Center. Sampling was conducted at the city level, excluding suburbs and geographic areas not located within city boundaries. The interview response rate for the total sample (i.e., percentage of selected eligible respondents who completed an interview) was 79.3 percent.

MEASURES

PSYCHOLOGICAL WELL-BEING. *Depression symptomatology* was measured by the twelve-item version of the Center for Epidemiologic Studies Depression Scale (CES-D) (Radloff 1977), developed by Ross, Mirowsky, and Huber (1983). The alpha reliability index for the CES-D in this study was .89 for the total sample and .90 for Black women. *Life satisfaction* was measured by a single item used in numerous national surveys: In general, how satisfied are you with your life as a whole these days (very satisfied, somewhat satisfied, somewhat dissatisfied, very dissatisfied). *Loneliness* was measured by a short version of the revised UCLA Loneliness Scale (Russell, Peplau, and Cutrona 1980). The loneliness coefficient alpha was .82 for the entire sample and .81 for Black women.

RELATIONSHIP CHARACTERISTICS AND SELF-ESTEEM. Three aspects of relationships were included: *relationship status* (married, divorced-separated, never married, and cohabitating) and marital importance and relationship importance. Marital importance was assessed by the question: How important is being married to you? Similarly, relationship importance was measured by the question: How important to you are romantic relationships in general? The responses were coded 1, not important at all, to 10 extremely important. (Those not in relationships were scored 0.) We used a six-item measure of the self-acceptance aspect of *self-esteem* that employs items from the Rosenberg Self-Esteem Scale (1965). Reliability for this scale is .75 overall and .72 for Black women.

SOCIOECONOMIC STATUS, FINANCIAL STANDING, AND OTHER DEMOGRAPHIC CHARACTERISTICS. *Personal income* was a measure of 1994 income from all sources, including salaries, wages, Social Security, welfare, and any other income received. Education was a categorical variable that combined total years of education with the highest degree received, resulting in a variable that ranged from ten years, indicating that the participant did not complete high school, to twenty years, indicating an advanced degree. *Perceived impoverishment* consisted of mean scores from a three-item measure used by Pearlin and Johnson (1977) in their Chicago stress study. Respondents were asked how often they did not have money for food, clothing, or medical care. A four-category response scale of *never, rarely, sometimes,* or *often* was used. *Age* was measured by age in years at last birthday. *Parenthood* was coded as 0 if a respondent had no living children and 1 if the respondent had at least one child. (Previous analyses determined that parenthood was more predictive of our variables of interest than number of children.)

RELIGION AND SOCIAL SUPPORT. *Religiosity* was measured by this question: "Using a 1 to 10 scale, with 1 meaning not religious at all and 10 meaning extremely religious, how religious would you say you are?" *Social support* is the mean of three items from the Provision of Social Relations Scale (Turner 1992): perceived family support ("My family will always be there for me should I need them"), the existence of a confidante ("I have at least one friend or family member I could tell anything"), and social companionship ("When I want to go out and do things, I have someone who would enjoy doing these things with me"). The response scale ranged from 1 to 10, indicating *not at all true* to *very much true.* The Cronbach alpha for the three-item measure was .59 overall and .63 for Black women.

CONTEXTUAL MEASURES. The contextual measures were city-level variables taken from the Census Summary Tape File 3 (STF3B) including sex- and race-specific unemployment levels, proportion of racial groups with some college, racial proportions in the population, proportions of the population who were divorced, race-specific median income, and proportions of racial groups below the poverty level.

DATA ANALYSIS

First, using analysis of variance and multiple classification analysis, I examined the adjusted means on key variables for each marital status group, controlling for age, education, and income. Next, regression models were tested for each indicator of psychological well-being, entering marital status as a dummy variable. The regression program in the STATA statistical package was used because it provides "Huber-White" covariance matrices (producing robust standard errors) and allowed us to control for the effects of clustering (i.e., based on the use of 21 sites). The analyses presented do not make distinctions on the basis of sexual preference, so persons in both heterosexual and same-sex relationships are included in all results.

RESULTS

Of the 833 African American women who participated in the study, 29 percent were married, 25 percent were separated or divorced, 39 percent had never been married, and 7 percent were living with a partner to whom they were not married. Table 7.1 presents mean scores by marital status on measures of psychological well-being and family formation attitudes adjusted for age, education, and income. Also presented are the F-values testing for a main effect of marital status. Since there were so few widowed women who did not fall into other categories (e.g., now living with a partner), they were excluded from these analyses. The results show that when these key resource variables are controlled, significant differences on the basis of marital status remain for depressive symptomatology, life satisfaction, and loneliness. Consistently, divorced and separated persons were less well off than the other groups. And on depression and loneliness, the scores of never married women fell between those of partnered women and those who were divorced or separated. Importantly, the groups did not differ on self-esteem. Means for the other variables are revealing, however. Never married, divorced, and separated, as well as cohabiting women, had significantly less social support than did married persons. Women without partners, understandably, placed less value on both marriage and relationships. Some striking similarities across groups are the same level of emphasis on factors believed to be important (or less important) for the success of a marriage: having an adequate income and having and raising children. In other areas, a somewhat distinctive value system of cohabiting and never married women seems evident, as when evaluating factors thought necessary for marital success, they place

TABLE 7.1 Means for Psychological Well-Being Measures and Family Formation Attitudes Adjusted for Age, Education, and Income with F-Values Testing Main Effects of Relationship Status

VARIABLE	MARITAL STATUS				F
	MARRIED	COHABITATING	DIVORCED/ SEPARATED	NEVER MARRIED	
Depression	1.23	1.34	1.75	1.57	5.90***
Life satisfaction	3.39	3.35	3.01	3.25	10.39***
Loneliness	1.71	1.71	1.91	1.83	3.35*
Self-esteem	3.71	3.59	3.65	3.63	2.15
Social support	9.30	8.80	8.87	8.89	3.51*
Perceived mate availability	5.63	5.50	4.53	4.71	6.56***
Dating satisfaction			2.70	2.83	1.59
Importance of marriage	9.19	7.04	6.49	5.94	61.02***
Importance of relationships	8.62	7.95	7.52	7.03	18.24***
For successful marriage, importance of:					
Social class	6.54	5.85	6.16	5.52	5.31***
Adequate income	8.64	8.97	8.72	8.71	0.51
Same religion	7.14	5.63	7.27	6.58	5.09**
Same ethnic group	6.18	5.24	5.99	5.33	3.28*
Having/raising children	8.33	8.24	8.07	7.88	1.26

Source: Study of Families and Relationships, 1995–1996.

Note: Married $N = 236–241$; cohabitating $N = 57–59$; divorced/separated $N = 203–207$; never married $N = 321–327$

$^*p \leq .05$ $^{**}p \leq .01$ $^{***}p \leq .001$ $+p = .05$

less emphasis on background characteristics such as social class, religion, and ethnicity.

Table 7.2 shows the results of the regression analyses for each indicator of subjective well-being. As shown in the table, each final model included the individual-level variables of age, education level, social support, religiosity, self-esteem, gender role ideology, importance of marriage, and marital status.

In early models, personal income was entered with the other predictor variables. However, it became clear that perceived poverty was a more powerful predictor of the outcome variables than personal income was. With the set of variables used in the model, which includes key instrumental and social resources, the contribution of marital status to outcome nearly disappears. After controlling for such variables, only divorced or separated women were significantly more depressed and expressed significantly less life satisfaction. Marital status made no contribution to loneliness. Contextual economic variables were also predictive. (Since city-level variables were entered one at a time, only those that made significant contributions to the models are presented in the table.) Women who lived in cities in which the Black median income was higher tended to be more depressed and more lonely. However, women who lived in cities in which Black male unemployment was higher were less satisfied with life. Notably, Black female unemployment was not even closely associated with the outcome measures (not shown).

DISCUSSION

The results of these analyses, when controlling for the availability of social and socioeconomic resources, demonstrate quite clearly that among the participants in this study, women who have never married are not more psychologically distressed than those who are married, widowed, or in cohabitating nonmarital relationships. The only group that suffers somewhat by the comparison is the divorced or separated group, and even here, the only area of striking difference was that of life satisfaction. Given the stress inherent in the divorce or separation process, we would expect women who have recently experienced these events to be under greater stress (we have no data on the timing of the divorce or separation). It seems likely, then, that observed differences in subjective well-being on the basis of marital status are most likely a function of economic differences and the differential availability of social support. Another factor in the absence of relationship status effects is the fact that never married African American women make up the largest relationship status group in the study (39%). Only a few decades ago, nearly all Black women married at least once in their lives. Not only is nonmarriage no longer a stigmatized status, it has become commonplace, and never married women now have plenty of very visible role models (e.g., Oprah Winfrey). Note that valuing marriage highly was only predictive of greater loneliness—that is, women who were most invested in marriage as an institution experienced more loneliness but were not more depressed or less satisfied with life.

TABLE 7.2 Multiple Regression Estimates for Predictors of Subjective Well-Being

VARIABLE	DEPRESSION		LIFE SATISFACTION		LONELINESS[a]	
	B	BETA	B	BETA	B	BETA
Age	−.016*	−.113	.004	.057	.000	.005
Education	−.032	−.047	−.030*	−.082	.013	.037
Poverty	.376***	.190	−.184***	−.179	.170***	.168
Social support	−.095**	−.114	.022	.051	−.074***	−.175
Religiosity	−.017	−.031	.030*	.105	−.019	−.068
Self-esteem	−.696***	−.201	.333***	.185	−.646***	−.367
Traditional gender role	.008	.045	.004	.043	−.003	−.032
Importance of marriage	.007	.015	−.010	−.041	.021*	.091
Marital status[b]						
Divorced/separated	.357*	.108	−.292**	−.170	.120	.072
Never married	.163	.056	−.073	−.048	.050	.034
Cohabitating	−.038	−.007	.060	.021	−.100	−.035
Black median income	.000+	.048	—	—	.000*	.036
Black male unemployment	—		−.013**	.021	—	
Constant	4.736		2.441		4.203	
R^2	.20		.14		.28	

[a] Depression $N = 817$; life satisfaction $N = 821$; loneliness $N = 821$
[b] The omitted category for marital status is Married.
*$p \leq .05$.   **$p \leq .01$;   ***$p \leq .001$; +$p = .05$.

The strongest predictors of subjective well-being were perceived poverty and self-esteem. Regardless of marital status, women who are unable to feed, clothe, and tend to the medical needs of their families are psychologically stressed, and those who feel better about themselves exhibit healthier psychological states. Social support was also strongly predictive of depression and loneliness, but not life satisfaction. Life satisfaction was also the only indicator associated with religiosity and education. It may be that because life satisfaction is more evaluative than mood-like (as with depression and loneliness), it is more determined by one's ideological perspective on life and the world (which would be more reflective of religious teachings and educational experiences).

These findings also demonstrate that certain features of the economic environment may contribute more to subjective well-being than more commonly used indicators, such as age, religiosity, and education. The positive association between Black median income and subjective well-being may seem counterintuitive at first. However, the relationship may reflect other aspects of environments in which Blacks are more well off. That is, cities in which Blacks have lower income may have more existing support structures than higher-income cities (e.g., churches, interdependent neighborhoods, community organizations, clubs). Also, higher-Black-income cities tend to have smaller African American populations (e.g., Seattle, Denver, Sacramento), which may also account for a lack of available supports. Finally, these cities tend to have substantial populations of migrants—i.e., persons who have moved there from other parts of the county or elsewhere. To the extent that many Blacks in these cities may have no or few local relatives to call on, they may exhibit more stress. Examination of these more detailed possibilities is beyond the scope of the present study but may provide fodder for future work.

The other contextual variable that predicted subjective well-being was Black male unemployment. Women in communities with higher male unemployment were less satisfied with life. This variable has emerged in a number of our other analyses as a significant determinant of a range of key outcomes. We interpret this variable as an indicator of economic uncertainty, since it is often predictive when personal income is not. This finding, together with our other findings, suggests that uncertainty about the economic environment for men has an association with the attitudes of city residents in a manner independent of one's personal socioeconomic resources. This is an issue that has not been studied in psychological research and one that should have particular relevance for African American populations, since economic uncertainty has become a fact of life for Blacks in many communities.

CONCLUSIONS

This review has indicated that there are major gaps in our understanding of how relationships or their absence affect the psychological well-being of African American women. Clinical and popular writings, and even fictional accounts, have isolated key areas where more research is needed; among them are the precise nature of the effects of racism, sexism, and homophobia on relationship formation and maintenance; how societal notions of attractiveness and beauty affect the psychological well-being of Black women and the course of relationships; the nature of Black women's negotiation of relationships in the context of conflicting gender-role and racial-role considerations and how such negotiations affect psychological well-being; and the mental health implications of a decline in the availability of "marriageable" men, defined here as those with compatible belief systems and economic viability. Though certain recent writings seem to suggest that a "war of the sexes" is under way in the African American community nationwide (Morin 1998), there is evidence that marriage and intimate relationships remain highly valued by African American women (Tucker 2000b) and, furthermore, that although marriage has declined, Black women are still highly likely to be involved in committed relationships (Tucker and Taylor 1989). Yet, as I have outlined, the barriers to relationship success for African American women are formidable. The good news, however, is that relationship status issues do not appear to have diminished self-esteem levels of African American women and, unlike women of other ethnic groups, Black women do not seem to be dependent on being married for maintenance of psychological well-being. This could well be an adaptive response to existing conditions, but it is also likely a reflection of the powerful and enduring support that African American women receive from family and friends.

REFERENCES

Bowman, P. J. and T. A. Forman. 1997. Instrumental and Expressive Family Roles Among African American Fathers. In R. J. Taylor, J. S. Jackson, and L. M. Chatters, eds., *Family Life in Black America*, 216–247. Thousand Oaks, Calif.: Sage.

Boyd-Franklin, N. 1989. *Black Families in Therapy: A Multisystems Approach.* New York: Guilford.

Broman, C. 1988. Satisfaction among Blacks: The significance of marriage and parenthood. *Journal of Marriage and Family* 50:45–51.

Brown, D. 1996. Marital Status and Mental Health. In H. W. Neighbors and J. S. Jackson, eds., *Mental Health in Black America*, 77–94. Thousand Oaks, Calif.: Sage.

Bureau of Labor Statistics and the Bureau of the Census. 1997. Table A-2. Employment status of the civilian population by race, sex, age, and Hispanic origin. Last revised June 6. <http://stats.bls.gov/news.release/empsit.to2.htm.

Buss, D., and M. Barnes. 1986. Preferences in human mate selection. *Journal of Personality and Social Psychology* 50 (3): 559–570.

Chadiha, L. A. 1992. Black husbands' economic problems and resiliency during the transition to marriage. *Families in Society: Journal of Contemporary Human Services* 73:542–552.

Chatters, L. M. (1988). Subjective well-being evaluations among older Black Americans. *Psychology and Aging* 3:184–190.

Clarke, S. C. 1995. Advance report of final divorce statistics, 1989 and 1990. *Monthly Vital Statistics Report: Final data from the Centers for Disease Control and Prevention* 43 (9, Supplement, March 22).

Coley, S. M. and J. O. Beckett. 1988a. Black battered women: A review of the empirical literature. *Journal of Counseling and Development* 66:266–270.

———. 1988b. Black battered women: Practice issues. *Social Casework* 69:483–490.

Coombs, R. H. 1991. Marital status and personal well-being: A literature review. *Family Relations* 40:97–102.

Darity, W. and S. L. Myers. 1995. Family Structure and the Marginalization of Black Men: Policy Considerations. In M. B. Tucker and C. Mitchell-Kernan, eds., *The Decline in Marriage Among African Americans: Causes, Consequences, and Policy Implications*, 263–308. New York: Russell Sage Foundation.

Ellis, B. J. 1992. The Evolution of Sexual Attraction: Evaluative Mechanisms in Women. In J. H. Barkow, L. Cosmides, and J. Tooby, eds., *The Adapted Mind: Evolutionary Psychology and the Generation of Culture*. New York: Oxford University Press.

Farley, R. 1995. *State of the Union: America in the 1990s.* Vol. 1, *Economic Trends.* New York: Russell Sage Foundation.

Greene, B. 1994. Lesbian Women of Color: Triple Jeopardy. In L. Comas-D°az and B. Greene, eds., *Women of Color: Integrating Ethnic and Gender Identities in Psychotherapy*, 389–427. New York: Guilford Press.

Grier, W. H. and P. M. Cobbs. 1968. *Black Rage.* New York: Basic Books.

Guttentag, M. and P. F. Secord. 1983. *Too Many Women.* Beverly Hills: Sage.

Hampton, R. L. and R. J. Gelles. 1994. Violence toward Black women in a nationally representative sample of Black families. Special Issue: Family violence. *Journal of Comparative Family Studies* 25:105–119

Hatchett, S., J. Veroff, and E. Douvan. 1995. Marital Instability Among Black and White Couples in Early Marriage. In M. B. Tucker and C. Mitchell-Kernan, eds., *The Decline in Marriage Among African Americans: Causes, Consequences, and Policy Implications*, 177–218. New York: Russell Sage Foundation.

John, D., B. A. Shelton, and K. Luschen. 1995. Race, ethnicity, gender, and perceptions of fairness. *Journal of Family Issues* 16:357–379.

Joseph, J. 1997. Woman Battering: A Comparative Analysis of Black and White Women. In G. K. Kantor and J. L. Jasinski, eds., *Out of Darkness: Contemporary Perspectives on Family Violence*, 161–169. Thousand Oaks, Calif.: Sage.

Kane, E. W. 1992. Race, gender, and attitudes toward gender stratification. *Social Psychology Quarterly* 55:311–320.

Keith, V. M. 1997. Life Stress and Psychological Well-Being Among Married and Unmarried Blacks. In R. J. Taylor, J. S. Jackson, and L. M. Chatters, eds., *Family Life in Black America*, 95–116. Thousand Oaks, Calif.: Sage.

Kiecolt, K. J. and M. A. Fossett. 1995. Mate Availability and Marriage Among African Americans: Aggregate- and Individual-Level Analyses. In M. B. Tucker and C. Mitchell-Kernan, eds., *The Decline in Marriage Among African Americans: Causes, Consequences, and Policy Implications,* 121–135. New York: Russell Sage Foundation.

King, A. E. 1993. The impact of incarceration on African American families: Implications for practice. *Families in Society* 74:145–153.

Lidell, A. L. 1998. "Length of Incarceration, Perceived Discrimination, and Social Support as Predictors of Psychological Distress in African American Spouses of Inmates." Ph.D. diss., California School of Professional Psychology.

Morin. R. (March 25, 1998). A Crisis: Among Blacks, Major Changes in the Family Structure. *Washington Post,* A-15. http://www.washingtonpost.com/wp-srv/WPlate/1998-03/25/150/-032598-idx.html.

Murray, C. B. and G. B. Stahly. 1987. Some victims are derogated more than others. *Western Journal of Black Studies* 11:177–180.

Neal, A. and M. Wilson. 1989. The role of skin color and features in the Black community: Implications for Black women in therapy. *Clinical Psychology Review* 9:323–333.

Okazawa-Rey, M., T. Robinson, and J. V. Ward. 1987. Black women and the politics of skin color and hair. *Women and Therapy* 6:89–102.

Oliver, M. L. and T. M. Shapiro. 1995. *Black Wealth/White Wealth: A New Perspective on Racial Inequality.* New York: Routledge.

Peplau, L. A., S. D. Cochran, and V. M. Mays. 1997. A National Survey of the Intimate Relationships of African American Lesbians and Gay Men. In B. Greene, ed., *Ethnic and Cultural Diversity Among Lesbians and Gay Men,* 11–38. Thousand Oaks, Calif.: Sage.

Pearlin, L. and J. S. Johnson. 1977. Marital status, life strains, and depression. *American Sociological Review* 42:704–715.

Radloff, L. S. 1977. The CES-D Scale: A self-report depression scale for research in the general population. *Journal of Applied Psychological Measurement* 1:385–401.

Rodgers, W. L. and A. Thornton. 1985. Changing patterns of first marriage in the United States. *Demography* 22:265–279.

Rosenberg, M. 1965. *Society and Adolescent Self-image.* Princeton, N.J.: Princeton University Press.

Ross, C. E., J. Mirowsky, and J. Huber. 1983. Dividing work, sharing work, and in between: Marriage patterns and depression. *American Sociological Review* 48: 809–823.

Russell, D., L. A. Peplau, and C. E. Cutrona. 1980. The revised UCLA Loneliness Scale: Concurrent and discriminant validity evidence. *Journal of Personality and Social Psychology* 39:472–480.

Sampson, R. J. 1995. Unemployment and Imbalanced Sex Ratios: Race-Specific Consequences for Family Structure and Crime. In M. B. Tucker and C. Mitchell-Kernan, eds., *The Decline in Marriage Among African Americans: Causes, Consequences, and Policy Implications,* 229–254. New York: Russell Sage Foundation.

Spanier, G. B. and P. Glick. 1980. Mate selection differentials between Whites and Blacks in the United States. *Social Forces* 58:707–725.

Staples, R. and L. B. Johnson. 1993. *Black Families at the Crossroads: Challenges and Prospects.* San Francisco: Jossey-Bass.

Straus, M. A. and R. J. Gelles. 1990. *Physical Violence in American Families: Risk Factors and Adaptations to Violence in 8,145 Families.* New Brunswick, N.J.: Transaction.

Taylor, P. L. 1998. "Attitudes Toward Marriage Among African American Singles: A Test of Four Perspectives." Ph.D. diss., UCLA.

Taylor, P. L., M. B. Tucker, and C. Mitchell-Kernan. 1999. Ethnic variations in perceptions of men's provider role. *Psychology of Women Quarterly* 23:759–779.

Thornton, A. 1989. Changing attitudes toward family issues in the United States. *Journal of Marriage and the Family* 51:873–893.

Tucker, M. B. 2000. Marital Values and Expectations in Context: Results from a 21 City Survey. In L. Waite, C. Bacharach, M. Hindin, E. Thomson, and A. Thornton, eds., *The Ties that Bind: Perspectives on Marriage and Cohabitation,* 166–187. New York: Aldine de Gruyter.

Tucker, M. B. and C. Mitchell-Kernan. 1990. New trends in Black American interracial marriage: The social structural context. *Journal of Marriage and the Family* 52: 209–218.

———. 1995a. Interracial dating and marriage in Southern California. *Journal of Social and Personal Relationships* 12:341–361.

———. 1995b. Marital Behavior and Expectations: Ethnic Comparisons of Attitudinal and Structural Correlates. In M. B. Tucker and C. Mitchell-Kernan, eds., *The Decline in Marriage Among African Americans: Causes, Consequences, and Policy Implications,* 145–171. New York: Russell Sage Foundation.

———. 1998. Psychological well-being and perceived marital opportunity among single African American, Latina, and White women. *Journal of Comparative Family Studies* 29:57–72.

Tucker, M. B. and R. L. Taylor. 1989. Demographic correlates of relationship status among Black Americans. *Journal of Marriage and the Family* 51:655–665.

Turner, R. J. 1992. Measuring Social Support: Issues of Concept and Method. In H. Veiel and U. Bauman, eds., *The Meaning and Measurement of Social Support,* 217–234. New York: Hemisphere.

Umberson, D. and K. Williams. 1999. Family status and mental health. In C. S. Anenshensel and J. C. Phelan, eds., *Handbook of the Sociology of Mental Health.* New York: Kluwer/Plenum.

U.S. Bureau of the Census. 1979. The social and economic status of the Black population in the United States: An historical view, 1790–1978. *Current Population Reports,* Series P-23, No. 80. Washington, D.C.: U.S. Government Printing Office.

———. 1992. Marriage, divorce, and remarriage in the 1990's. *Current Population Reports,* Series P-23, No. 80. Washington, D.C.: U.S. Government Printing Office.

———. 1996. Interracial Married Couples: 1960 to Present. Published September 20. www.census.gov/population /socdemo/ms-la/95hiso4.txt.

————. 1997. Table P-2. Race and Hispanic Origin—Persons 15 Years Old and Over, by Median Income and Sex: 1947 to 1996. Last revised November 7. www.census. gov/ hhes/income/histinc/p)2.html

Williams, D. R., D. T. Takeuchi, R. K. Adair. 1992. Marital status and psychiatric disorders among Blacks and Whites. *Journal of Health and Social Behavior* 33:140–157.

Wilson, W. J. 1996. *When Work Disappears: The World of the New Urban Poor.* New York: Knopf.

8 LOW-INCOME SINGLE BLACK MOTHERS: THE INFLUENCE OF NONRESIDENT FATHERS' PRESENCE ON MENTAL WELL-BEING

Aurora P. Jackson

Relations between Black fathers and their children have become an issue of public concern because children in families headed by single Black women have extraordinarily high rates of poverty (McLanahan 1997; Wilson 1996). Furthermore, single mothers who are employed rarely earn enough to bring their families out of poverty (Edin and Lein 1997; Ellwood 2000), and there is a high likelihood that child support, the most common means by which economic resources are transferred from nonresident fathers to their children, will not be awarded to Black mothers (Teachman 1990).

Largely neglected in the discourse about the parental responsibilities of Black nonresident fathers, however, are factors other than economic contributions that might affect the well-being of single Black mothers and, thereby, young Black children. Drawing upon a range of indicators of fathers' involvement, this chapter investigates the effects of nonresident fathers' presence on the psychological well-being of single Black mothers of a preschool child who were employed in low-wage jobs or receiving welfare benefits in the fall of 1995. It also explores whether the influence of nonresident fathers' involvement or noninvolvement on the psychological well-being of the mother varies according to the mother's employment status. Data from the first wave of an ongoing study of current and former welfare recipients are used to see whether mothers who maintain a relationship with nonresident fathers are better off on indicators of parenting stress and depressive symptoms than mothers who do not, and, if so, whether maternal employment status makes a difference. These variations are important because the 1996 welfare reform places time limits on welfare receipt and imposes harsh penalties on poor single mothers who are unable to ward off poverty by doing low-wage work. Single Black mothers are disproportionately poor

(Wilson 1996), and policy makers often view these women and their families in monolithic terms. Since fathers and mothers influence each other's parenting and, thereby, child outcomes in married-couple families (Belsky 1981; Belsky and Vondra 1989), it is plausible that the nonresident father–mother relationship might influence children in single-parent families through its effects on mothers.

BACKGROUND

This study adopts a risk-and-resiliency or individual difference approach. Rather than regarding single Black mothers and young Black children in high-risk environments as uniformly at risk for negative well-being and developmental outcomes, the risk-and-resiliency perspective highlights the differential and interactive influences of individual, family, and environmental factors in efforts to determine which individuals are at risk for negative outcomes and the contexts within which resilience is most likely (McLoyd 1990; Spencer 1990). Inasmuch as some individuals maintain good mental health despite facing the same hardships that bring about distress in others, an important issue is what factors operate as protective mechanisms in people's response to risk circumstances (Rutter 1987). The research literature provides clues. For example, whereas studies have found that depression is associated with women's perceptions of parenting as stressful and unsatisfying (Downey and Coyne 1990), social supports have been found to moderate depression in welfare-dependent mothers, to have a beneficial effect on parenting behavior, and to be associated with more positive attitudes toward children (Colletta and Lee 1983; Conger et al. 1992; Crnic and Greenberg 1987; Jackson 1998; Jackson et al. 2000; Simons et al. 1983; Zur-Szpiro and Longfellow 1982). In this investigation, nonresident fathers' involvement is considered an aspect of social support.

Although single mothers are capable of raising well-adjusted children, especially if economic resources are sufficient (Hawkins and Eggebeen 1991), there is evidence that growing up in a single-parent family can diminish children's well-being and development (McLanahan 1988). Studies have demonstrated that fathers can have a positive effect on children's development (Parke 1981; Patterson, Kuperschmidt, and Vaden 1990; Radin 1981). Indeed, the links between fathers' absence and negative child outcomes have led some to assume that involving fathers, including nonresident fathers, in their children's upbringing can moderate the likely harmful effects of single parenting

(Furstenberg and Harris 1992; Hawkins and Eggebeen 1991). Although there is limited evidence to support this hypothesis (King 1994), it is plausible to expect that single Black mothers who maintain a positive relationship with the nonresident father of their preschooler will be better off on well-being indicators, including parenting stress, than those who do not. This expectation motivated the present investigation. In the discussion that follows, nonresident fathers will be referred to as fathers and single Black mothers will be referred to as mothers.

METHODS AND PROCEDURE

Prospective respondents were 150 employed and 150 nonemployed mothers of a three- or four-year-old child. The mothers were current and former welfare recipients in New York City, recruited through the New York City Human Resources Administration's Office of Employment Services (OES). The OES offers a range of services, including vouchers for subsidized child care for employed former welfare recipients and facilitation of job training, job placement, and basic education classes for nonemployed current welfare recipients.

Recruitment involved the following procedure. First, the names of employed mothers eligible for child-care vouchers were obtained. The list included all such mothers with a three- or four-year-old child in zip codes representing Central Harlem in Manhattan, Bedford-Stuyvesant in Brooklyn, and Jamaica in Queens, areas with substantial numbers of low-income Black families. Next, 150 randomly selected mothers who also were former welfare recipients were sent a letter describing the study and requesting their participation. Those who agreed to participate were subsequently visited at their home. Nonemployed mothers were recruited in the same way, selected randomly from a list of welfare recipients involved in education, training, and/or job placement programs in the same zip codes. This author and a research assistant simultaneously conducted a structured interview with each mother and an objective assessment of each focal child. The interviews, which were carried out between February 1996 and January 1997, each took approximately one and a half to two hours. The final sample consisted of 188 mothers. Since 34 of the 300 prospective respondents were either married (8), Latino (3), or had moved and did not receive the solicitation letter (23), the response rate for the study was 71 percent of the remaining 266 prospective respondents. Respondents were paid twenty-five dollars.

DESCRIPTION OF THE SAMPLE

Employed mothers ($N = 93$) worked at least 10 hours a week. On average, they were 29 years old ($SD = 4.8$). Most, 79 percent, had some education beyond high school. Although the latter included any education or training past high school, 7 percent of employed mothers had a bachelor's degree. Working hours ranged from 10 to 72 hours a week, with a mean of 34 hours ($SD = 11$). On average, the mothers earned $8.72 an hour ($SD = 3.08; range was from $2.50 to $19.20). Fifty-four percent of the focal children were boys and 46 percent were girls. Employed mothers had an average of two children (range was one to four). For these mothers and children, the mean age of nonresident fathers was 31 years ($SD = 6.5$). Most, 85 percent, had no child support award. In 41 percent of the cases, the father was not present in the child's life.

Nonemployed mothers ($N = 95$) averaged 28 years of age ($SD = 5.3$). Most, 60 percent, had some education beyond high school; of these, 2 mothers had a bachelor's degree. Among the focal children, 57 percent were boys and 43 percent were girls. On average, these mothers had two children (range was one to seven). The fathers were, on average, 31 years old ($SD = 6.9$). Most, 84 percent, had no child support award. In 47 percent of the cases, the father was not present in the child's life.

MEASURES

PARENTING STRESS. A seven-item, Likert-like scale, developed by Abidin (1990), was used to measure feelings of stress in the parenting role. This six-point scale, with response options ranging from 0 = *not at all true* to 5 = *completely true,* asked respondents to indicate the extent to which statements such as the following held for them: "My child seems to be much harder to care for than most," "There are some things my child does that really bother me a lot," "I find myself giving up more of my life to meet my child's needs than I ever expected." Higher scores indicated greater parenting stress. Cronbach's alpha was .64 in this study.

DEPRESSIVE SYMPTOMS. The Center for Epidemiologic Studies Depression (CES-D) Scale was used to measure depressive symptoms. This 20-item self-report inventory was designed to measure depressive symptoms in the general population (Radloff 1977). Respondents were asked to indicate on a four-point scale, ranging from 0 = *less than once a day* to 3 = *most or all of the time,* how often during the past week they felt depressed, lonely, sad, unusually bothered by things. Higher scores indicated more depressive symptoms. Cronbach's alpha was .88 in this study.

RELATIONS WITH NONRESIDENT FATHERS. Seven measures were used to assess relations with nonresident fathers. The presence of the child's father in the child's life was operationalized as a single dummy variable coded 1 if *yes* and 0 if *no.* To measure the frequency and extent of the child's contact with the father, mothers were asked to indicate on an eight-point scale, ranging from 1 = *child has never seen father* to 8 = *almost every day,* how often the father saw the child.

Three questions measured mothers' satisfaction with the fathers' support. Respondents were asked to indicate on a six-point scale, ranging from 0 = *very dissatisfied* to 5 = *very satisfied,* the extent of their satisfaction with the amount of love and caring the father showed their child, the amount of time the father spent with the child, and the amount of money and help the father had provided for raising the child. The higher the score, the greater the satisfaction. Mothers also were asked whether child support payments for their preschooler had ever been agreed to or awarded to them. Answers to this question were operationalized as a single dummy variable coded 1 if *yes* and 0 if *no.*

Two scales measured the quality of the relationship between mothers and fathers. First, mothers were asked to indicate on a five-point scale, ranging from 1 = *completely dissatisfied* to 5 = *completely satisfied,* how satisfied they had been with their own relationship with their focal child's father over the past two months. Higher scores indicated greater satisfaction with this relationship. Then, to measure the level of conflict between fathers and mothers, respondents were asked to indicate on a six-point scale, ranging from 0 = *no conflict* to 5 = *a great deal of conflict,* how much conflict they had with the father about things having to do with their child. Higher scores indicated greater conflict.

DEMOGRAPHIC MEASURES. Educational attainment for both mothers and fathers was measured on a five-point scale, ranging from 1 = *grade school* to 5 = *some education beyond high school/specify degree and major,* that asked mothers to indicate the highest level of education they themselves (and the fathers) had completed. Among employed mothers, hourly pay was constructed from respondents' answers to questions about their weekly working hours and salary. The child's gender was coded 1 if a girl and 0 if a boy.

TABLE 8.1 T-tests: Differences Between Employed and Nonemployed Mothers

VARIABLE	MEAN	SD	T
Depressive symptoms			
Employed	14.45	9.68	
Nonemployed	17.01	11.23	1.67*
Parenting stress			
Employed	1.59	.89	
Nonemployed	1.90	.90	2.37**
Satisfaction with mother-father relationship			
Employed	2.51	1.31	
Nonemployed	2.46	1.39	−.27
Mother-father conflict			
Employed	2.48	2.02	
Nonemployed	2.45	2.08	−.10

Note: degree of freedom = 186; employed mothers N = 93; nonemployed mothers N = 95
*$p < .05$ **$p < .01$

RESULTS

Preliminary examination of the data involved a series of t-tests to evaluate between-group differences on the major variables by maternal employment status. Next, multivariate analyses were carried out separately for employed and nonemployed mothers, since some believe these groups may differ a priori (Hoffman 1984).

T-test results are depicted in table 8.1. Employed mothers were lower both in parenting stress and in depressive symptoms than their nonemployed counterparts. Although the CES-D Scale is not a measure of clinical depression, groups with scores of 16 or more are considered to be at particularly high risk for depression (Radloff 1977). Note that nonemployed mothers had a mean score of 17 on this scale. There were no differences between employed and nonemployed mothers, however, with regard to their feelings about their own relations with the fathers of their child or the amount of conflict they experienced with fathers about things having to do with their child.

EMPLOYED MOTHERS. Correlational analyses indicated that parenting stress for employed mothers was positively related to lower educational attainment, a male child, and higher levels of depressive symptoms. Depressive symptoms, in turn, were related to maternal educational attainment ($-.21$, $p < .05$), hourly pay ($-.29$, $p < .01$), and the degree to which mothers were satisfied with the amount of time the fathers spent with their child ($-.20$, $p < .05$). In other words, the less educated the mothers were, the less pay they earned, and the less satisfied they were with the amount of time the fathers spent with their child, respectively, the greater was their risk for depression.

Multivariate analyses are depicted in table 8.2. Model 1 shows that when mothers' and fathers' educational attainment, the child's gender, and the mothers' hourly pay were entered together in multiple regression analyses along with the father-relationship variables, as independent and joint predictors of parenting stress, mothers' educational attainment and the child's gender significantly explained 12 percent of the variance in parenting stress. More explicitly, mothers with lower educational attainment and those with a preschool son scored higher for parenting stress.

Next, the same variables, along with parenting stress, were entered together as predictors in the multiple regression of depressive symptoms. The results in Model 2 show that greater parenting stress and lower hourly pay together explained 11 percent of the variance in depressive symptoms. None of the father-relationship variables achieved significance in these analyses.

NONEMPLOYED MOTHERS. As was the case for employed mothers, the correlational analyses indicated that parenting stress for nonemployed mothers was related to lower educational attainment (2.26, $p < .01$) and higher depressive symptoms ($.30$, $p < .001$). Conversely, however, for these mothers, parenting stress also was related to the lack of a child support award from the father ($-.22$, $p < .05$). Higher levels of depressive symptoms were related to the father's absence from the child's life ($-.35$, $p < .001$), infrequent contact between the father and the child ($-.37$, $p < .001$), and the mother's dissatisfaction with the amount of love (-22, $p < .05$), time (-28, $p < .01$), and money ($-.37$, $p < .001$) the father provided for their child.

Multivariate analyses for nonemployed mothers are depicted in Models 3 and 4 in table 8.2. Results in Model 3 show that none of the predictors significantly explained parenting stress. However, when the same predictors, along with parenting stress, were entered together in the multiple regression of depressive symptoms, parenting stress, father-child contact, maternal satisfaction with the amount of money the father provided for the child, and mothers' satisfaction with their own relationship with the father remained in the equation, significantly explaining 19 percent of the variance (see Model

TABLE 8.2 Regression of Parenting Stress and Depressive Symptoms

	EMPLOYED MOTHERS		NONEMPLOYED MOTHERS	
	(1)	(2)	(3)	(4)
VARIABLE	PARENTING	DEPRESSION	PARENTING	DEPRESSION
	beta	beta	beta	beta
Mother's education	−.29**	...	...	...
Father's education	...	...	...	...
Child's gender	−.29**	...	...	...
Hourly pay		...	−.26*	
Father present	...	...	...	...
Father sees	...	...	...	-.30*
Child support	...	...	...	...
Satisfaction/love	...	...	...	...
Satisfaction/time	...	...		
Satisfaction/money	...	...	...	−.50***
Satisfaction/father-mother relationship	...	...	...	.33*
Parental conflict	...	...	...	...
Parenting stress		.23*		.29**
F	6.34**	6.10**		6.92***
R^2	.12	.11		.19

Note: Dummy coding for child's gender: 0 = boy; 1 = girl. Dummy coding for father's presence: 0 = no; 1 = yes. Dummy coding for child support: 0 = no; 1 = yes.
*$p \leq .05$ **$p \leq .01$ ***$p \leq .001$

4). More precisely, greater parenting stress, infrequent contact between fathers and their child, lower maternal satisfaction with the amount of money fathers provided for their child, and mothers' greater satisfaction with their own relationship with their child's father predicted higher levels of maternal depressive symptoms. The meaning of the independent effect of nonemployed mothers' greater satisfaction (note the positive coefficient) with their own relationship with the nonresident father in these analyses is unclear. However, if they were "satisfied" with a relationship they believed was less optimal than it should be for their child, then maintaining such a relationship might well contribute to higher levels of depressive symptoms. Note that none of the father-relationship variables achieved significance in parallel analyses for employed mothers.

DISCUSSION AND CONCLUSION

The primary purpose of this investigation was to examine the influence of nonresident fathers' presence on low-income employed and non-employed single Black mothers' parenting stress and depressive symptoms. Because the father's presence or absence may have different effects for children in single-parent families by virtue of its effects on mothers, the expectation was that mothers who maintained a relationship with the father would be better off on indicators of parenting stress and depression than those who maintained no relationship with the father. Motivated, as well, by the 1996 welfare reform law, which places strict time limits on welfare receipt and demands that the poor—even mothers with very young children and low skills—go to work, I examined individual and group differences based on maternal employment status, inasmuch as the sample comprises current and former welfare recipients (and their preschool children) in New York City.

Consistent with the findings of a recent evaluation of welfare-to-work programs in six states, which indicate that welfare reforms can have positive effects if they increase both employment and income (Morris et al. 2001), the present data clearly suggest that mothers are better off when employed, even in low-wage jobs. Specifically, the pattern of findings indicates that nonemployed mothers scored significantly higher in both parenting stress and depressive symptoms than their employed counterparts. Moreover, multivariate analyses indicated that infrequent contact between father and child, the mothers' dissatisfaction with the fathers' financial contributions for the child, and, unexpectedly, their satisfaction with their own relationship with the father accounted for the variation in nonemployed mothers' depressive symptoms. Although the meaning of the finding that these mothers' satisfaction with their own relationship with their child's father made an independent contribution to higher levels of depression is unclear, it is possible that nonemployed mothers felt compelled—buttressed, perhaps, by fewer resources than their employed counterparts had—to maintain a relationship with their child's father that was less supportive (vis-à-vis their child's well-being) than they preferred—a compunction not shared by employed mothers. Recall that nonemployed mothers' risk for depression was particularly high.

In contrast, nonresident fathers seem to be less consequential vis-à-vis the psychological functioning of employed mothers, perhaps—as suggested above—because of their greater financial resources. For these mothers, however, the child's gender (together with lower maternal educational attainment) contributed to greater parenting stress, which, together with lower hourly pay, explained increased symptoms of depression. Taken together, these findings might mean that mothers with lower education (and possibly jobs that paid less) find their preschool boys more difficult to parent because these children are more active than preschool girls and, as such, require more time and energy to manage (Jackson 1993; Maccoby and Martin 1983). Jackson and Huang (1998) found, as well, that low-income, employed, single, Black mothers were less comfortable with their main child-care arrangement when their child was a boy. They interpreted this to mean that the greater activity and aggressiveness of young boys (in comparison to girls) may contribute to mothers' increased concerns about the care their sons get from less capable (and probably less expensive) child-care providers. If these findings are valid, then wages for the mothers that allay such concerns might improve both parental and child well-being.

A word about the nonsignificance of all the variables in this study in explaining the variance in parenting stress among nonemployed mothers is in order. Clearly, these mothers are different from their employed counterparts. It also is clear that parenting stress, which was significantly higher for them, needs to be explored further. Possibly, a design that takes into account other aspects of social support (e.g., social isolation) and other indicators of psychological functioning (e.g., self-efficacy; see, for example, Jackson 2000 and Jackson and Huang 2000) would shed more light on this issue. Still, no single analysis can provide firm conclusions about the large questions raised in this study. These questions need further exploration through longitudinal data on the effects over time of mothers' employment and nonresident fathers' presence and absence on the well-being of single Black mothers and the development of young Black children. Finally, this study has several limitations that should be acknowledged. For one thing, it relied on self-report data, and the extent to which these data represent actual feelings is not known. For another, the data are cross-sectional and, as such, provide no basis for inferences about causality. For example, mothers' employment may both be influenced by maternal psychological functioning and influence maternal psychological functioning. Thus, future research should explore the temporal relations between and among low-income employment, mothers' psychological functioning, parenting, and child outcomes.

REFERENCES

Abidin, R. R. 1990. *The Parenting Stress Index Short Form*. Charlottesville, Va.: Pediatric Psychology Press.

Belsky, J. 1981. Early human experience: A family perspective. *Developmental Psychology* 17:3–23.

Belsky, J. and J. Vondra. 1989. Lessons from Child Abuse: The Determinants of Parenting. In D. Cicchetti and V. Carlson, eds., *Child Maltreatment: Theory and Research on the Causes and Consequences of Child Abuse and Neglect*, 153–202. New York: Cambridge University Press.

Colletta, N. and D. Lee. 1983. The impact of support for Black adolescent mothers. *Journal of Family Issues* 4:127–143.

Conger, R. D., K. J. Conger, G. H. Elder, Jr., F. O. Lorenz, R. L. Simons, and L. B. Whitbeck. 1992. A family process model of economic hardship and adjustment of early adolescent boys. *Child Development* 63:526–541.

Crnic, K. and M. Greenberg. 1987. Maternal Stress, Social Support, and Coping: Influences on Early Mother-Child Relationship. In C. Boukydis, ed., *Research on Support for Parents and Infants in the Postnatal Period*, 25–40. Norwood, N.J.: Ablex.

Downey, G. and J. Coyne. 1990. Children of depressed parents: An integrative review. *Psychological Bulletin* 108:50–76.

Edin, K. and L. Lein. 1997. *Making Ends Meet: How Single Mothers Survive Welfare and Low-Wage Work*. New York: Russell Sage Foundation.

Ellwood, D. 2000. Anti-poverty policy for families in the next century: From welfare to work and worries. *Journal of Economic Perspectives* 14:187–198.

Furstenberg, F. F. and K. M. Harris. 1992. The Disappearing American Father: Divorce and the Waning Significance of Biological Parenthood. In S. South and S. Tolnay, eds., *The Changing American Family: Sociological and Demographic Perspectives*, 197–223. Boulder, Col.: Westview.

Hawkins, A. J. and D. J. Eggebeen. 1991. Are fathers fungible? Patterns of coresident adult men in maritally disrupted families and young children's well-being. *Journal of Marriage and the Family* 53:958–972.

Hoffman, L. W. 1984. The Study of Employed Mothers Over Half a Century. In M. Lewin, ed., *In the Shadow of the Past: Psychology Portrays the Sexes*, 295–320. New York: Columbia University Press.

Jackson, A. P. 1993. Black single working mothers in poverty: Preferences for employment, well-being, and perceptions of preschool-aged children. *Social Work* 38: 26–34.

————. 1998. The role of social support in parenting for low-income, single, black mothers. *Social Service Review* 72:365–378.

————. 2000. Maternal self-efficacy and children's influence on stress and parenting among single Black mothers in poverty. *Journal of Family Issues* 21:3–16.

Jackson, A. P., J. Brooks-Gunn, C. Huang, and M. Glassman. 2000. Single mothers in low-wage jobs: Financial strain, parenting, and preschoolers' outcomes. *Child Development* 71:1409–1423.

Jackson, A. P. and C. C. Huang. 1998. Concerns about children's development: Implications for single employed Black mothers' well-being. *Social Work Research* 22:233–240.

————. 2000. Parenting stress and behavior among single mothers of preschoolers: The mediating role of self-efficacy. *Journal of Social Service Research* 26:29–42.

King, V. 1994. Nonresident father involvement and child well-being: Can dads make a difference? *Journal of Family Issues* 15:78–96.

Maccoby, E. D. and J. A. Martin. 1983. Socialization in the Context of the Family: Parent-Child Interaction. In E. M. Hetherington, ed., *Mussen Manual of Child Psychology*, 4:1–102. 4th ed. New York: Wiley.

McLanahan, S. 1988. The consequences of single parenthood for subsequent generations. *Focus* 11:16–21.

————. 1997. Parent Absence or Poverty: Which Matters More? In G. J. Duncan and J. Brooks-Gunn, eds., *Consequences of Growing Up Poor*, 35–48. New York: Russell Sage Foundation.

McLoyd, V. C. 1990. The impact of economic hardship on Black families and children: Psychological distress, parenting, and socioemotional development. *Child Development* 61:311–346.

Morris, P. A., A. C. Huston, G. J. Duncan, D. A. Crosby, and J. M. Bos. 2001. *How Welfare and Work Policies Affect Children: A Synthesis of Research.* New York: Manpower Demonstration Research Corporation.

Parke, R. D. 1981. *Fathers.* Cambridge: Cambridge University Press.

Patterson, C. J., J. B. Kuperschmidt, and N. A. Vaden. 1990. Income level, gender, ethnicity, and household composition as predictors of children's school-based competence. *Child Development* 61:485–494.

Radin, N. 1981. The Role of the Father in Cognitive, Academic, and Intellectual Development. In M. E. Lamb, ed., *The Role of the Father in Child Development*, 379–428. New York: Wiley.

Radloff, L. 1977. The CES-D Scale: A self-report depression scale for research in the general population. *Journal of Applied Psychological Measurement* 1:385–401.

Rutter, M. 1987. Psychosocial resilience and protective mechanisms. *American Journal of Orthopsychiatry* 57:316–331.

Simons, R. L., J. Beaman, R. D. Conger, and W. Chao. 1993. Stress, support, and antisocial behavior trait as determinants of emotional well-being and parenting practices among single mothers. *Journal of Marriage and the Family* 55:713–723.

Spencer, M. B. 1990. Development of minority children: An introduction. *Child Development* 61:267–269.

Teachman, J. D. 1990. Socioeconomic resources of parents and award of child support in the United States: Some exploratory models. *Journal of Marriage and the Family* 52:689–700.

Wilson, W. J. 1996. *When Work Disappears: The World of the New Urban Poor.* New York: Knopf.

Zur-Szpiro, S. and C. Longfellow. 1982. Fathers' Support to Mothers and Children. In D. Belle, ed., *Lives in Stress: Women and Depression,* 145–153. Beverly Hills: Sage.

9 SHO' ME THE MONEY: THE RELATIONSHIP BETWEEN SOCIAL CLASS AND MENTAL HEALTH AMONG MARRIED BLACK WOMEN

Pamela Braboy Jackson

A person's social class position affects that person in nearly every aspect of life. Class distinctions determine the nature of our work, the division of labor in the family, and our health and safety. Inequalities in the class structure are also related to individual power, where class differences carry over to gender (Mantsios 1995). It is not too surprising to find, for example, that a woman's social class position is often defined on the basis of her husband's and/or her father's characteristics (e.g., see Rubin 1976; Ulbrich, Warheit, and Zimmerman 1989). In fact, Crompton and Mann argued that "married women have a dual class position" derived from their paid work and a social-class position as housewives in relation to their husbands (1986:39). White married women define their social class position partly according to personal characteristics and those of their husband (Hiller and Philliber 1986). These women have been identified as more psychologically vulnerable than married men partly because of this derived identity (Warren and McEachren 1985).

Despite the growing interest in the way women experience social class, much of it has focused on White women. There is some discussion of the fact that Black women in America face double jeopardy, triple jeopardy, and/or gendered racism as a result of their combined disadvantaged statuses (e.g., see Beale 1970; Essed 1991; Mantsios 1995). Nonetheless, there remains a dearth of empirical work on the factors that shape the emotional experiences of Black women, especially those who are married. This study provides a simple description of the way in which social class comes to matter for African American women. The results from this research are placed in perspective of the broader sociological literature by comparing them to results found for a comparable group of non-Hispanic White women who were also included in the sample.[1]

Following previous work in this area, I consider the different dimensions of social class: education, occupational prestige, and income. Although people in the lower social classes have higher rates of psychological distress (Kessler and Cleary 1980), more recent research has shown that the components of social class are not equal in their effects on mental health (Broman 1991; McLeod and Kessler 1990). Thus, the focus here will be on the relative importance of resources that may be "mine, his, and ours." I then explore two mechanisms through which social class may come to matter for women's mental health: (1) marital conflict and (2) self-esteem. Identifying the mediators of the effects of social class on women's mental health is important in providing some insight into the meaning of the resources gained from social class position.

EDUCATION

Education, a major social institution in society, is the means by which knowledge, beliefs, and values are transmitted in an organized manner across generations (Goode 1988). But education serves also as an important coping resource in times of trouble. That is, certain knowledge and skills gained through education help us to manage stressful situations. Education has been linked to self-esteem (Rosenberg and Pearlin 1978), social competence (Veroff, Douvan, and Kulka 1981), and a self-directed orientation (Schoenbach 1985). The negative relationship found between education and depression has come to be understood in terms of the cognitive skills developed through extended schooling (Ross and Huber 1985). Education is more important than personal occupation or income in predicting marital conflict (Booth, Johnson, and White 1984) and psychological distress (Gove, Hughes, and Style 1983; Kessler and McRae 1982; Radloff 1975) among White women.[2]

According to many of the scholarly discussions about the obstacles faced by Black women, the cognitive skills acquired through education may not be sufficient to overcome the emotional toll of discrimination (Etter-Lewis 1994). In order to achieve some level of success, a Black woman must often conform to a model that was designed for White men. This can lead to identity struggles where she must choose between "staying real" (maintaining her cultural identity) and "selling out" (total assimilation). Either choice can make a difference for her psychological well-being. In essence, the Black woman may "face racial discrimination at the hands of Whites and sex discrimination at the hands of men" (Benokraitis and Feagin 1995:152). This study will take a preliminary look at the impact education has on Black women's mental health.

EMPLOYMENT STATUS

One line of sociological research has concentrated on the individual's employment status and occupational prestige (among those in the labor force), contrasting working wives with housewives. These studies have found that women who work outside of the home have better marital communication (Burke and Weir 1976), higher self-esteem (Barnett and Baruch 1985), and lower levels of depression (Glass and Fujimoto 1994) than women who are engaged in unpaid domestic work. The psychological benefits of working for pay seem also to hold for Black women (Reskin and Coverman 1985). Nonetheless, there is some evidence that employment is most beneficial to women who have a positive attitude toward their jobs (see Repetti, Matthews, and Waldron 1989 for a review) or face few family demands (Rosenfield 1989). Simply being employed is not beneficial if the job is unrewarding or the job responsibilities somehow conflict with other familial obligations. Retail and service occupations are more clearly associated with low pay, low autonomy, and less workplace control (see Menaghan and Parcel 1990 for a review). To the extent that Black women are overrepresented in the service industry, we may see fewer benefits of working in these jobs than the literature would suggest. I explore this hypothesis by contrasting women who hold certain positions in the occupational structure and women who are not in the paid labor force.

Another line of research addressing the link between occupational prestige and women's well-being considers the importance of the husband's occupation. Some studies suggest that wives whose husbands occupy prestigious positions in the workplace are less satisfied with their marital relationship than wives whose husbands occupy positions at the lower levels of the occupational hierarchy (e.g., see Clark, Nye, and Gecas 1978). There could be several explanations for this finding. First, these wives may be competing for their husband's attention if his job is very demanding. Second, women who are married to men who hold demanding jobs may find themselves engaged in a less than equitable exchange with regard to household tasks. Or third, women who are married to men who hold prestigious jobs may also hold a demanding job that requires time and energy. If the wife is spending her free time on family obligations rather than personal interactions with her spouse, she may feel that the marriage is suffering. In general, other research does not clarify or provide a parsimonious explanation for these empirical findings. In fact, qualitative research by Rubin (1976) suggests that middle-class marriages are more clearly characterized by open discussions and less marital discord than working-class marriages. Although Rubin's work provides a more in-depth profile of the class differences evident in many marital exchanges, her interviews focused on a very select sample of couples. More important, there is a dearth of knowledge on the impact that "his" and "her" occupations have on the marriage. This study addresses this gap in the literature and also explores the importance of occupational prestige on women's self-esteem.

The relationship between husband's occupational prestige and wife's emotional well-being also remains unsettled. For example, Keith and Schafer (1983) found no effect of husband's occupation on wife's level of depression in a sample of White, dual-earner couples in Iowa. However, using data from a national sample of White adults, Kessler and McRae (1982) found that husband's occupation has a more consistent relationship to wife's psychological well-being than the wife's own occupation. A study by Freudiger (1983) further specified this relationship, differentiating the work status of unemployed women by separating those who were traditional housewives (little or no work experience) from those who temporarily exited the paid labor force. Unlike previous research, she found that working wives' personal occupational prestige was more important in predicting life satisfaction than whether their husbands held prestigious occupations. She also found that wives who were previously or never employed derived the most satisfaction from their husbands' occupational status. The contradictory findings from these studies highlight the complexity of the role occupation can play in women's lives. I will reexamine the relative importance of "his" and "her" occupation on women's mental health, exploring both life satisfaction and depressive symptomatology as potential outcomes.

INCOME

As the large body of stress research has clearly demonstrated, financial resources allow people to solve distressing problems and eliminate major life stress (see Thoits 1995 for a review). Income is more closely linked to exposure to undesirable financial events (e.g., mortgage foreclosure) than any other dimension of social class (McLeod and Kessler 1990). Money provides the means to pay the bills, feed the children, and obtain shelter and medical care for the members of the household. Financial stress has been linked to feelings of self-worth (e.g., see Pearlin et al. 1981), and according to many family sociologists, money stabilizes a marriage (Cherlin 1979). There is also consistent evidence that personal income is associated with general life satisfaction (Adelmann 1987) and psychological well-being (Kessler and McRae 1982).

The title of this essay was inspired by the words spoken between two men during a scene in the film *Jerry McGuire*. In this movie, Cuba Gooding, Jr., plays Rod Tidwell, a professional football player who is trying to communicate to his agent, Jerry McGuire (Tom Cruise), that his contract negotiations partially determine his ability to perform to his utmost ability. In one of the most comedic scenes in the film, Rod articulates (through his behaviors) the following realities to Jerry: "If you sho' me the money, I will behave according to your normative expectations (e.g., dance when I make a touchdown); if you sho' me the money, I will increase my personal self-confidence (e.g., stop complaining that I'm not appreciated by the league); if you sho' me the money, I will be more satisfied with my family life (e.g., move my family into a decent house). Just sho' me the money!" The feelings expressed by Rod Tidwell in this film capture the reality of what money can do for an individual. The ability to meet the demands of family life has important consequences for psychological well-being.

Nonetheless, we must also note that Rod is a working man expressing the reality of the way in which "his" money can affect him and his family. To the extent that women experience wage discrimination and view their income as supplemental to their husband's, personal income may not be as relevant for overall well-being. For wives, a combined family income may be the more realistic feature of social class position that helps to reduce stress. For example, a woman who is engaged in many roles (e.g., worker, parent, spouse) can alleviate some aspects of familial stress by hiring someone or buying products (e.g., dishwasher) to help with homemaker responsibilities, hiring a sitter so she can go out and enjoy time alone with her husband, and/or using money to entertain herself. All of these actions translate into a more active social life and more leisure time for the woman who has mo' money.

Because of the many ways in which women can use money, it is my position that family income is the most important resource gained from social class position. Although a high level of education is related to the use of more effective coping strategies during times of high stress, money speaks louder than words. For example, my education may dictate that I face a problem and deal with it squarely, but my money will put gasoline in the car so that I can drive away to the coast to relax on the beach. Similarly, my occupation may offer me a sense of control over my work environment, but my money will allow me to plan a vacation far away from my "wonderful" job. In the analysis that follows, I examine the impact of these different dimensions of social class position on married women's reports of marital conflict, self-esteem, and mental health. The question addressed here is, What dimension(s) of social class is (are) most important for the married woman's life experiences?

METHODS

DATA AND SAMPLE

This study uses data from the National Survey of Families and Households (NSFH), conducted in 1987 and 1988 (Sweet, Bumpass, and Call 1988). The survey was based on respondents from a multistage probability sample of households in the United States. The main sample included 9,643 households. The survey also included an oversample of minorities, single-parent families, families with stepchildren, cohabiting couples, and recently married persons (N = 3,374), yielding a total sample of 13,017 respondents. The response rate for the study was 75 percent. The sample can be viewed as representative of noninstitutionalized persons in the United States. Two-hour structured interviews with respondents were conducted by trained interviewers in each respondent's home. Since the issues studied here may be somewhat different for couples in which the husband is not employed, the analysis is limited to married couples in which the husband is employed full-time (35+ hours/week). The sample includes wives who are either full-time homemakers or employed full-time (35+ hours/week) and are younger than age 65. There are 131 African American wives and 966 non-Hispanic White wives who meet these criteria.

Table 9.1 compares the sociodemographic characteristics of the two samples of wives in the NSFH. As shown here, the wives are similar in age. Black women are more likely to have young children in the household, to be in the paid labor force, and to have lower social status than their White counterparts. There are no significant differences in reports of self-esteem between these samples, but African American wives report slightly higher levels of marital conflict. And finally, African American wives report higher levels of psychological distress (as indicated by the depression and happiness scores) than their White counterparts (see Jackson 1997 for a similar pattern).

VARIABLE MEASUREMENT

DEPENDENT VARIABLES. *Depression* refers to self-reported feelings of melancholic moods and is assessed using a subscale taken from the Center for Epidemiologic Studies Depression (CES-D) Scale (Radloff 1977). Respondents were asked how many days, during the past week, they (1) did not feel like eating; (2) had trouble keeping their mind on what they were doing; (3) had trouble shaking off the blues, even with help from family and friends;

TABLE 9.1 Descriptive Characteristics of Selected Samples of Married Women in the National Survey of Families and Households (NSFH)

| | AFRICAN AMERICANS | | NON-HISPANIC WHITES | |
| | (N = 131) | | (N = 966) | |
	MEAN (SD)	%	MEAN (SD)	%
Control variables				
1. Age	35.49 (9.46)		35.38 (11.22)	
2. Preschooler in household		79.0		61.0
3. Number of children	2.35 (1.94)		1.81 (1.49)	
4. Long-term health problems	.22 (.74)		.14 (.59)	
Independent variables				
Social class resources				
" Mine"				
5. Education	12.66 (2.72)		13.40 (2.47)	
6. Job status (% employed)		64.8		54.4
Occupation				
Operators, fabricators, laborers		14.1		6.8
Precision workers		1.2		3.4
Service work		17.6		12.7
Technical, sales, administration		47.1		40.0
Managers, professionals		20.0		37.0
"His"				
7. Occupational prestige				
Operators, fabricators, laborers		36.6		17.4
Precision workers		17.9		19.6
Service work		13.0		6.3
Technical, sales, administration		15.4		19.1
Managers, professionals		17.1		37.6
"Ours"				
8. Household income	6.05 (3.29)		7.38 (3.48)	
(example: 1 = $15,000; 5 = $20,001—-$25,000; 7 = $30,001—-$35,000)				
Mediating variables				
9. Self-esteem	11.83 (2.09)		11.89 (1.65)	
10. Marital conflict	1.13 (1.28)		.94 (1.20)	
Dependent Variables				
11. Depression	26.62 (14.56)		24.71 (13.56)	
12. Happiness	5.54 (1.23)		5.69 (1.10)	

(4) slept restlessly; (5) talked less than usual; (6) felt depressed; (7) felt lonely; (8) felt sad; (9) felt fearful; (10) felt that everything they did was an effort; (11) felt that they could not get going; (12) felt bothered by things that usually don't bother them. Twelve items of the CES-D were summed to form a total depression score ranging from 0 to 84. This scale does not measure a clinical disorder, but it is a highly reliable (alpha = .91) and valid measure of depressive symptoms (see Jackson 1997 for further discussion). *Happiness* is a single-item indicator measured by asking respondents: "Taking things altogether, how would you say things are these days?" Responses ranged from 1 (*very unhappy*) to 7 (*very happy with how things are these days*). Table 9.1 shows that African American women report significantly higher levels of depression than non-Hispanic White wives, but there is no significant difference between these women in levels of happiness.

INDEPENDENT VARIABLES. *Education* is a single-item measure representing the highest level of schooling completed by the respondent (coded in years). *Occupational prestige* is measured using five dummy variables that compare those who fall within the following job categories (operators, precision, service, technical, and managerial, each coded 1) with the unemployed housewife (coded 0). *Spouse's occupational prestige* scores are assigned as follows: (1) operators, fabricators, laborers; (2) precision work; (3) service work; (4) technical, sales, administrative work; and (5) managers, professionals. *Household income* was collapsed into 13 categories, each having a $4,999 range (e.g., 1 = $1–$5,000; 2 = $5,001–$10,000) except the last category, which includes those who report household incomes higher than $60,000.

MEDIATING VARIABLES. *Self-esteem* refers to positive or negative feelings of self-worth. This scale consists of three items assessed in a *strongly agree* to *strongly disagree* format. Respondents were asked their level of agreement with the following statements: "On the whole, I am satisfied with myself"; I am able to do things as well as other people"; and "I have always felt pretty sure my life would work out the way I wanted it to." The first two items are drawn from Rosenberg's (1965) self-esteem scale. Negatively worded items were back-coded so that a high summed score on the scale represented high self-esteem. This scale has an alpha reliability of .60 and .54 for the sample of African American and non-Hispanic White wives, respectively.

   Marital conflict is an index constructed from six areas describing the marital relationship. Married respondents were asked how often, if at all, in the last year they had open disagreements with their spouses in the areas of household tasks, money, sex, spending time together, the in-laws, and having a (other) child(ren). Respondents selecting *never* or *less than once a month* were assigned a score of 0. Those selecting *several times a month, about once a week, several times a week,* or *almost every day* were assigned a score of 1 on that item. Individual items were then summed to form an index of marital conflict (alpha = .64 and .61 for the samples of African American and non-Hispanic White wives, respectively) with scores ranging from 0 to 6.

CONTROL VARIABLES. *Age* is coded as an interval variable. Previous research indicates that children affect women's psychological well-being; therefore two measures were included to assess parental status. The first considered whether there was a *preschooler in the household* (0 = no, 1 = yes). The second assessed the *number of children* ever born to the respondent. To partially control for selection into the workforce, a measure was constructed to assess the presence of *long-term health problems.* Respondents were asked if they had a mental or physical health condition that limited their daily activities. Those who answered *yes* to this question were then asked how long the condition existed. An index was derived that combined these questions and was coded as follows: 0 = *no conditions,* 1 = *has a condition but not limited,* 2 = *activity restriction for less than a year,* and 3 = *activity restriction for a year or more.* In the regression analyses, missing data are coded to the mean according to the respondent's racial category and employment status.

RESULTS

The relationships proposed in this study were examined using multiple regression analysis. These tests proceeded in three steps, holding constant the background variables at each step. First, the effects of the social class variables on the indicators of mental health were determined (baseline model). Second, the impact of social class on the mediating variables of self-esteem and marital conflict was examined (mediating model). And third, the effects of self-esteem and marital conflict on mental health were explored, controlling for the measures of social class (final model). All analyses were performed separately for African American and White wives.

AFRICAN AMERICAN WOMEN

As shown in table 9.2 (section A), none of the indicators of social class position is related to depression among this sample of married women. However, there is an association between education and life happiness (*beta* = −.29, *p* < .05). African American women who have achieved a high level of education are not as happy with their lives as those with less education. Turning to the mediating model (section B), we see that the indicators of

TABLE 9.2. Regression Analysis of Mental Health for African American Married Women (N = 131)

	SECTION A MODEL I—BASELINE				SECTION B MODEL II—MEDIATING				SECTION C MODEL III—FINAL			
	DEPRESSION		HAPPINESS		SELF-ESTEEM		MARITAL CONFLICT		DEPRESSION		HAPPINESS	
	beta	s.e.	beta	s.e.	beta	s.e.	beta	s.e.	beta	s.e.	beta	s.e.
Social class variables												
"Mine"												
Education	.11	.68	-.29*	.06	-.14	.10	.08	.06	.08	.71	-.27*	.06
Occupation[a]												
Laborers	-.02	4.97	.01	.43	-.14	.72	-.00	.45	-.02	4.95	.02	.39
Precision work	.08	14.99	.10	1.29	.13	2.17	-.03	1.34	-.06	14.88	.04	1.20
Service	-.08	4.33	-.14	.37	.06	.64	-.03	.39	-.06	4.33	-.21*	.35
Sales, administration	.02	3.62	-.01	.31	.01	.54	-.04	.34	.08	3.75	-.05	.30
Managerial, professional	-.06	5.12	.04	.44	.03	.74	-.12	.46	.01	5.10	-.03	.09
"His"												
Occupational prestige	-.14	.81	.01	.07	-.02	.12	.11	.07	-.19+	.82	.02	.07
"Ours"												
Household income	-.02	.49	.09	.04	.09	.07	-.22*	.05	.00	.51	.03	.04
Mediating variables												
Self-esteem	—		—		—		-.13	.06	-.02	.67	.23*	.05
Marital conflict	—		—		-.14	.16	—		.26**	1.11	-.28**	.09
R²	.08		.08		.13		.12		.15		.25	
Adjusted R²	.03		.02		.02		.01		.03		.14	

Note: Each equation controls for age, presence of preschooler in the household, number of children, and previous health condition.

[a] Comparison group is housewives.

+ p ≤ .10; * p ≤ .05; ** p ≤ .01; *** p ≤ .001.

Source: National Survey of Families and Households, 1987–1988.

social class are not related to self-concept for Black women. Women who report a higher family income experience less marital conflict than women who have fewer financial resources, as hypothesized.

In examining the final model (section C) we find a moderate difference in levels of depression between women whose husbands occupy prestigious jobs and those whose husbands do not hold such positions (*beta* = −.19, *p* < .10). And, as expected, marital conflict is positively associated with depression (*beta* = .26, *p* < .01). We also see in this table that the importance of education for happiness remains even after considering the woman's self-esteem and marital problems. Women who report high levels of education are not as happy as their less-educated peers (*beta* = −.27, *p* < .05). The effect of wife's occupation also emerges in this final model. Women who work in service occupations are not as happy with their lives as women who are full-time homemakers (*beta* = −.21, *p* < .05). As suggested by the stress literature, both self-esteem and marital conflict are related to life happiness. Women high in self-confidence are happier with their lives (*beta* = .23, *p* < .05), while those who experience few marital problems report more life happiness (*beta* = −.28, *p* < .01). In essence, the most important dimension of social class position for African American women's positive mental health is household income. But money seems to matter for Black women because of its relationship to marital conflict. Black, married women who have a substantial amount of disposable income have fewer arguments with their spouses than Black women who have less money to run the household. And, the less they argue, the better the wife feels psychologically.

NON-HISPANIC WHITE WOMEN

The same set of regression models was tested for the sample of White married women. These results are presented in table 9.3. As shown in section A of the table, educated women report slightly lower levels of depression than their less educated peers (*beta* = −.07, *p* < .10). Women who occupy positions characterized as manual labor (e.g., machine operators) are somewhat more depressed than housewives (beta = .06, *p* < .10). Women who report a high family income are also somewhat less depressed than their counterparts who fall into the lower income brackets (*beta* = −.06, *p* < .10). Women who work in precision jobs (e.g., mechanics, electricians) are not as happy as the sample of housewives (*beta* = −.06, *p* < .10). And, as expected, women whose husbands hold prestigious jobs are happier with their lives than women whose husbands hold less prestigious jobs (*beta* = .09, *p* < .05).

TABLE 9.3. Regression Analysis of Mental Health for Non-Hispanic White Married Women ($N = 966$)

	SECTION A				SECTION B				SECTION C			
	MODEL I—BASELINE				MODEL II—MEDIATING				MODEL III—FINAL			
	DEPRESSION		HAPPINESS		SELF-ESTEEM		MARITAL CONFLICT		DEPRESSION		HAPPINESS	
	beta	s.e.	beta	s.e.	beta	s.e.	beta	s.e.	beta	s.e.	beta	s.e.
Social class variables												
"Mine"												
Education	-.07+	.19	-.02	.02	-.03	.03	-.05	.02	-.03	.21	-.05	.02
Occupation[a]												
Laborers	.06+	2.41	-.01	.19	-.02	.31	.09**	.22	.03	2.43	-.01	.19
Precision work	.01	3.40	-.06+	.27	-.01	.42	-.01	.29	.02	3.22	-.06*	.25
Service	.03	1.82	.03	.14	.03	.23	.01	.16	.03	1.79	.01	.14
Sales, administration	-.04	1.21	-.02	.09	-.06	.15	.08**	.10	-.09*	1.15	.01	.09
Managerial, professional	-.04	1.35	-.04	.10	.05	.16	.09*	.12	-.05	1.29	-.04	.10
"His"												
Occupational prestige	.06	.25	.09*	.02	.03	.03	-.01	.02	-.05	.24	.09**	.02
"Ours"												
Household income	-.06+	.14	-.01	.01	.10**	.01	-.03	.01	-.03	.14	-.04	.01
Mediating variables												
Self-esteem	—	—	—	—	—		-.11**	.02	-.18***	.26	.30***	.02
Marital conflict	—	—	—	—	-.12***	.01	—		.26**	.37	-.19***	.03
R^2	.06		.05		.05		.11		.17		.18	
Adjusted R^2	.05		.04		.03		.09		.15		.16	

Note: Each equation controls for age, presence of preschooler in the household, number of children, and previous health condition.

[a] Comparison group is housewives.

+ $p \leq .10$; * $p \leq .05$; ** $p \leq .01$; *** $p \leq .001$.

Source: National Survey of Families and Households, 1987–1988.

Results from the mediating models reveal that the only indicator of social class related to self-esteem is household income. Women who fall within the higher household income categories have higher levels of self-esteem than those whose household income falls into the lower categories (*beta* = .10 , $p < .01$). On the other hand, married women who occupy certain job positions are significantly different from housewives in regard to marital conflict. As shown in section B of table 9.3, women who work in manual labor (*beta* = .09, $p < .01$), sales (*beta* = .08, $p < .05$), or professional jobs (*beta* = .09, $p < .05$) have more arguments with their husbands than women who are housewives.

And finally, section C of table 9.3 demonstrates the overall impact of social class on women's mental health. In terms of depression, women who occupy sales positions are less depressed than housewives (*beta* = $-.09$, $p < .05$). Both self-esteem and marital conflict are related to depression, as expected. Women who report high self-esteem are less depressed (*beta* = $-.18$, $p < .001$) and those who report marital problems are more depressed (*beta* = .26, $p < .001$) than their peers. In the regression model predicting life happiness, we see that occupational status is somewhat important for these married women. Those who work in service jobs are not as happy with their lives as are housewives (*beta* = $-.06$, $p < .05$). The husband's occupational prestige remains an important predictor of the wife's life happiness. Wives whose husbands work in prestigious jobs are happier than those whose husbands work in less prestigious occupations (*beta* = .09, $p < .01$). And again, self-esteem and marital conflict are related to life happiness. Women who report high self-esteem are happier with their lives compared to women low in self-esteem (*beta* = .30, $p < .001$). And those who report marital problems are not as happy with their lives compared to women with few problems in this area (*beta* = $-.19$, $p < .001$).

In essence, we find that "her," "his," and "their" resources matter for White women's emotional well-being. Her choice of occupation affects the marriage. His occupation is directly related to the extent to which she is happy with her life. And their money affects her self-concept. Social class position has a much more pervasive effect on White women's mental health than we found for African American women, but money remains an important feature of social class position.

CONCLUSIONS

This research provided an investigation of the relationship between social class and mental health among married women. The results from this study demonstrate that social class is related to mental health among both

Black and White wives, but the particular dimension of class and the mechanisms through which it operates are quite different for these two groups.

BLACK WIVES

Two interesting patterns emerge in the findings for Black women. First, education was a significant factor in the models predicting life happiness. However, unlike the findings in the broader stress literature, this relationship was in the opposite direction for Black wives. That is, educated Black women are not as happy with their lives as their peers with less education are. There are several possibilities for this particular finding. For example, Black women may not be very happy if their experience is that their additional schooling does not translate into higher income. Although Black women have reached parity in income attainment with White women, both groups continue to lag behind men (National Committee on Pay Equity 1995). Another reason education may not serve as an advantage for Black women is that they still face discrimination in the workplace, despite their educational achievements. Such treatment could easily result in disillusionment with the system (see Jackson, Thoits, and Taylor 1995). Yet a third possibility is that educated women might find themselves confronted with some unchanging realities in the home, despite their educational attainment. If these women were expecting to have a more egalitarian relationship with their husbands (rather than the traditional division of labor), they may be trying to cope with the fact that they are still doing most of the work (even though research indicates that Black men engage in more household task sharing than White men) (Broman 1991). Future research should consider the type of stressors faced by educated women, both in the home and in the workplace.

The second pattern in the results for Black women can be found in occupational choice. African American women who work in service occupations seem to be at a psychological disadvantage compared to those who are full-time housewives. The low pay and lack of job mobility associated with these occupations may undermine the sense of competence that is supposed to be derived from paid employment. This is an important area of inquiry given the proliferation of the service sector in the United States. It would be interesting to note how Black women in these occupations view their jobs. Perhaps these women experience the most conflict between working and taking care of the household. These elaborations highlight the need for more rigorous research on the meaning of work and the ways in which work and family life get negotiated in the African American household.

WHITE WIVES

The most interesting finding for the sample of White women has to do with the importance of their occupation. Compared to housewives, women who work in nontraditional occupations are more distressed. Here we may have a situation in which husbands are having a difficult time reconciling their wives' nontraditional occupations. The only group that seems to be at a psychological advantage are women who work in sales and administrative positions (although they still report more marital conflict than housewives do). Recall that this aspect of the study builds on the body of work that contrasts the type of occupation with nonemployment (see Freudiger 1983; Schoenbach 1985). Here we have identified an important mechanism by which work comes to matter for White women's mental health. The type of job women hold is related to the level of discord in their marriages. Perhaps it is because White women are more recent entrants into the paid labor force (compared to most Black women) that White women are having problems with their husbands regarding their employment. Their husbands may be trying to cope with the changing roles of women in society.

BLACK AND WHITE

One of the most striking, but expected, findings from this research is the importance of family income for women's mental health. The amount of money contributed to the household economy reduces the level of marital conflict between African American wives and their husbands. Women who have few marital problems are, in turn, less depressed and happier with their lives. These data substantiate much of the family literature, which finds that money helps to decrease marital tension. At the same time, money matters in a different way for White women. It increases feelings of self-worth. Making mo' money can increase your social standing among neighbors and friends. Having mo' money will provide the means to purchase beauty products or pay for surgical procedures that enhance your outward appearance. These findings suggest that an especially fruitful area of investigation would be the ways in which Black and White married couples use their disposable income. What activities do wives engage in that then facilitate marital harmony or improve self-esteem?

Although the final model predicting women's mental health is somewhat different for Black and White wives, money stands out as an important determinant for both groups. And marital conflict is a critical mediating factor.

Married women's mental health is strongly affected by their relationships with their husbands. These relationships are clearly indicative of the broader system of oppression in which women must operate. Because men control the valued resources, they also determine the general expectations for the behavior of women. But if women are able to utilize a pooled resource (family income) to improve their psychological health, they are able to take back some control over their life circumstances.

NOTES

1. The comparisons made to White wives will also allow us to determine if the same conceptual model holds across these ethnic populations. Because much of the research in this area is based on samples of non-Hispanic White adults, we do not know if the same social psychological processes are consistent regardless of racial/ethnic category.
2. Many studies find no association between husband's education and wife's psychological well-being (e.g., see Schoenbach 1985); therefore this dimension of husband's social class position is not included in this study.

REFERENCES

Adelmann, P. K. 1987. Occupational complexity, control, and personal income: Their relation to psychological well-being in men and women. *Journal of Applied Psychology* 72:529–537.

Barnett, R. C. and G. K. Baruch. 1985. Women's involvement in multiple roles and psychological distress. *Journal of Personality and Social Psychology* 49:135–145.

Beale, F. 1970. Double-Jeopardy: To Be Black and Female. In T. Cade, ed., *The Black Woman*, 90–110. New York: Signet.

Benokraitis, N. V. and J. R. Feagin. 1995. Women of Color: Fighting Sexism and Racism. In N. V. Benokraitis and J. R. Feagin, eds., *Modern Sexism: Blatant, Subtle, and Covert Discrimination*, 144–163. Englewood Cliffs, N.J.: Prentice Hall.

Booth, A., D. R. Johnson, and L. White. 1984. Women, outside employment, and marital instability. *American Journal of Sociology* 90:567–583.

Broman, C. L. 1991. Gender, work-family roles, and psychological well-being. *Journal of Marriage and the Family* 53:509–520.

Burke, R. J. and T. Weir. 1976. Relationship of wives' employment status to husband, wife, and pair satisfaction and performance. *Journal of Marriage and the Family* 38:279–287.

Cherlin, A. 1979. Work Life and Marital Dissolution. In G. Levinger and O. C. Moles, eds., *Divorce and Separation: Context, Causes, and Consequences*, 151–166. New York: Basic Books.

Clark, R. A., F. I. Nye, and V. Gecas. 1978. Husbands' work involvement and marital role performance. *Journal of Marriage and the Family* 40:9–21.

Crompton, R. and M. Mann. 1986. *Gender and Stratification.* New York: Blackwell.

Essed, P. 1991. *Understanding Everyday Racism.* Newbury Park, Calif.: Sage.

Etter-Lewis, G. 1994. African American Women in the Work Place: Double Standards/ Double Lives. In V. Demos and M. T. Segal, eds., *Ethnic Women: A Multiple Status Reality,* 155–168. Dix Hills, N.Y.: General Hall.

Freudiger, P. 1983. Life satisfaction among three categories of married women. *Journal of Marriage and the Family* 45:213–219.

Glass, J. and T. Fujimoto. 1994. Housework, paid work, and depression among husbands and wives. *Journal of Health and Social Behavior* 35:179–191.

Goode, E. 1988. *Sociology.* Englewood Cliffs, N.J.: Prentice Hall.

Gove, W. R., M. Hughes, and C. B. Style. 1983. Does marriage have positive effects on the psychological well-being of the individual? *Journal of Health and Social Behavior* 24:122–131.

Hiller, D. V. and W. W. Philliber. 1986. Determinants of social class identification for dual-earner couples. *Journal of Marriage and the Family* 48:583–587.

Jackson, P. B. 1997. Role occupancy and minority mental health. *Journal of Health and Social Behavior* 38:237–255.

Jackson, P. B., P. A. Thoits, and H. Taylor. 1995. Composition of the workplace and psychological well-being: The effects of tokenism on America's Black elite. *Social Forces* 74:543–557.

Keith, P. M. and R. B. Schafer. 1983. Employment characteristics of both spouses and depression in two-job families. *Journal of Marriage and the Family* 45:877–884.

Kessler, R. C. and P. D. Cleary. 1980. Social class and psychological distress. *American Sociological Review* 45:463–478.

Kessler, R. C. and J. A. McRae, Jr. 1982. The effect of wives' employment on the mental health of married men and women. *American Sociological Review* 47:216–227.

Mantsios, G. 1995. Class in America: Myths and Realities. In P. S. Rothenberg, ed., *Race, Class, and Gender in the United States,* 131–143. New York: St. Martin's.

McLeod, J. D. and R. C. Kessler. 1990. Socioeconomic status differences in vulnerability to undesirable life events. *Journal of Health and Social Behavior* 31:162–172.

Menaghan, E. G. and T. L. Parcel. 1990. Parental employment and family life: Research in the 1980's. *Journal of Marriage and the Family* 52:1079–1098.

National Committee on Pay Equity. 1995. The Wage Gap: Myths and Facts. In P. S. Rothenberg, ed., *Race, Class, and Gender in the United States,* 144–151. New York: St. Martin's.

Pearlin, L. I., E. G. Menaghan, M. A. Lieberman, and J. T. Mullan. 1981. The stress process. *Journal of Health and Social Behavior* 22:337–356.

Radloff, L. 1975. Sex differences in depression: The effects of occupation and marital status. *Sex Roles* 1:249–265.

———. 1977. The CES-D Scale: A self-report depression scale for research in the general population. *Journal of Applied Psychological Measurement* 1:385–401.

Repetti, R. L., K. A. Matthews, and I. Waldron. 1989. Employment and women's health. *American Psychologist* 44:1394–1401.

Reskin, B. F. and S. Coverman. 1985. Sex and race in the determinants of psychophysical distress: A reappraisal of the sex-role hypothesis. *Social Forces* 63:1038–1059.

Rosenberg, Morris. 1965. *Society and the Adolescent Self-Image.* Princeton: Princeton University Press.

Rosenberg, M. and L. I. Pearlin. 1978. Social class and self-esteem among children and adults. *American Journal of Sociology* 84:53–77.

Rosenfield, S. 1989. The effects of women's employment: Personal control and sex differences in mental health. *Journal of Health and Social Behavior* 30:77–91.

Ross, C. E. and J. Huber. 1985. Hardship and depression. *Journal of Health and Social Behavior* 26:312–327.

Rubin, L. 1976. *Worlds of Pain.* New York: Basic Books.

Schoenbach, C. 1985. Effects of husband's and wife's social status on psychological functioning. *Journal of Marriage and the Family* 47:597–607.

Sweet, J., L. Bumpass, and V. Call. 1988. "The Design and Content of the National Survey of Families and Households." Working Paper NSFH-1. Center for Demography and Ecology, University of Wisconsin–Madison.

Thoits, P. 1995. Stress, coping, and social support processes: Where are we? What next? *Journal of Health and Social Behavior* (Extra Issue): 53–79.

Ulbrich, P. M., G. J. Warheit, and R. S. Zimmerman. 1989. Race, socioeconomic status, and psychological distress: An examination of differential vulnerability. *Journal of Health and Social Behavior* 30:131–146.

Veroff, J., E. Douvan, and R. Kulka. 1981. *The Inner American: A Self-Portrait from 1957 to 1976.* New York: Basic Books.

Warren, L. W. and L. McEachren. 1985. Derived identity and depressive symptomatology in women differing in marital and employment status. *Psychology of Women Quarterly* 9:133–144.

10 LIFE AIN'T BEEN NO CRYSTAL STAIR: EMPLOYMENT, JOB CONDITIONS, AND LIFE SATISFACTION AMONG AFRICAN AMERICAN WOMEN

Anna L. Riley and Verna M. Keith

I don't know any more about the future than you do. I hope that it will be full of work, because I have come to know by experience that work is the nearest thing to happiness that I can find. No matter what else I have among the things that humans want, I go to pieces in a short while if I do not work. —ZORA NEALE HURSTON (1942:293)

A sense of satisfaction with life is heavily influenced by one's experiences in different domains of life. The above quote from the autobiography of Zora Neale Hurston, an early twentieth-century African American feminist writer, identifies work as a key domain that impinges on one's general assessment of life. For Hurston, work is central for achieving happiness and for maintaining an overall sense of emotional balance. Many African American women can relate to Hurston's statement, in that life satisfaction involves finding fulfillment not only in family and friend networks but also in their work.

Studies note that rewarding work experiences can foster a sense of competence and self-direction as well as influence one's sense of personal efficacy and control over life situations (Kohn and Schooler 1983). Research on psychological distress also generally finds a positive relationship between employment and women's mental health (e.g., Reskin and Coverman 1985), but the direction of this relationship can depend upon a number of factors, including work conditions and rewards (e.g., Lennon and Rosenfield 1992). Extensive research on the sociology of work links intrinsic (e.g., autonomy and fulfillment) and extrinsic (e.g., pay and job security) rewards to higher levels of job satisfaction (Mortimer and Lorence 1995; Rain, Lane, and Steiner 1991; Rice, Near, and Hunt 1980), and satisfying work tends to produce greater global life satisfaction (Rain, Lane, and Steiner 1991).

While work is rewarding for many African American women, for others it is not the "nearest thing to happiness" that they can find. Hurston herself was well aware that work can be oppressive for African American women, as is evident when a character in one of her novels describes the Black woman as "de mule uh de world" (Hurston 1937:16). The interconnections between work and life satisfaction are often complicated by difficulties in finding work and by unsatisfactory working conditions. This is especially the case for African American women, whose work experiences often deny them promotion opportunities and earning power, underutilize their skills and abilities, and require them to toil for long hours under physically demanding conditions (Rollins 1985; St. Jean and Feagin 1998). Rather than being a source of happiness and fulfillment, work is often a burden that Black women bear for the economic survival of themselves and their families. For many, their work experiences are best captured by a line from a Langston Hughes poem in which a mother tells her son:

> Well, son, I'll tell you:
> Life for me ain't been no crystal stair.
> —LANGSTON HUGHES (1974)

The effects of employment and work conditions on African American women's life satisfaction have received relatively little attention. While some research examines the combined effect of work and family roles on African American women's life satisfaction (e.g., Broman 1988), this research did not include measures of job conditions, such as autonomy. In addition, much of the literature on job satisfaction focuses on either gender or racial differences, while studies of job conditions and women's mental health include statistical controls for race but no racial comparisons (e.g., Lennon 1994).

The aim of this study is to examine the relationship between employment and life satisfaction among African American women. Specifically, the goals are to investigate whether working women are more satisfied with their lives than nonworking women, to assess the effects of intrinsic job conditions such as autonomy on job satisfaction and life satisfaction among employed women, and to assess the relative importance of job satisfaction for general life satisfaction among those who work.

AFRICAN AMERICAN WOMEN AND WORK

Historically, work has been an important facet of life for African American women. Until the 1950s, married women of color had labor-force participation rates that were more than twice those of their White counterparts (Beckett 1976). Although racial differences in female employment have converged since the 1960s, discrepancies in the work experiences of Black and White women remain. Compared to White women, African American women are generally twice as likely to be unemployed (Woody 1992), and they also encounter greater difficulty in finding full-time jobs (Hughes and Dodge 1997). When seeking work, Blacks of both sexes encounter discriminatory barriers such as employer perceptions that African American workers lack necessary skills, do not have a strong work ethic, and are less dependable. These negative evaluations are often based on inferences drawn from the "inner city" address of the applicant rather than on a specific applicant's job history (Neckerman and Kirschenman 1991). An additional barrier often faced by African American women, especially those with darker skin tones, is that they do not conform to the larger society's standards of beauty—an asset that is important for accessing high-visibility jobs at upper administrative levels (Russell, Wilson, and Hall 1992:132; St. Jean and Feagin 1998:45, 74).

When employed, African American women fare less well than White women and males in both job quality and rewards. African American women are underrepresented in the more highly paid professional-managerial, clerical, and sales jobs and are concentrated in the generally lower-paid blue-collar operative and service jobs (Anderson and Shapiro 1996; Woody 1992). The low-level service jobs of today (e.g., food service, day care worker, nursing home aide) often resemble domestic service jobs (Collins 1991:63), the largest category for Black women until the 1970s. Rollins (1985) describes domestic work as being characterized by hard physical labor, monotony, loneliness, low pay, and no health, vacation, or retirement benefits. At the psychological level, domestic and "domestic-like" work requires deference in speech, in dress, and in terms of address as well as an overall expectation of knowing one's place—which is below that of the employer.

Within the professional ranks, Black women are often concentrated in less-prestigious, female-dominated occupations such as nursing, teaching, and social work (Amott and Matthaei 1991). African American women holding higher-level positions command decent salaries and benefits but also face career challenges and on-the-job impediments. These women encounter the glass ceiling, where opportunities for promotion are blocked, trapping many in entry-level positions for which they are overqualified (Sokoloff 1992; St. Jean and Feagin 1998). Professional African American women often hold prestigious job titles that offer very little power and that are undercompensated. They also have less job authority and lower earnings relative to their credentials than Whites and African American men do (McGuire and Reskin 1993). Anderson and Shapiro (1996) found that in order to gain access to higher-paying jobs, African American women must have not only high levels of education but also job tenure and experience. In other words, they have to prove themselves more than other groups do. In the public sector, many Black professional women are employed in institutions that serve other Blacks, but they have little control over budgets, hiring, or policy, which limits their ability to provide effective assistance to their clients (Omolade 1994:54). For both professional and nonprofessional employed Black women, the discrimination and conditions encountered on the job often deplete their self-confidence and spirit. In addition, these job-associated burdens make it more difficult for them to cope with the experiences and challenges of daily life, creating a situation that may ultimately threaten their emotional well-being.

EMPLOYMENT, JOB CONDITIONS, AND LIFE SATISFACTION

The limited research on the relationship between employment and well-being among African American women yields inconsistent results. Reskin and Coverman (1985) report that employed African American women have lower levels of psychological distress than Black women who do not work. Brown and Gary (1988) also find that depressive symptoms are less prevalent among employed Black women, but note that there are important distinctions among nonworking women. African American homemakers, women who do not work by choice, have lower symptom levels than unemployed women whose nonworking status is involuntary. Thus, Black women who desire and/or need work but who are unable to find it are at greatest risk emotionally. Broman (1991), on the other hand, finds no significant relationship between employment status and global life satisfaction, but does report that employed African American women have lower levels of family life satisfaction than Black women who are not employed. The implications of Broman's findings are that combining work and family roles is detrimental to African American women's satisfaction with family life. These conflicting results across distress, global life satisfaction, and family life satisfaction remain unresolved and suggest that more research is needed. The first goal of this research is to assess the effects of employment status on African American women's life satisfaction.

Women—African Americans as well as others—are concentrated in female-dominated or "pink-collar" jobs. Structurally, these jobs tend to be less rewarding and less secure than those jobs in which men predominate. Yet, employed women vary in the rewards and demands that they encounter in the workplace, and these day-to-day work experiences have implications for their mental health. Numerous investigations find that control over the work process, an intrinsic reward, is central to healthy psychological functioning. Lennon and Rosenfield (1992), for example, report that employed married women with low levels of perceived job control/autonomy have higher levels of distress than married homemakers. Among employed women, Loscocco and Spitze (1990) find that jobs high in substantive complexity and autonomy increase feelings of happiness. On the other hand, time pressures, physically taxing jobs, jobs with high demand but little control, and jobs that are routinized increase job strains, which can lead to higher levels of distress and unhappiness (Lennon 1994; Karasek and Theorell 1990; Pugliesi 1995).

Most studies of the relationship between job conditions and well-being have included statistical controls for race, but extensive analyses of African American women are generally not presented. Research by Snapp (1992), however, did focus on the effects of workload, unfair/impersonal treatment, and trouble with boss or subordinates on depressive symptoms among African American and White professional managerial women. No clear racial differences in depression emerged, although for all women trouble with boss and subordinates increased depressive symptoms, and there were racial differences in levels and type of support. Perhaps including women with greater occupational diversity would yield different results given black-white differences in occupational standing. Thus, another goal of this research is to evaluate how perceived job conditions affect life satisfaction among African American women using a sample of women with varying types of jobs.

JOB CONDITIONS, JOB SATISFACTION, AND LIFE SATISFACTION

Research shows that both extrinsic and intrinsic work conditions are linked to women's job satisfaction. Extrinsic work conditions such as salary, job security, and fringe benefits are especially important for women working in nontraditional occupations or working because of financial necessity (Bokemeier and Lacy 1987; Lincoln and Kalleberg 1990; Loscocco and Spitze 1990). Intrinsic features of work such as autonomy, responsibility, interest, challenge, and fulfillment are associated with higher levels of job satisfaction in many studies (Hodson 1989; Miller 1988; Mortimer, Finch, and Maruyama 1988; Mortimer and Lorence 1989). There is evidence that women find both intrinsic and extrinsic features of work important when evaluating their jobs.

The research on African Americans and job satisfaction is generally limited. However, the few existing studies reveal that African Americans have lower levels of job satisfaction than Whites, owing to their lower structural position in the labor market (Tuch and Martin 1991). Relative to White males and females, Black males and females are overrepresented in jobs that are less stable, lower paying, and lower in prestige. As a consequence of this disadvantaged position, African Americans place more importance on extrinsic job conditions than intrinsic job conditions as the main sources of job satisfaction. African Americans are more likely to place greater emphasis on having a job and making a decent wage than on autonomy and fulfillment, owing to their labor market history, which has been characterized by discrimination and uncertainty. It is unclear, however, to what extent this pattern differs for African American males and females. Thus, one issue that we address here is the impact of work conditions on African American women's job satisfaction. We are especially concerned with intrinsic conditions, given the emphasis placed on this issue in some studies of women's mental health (Lennon and Rosenfield 1992; Lennon 1994). It is likely that for many Black women these conditions act as stressors that substantially compromise their overall satisfaction with life.

Job satisfaction may be a key factor linking job conditions and life satisfaction. Work is an important activity of life and entails a considerable expenditure of time and energy. As a consequence, work difficulties and attitudes toward work life can create problems in other domains of life and impinge on an individual's overall psychological well-being (Campbell, Converse, and Rodgers 1976). The spillover hypothesis implies that satisfaction with work has consequences for behaviors in other life spheres, which can, in turn, affect one's overall satisfaction with life (Rice, Near, and Hunt 1980; Rain, Lane, and Steiner 1991; Steiner and Truxillo 1987). The literature suggests that there is a consistent positive relationship between job satisfaction and life satisfaction. A study of middle-aged African Americans and Whites indicates that high levels of job satisfaction are associated with increased life satisfaction among African American women, as well among African American males and Whites of both gender groups (Crohan et al. 1989). In these analyses, we examine this relationship for both younger and midlife African American women. We argue that the relationship between job conditions and life satisfaction is mediated, in part, by job satisfaction.

METHODS

DATA

The data for this study are taken from Wave I of the Americans' Changing Lives (ACL) Survey (House 1986). The data were collected in 1986 using face-to-face interviews of respondents from a nationwide probability sample. A total of 3,617 respondents were interviewed, for an overall response rate of 67 percent. For this study, we selected African American women only ($N = 778$) and then weighted the data to account for the over-sample of older women. Similar to other studies of women's employment and mental health (e.g., Lennon 1994), we confine the analyses to younger and midlife women, for a total of 599 respondents. Of the total, 67 percent are working and 33 percent describe themselves as not working.

MEASURES

Life satisfaction, the dependent variable, is measured with a single-item indicator that asks respondents to indicate how satisfied they are with their life as a whole. Responses are reverse coded: (1) *not at all,* (2) *not very,* (3) *somewhat,* (4) *very,* and (5) *completely satisfied.*

The major independent variables are employment status, work conditions, and job satisfaction. *Employment status* is dichotomized as currently working ($N = 401$) or not currently working ($N = 196$), with the latter including women who are disabled (9.8%), retired (3.4%), unemployed (34.8%), or engaged in full-time housekeeping (52%). Like recent studies of women's job conditions and mental health (Lennon 1994), this study focuses on intrinsic work conditions—autonomy, physical demands, and time demands. The work conditions questions were asked of respondents who worked at least twenty hours per week. Responses to all three constructs range from (1) *strongly agree* to (4) *strongly disagree. Autonomy* (alpha = .49) is the sum of: (1) I have little chance to decide how to do my work, (2) I get to do a variety of things in my work, and (3) I have a lot to say about my work. *Time demands* (correlation coefficient = .30) is the sum of: (1) I am free from conflicting demands that others make and (2) I have enough time to do my work. The *physical demands* (alpha = .78) measure is based on: (1) My work requires working very fast, (2) My work requires physical effort, and (3) My work requires continuous physical activity. High scores indicate high autonomy and high levels of time and physical demands. *Job satisfaction* is measured with a single-item indicator that asks employed respondents to indicate how satisfied they are with their jobs. Response categories mirror those of life satisfaction and are reverse coded.

Control variables include age (in years), marital status (married, formerly married, never married), parental status (the number of respondents' own children residing in the household), education (years of schooling completed, ranging from 0 to 17); and family income (midpoint of ten income categories ranging from $2,500 to $110,000, divided by 1,000 for more interpretable results). Both *financial satisfaction* and *satisfaction with health* are measured by single-item indicators that ask respondents to indicate how satisfied they are with their financial situation and their health status, respectively. Responses are the same as those for global life satisfaction. The literature indicates that each of these has a bearing on overall life satisfaction and is likely to vary by employment status. Correlations between the satisfaction variables did not exceed .40, giving some indication that these are independent constructs.

RESULTS

DESCRIPTIVE RESULTS

Using the t-test to examine differences between nonworking and employed African American women, findings show (data not presented) that working women are more satisfied with life than are nonworking women, although the difference is not large. Generally, women's average satisfaction scores fall in the *somewhat satisfied* category. Working and nonworking women were on average around 40 years of age, and 44 and 49 percent, respectively, were married. Compared to working women, nonworking women have more children on average than those who work (1.64 versus 1.22), about 1.5 fewer years of educational attainment (11.10 versus 12.69), lower family income ($10,885 versus $26,369), and are less satisfied with both their financial situation and their health. Among employed women, average job autonomy is relatively high given that the mean score is 9.37 out of a possible range of 3 to 12. Average time demands fall into the middle range, with a mean of 4.23 (scores range from 2 to 8), and physical demands fall at the higher end of the distribution, an average of 8.29 with scores ranging from 3 to 12. Average job satisfaction is also fairly high (mean = 3.74).

EMPLOYMENT AND LIFE SATISFACTION

To address the issue of why employed African American women are more satisfied with their lives than their nonworking counterparts, we present results from hierarchical multivariate regression analyses. This procedure permits us to examine changes in the effect of being employed as we consider other factors that are related to life satisfaction, some of which also differ by employment status. Model 1 in table 10.1 simply confirms that employed African American women have higher levels of life satisfaction. When age, marital status, and parental status are considered in Model 2, the effect for employment is reduced somewhat but remains statistically significant. Older women are more satisfied than their younger counterparts, while formerly married women are less satisfied than married women. In Model 3, the effect of being employed also remains significant when education, family income, and financial satisfaction are added to the regression equation. Highly educated women are less satisfied with their lives, while those satisfied with their financial situation are more likely to indicate higher levels of global life satisfaction. Indeed, the effect of employment actually increases in Model 3. Model 4 introduces satisfaction with health, and in this model life satisfaction differences between employed and nonemployed women become only marginally significant. Thus a major reason why employed women have higher levels of satisfaction is that they are more satisfied with their health. Further analyses (not shown) indicate that in this sample of African American women, only 10 percent of employed women rate their health as fair or poor while almost twice that proportion (19.8%) of nonworking women rate their health as being fair or poor. The gap is large even when the disabled are excluded. These findings suggest that poor health plays a significant role in determining African American women's employment status, and ultimately in their life satisfaction. Collectively, employment, social demographic characteristics, and satisfaction with other domains of life explain about 19 percent of the variance in African American women's global life satisfaction.

JOB CONDITIONS AND JOB SATISFACTION

Earlier we hypothesized that for employed African American women job conditions are likely to be important in explaining their overall job satisfaction. Therefore, we again employ hierarchical multivariate regression analyses and assess the extent to which work conditions—autonomy, time demands, and physical demands—affect job satisfaction net of other social and demographic factors. When we enter the job condition variables into the equation first, the results (data not shown) confirm the hypothesis that job autonomy increases job satisfaction, while time demands and physical demands reduce job satisfaction. These relationships remain significant when age, marital status, and number of children are introduced, and when education and family income are subsequently controlled. Although not significant, both education and income have negative signs. Conceptually, one would not expect job satisfaction to affect financial and health satisfaction, so these factors are not controlled. However, we also estimated two additional models by first introducing financial satisfaction and then health satisfaction into the regression equations. The results remained essentially the same for autonomy and time demands, but the coefficient for physical demands was only marginally significant when satisfaction with health was controlled. Thus, once satisfaction with health is taken into consideration, physically demanding work has little impact on job satisfaction.

JOB CONDITIONS, JOB SATISFACTION, AND LIFE SATISFACTION

Table 10.2 presents the effects of job conditions and job satisfaction on global life satisfaction among employed African American women. Model 1 indicates that, of the three job conditions, only job autonomy is significant. African American women who perceive higher levels of control over their work process are more likely to be satisfied with their lives. Model 2 also reveals the expected positive association between job satisfaction and life satisfaction. The coefficient for autonomy is reduced by about 24 percent when job satisfaction is added, indicating that job satisfaction moderates some of the effects of autonomy. Both autonomy and satisfaction remain significant when other factors are considered in subsequent models. Job conditions alone, primarily autonomy, explain about 4 percent of the variance in life satisfaction among employed African American women, and the explained variance increases to 9 percent when job satisfaction is added in Model 2. Thus, consistent with previous studies, there is support for the spillover hypothesis. The assessment of one's job influences how one evaluates life generally. Neither time nor physical demands have a direct bearing on assessment of overall life satisfaction. The relatively small sample size may not provide enough power for the effects of time and physical demands to achieve statistical significance, but the relative weakness of the coefficients suggests that this is not the case. However, it is important to note that these job conditions may have indirect effects on life satisfaction through their impact on job satisfaction. Recalling the relationship between job conditions and job satisfaction, women who experience time pressures and who evaluate their jobs as being physically demanding are less satisfied with their jobs, and lower levels of job satisfaction decrease global life satisfaction. It must be noted that financial satisfaction has the strongest impact on global life satisfaction. Indeed, when this variable is introduced, the explained variance increases from 10 percent to almost 20 percent. Thus, although autonomy and job satisfaction are important aspects of global life satisfaction, financial security weighs in more heavily. This

TABLE 10.1 The Effect of Employment Status on Life Satisfaction Among African American Women

	MODEL 1	MODEL 2	MODEL 3	MODEL 4
Employed	.093*	.084*	.098*	.077+
	(.187)	(.169)	(.197)	(.154)
Age		.130*	.092+	.096+
		(.013)	(.009)	(.009)
Formerly married		−.092*	−.017	−.016
		(−.189)	(−.003)	(−.031)
Never married		−.061	−.066	−.071
		(−.142)	(−.152)	(−.164)
Parental status		.002	.034	.037
		(.001)	(.002)	(.027)
Education			−.096*	−.097*
			(−.034)	(−.034)
Family income			−.082	−.072
			(−.004)	(−.004)
Financial satisfaction			.419***	.389***
			(.369)	.343
Health satisfaction				.109***
				(.094)
Intercept	3.326	2.931	2.460	2.191
Adjusted R^2	.007	.027	.181	.190

Source: House, *Americans' Changing Lives*, 1986.

Note: Unstandardized coefficients in parentheses
$^+p \leq .10$ * $p \leq .05$ **$p \leq .01$ ***$p \leq .001$

domain is therefore critical to understanding African American women's subjective well-being. As noted previously, the modest correlation between life satisfaction and financial satisfaction suggests that multicollinearity is not an issue, and that these are related but separate dimensions of well-being. Thus, Black women find less fulfillment overall when economic aspects of their lives are unsatisfactory.

DISCUSSION AND CONCLUSION

This study examined the consequences of employment and work conditions for African American women's life satisfaction. The results indicate that employed Black women express higher levels of satisfaction than those who are not employed, even when differences in demographic characteristics and financial standing are taken into account. Higher satisfaction with health among employed women largely accounts for this difference, and further analyses reveal that nonemployed women report lower perceived health status than employed women. These findings suggest that while paid work enhances African American women's life satisfaction, poor physical health may limit the ability of many to work and to experience the rewards that work can bring.

Consistent with previous research, this study found a link between intrinsic job conditions and job satisfaction. African American women with higher levels of job autonomy and fewer physical and time demands are more satisfied with their jobs. In addition, there is some support for the spillover hypothesis in that high levels of autonomy and job satisfaction are positively associated with life satisfaction. When women perceive some control over their working conditions and enjoy their jobs, they evaluate their lives more positively. Although time and physical demands do not have a direct bearing on life satisfaction, they are both related to job satisfaction, which suggests that they have indirect effects on life satisfaction. Having a job that is physically demanding and/or that provides little time discretion increases dissatisfaction with the job, which, in turn, decreases satisfaction with life. Thus, working conditions, particularly the degree of autonomy, have substantial effects on African American women's subjective well-being by spilling over into other spheres of life.

Interestingly, financial satisfaction plays the most influential role in determining whether African American women find their life generally satisfying. Perhaps this finding reflects the economic problems that Black women continue to struggle with. Poverty rates are higher among African American women, especially when they are single parents, than among any other ethnic-gender group in the United States. Further, owing to discrimination and structural changes in the economy the economic position of African American males has deteriorated over the last two decades. As a consequence, Black women, even when married, are more likely to experience lower levels of financial certainty than other women, especially White women. As a result of their personal and collective histories, African American women may give financial security priority when rating their overall life situation.

TABLE 10.2 The Effect of Job Conditions and Job Satisfaction on Life Satisfaction Among Employed Women

	MODEL 1	MODEL 2	MODEL 3	MODEL 4	MODEL 5
Job autonomy	.220***	.167**	.170**	.176***	.170***
	(.095)	(.072)	(.076)	(.076)	(.073)
Time demands	.003	.050	.041	.074	.079
	(.002)	(.029)	(.024)	(.043)	(.046)
Physical demands	.022	.049	.049	.049	.047
	(.008)	(.018)	(.018)	(.018)	(.017)
Job satisfaction		.245***	.253***	.155**	.155**
		(.210)	(.217)	(.133)	(.133)
Age			−.010	−.033	−.040
			(−.001)	(−.003)	(−.004)
Formerly married			−.154**	−.115+	−.113+
			(−.300)	(−.223)	(−.220)
Never married			−.051	−.083	−.087
			(−.109)	(−.177)	(−.186)
Parental status			−.028	.009	.017
			(−.010)	(.007)	(.012)
Education				−.091	−.093
				(−.030)	(−.031)
Family income				−.090	−.085
				(−.004)	(−.004)
Financial satisfaction				.346***	.326***
				(.288)	(.271)
Health satisfaction					.079
					(.068)
Intercept	2.570	1.803	1.959	1.892	1.728
Adjusted R^2	.039	.090	.100	.195	.199

Note: Unstandardized coefficients in parentheses
$^+p \leq .10$ $^*p \leq .05$ $^{**}p \leq .01$ $^{***}p \leq .001$

Source: House, *Americans' Changing Lives*, 1986.

One unexpected finding in this study is that life satisfaction declines as educational attainment increases. Among employed women, this relationship is not significant, but the sign remains negative throughout the analyses. When both unemployed and employed women are taken as a group, the negative relationship between education and life satisfaction may reflect dissatisfaction among highly educated women who are not currently working, perhaps because of family obligations. Among employed women, perhaps this finding is a result of high educational attainment stimulating high job expectations, especially among those in prestigious occupations. When expectations of authority and control over work, rewards that are generally associated with higher-status jobs, are not met, it may be more emotionally troubling than when one does not have such expectations. Further, it is likely that highly educated women view their jobs as part of their overall identity. When things are not going well on the job, they may be less able to evaluate other aspects of life positively. In contrast, women who have less-prestigious jobs and who identify with their jobs less closely may be more immune to the "spillover" effects of unsatisfactory work.

This research identified employment as central to African American women's life satisfaction and found that work conditions (especially autonomy), high levels of job satisfaction, and high levels of financial satisfaction contribute to employed women's evaluation of their lives. A number of issues remain unexplored, suggesting topics for future research. For example, because of the sample size, we are unable to compare various groups of nonworking women (e.g., housewives versus the unemployed) with employed women. Similarly, we do not make distinctions between employed women on such characteristics as part-time versus full-time employment and occupational standing. Such detailed analyses would likely alter some of our findings. We also did not assess how nonworking women evaluate their "housework." Lennon (1994) found that when perceptions of both work and housework conditions (e.g., autonomy in work and autonomy in housework) are considered, the emotional advantages associated with work are reduced considerably. It is also important to consider issues like the availability of social support and interaction effects, such as whether or not respondents are both employed and married.

REFERENCES

Amott, T. and J. Matthaei. 1991. *Race, Gender, and Work: A Multicultural Economic History of Women in the United States.* Boston: South End Press.

Anderson, D. and D. Shapiro. 1996. Racial differences in access to high-paying jobs and the wage gap between Black and White women. *Industrial and Labor Relations Review* 49:273–286.

Beckett, J. O. 1976. Working wives: A racial comparison. *Social Work* 43:463–471.

Bokemeier, J. L. and W. B. Lacy. 1987. Job values, rewards, and work conditions as factors in job satisfaction among men and women. *Sociological Quarterly* 28:189–204.

Broman, C. L. 1988. Satisfaction among Blacks: The significance of marriage and parenthood. *Journal of Marriage and the Family* 50:45–51.

———. 1991. Gender, work-family roles, and psychological well-being of Blacks. *Journal of Marriage and the Family* 53:509–520.

Brown, D. R. and L. E. Gary. 1988. Unemployment and psychological distress among Black American women. *Sociological Focus* 21:209–221.

Campbell, A., P. E. Converse, and W. L. Rodgers. 1976. *The Quality of American Life: Perceptions, Evaluations, and Satisfactions.* New York: Russell Sage.

Collins, P. H. 1991. *Black Feminist Thought: Knowledge, Consciousness, and the Politics of Empowerment.* New York: Routledge.

Crohan, S., T. Antonucci, P. K. Adelmann, and L. Coleman. 1989. Job characteristics and well-being at midlife. *Psychology of Women Quarterly* 13:223–235.

Hodson, R. 1989. Gender differences in job satisfaction: Why aren't women more dissatisfied? *Sociological Quarterly* 30:385–399.

House, J. S. 1986. *Americans' Changing Lives: Wave I.* Ann Arbor: Survey Research Center (producer), Inter-University Consortium for Political and Social Science Research (distributor).

Hughes, D. and M. A. Dodge. 1997. African American women in the workplace: Relationships between job conditions, racial bias at work, and perceived job quality. *American Journal of Community Psychology* 25:581–599.

Hughes, L. 1974. "Mother to Son" (1926, renewed in 1954). In A. Bontemps, *American Negro Poetry,* 67. 2d ed. New York: Hill and Wang.

Hurston, Z. N. 1942. *Dust Tracks on a Road.* Reprint, New York: Arno Press, 1969.

———. 1937. *Their Eyes Were Watching God.* Reprint, Greenwich, Conn.: Fawcett, 1969.

Karasek, R. and T. Theorell. 1990. *Healthy Work: Stress, Productivity, and the Reconstruction of Working Life.* New York: Basic.

Kohn, M. L. and C. Schooler, eds. 1983. *Work and Personality: An Inquiry Into the Impact of Social Stratification.* Norwood, N.J.: Ablex Publishing.

Lennon, M. C. 1994. Women, work, and well-being: The importance of work conditions. *Journal of Health and Social Behavior* 35:235–247.

Lennon, M. C. and S. Rosenfield. 1992. Women and mental health: The interaction of job and family conditions. *Journal of Health and Social Behavior* 33:316–327.

Lincoln, J. R. and A. L. Kalleberg. 1990. *Culture, Control, and Commitment: A Study of Work Organization and Work Attitudes in the United States and Japan.* Cambridge: Harvard University Press.

Loscocco, K. A. and G. Spitze. 1990. Working conditions, social support, and the well-being of female and male factory workers. *Journal of Health and Social Behavior* 31:313–327.

McGuire, G. M. and B. F. Reskin. 1993. Authority hierarchies at work: The impacts of race and sex. *Gender Society* 7:487–506.

Miller, J. 1988. Jobs and Work. In N. J. Smelser, ed., *Handbook of Sociology*, 327–359. Newbury Park, Calif.: Sage.

Mortimer, J. T., M. D. Finch, and G. Maruyama. 1988. Work Experience and Job Satisfaction: Variation by Age and Gender. In J. T. Mortimer and K. M. Borman, eds., *Work Experience and Psychological Development Through the Life Span*, 109–155. Boulder: Westview.

Mortimer, J. T. and J. Lorence. 1989. Satisfaction and involvement: Disentangling a deceptively simple relationship. Social Psychology Quarterly 52:249–265.

———. 1995. *Social Psychology of Work*. In K. S. Cook, G. A. Fine, and J. S. House, eds., Sociological Perspectives on Social Psychology, 497–523. Boston: Allyn and Bacon.

Neckerman, K. M. and J. Kirschenman. 1991. Hiring strategies, racial bias, and inner-city workers. *Social Problems* 38:433–447.

Omolade, B. 1994. *The Rising Song of African American Women*. New York: Routledge.

Pugliesi, K. 1995. Work and well-being: Gender differences in the psychological consequences of employment. *Journal of Health and Social Behavior* 36:57–71.

Rain, J. S., I. M. Lane, and D. D. Steiner. 1991. A current look at the job satisfaction/life satisfaction relationship: Review and future considerations. *Human Relations* 44:287–307.

Reskin, B. and S. Coverman. 1985. Sex and race in the determinants of psychophysical distress: A reappraisal of the sex-role hypothesis. *Social Forces* 64:1038–1059.

Rice, R. W., J. P. Near, and R. G. Hunt. 1980. The job satisfaction/life satisfaction relationship: A review of empirical research. *Basic and Applied Social Psychology* 1:37–64.

Rollins, J. 1985. *Between Women: Domestics and Their Employers*. Philadelphia: Temple University Press.

Russell, K., M. Wilson, and R. Hall. 1992. *The Color Complex: The Politics of Skin Color Among African Americans*. New York: Harcourt Brace Jovanovich.

Snapp, M. B. 1992. Occupational stress, social support, and depression among Black and White professional-managerial women. *Women and Health* 18:41–74.

Sokoloff, N. 1992. *Black Women and White Women in the Professions*. New York: Routledge.

Steiner, D. D. and D. M. Truxillo. 1987. Another look at the job satisfaction–life satisfaction relationship: A test of the disaggregation hypothesis. *Journal of Occupational Behavior* 8:71–77.

St. Jean, Y. and J. R. Feagin. 1998. *Double Burden: Black Women and Everyday Racism*. Armonk, N.Y.: M. E. Sharp.

Tuch, S. A. and J. K. Martin. 1991. Race in the workplace: Black/White differences in the sources of job satisfaction. *Sociological Quarterly* 32:103–116.

Woody, B. 1992. *Black Women in the Workplace: The Impacts of Structural Change in the Economy*. New York: Greenwood.

11 MULTIPLE SOCIAL ROLES AND MULTIPLE STRESSORS FOR BLACK WOMEN

Diane R. Brown and Donna L. Cochran

> Get any five sisters in a room and at least four will tell stories of how their mothers worked all day (or all night), cooked and cleaned, raised several children, nurtured a man who was mistreated by the system. . . . And almost all will talk about their mother's strength.
>
> —MITCHELL (1998:66–67)

African American women have historically held multiple social roles, encompassing their personal and family life, community and workplace (Ralston 1997). The ability to manage multiple roles, often under oppressive circumstances, has come to symbolize the "strength" of African American women (hooks 1981). Yet few empirical studies have examined the mental health consequences of multiple role management among African American women. Unfortunately, much of the research has focused almost exclusively on White, middle-class, middle-aged women (Staples and Boulin-Johnson 1993). Thus little is known about the influence of multiple social roles on the psychological well-being of women of color, specifically African American women.

A number of factors provide explanations for the multiple roles held by African American women. In some cases, because of the economic marginality of many African American men, African American women have been forced to seek employment in order to contribute financially to the household (Staples 1988). At the same time, African American women have always been actively involved in care-providing responsibilities. Providing for immediate, extended, and fictive kin has been a long-standing tradition among African Americans (Dilworth-Anderson, Williams, and Cooper 1999; McCray 1980). Consequently, many African American communities show higher levels of multigenerational households, fosterage of kin and non-kin children, and care for dependent family members (Staples and Boulin-Johnson 1993). Additionally, in an effort to enhance the general welfare of family members and community, many African American women contribute significant voluntary efforts to their church and to their community (Harrison 1989; Ralston 1997).

Demographic factors also affect the number and types of roles occupied by African American women. For example, many African American women are not married because of a shorter life expectancy (National Vital Statistics Report 2002) and the limited pool of marriageable African American men (Tucker and Mitchell-Kernan 1993). This decreases the probability that African American women will occupy the marital role during most or part of their adult lives and that they will have the economic and psychological benefits associated with marriage (Brown 1996). The disadvantageous sex ratio and population demographics also increase the likelihood that African American women will be nonmarried parents as well as the primary care providers for grandchildren (Brown and Monye 1995).

THEORETICAL PERSPECTIVES ON ROLES AND WELL-BEING

Resulting from more than forty years of debate about the relationship of multiple roles to psychological well-being (Hong and Selzer 1995), two opposing hypotheses have emerged. Both evolve from role theory and are distinguished by the proposed impact of social roles on well-being. According to the role enhancement hypothesis, multiple social roles provide meaning and purpose for daily living. Engaging in more than one role yields positive effects for mental well-being regardless of the nature of the roles occupied (Rushing, Ritter, and Burton 1992). The overwhelming number of research studies on social roles and psychological well-being conclude that the healthiest individuals have the most complex social role configurations (Hong and Seltzer 1995; Rushing, Ritter, and Burton 1992; Waldron and Jacobs 1989). The more roles people fill, the greater their ability to maintain positive thoughts about aspects of self and the greater their resources for trading off negative aspects of each role (Adelmann 1994). On the other hand, the role strain hypothesis asserts that multiple roles cause role overload or strain (Goode 1960). Specifically, role strain or overload emerges as a consequence of incompatible or a large quantity of role demands (Adelmann 1994). Role strain results in pernicious mental health consequences for individuals with multiple social roles. The few previous studies of African American women provide support for both the role strain and the role enhancement hypotheses as factors that affect the well-being of African American women (Staples and Boulin-Johnson 1993). However, Staples and Boulin-Johnson (1993) contend that fulfilling excessive role obligations may have a greater mental health impact than does the actual number of social roles.

RESEARCH ON SOCIAL ROLES

Parenthood, marriage, and employment are the most commonly examined social roles in the literature. Of the three roles, employment is consistently found to be the most significant predictor of mental well-being among women in several studies (Coleman, Antonuccci, and Adelmann 1987). In their study of middle-aged and older African American women, Coleman and colleagues (1987) found that there were few who participated in all three of the traditional roles of spouse, parent, and worker. Parent and worker were the two roles mostly likely to be performed by middle-aged and older African American women. That study further noted that the work role (i.e., being gainfully employed), was especially important for the mental and physical well-being of African American women.

In recent years researchers have begun to acknowledge and examine a broader range of social roles undertaken by women. For example, such roles as volunteer (Fischer, Mueller, and Cooper 1991), grandmother (Miller and Cavanaugh 1990), and care provider (Moen, Robison, and Dempster-McClain 1995; Stephens, Franks, and Townsend 1994) are increasingly being investigated in the literature to discover their impact on mental and physical well-being. Overall, this emerging literature, which extends beyond the traditional social role triad of parent, spouse, and worker, tends to support the role enhancement hypothesis. However, few studies have explored the impact of contemporary social roles in relation to traditional social roles and well-being among African American women.

The purpose of the current analysis is to examine how the types and number of social roles held by African American women are related to their mental health—specifically, to depressive symptoms. The analysis focuses on midlife and older African American women because they are most likely to occupy a spectrum of social roles from parent and spouse to worker, grandmother, volunteer, and caregiver.

METHODS

DATA AND SAMPLE

The analyses are based on cross-sectional data from the first wave of the Health and Retirement Study (HRS) (Juster and Suzman 1995). The HRS contains contemporaneous data on health, employment, income, and family structure for a nationally representative sample of individuals born between 1931 and 1941 (see Juster and Suzman 1995 for a detailed discussion of the HRS data). Only data from the 547 African American women, 55–64 years of age, were used for this analysis.

The shortened, fourteen-item version of the Center for Epidemiologic Studies Depression (CES-D) Scale was used to measure depressive symptoms (Juster and Suzman 1995; Kohout et al. 1993; Wallace and Herzog 1993). Depressive symptoms are assessed over the period of a week. The social roles included in the analysis were spouse or partner, employee, care provider, grandmother, and volunteer. Depending upon the statistical technique, marriage and employment status were used as multi-categorical or dichotomized variables. Care provider, grandmother, and volunteer variables were dichotomized throughout all analyses. If a respondent occupied a role, it was coded 1; unoccupied roles were coded 0.

The role of care provider was constructed in several steps. Three specific questions were used to assess whether (a) a child lived in the household (including those away at school); (b) 100 hours or more during the past year were spent taking care of one's own parent; or (c) at least 100 hours during the last twelve months were spent caring for an in-law. A score of 1 was assigned if one or more of these statements was true; a 0 was assigned to respondents who answered *no* to all of the questions. In terms of the role of grandmother, respondents were asked if they provided more than 100 hours of care to a grandchild or to grandchildren during the past twelve months. Affirmative responses were coded 1. The role of volunteer was measured by asking respondents to indicate whether they had spent 100 hours or more during the past twelve months doing volunteer work for a religious or charitable organization. Those who responded yes were coded 1 for participating in a volunteer role, while the marital role was coded 0 = married and 1 for the other marital status categories. Similarly, the employment role was coded 1 = *employed* and 0 = *other* or not employed. A variable was constructed to assess the total number of roles in which women participated during old age. The variable reflected the five social roles (i.e., spouse, employee, care provider, grandmother, and volunteer) examined in this study. Responses ranged from 0 to 5 roles.

Demographic variables used in this analysis include age, income, and education. Income was used for the descriptive analysis only, with four categories ranging from less than $9,000 to more than $40,000. Depending on the statistical method used, age and education were treated as both continuous and categorical variables and included in the descriptive and multiple regression analyses. The mean age for African American women was 57.6 years ($SD =$ 1.87), while the mean number of years of educational attainment was 11.06 ($SD = 3.26$). The average income was $19,696 ($SD = $15,026$), with approximately a quarter of women having incomes of less than $10,000.

RESULTS

Table 11.1 provides the distribution of African American women according to the five social roles. With regard to marital status, slightly fewer than half (44.0%) were married, while nearly half (48.0%) were previously married (separated, widowed, or divorced) and fewer than 10 percent (7.9%) had never married. In terms of employment status, about half (49.5%) were currently employed. Those who were not employed were most apt to be homemakers (18.4%), disabled (18.0%), or retired (9.5%). A substantial number of women (42.8%) were providing care to a child, parent, or in-law. Only 23.2 percent were caring for a grandchild, and even fewer (12.6%) were engaged in a volunteer role. Overall, African American women had an average of 1.71 ($SD = 1.02$) social roles. The role most likely to be occupied was that of worker, followed by spouse and care provider. It is important to note, however, that 12 percent occupied no social roles.

SOCIAL ROLES AND MENTAL HEALTH

Table 11.2 gives the distribution of depressive symptoms for each social role. The association between depressive symptoms and the marital role was significant, $F = 26.13$, $p \leq .01$. Married African American women had fewer depressive symptoms than did those who were not married. Depressive symptoms were highest for separated/divorced and never married women. A significant association between the worker role and depressive symptoms was also found, $F = 81.09$, $p \leq .00$. African American women who were employed reported the lowest depressive symptoms while depressive symptoms were highest for women who were sick and disabled.

TABLE 11.1 Distribution of Social Roles for Midlife and Older African American Women

SOCIAL ROLES	N	%
Marital status		
Married/partner	240	44.0
Separated	47	8.6
Divorced	95	17.4
Widowed	120	22.0
Never married	43	7.9
Total	545	100.0
Employment status		
Working	248	49.5
Unemployed	10	2.0
Sick	12	2.4
Disabled	91	18.2
Retired	48	9.5
Homemaker	92	18.4
Total	501	100.0
Care provider		
Yes	234	42.8
No	313	57.2
Total	547	100.0
Grandmother		
Yes	127	23.2
No	420	76.8
Total	547	100.0
Volunteer		
Yes	69	12.6
No	478	87.4
Total	547	100.0
Number of roles		
0	67	12.2
1	169	31.0
2	202	37.0
3	83	15.2
4	23	4.2
5	2	0.4
Total	546	100.0

Source: Health and Retirement Study, 1995.

Regarding the care provider role, there was no significant relationship with depressive symptoms, $F = .02$, ns. This finding indicates that care providers and non–care providers have similar levels of depressive symptoms. Similarly, there was no significant association between undertaking the grandmother role and depressive symptoms ($F = .85$, ns). The level of depressive symptoms reported by grandmothers was similar to that reported by non-grandmothers. On the other hand, the association between the volunteer role and depressive symptoms was significant ($F = 20.07$, $p \leq .001$). This suggests that African American women who are volunteers have fewer depressive symptoms than non-volunteers.

When the total number of social roles was examined, the results show a significant association ($F = 34.99$, $p \leq .001$). This finding indicates that African American women with a greater number of social roles report fewer depressive symptoms than women with fewer social roles. African American women occupying all five roles had the least depressive symptoms ($M = 19.5$, $SD = 3.5$) while those occupying no social role had the highest level of depressive symptoms with a mean of 27.7 ($SD = 8.4$).

MULTIPLE REGRESSION ANALYSIS

A multiple regression analysis was performed to ascertain those types of social roles that had the strongest association with depressive symptoms while controlling for age and education. For the multiple regression analysis, the role of grandmother was combined with that of care provider. As shown in table 11.3, the three social roles of marital status, employment status, and volunteer were significant predictors of depressive symptoms. Being a care provider was not a significant predictor. With regard to marital status, being divorced (B = 1.892, $p \leq .01$) contributed to higher levels of depressive symptomatology. At the same time, being employed (B = -4.185, $p \leq .001$) was associated with a decline in depressive symptoms while having a volunteer role (B = -1.717, $p \leq .01$) was also associated with decreasing depressive symptoms.

A second multiple regression equation was conducted using the total number of social roles as the predictor of depressive symptoms. As shown in table 11.4, the total number of social roles was a significant predictor of depressive symptoms (B = -1.236, $p \leq .001$). The findings indicate that occupying a greater number of roles was associated with a decreasing level of depressive symptoms.

TABLE 11.2 Distribution of Depressive Symptoms by Social Roles

SOCIAL ROLES	MEAN	SD	N
Marital Status			
Married/partner	21.978	5.164	233
Separated/divorced	25.289	8.095	138
Widowed	24.948	6.492	117
Never married	25.300	7.965	40
Employment status			
Working	21.759	4.482	245
Unemployed	22.900	5.626	10
Sick and disabled	29.244	7.553	98
Retired	22.148	5.137	47
Homemaker	22.759	6.545	84
Care provider			
Yes	23.728	6.763	306
No	23.750	6.679	224
Grandmother			
Yes	23.856	6.922	405
No	23.352	6.035	125
Volunteer			
Yes	24.071	6.843	463
No	21.432	5.306	67
Number of roles			
0	27.734	8.429	64
1	25.452	7.947	157
2	22.437	5.580	199
3	21.647	4.612	85
4	20.200	2.857	25
5	19.500	3.536	2

Source: Health and Retirement Study, 1995.

TABLE 11.3 Regression of Depressive Symptoms on Social Roles

	B	SE B
Age	−.280*	.125
Education	−.250***	.085
Marital status		
Cohabitating[a]	.644	1.852
Separated/divorced	1.892**	.633
Widowed	.952	.681
Never married	.774	.971
Employed	−4.185***	.534
Volunteer	−1.717**	.667
Care provider	.010	.531
$R^2 = .160$		

[a] Married is reference category. Unstandardized coefficients shown.
$^+p \leq .05$ $^*p \leq .01$ $^{**}p \leq .01$ $^{***}p \leq .001$

DISCUSSION

This investigation examined the influence of multiple social role participation on the level of depressive symptoms reported by midlife and older African American women. No support was found for the role strain hypothesis, that an increased number of social roles is associated with greater depression. On the other hand, these analyses provided general support for the role enhancement hypothesis, which contends that mental health benefits are derived from multiple role management (Rushing, Ritter, and Burton 1992). Specifically, African American women who are engaged in more than one social role report better mental health in terms of fewer depressive symptoms. It is likely that African American women who have two or more social roles do not have to commit all of their psychological resources to one particular role. Having multiple social roles may allow them to balance stresses and rewards among the various roles. For example, if the demands of one role, such as a job, become especially stressful, the rewards of another role, such as parenting, may help them to achieve a level of psychological and emotional balance.

TABLE 11.4 Regression of Depression on Total Number of Social Roles

	B	SE B
Age	−.189	.128
Education	−.338***	.085
Total number of roles	−1.236***	.224
$R^2 = .092$		

***$p \leq .001$

Findings from these analyses also show that the types of social roles are important for mental well-being. Of the five social roles examined in this analysis, the role associated with the least depressive symptoms for African American women was employment. Employment had a more powerful influence on diminishing depressive symptoms for African American women than any of the other social roles. Employment is associated with greater economic benefits, which are predictive of lower levels of depressive symptoms (Kandel, Davies, and Raveis 1985). However, age and gender discrimination, in addition to racism, are likely to decrease the possibility of older African American women having the employment role, and experiencing the high levels of reward and satisfaction that are associated with that role. It should be noted that marital status was also a significant predictor of depressive symptoms, but specifically for those who were separated or divorced, as African American women who are separated and divorced report higher levels of depressive symptoms.

An examination of type of social role occupied and its relationship to depressive symptoms is particularly important for women who engage in only one role. Recall that these analyses show that African American women with only one role had higher depressive symptoms than those with two or more roles. Further analyses (not shown) indicate that African American women with only one social role are more likely to be in the roles of care provider or grandmother. In essence, they are undertaking care provider responsibilities without having the economic and psychological resources provided by employment and/or marriage. Midlife and older African American women who are unmarried, unemployed, and providing care for others may particularly face economic hardship—circumstances that have consistently been linked to higher levels of depression in the literature (Coleman, Antonucci, and Adelmann 1987).

From these analyses it is evident that occupying certain social roles such as employee and spouse tends to be associated with lower levels of depressive symptoms and, consequently, with better mental health in comparison to women who are unemployed or without partners. However, given the social structural disadvantages imposed on African American women, they have less opportunity than White women to occupy these roles and to reap high levels of reward and satisfaction with these roles. For example, the percentages of African American women who were widowed (22%) and never married (8.6%) compared with those of White women (10.6% and 1.9%, respectively) indicate that African American women are less likely to occupy the marriage role. Even when African American women are married, they report lower levels of life satisfaction than do White women (Thomas and Holmes 1992).

It is important to note that a nontrivial number of African American women in this analysis occupied none of the five social roles. This means that they were not in the traditional social roles held by women in American society, specifically marriage and employment, nor in the roles of volunteer, care provider, or grandmother. Given that women with no social role were also those with the highest level of depressive symptoms, this suggests that they are likely to be socially isolated and have fewer sources of social support than women with at least one social role.

The findings from this study contribute to the previous literature by examining the number and types of social roles and their impact on the mental health of midlife and older African American women. Nevertheless, this study had several limitations. Only two aspects of role occupancy were examined: number and type of social roles. Future studies of mental well-being need to investigate role quality as well as scope of role demands. In addition to the type and number of social roles, future research needs to examine the types of stressors and the scope of demands and rewards associated with the roles that African American women occupy. In many cases, African American women experience excessive demands of role overload or role conflict that have detrimental effects on their mental health (Staples and Boulin-Johnson 1993). For example, for many African American women, caregiving may encompass providing various sorts of assistance not only to multiple adult children but also simultaneously to multiple grandchildren, great-grandchildren, aging parents, and siblings, as well as other kin and non-kin. In other instances, the demands of one social role may conflict with the demands of another.

A limitation of this analysis is that the data were cross-sectional and did not examine causal links. Accordingly, it is possible that high levels of depressive symptoms among African American women may have led to their having fewer social roles and to their lower likelihood of marriage and employment. In addition, future studies of African American women need to include measures of social roles that encompass a sociocultural context. As an example, the care provider measure used in this study did not capture the tasks of women providing care to extended family (e.g., nieces, nephews, grandparents, siblings, aunts, cousins, fictive kin). This is particularly important for African Americans, who traditionally have provided care for a broad spectrum of kin and non-kin (McCray 1980). Thus, future studies on the caregiving role should move beyond the traditional family members currently discussed in the literature and include information about members of the extended family and non-kin who may be receiving care.

Another limitation of this study is that it looked only at women between the ages of 55 and 64. With the inclusion of younger women, findings may differ with regard to the social roles that have the strongest influence on level of depressive symptoms. Future studies also need to include the social role of "householder," with or without spouse. Many African American women are heads of households, which brings with it specific role demands and rewards. A more comprehensive measure of the volunteer role is also needed. Many African American women participate, hold office, and have various levels of responsibilities in social organizations besides the church. Unfortunately, the current measures of volunteer participation do not capture the many areas where older African American women volunteer their time (Ralston 1997). Thus, in future studies, consideration of the volunteer role should extend beyond church participation to include such activities as social and recreational organizations, senior centers, community organizations, and advocacy groups.

REFERENCES

Adelmann, P. K. 1994. Multiple roles and physical health among older adults: Gender and ethnic comparisons. *Research on Aging* 16:142–166.

Broman, C. 1991. Gender, work-family roles, and psychological well-being of Blacks. *Journal of Marriage and the Family* 53:509–520.

Brown, D. R. 1996. Marital Status and Mental Health. In H. W. Neighbors and J. S. Jackson, eds., *Mental Health in Black America*. 77–94. Newbury Park, Calif.: Sage.

Brown, D. R. and D. Monye. 1995. *Mid-Life and Older African Americans as Intergenerational Caregivers of School-Aged Children*. Center for Urban Studies, College of Urban, Labor and Metropolitan Affairs. Detroit: Wayne State University.

Coleman, L., T. Antonucci, and P. Adelmann. 1987. Social roles in the lives of middle-aged and older Black women. *Journal of Marriage and the Family* 49:761–771.

Dilworth-Anderson, P., S. W. Williams, and T. Cooper. 1999. Family caregiving to elderly African Americans: Caregiver types and structures. *Journals of Gerontology: Social Sciences* 54 (4): S237–S241.

Fischer, L. R., D. P. Mueller, and P. W. Cooper. 1991. Older volunteers: A discussion of the Minnesota Senior Study. *Gerontologist* 31:183–195.

Goode, W. 1960. A theory of role strain. *American Sociological Review* 25:483–496.

Harrison, A. O. 1989. Black Working Women: Introduction to a Life Span Perspective. In R. L. Jones, ed., *Black Adult Development and Aging*. Berkeley: Cobb and Henry.

Hong, J. and M. Seltzer. 1995. The psychological consequences of multiple roles: The normative case. *Journal of Health and Social Behavior* 36:386–398.

hooks, b. 1981. *Ain't I a Woman: Black Women and Feminism*. Boston: South End Press.

Juster, F. T. and R. Suzman. 1995. The Health and Retirement Study: An overview. *Journal of Human Resources* 30 (Supplement): 7–56.

Kandel, D., M. Davies, and V. Raveis. 1985. The stressfulness of daily social roles for women: Marital, occupational, and household roles. *Journal of Health and Social Behavior* 26:64–78.

Kohout, F. J., L. F. Berkman, D. A. Evans, and J. Cornoni-Huntley. 1993. Two shorter forms of the CES-D (Center for Epidemiologic Studies–Depression) depression symptoms index. *Journal of Aging and Health* 5:179–193.

McCray, C. A. 1980. The Black Woman and Family Roles. In L. Rodgers-Rose, ed., *The Black Woman*, 67–78. Beverly Hills: Sage.

Miller, S. and C. Cavanaugh. 1990. The meaning of grandparenthood and its relation to demographic, relationship, and social participation variables. *Journal of Gerontology: Psychological Sciences* 45: P244–P246.

Mitchell, A. 1998. *What the Blues Is All About*. New York: Berkeley Publishing Group.

Moen, P., J. Robison, and D. Dempster-McClain. 1995. Caregiving and women's well-being: A life course approach. *Journal of Health and Social Behavior* 36:259–273.

National Vital Statistics Report 2002. Table 12. Estimated Life Expectancy at Birth in Years by Race and Sex. http://www.cdc.gov/nchs/fastats/pdf/nysr50_06tb12.pdf.

Ralston, P. 1997. Midlife and Older Black Women. In J. M. Coyle, ed., *Handbook of Women and Aging*. 283–289. Westport, Conn.: Greenwood.

Rushing, B., C. Ritter, and R. Burton. 1992. Race differences in the effects of multiple roles on health: Longitudinal evidence from a national sample of older men. *Journal of Health and Social Behavior* 33:126–139.

Saluter, A. 1991. Marital status and living arrangements. Current Population Reports. *Population Characteristics*. Series P-20, No. 46. Washington, D.C.: U.S. Government Printing Office.

Staples, R. 1988. An Overview of Race and Marital Status. In H. P. McAdoo, ed., *Black Families*, 187–189. Newbury Park, Calif.: Sage.

Staples, R. and L. Boulin-Johnson. 1993. *Black Families at the Crossroads: Challenges and Prospects*. San Francisco: Jossey-Bass.

Stephens, M., M. Franks, and A. Townsend. 1994. Stress and rewards in women's multiple roles: The case of women in the middle. *Psychology and Aging* 9:45–52.

Thoits, P. 1983. Multiple identities and psychological well-being: A test of the social isolation hypothesis. *American Sociological Review* 48:174–187.

Thomas, M. E. and B. J. Holmes. 1992. Determinants of satisfaction for Blacks and Whites. *Sociological Quarterly* 33:459–472.

Tucker, M. B. and C. Mitchell-Kernan. 1993. Marriage and romantic involvement among aged African Americans. *Journal of Gerontology: Social Sciences* 48:S123–S132.

Waldron, I. and J. Jacobs. 1989. Effects of multiple roles on women's health: Evidence from a national longitudinal study. *Women and Health* 15:3–19.

Wallace, R. and A. R. Herzog. 1993. "Overview of the Health Measures in the Health and Retirement Survey." Paper presented at the Health and Retirement Survey Workshop, Ann Arbor, September.

PART V
KEEPING ON ... KEEPING ON

The fact that the adult American Negro female emerges a formidable character is often met with amazement, distaste, and even belligerence. It is seldom accepted as an inevitable outcome of the struggle won by survivors, and deserves respect if not enthusiastic acceptance.

—Maya Angelou

12 KEEPING THE FAITH: RELIGION, STRESS, AND PSYCHOLOGICAL WELL-BEING AMONG AFRICAN AMERICAN WOMEN
Karen D. Lincoln and Linda M. Chatters

O ne of the most consistent findings on Black religious involvement is that women are more likely than men to engage in a
variety of religious behaviors and to endorse religious attitudes
and beliefs at higher levels. The gender differential is evident for virtually
every type of religious behavior (i.e., organizational, private devotions) and
attitudinal measures (e.g., importance of church, self-described religiosity).
The differential also is apparent across different samples and data collection
points and is comparable to the gender differential found in research among
Whites (Batson, Schoenrade, and Ventis 1993; Beit-Hallahmi and Argyle 1997;
Bergan and McConatha 2000). These elevated levels of religious involvement
suggest that religion may have special salience and relevance for African
American women (Ellison and Taylor 1996). Further, anecdotal accounts, as
well as a small number of empirical investigations, suggest that among Black
women, religious involvement has a positive association with mental health
and well-being (Ellison and Taylor 1996).

The purpose of this study is to test a specific conceptual model of the relationships among religious involvement, life stress, and psychological well-being
among African American women. Several relevant literatures serve as the background for this investigation, such as (1) patterns of religious involvement
among African American women; (2) connections between religious involvement and well-being; and (3) relationships among religion, life stress, and
psychological well-being.

AFRICAN AMERICAN WOMEN AND RELIGION

Women's greater investment in religious concerns has prompted
researchers to ask what factors might underlie the gender difference in religious

involvement. The literature identifies a number of possible explanations. One class of explanations is based on the customary social roles and activities performed by women and men that result in gender-based differences in family and work roles and labor force participation (de Vaus and McAllister 1987). Another perspective suggests that religious teachings, beliefs, and practices are compatible with gender-based socialization messages as to the types of personality traits, attributes (e.g., sociability, cooperation), and roles (e.g., nurturance, supportive caregiver) that are deemed appropriate for women. Religious content, symbols, and meanings may have special relevance for women, given their greater identification with prosocial traits and involvement in family, social, and caregiving roles and activities. Further, because women remain the primary socialization agents for young children (Thornton et al. 1990) and are involved in moral instruction and the inculcation of religious values, they have more exposure to and familiarity with religious information and contexts. Women also tend to be more prominent members of the social networks that make up religious settings (i.e., churches), thus providing more opportunities to become involved in religious pursuits and activities and to be exposed to pro-religious social norms and values inherent to these groups.

Finally, in a slightly different vein, observed gender differences may reflect the functional benefits that women derive from religious involvement. That is to say, women may participate in religious activities because they find them to be beneficial for coping with the demands and stresses associated with their various social roles and obligations. As compared to men, women may be exposed to qualitatively different types of stressors and/or higher levels of overall stress by virtue of their greater involvement in family social roles and obligations. Consequently, religious activities, symbols, and content may have relevance for women because they provide a means of understanding and coping with life stresses. Religious coping strategies, particularly those focused on problem reappraisal (i.e., reframing) and mood regulation, may be especially effective in dealing with the stresses arising from these roles. This explanation suggests a link between religious involvement and overall well-being—a topic that has some prominence in the literature.

RELIGION AND MENTAL HEALTH/PSYCHOLOGICAL WELL-BEING

In recent years there has been renewed interest in the relationship between religious involvement and physical and mental health and well-being, as demonstrated by the growing literature on this topic (Chatters, Levin, and

Ellison 1998; Levin and Chatters 1998; Levin et al. 1996). Levin and Chatters's review (1998) of the clinical, epidemiological, social, and gerontological research indicates that religious involvement has preventive and positive therapeutic effects on mental health outcomes. Specific research on the relationship between religious involvement and mental health/psychological well-being indicates a general positive association (Levin and Chatters 1998; Levin, Chatters, and Taylor 1995; Levin and Schiller 1987). However, Batson, Schoenrade, and Ventis's (1993) review of the literature suggested that findings for the relationship between religion and mental health were mixed. Specifically, religion, when it is used as a means to achieve some end, such as emotional or social support or social status, is negatively associated with mental health. On the other hand, when religion is viewed as a guiding principle in one's life, it is positively associated with mental health. Importantly, studies of the connection between religion and well-being suggest that specific religious indicators may be differentially associated with well-being and, further, that the relationship may be contingent on other factors such as age, gender, and region (Ellison and Gay 1990; Ellison, Gay, and Glass 1989).

Although research specifically examining the relationship between religion and mental health/psychological well-being among women is scarce, the few available studies suggest that religion has a beneficial influence. Shaver, Lenauer, and Sadd's (1980) study of 2,500 American women found that high levels of religious involvement were related to enhanced mental and physical health. A study of African American women from Missouri (Handal, Black-Lopez, and Moergen 1989) found that those with low levels of religious involvement reported significantly more psychological symptoms than women with high levels of religious involvement. In their study of 30 elderly women (65+ years of age) recovering from hip replacement surgery, Pressman and colleagues (1990) found that higher levels of religious involvement (e.g., attendance at religious services, perceived religiousness, degree to which religion is a source of strength/comfort) were associated with lower levels of depressive symptoms at the time of discharge from the hospital (Pressman et al. 1990). Finally, Chang and colleagues (2001) found that frequency of religious service attendance buffered the effects of sexual assault on mental health and depression among a national sample of women veterans. Although the buffering effect of subjective religiosity (i.e., religious beliefs as a source of strength/comfort) was not observed, subjective religiosity was positively associated with better mental health in women with and without a history of sexual assault (Chang, Skinner, and Boehmer 2001).

Overall, the evidence suggests that religious involvement is positively associated with mental health and psychological well-being among women. Despite these positive findings, however, the research is plagued with methodological and conceptual inconsistencies. Primary among these is the fact that the con-structs of religion and mental health are defined and operationalized in a variety of ways, with little consistency across studies (Levin and Chatters 1998). Chatters (2000) suggests that many of the discrepancies can be attributed to the various ways in which religion and psychological well-being/mental health have been measured. Further, with few exceptions (Markides, Levin, and Ray 1987), studies of religion and mental health employ a cross-sectional design, which makes it difficult to determine the nature of causal relationships.

RELIGION AND LIFE STRESS

Although research documents an overall positive relationship between religion and mental health and psychological well-being, the specific mechanisms through which religious involvement influences these factors remain unclear. Several hypotheses give particular attention to the potential role(s) that religion plays in the stress process (Levin and Chatters 1998). First, religious involvement is important in shaping behavioral patterns and lifestyles in ways that may prevent or reduce the risk of experiencing certain social stressors. In this respect, religious beliefs, practices, and institutions may be effective in a stress-preventive role (Jenkins 1992; Payne et al. 1992). Second, religion offers its members a coherent and meaningful framework that helps to interpret and manage problematic situations (Capps 1990). Several investigators suggest that religion provides a framework that gives meaning and purpose to life (e.g., Pargament 1997). Research findings suggest that having a sense of meaning in life is associated with positive mental health outcomes, whereas a lack of meaning is associated with negative outcomes (Coleman, Kaplan, and Downing 1986). Further, persons who are religiously committed are more likely to reframe negative events as challenges and oppor-tunities for growth, as compared to those with lower levels of religious com-mitment (Pargament et al. 1992).

Third, religion may be important in generating relatively high levels of social resources (e.g., social support from clergy and fellow church mem-bers) that act to buffer the impact of stressful events. Chalfant and colleagues (1990) found that people in distress often prefer to seek help from their clergy or religious congregations, as opposed to mental health professionals. Similarly, 13 percent of older adults seek assistance from clergy in times of personal crisis, as compared to 2 percent who consult formal mental health professionals (Veroff, Douvan, and Kulka 1981). Among church members who were coping with a major negative life event, support from the clergy and church was associated with better psychological status (Pargament et al. 1990). One study (Ortega, Crutchfield, and Rushing 1983) noted that frequency of contact with church-related friends was a critical factor in reports of positive well-being among older minorities, suggesting that support from church members may be important for health and functioning. Religion may also function as a means of maintaining or enhancing a sense of positive self-regard involving feelings of personal control or self-esteem. Involvement with religious communities and/or endorsement of specific religious beliefs and tenets may instill a sense of self-worth and value among adherents (Ellison 1993) that protects them from the effects of stress.

Alternatively, religious involvement may function to modify the relationship between stress and mental health and psychological well-being. Religion is often intimately associated with life's most stressful occurrences. People may be especially likely to turn to religion for solace in coping with illness (Koenig, Pargament, and Nielsen 1998; Levin and Vanderpool 1992), physical disability (Idler and Kasl 1997; Koenig 1994), serious injury (Pressman et al., 1990), major surgery (Oxman, Freedman, and Manheimer 1995), or the death of a loved one (Krause 1992; McIntosh, Silver, and Wortman 1993). Religious forms of coping are especially helpful to people who are confronted with uncontrollable, unmanageable, or otherwise difficult situations (Pargament et al. 1998; Williams et al. 1991). For instance, some researchers (e.g., Mattlin, Wethington, and Kessler 1990) find that religious cognitions and behaviors are more effective than other types of coping strategies in reducing depression and other negative psychosocial states that often develop following bereavement events and health-related stressors.

As compared to general indicators of religiousness, specific measures of religious coping are thought to be stronger predictors of adjustment to life crises (Pargament 1995) and better predictors of adjustment over and above the effects of nonreligious coping. Williams and colleagues' (1991) study of religion and psychological distress in a community sample found that religion was a potent coping strategy that facilitated adjustment to life stress. An interaction among religion, social stress, and measures of psychological distress indicated that stress was associated with higher levels of psychological distress among those with low levels of religious attendance. For persons with high levels of religious attendance, however, the adverse effects of stress were reduced (religious involvement had no direct effect on psychological distress).

Only a few studies examine the relationships among religion, stress, and well-being among African Americans. Available findings indicate that religious coping, particularly the use of prayer and church support, is especially common among African Americans (Bearon and Koenig 1990; Ellison and Taylor 1996; Koenig 1994), but the ability to generalize the findings to the Black population is limited because these studies are based on community or regional samples and the numbers of African Americans are small. However, a group of studies that are based on the National Survey of Black Americans (NSBA) confirms the role of religion during times of stress. Specifically, Chatters and Taylor (1989) found that elderly persons frequently used prayer in coping with money and health problems. Blacks are especially likely to turn to religion when experiencing high levels of stress (Ellison and Taylor 1996; Krause 1992), and prayer is the most frequently mentioned coping resource among African Americans who were confronted with a personal problem. Consistent with established gender differences in overall religious involvement, women are more likely than men to use prayer to cope with a problem (Ellison and Taylor 1996).

Despite a long tradition of interest in these questions and strong evidence that religious involvement plays an important role in the stress process, the specific mechanisms through which religious involvement operates to affect psychological well-being are not well understood. Research on the topic is plagued by the lack of conceptual clarity concerning religious involvement and the absence of a clear theoretical framework outlining the potential functions of religion in the stress process. This study attempts to clarify these relationships by employing more precise measures of religious involvement and testing a conceptual model linking religious involvement, social stressors, and psychological well-being within a national sample of African American women.

THE PROPOSED MODEL

Figure 12.1 illustrates the conceptual model of the proposed relationships among stress, religious involvement, and psychological well-being. Religious involvement is represented in the model by non-organizational behaviors (e.g., prayer and other devotional practices, use of print and electronic media). Non-organizational religious involvement is one of three dimensions of religiosity that have been investigated in the literature, the others being organizational and subjective religious involvement (Levin, Taylor, and Chatters 1995). The inclusion of non-organizational religious involvement in the model was based on several considerations. First, organizational religious involvement, such as church attendance, may be influenced by factors such as health status that are largely secondary to religious concerns

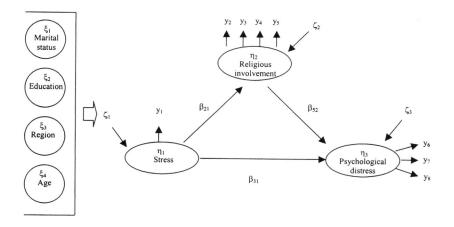

FIGURE 12.1 Conceptual Model of Nonorganizational Religious Involvement, Stressful Life Events and Psychological Well-being

ηs (etas) represent latent factors that the observed indicators (Y_i) are believed to represent.

γs (gammas) represent observed or measured indicators.

ζs (zetas) represent structural disturbance terms.

βs (betas) denote the relationships among the latent factors.

(Ellison and Gay 1990). Subjective religious involvement, often conceptualized as reflecting strength of religious commitment and self-attributions and identification as a religious person, may be less directly pertinent to questions of how religious factors are related to a person's experience of and effort to cope with stressful events and circumstances.

Non-organizational religious involvement, because it consists of devotional activities that can be performed privately and at the discretion of the individual, is presumed to be less directly influenced by extraneous factors (e.g., health, social expectations, community norms). Consequently, non-organizational religious involvement is a more suitable behavioral indicator of personal religious commitment than is organizational religious involvement. Further, non-organizational religious involvement reflects a group of devotional behaviors (e.g., prayer, reading religious materials) that are often cited in the literature in relation to coping with life problems and stresses (e.g., Ellison and Taylor 1996). As such, they are likely to be especially relevant in relation to the stressful life conditions and events that respondents report experiencing.

A select group of exogenous factors (i.e., age, marital status, education, and region) are identified as control variables in the model. On the basis of previous research, we expect that older and married women will report fewer stressors (Chatters 1988) but demonstrate higher levels of both non-organizational religious involvement (Chatters and Taylor 1989) and psychological well-being (Chatters 1988; Ellison and Gay 1990). Women residing in the South (as compared to women living outside the South) and those with higher levels of education will report fewer stressors (Chatters 1988) and higher levels of non-organizational religious involvement (Chatters and Taylor 1989). Previous research is equivocal concerning expectations for educational and regional influences on psychological well-being. Analyses involving the NSBA data set (Chatters 1988; Levin, Chatters, and Taylor 1995) and findings from three national surveys (Levin and Chatters 1998) failed to find significant effects for education on overall assessments of well-being. Consequently, no specific predictions are made concerning the effects of region and education on well-being.

METHODS

DATA

Analyses for this study are based on data from the National Survey of Black Americans (NSBA). The NSBA sample was developed by the Survey Research Center, Institute for Social Research at the University of Michigan and is the first nationally representative cross-section of the adult (18 years and older) Black population living in the continental United States. One adult member of each selected household was then chosen for interviewing. This sampling procedure resulted in 2,107 completed interviews collected in 1979 and 1980, representing a response rate of nearly 70 percent. The demographic distribution of the NSBA sample is comparable to that of the general African American population (see Jackson and Hatchett 1986). The sample consisted of 1,236 women who ranged in age from 18 to 101 years with a mean of 43.10 years ($SD = 17.52$). Mean education was 10.90 years ($SD = 3.30$), 35 percent were married, and 53.6 percent resided in the South.

CONFIRMATORY FACTOR ANALYSIS

All analyses were conducted using covariance matrices as input and the maximum likelihood estimator in LISREL 8.51 (Jîreskog and Sîrbom 2001). Results of a series of preliminary confirmatory factor analyses conducted for each latent construct (not shown) indicate that items clearly reflect the underlying construct included in the model. Table 12.1 presents the item descriptions and standardized factor loadings, along with the measurement error estimate next to each item. The factor loadings provide useful information regarding the psychometric properties of the indicators. Although there are no firmly established guidelines regarding cutoff points, the general consensus is that items above .40 have acceptable psychometric properties (e.g., Liang 1986). The data in table 12.1 reveal that individual factor loadings were moderate to high in magnitude, ranging from .539 to .921.

MEASURES

Psychological well-being, the outcome variable, is a three-item construct consisting of assessments of life satisfaction, happiness, and attainment of life goals (table 12.1). This factor has been used in previous research on older African Americans (Levin, Chatters, and Taylor 1995). *Religious involvement* is represented by a four-item construct of non-organizational religiosity (e.g., the frequency of devotional activity) that includes reading religious books or other materials, watching or listening to religious programs, frequency of prayer, and requests for prayer (table 12.1). Higher values on this construct correspond to higher levels of devotional activity.

Stressful life events is measured using a ten-item checklist containing negative or undesirable events. Respondents were asked to report whether they had experienced any of the following events: health problems, money problems, job problems, family or marriage problems, problems with non-family members, problems with children, with the police, with your love life, with crime, and with racism; each reported stressful event was given a score of 1. Previous research indicates that weighting of life events does not increase the amount of variance explained by measures of stress (e.g., Krause and Tran 1989). Consequently, life events were not weighted by the perceived impact of the event. A summary score was created by summing the number of events reported by each respondent. A high score indicates that the respondent experienced a greater number of stressful events.

TABLE 12.1 Factor Loadings of Observed Indicators

ITEM DESCRIPTIONS	FACTOR LOADINGS	ERROR TERMS
η_1 y_1 Stressful life events[a]	.921	.151
η_2 Nonorganizational religious involvement[b]		
y_2 Religious materials	.708	.499
y_3 Religious programming	.556	.690
y_4 Prayer	.851	.277
y_5 Requests for prayer	.539	.709
η_3 Psychological well-being		
y_6 Life satisfaction[c]	.660	.565
y_7 Happiness[d]	.687	.528
y_8 Attainment of life goals[e]	.768	.411

Notes: Standardized factor loadings; the first item was constrained to 1.0 in the metric solution.
[a] This item was a summary score of 10 items.
[b] These items were scored in the following manner: nearly every day (5), at least once a week (4), a few times a month (3), a few times a year (2), never (1).
[c] This item was scored in the following manner: very satisfied (4), somewhat satisfied (3), somewhat dissatisfied (2), dissatisfied (1).
[d] This item was scored in the following manner: very happy (3), pretty happy (2), not too happy (1).
[e] This item was scored in the following manner: gotten mostly what hoped for (2), gotten less than hoped for (1).

The stress measure was assumed to be measured imperfectly and, therefore, its reliability was set to be .70 on the basis of previous research (e.g., Krause and Tran 1989). Previous research also informed estimation of the influence of the demographic variables (Levin, Chatters, and Taylor 1995; U.S. Bureau of the Census 1975) on nonorganizational religious involvement and psychological well-being. This is a commonly used technique and provides a more accurate assessment of the effects of the demographic variables, since it is not assumed that age, education, or marital status is perfectly measured. Region is an ecologically coded variable, therefore its reliability is set at 1.0. It is recognized that the reliability estimates were obtained from previous research and not from the NSBA. Therefore, while the estimates may not be precise, they are believed to be preferable to estimates that assume perfect measurement.

RESULTS

On average, African American women had high levels of religious involvement and psychological well-being. Each religious involvement indicator ranged from 1 to 5. Respondents had mean scores of 3.61 for reading religious materials ($SD = 1.23$), 3.71 for watching religious programming ($SD = 1.12$), 4.40 for engaging in prayer ($SD = .80$), and 2.84 for requesting prayer ($SD = 1.37$). Average scores were 3.02 for life satisfaction (range = 1–4; $SD = .83$), 1.61 for happiness (range = 1–2; $SD = .49$), and 2.11 for attainment of life goals (range = 1–3; $SD = .65$). Table 12.2 presents the completely standardized maximum likelihood parameter estimates for the proposed model. According to the various fit indices computed, the proposed model fits the data quite well; X^2 (38, $N = 1,236$) = 197.719, GFI = .974, AGFI = .948, NFI = .948, NNFI = .926, CFI = .958, RMSEA = .058, SRMR = .035, and CN = 382.433.

The results reveal that, as predicted, stress has a significant influence on psychological well-being. Specifically, the findings indicate that as exposure to the number of stressors increases, African American women experience a decrease in psychological well-being (*beta* = -.552; $p < .001$). The data also indicate that religious involvement may play an important role in bolstering a sense of well-being. Particularly strong effects were observed between non-organizational religious involvement and psychological well-being, suggesting that higher levels of non-organizational religious involvement are associated with higher levels of psychological well-being (*beta* = .168; $p < .01$).

Although the influence of the exogenous variables on stress, non-organizational religious involvement, and psychological well-being is not the specific focus of this investigation, it provides important information on how social location influences these factors. These results indicate that age is associated with stress, religious involvement, and psychological well-being. That is, older African American women are exposed to fewer stressors (*beta* = −.397; $p < .001$), but report higher levels of non-organizational religious involvement (*beta* = .527; $p < .001$), which results in higher levels of psychological well-being. Education is also associated with exposure to stress, indicating that higher levels of education are associated with lower levels of exposure to stress (*beta* = −.143; $p < .01$). Marital status is significantly associated with all three latent constructs. Specifically, African American women who are married experience less exposure to life stressors (*beta* = −.128; $p < .05$) and have higher levels of non-organizational religious involvement (*beta* = .125; $p < .01$) and psychological well-being (*beta* = .299; $p < .001$). Finally, region is significantly associated with stress, religious involvement, and psychological well-being. Specifically, African American women who live in

TABLE 12.2 Completely Standardized Exogenous Effects of the Proposed Model

| | ENDOGENOUS CONSTRUCTS | | |
EXOGENOUS CONSTRUCTS	STRESS	NONORGANIZATIONAL INVOLVEMENT	WELL-BEING
Marital Status[a]			
Direct	−.128*	.132**	.206***
Indirect	.000	−.007	.093**
Total	−.128*	.125**	.299***
Education[b]			
Direct	−.143**	−.006	−.022
Indirect	.000	−.008	.078*
Total	−.143**	−.014	.056
Region[c]			
Direct	.154**	−.185***	−.040
Indirect	.000	.009	−.116***
Total	.154**	−.176***	−.156**
Age[b]			
Direct	−.397***	.549***	.076
Indirect	.000	−.022	.311***
Total	−.397***	.527***	.388***

ENDOGENOUS CONSTRUCTS			
Stress			
Direct		.056	−.562***
Indirect		.000	.009
Total		.056	−.552***
Nonorganizational			
Direct			.168**
Indirect			.000
Total			.168**

* $p < .05$; ** $p < .01$; *** $p < .001$
[a] Marital status is coded in the following manner: 1 = married; 0 = other.
[b] Education and age are coded continuously in years.
[c] Region is coded in the following manner: 0 = South; 1 = other.

regions outside of the South (as compared to Southerners) experience more exposure to life stressors (*beta* = .154; $p < .01$), while demonstrating lower levels of non-organizational religious involvement (*beta* = -.176; $p < .001$), which results in lower levels of psychological well-being (*beta* = $-.156, p < .01$).

DISCUSSION

The purpose of this study was to clarify the relationships among stress, religious involvement, and psychological well-being within a national sample of African American women. The use of a precise measure of religious involvement and the testing of a particular theoretical model helped to identify the potential role of religion in the stress process. The findings verified that experienced life stressors have detrimental consequences for the psychological well-being of African American women. The findings also indicated, however, that African American women who are more involved in non-organizational religious pursuits experience higher levels of psychological well-being than Black women who are less involved. It is important to emphasize that because the study examined private religious behaviors only, no statements can be made about the relative importance of other forms of religious involvement (i.e., church attendance) for psychological well-being among Black women. It is significant, however, that these private forms of religious activity were important for a sense of well-being.

The positive association between religious involvement and psychological well-being can be interpreted in several ways. First, religion may provide a framework that African American women use to interpret stressful situations. When faced with serious problems (i.e., illness, death of a loved one), Black women may view the stressful event as evidence of God's will or of a divine plan (e.g., Pargament 1997). While the exact meaning and purpose of personal suffering and difficulties may not be readily apparent, Black women may derive comfort from the personal conviction that their ultimate significance will be revealed in time. Religious teachings often highlight the personal suffering of biblical figures and their efforts (both secular and religious) to comprehend and overcome difficult and challenging circumstances. Further, one of the largest categories of popular religious literature is that of inspirational readings. Involvement in private religious practices (e.g., prayer, devotional readings) may provide Black women the opportunity to reflect upon the nature of their problems and place these occurrences within an explicitly religious context.

Alternatively, religious involvement may positively influence the psychological well-being of African American women because it embodies a set of attitudes, beliefs, and activities that instill a sense of value and self-worth. Ellison (1993) found a positive association between self-esteem and private devotional activities (e.g., prayer, reading religious materials, watching religious programming, Bible study), suggesting that these types of activities may foster feelings of self-worth by bolstering feelings of being loved and cared for by God. It may be that private religious activities reinforce and maintain a positive sense of self among African American women that then influences their psychological well-being.

Contrary to expectations, there was no significant indirect effect of stress on psychological well-being through private religious involvement (Krause and Tran 1989). Apparently, private religious practices (e.g., prayer, reading religious materials) do not mediate the impact of stress on psychological well-being among Black women. There are several possible explanations for this finding. First, the particular stressors included in this investigation may be less amenable to religious frameworks and coping. Related to this, it could be that the cross-sectional nature of the data does not allow for the emergence of long-term patterns of adjustment. In essence, a single "snapshot" of the life stressors facing Black women may not be sufficient to understand the potential role that private religious behaviors play in addressing these difficulties on an ongoing basis.

Finally, perhaps private religious practices do not mediate the effects of stress on well-being but, in fact, have independent effects on well-being. Along these lines, the findings demonstrated that stress had a strong negative influence on Black women's psychological well-being, while religious involvement was positively associated with well-being (apparently independent of the level of exposure to stress). Consequently, for Black women, the positive effect of non-organizational religious involvement may potentially counterbalance or offset the negative effect of stress on psychological well-being. Additional research is needed to further clarify the capabilities of different dimensions of religious involvement (e.g., organizational and subjective forms of religiosity) to mediate the effects of stress.

The pattern of findings for the effects of exogenous factors on stress, religious involvement, and psychological well-being are largely consistent with previous research. This analysis found that among African American women, those who were older, unmarried, and resided in the South were more involved in religious pursuits than their counterparts. Interestingly, although women with higher levels of education experienced fewer life stressors, they were no different from less-educated women with respect to psychological well-being (Chatters 1988). Black women who were unmarried reported fewer life stressors and overall higher levels of well-being than did married women. Finally, Southern women experienced fewer stressors than African American women who resided in other regions, and consequently, Southern women had higher levels of well-being.

The results of this investigation must be viewed within the context of the study's limitations. First, the use of cross-sectional data limits the ability to determine the causal direction in the tested model. Clarification of the causal relationships among the model components is critical for understanding the role of religion in coping with life stresses. Second, although the study employed specific measures of non-organizational religious involvement in the model, we can only speculate as to the meaning these activities have for African American women. In particular, despite an assumption that private religious behaviors of this sort are important for addressing stressful life problems, there is little direct evidence concerning what African American women actually do in stressful circumstances, the timing and sequencing of their efforts, the relationship of these activities to their overall coping strategy, and the bearing that their efforts have on the course of the stressful situation.

This analysis moved beyond the conventional analysis of direct and indirect effects and addressed conceptual and theoretical limitations of current research on religion and mental health. The role of religion in the stress process has been interpreted in the literature in a variety of ways (e.g., stress-preventive, stress-buffering, direct effects). Given this diversity, it is important that studies of the relationships among stress, religious involvement, and mental health be grounded in and formally test explicit theoretical frameworks. Conceptual clarity is necessary in order to identify and operationalize the specific mechanisms through which religion affects the stress–mental health relationship.

Finally, this analysis represented an initial attempt to test a specific model of the interrelationships among stress, private religious involvement, and psychological well-being among African American women. Future research would benefit from the development and employment of more-precise measures of religion, particularly those that take into account various dimensions of religious involvement (i.e., organizational, subjective). More generally, research examining the role of religion in the stress process should be concerned with what is the natural course of coping, with specific attention to measures that explicitly tap into diverse types of coping strategies and multiple assessments of the consequences of religious coping efforts (e.g., well-being, depression). These and other studies would contribute to under-standing the unique place of religious involvement in the lives of African American women.

REFERENCES

Batson, C. D., P. Schoenrade, and W. L. Ventis. 1993. *Religion and the Individual: A Social Psychological Perspective*. New York: Oxford University Press.

Bearon, L. B. and H. G. Koenig. 1990. Religion cognitions and use of prayer in health and illness. *Gerontologist* 30:249–253.

Beit-Hallahmi, B. and M. Argyle. 1997. *The Psychology of Religious Belief, Behaviour, and Experience*. London: Routledge.

Bergan, A. and J. T. McConatha. 2000. Religiosity and life satisfaction. *Activities, Adaptation, and Aging* 24:23–34.

Capps, D. 1990. *Reframing: A New Method in Pastoral Care*. Minneapolis: Fortress Press.

Chalfant, H. P., P. L. Heller, A. Roberts, D. Briones, S. Aguirre-Hochbaum, and W. Farr. 1990. The clergy as a resource for those encountering psychological distress. *Review of Religious Research* 31:305–313.

Chang, B. H., K. M. Skinner, and U. Boehmer. 2001. Religion and mental health among women veterans with sexual assault experience. International Journal of Psychiatry in Medicine. Special Issue. *Biopsychosocial Aspects of Patient Care* 31:77–95.

Chatters, L. M. 1988. Subjective well-being evaluations among older Black Americans. *Psychology and Aging* 3:184–190.

———. 2000. Religion and health: Public health research and practice. *Annual Review of Public Health* 21:335–367.

Chatters, L. M., J. S. Levin, and C. G. Ellison. 1998. Public health and health education in faith communities. *Health Education and Behavior* 25:689–699.

Chatters, L. M. and R. J. Taylor. 1989. Life problems and coping strategies of older Black adults. *Social Work* 34:313–319.

Coleman, S., J. Kaplan, and R. Downing. 1986. Life cycle and loss: The spiritual vacuum of heroin addiction. *Family Process* 25:5–23.

de Vaus, D. and I. McAllister. 1987. Gender differences in religion: A test of the structural location theory. *American Sociological Review* 52:472–481.

Ellison, C. G. 1993. Religious involvement and self-perception among Black Americans. *Social Forces* 71:1027–1055.

Ellison, C. G. and D. A. Gay. 1990. Region, religious commitment, and life satisfaction among Black Americans. *Sociological Quarterly* 31:123–147.

Ellison, C. G., D. A. Gay, and T. A. Glass. 1989. Does religious commitment contribute to individual life satisfaction? *Social Forces* 68:100–123.

Ellison, C. G. and R. J. Taylor. 1996. Turning to prayer: Social and situational antecedents of religious coping among African Americans. *Review of Religious Research* 31:111–131.

Handal, P. J., W. Black-Lopez, and S. Moergen. 1989. Preliminary investigation of the relationship between religion and psychological distress in Black women. *Psychological Reports* 65:971–975.

Idler, E. L. and S. V. Kasl. 1997. Religion among disabled and nondisabled persons. II. Attendance at religious services as predictors of the course of disability. *Journal of Gerontology: Social Sciences* 52B:S306–S316.

Jackson, J. S. and S. J. Hatchett. 1986. Intergenerational Research: Methodological Considerations. In N. Datan, A. L. Greene, and H. W. Reese, eds., *Intergenerational Relations*, 51–75. Hillsdale, N.J.: Erlbaum.

Jenkins, R. 1992. Toward a Psychosocial Conceptualization of Religion as a Resource in Cancer Care and Prevention. In K. Pargament, K. Maton, and R. E. Hess, eds., *Religion and Prevention in Mental Health: Research, Vision, and Action*, 179–194. New York: Haworth.

Jöreskog, K. G. and D. Sörbom. 2001. *LISREL 8.51 User's Reference Guide*. Chicago: Scientific Software.

Koenig, H. G. 1994. *Aging and God: Spiritual Pathways to Mental Health in Midlife and Later Years*. New York: Haworth.

Koenig, H. G., K. I. Pargament, and J. Nielsen. 1998. Religious coping and health status in medically ill hospitalized older adults. *Journal of Nervous and Mental Disease* 186:513–521.

Krause, N. 1992. Stress, religiosity, and psychological well-being among older Blacks. *Journal of Aging and Health* 4:412–439.

Krause, N. and T. V. Tran. 1989. Stress and religious involvement among older Blacks. *Journal of Gerontology: Social Sciences* 44:S4–S13.

Levin, J. S. and L. M. Chatters. 1998. Religion, health, and psychological well-being in older adults: Findings from three national surveys. *Journal of Aging and Health* 10:504–531.

Levin, J. S., L. M. Chatters, C. G. Ellison, and R. J. Taylor. 1996. Religious involvement, health outcomes, and public health practice. *Current Issues in Public Health* 2:220–225.

Levin, J. S., L. M. Chatters, and R. J. Taylor. 1995. Religious effects on health status and life satisfaction among Black Americans. *Journal of Gerontology: Social Sciences* 50B:S154–S163.

Levin, J. S. and P. L. Schiller. 1987. Is there a religious factor in health? *Journal of Religion and Health* 26:9–35.

Levin, J. S., R. J. Taylor, and L. M. Chatters. 1995. A multidimensional measure of religious involvement for African Americans. *Sociological Quarterly* 36:157–173.

Levin, J. S. and H. Y. Vanderpool. 1992. Religious Factors in Physical Health and the Prevention of Illness. In K. I. Pargament, K. I. Maton, and R. E. Hess, eds., *Religion and Prevention in Mental Health: Research, Vision, and Action*, 83–103. New York: Haworth.

Liang, J. 1986. Self-reported physical health among aged adults. *Journal of Gerontology* 41:248–260.

Markides, K. S., J. S. Levin, and L. A. Ray. 1987. Religion, aging, and life satisfaction: An eight-year, three-wave longitudinal study. *Gerontologist* 27:660–665.

Mattlin, J. A., E. Wethington, and R. C. Kessler. 1990. Situational determinants of coping and coping effectiveness. *Journal of Health and Social Behavior* 31:103–122.

McIntosh, D. N., R. C. Silver, and C. B. Wortman. 1993. Religion's role in adjustment to a negative life event: Coping with the loss of a child. *Journal of Personality and Social Psychology* 65:812–821.

Ortega, S., R. D. Crutchfield, and W. A. Rushing. 1983. Race differences in elderly personal well-being: Friendship, family, and church. *Research on Aging* 4:101–117.

Oxman, T. E., D. H. Freedman, and E. D. Manheimer. 1995. Lack of social participation or religious strength and comfort as risk factors after cardiac surgery in the elderly. *Psychosomatic Medicine* 57:5–15.

Pargament, K. I. 1995. "In the Dust of Our Trials: Methods of Religious Coping with Major Life Stressors." Paper presented at the American Psychosomatic Society, New Orleans.

———. 1997. *The Psychology of Religion and Coping: Theory, Research, Practice.* New York: Guilford.

Pargament, K. I., D. S. Ensing, K. Falgout, H. Olsen, B. Reilly, K. Van Haitsma, and R. Warren. 1990. God help me. I. Religious coping efforts as predictors of the outcomes to significant negative life events. *American Journal of Community Psychology* 18:793–824.

Pargament, K. I., H. Olsen, B. Reilly, K. Falgout, D. S. Ensing, and K. Van Haitsma. 1992. God help me. II. The relationship of religious orientations to religious coping with negative life events. *Journal for the Scientific Study of Religion* 31:504–513.

Pargament, K. I., B. W. Smith, H. G. Koenig, and L. Perez. 1998. Patterns of positive and negative coping with major life stressors. *Journal for the Scientific Study of Religion* 37:710–724.

Payne, I. R., A. E. Bergin, K. A. Bielema, and P. H. Jenkins. 1992. Review of religion and mental health: Prevention and the enhancement of psychosocial functioning. In K. I. Pargament, K. K. Maton, and R. E. Hess, eds., *Religion and Prevention in Mental Health: Research, Vision, and Action,* 57–82. New York: Haworth.

Pressman, P., J. S. Lyons, D. B. Larson, and J. J. Strain. 1990. Religious belief, depression, and ambulation status in elderly women with broken hips. *American Journal of Psychiatry* 147:758–760.

Shaver, P., M. Lenauer, and S. Sadd. 1980. Religiousness, conversion, and subjective well-being: The "healthy-minded" religion of modern American women. *American Journal of Psychiatry* 137:1563–1568.

Thornton, M. C., L. M. Chatters, R. J. Taylor, and W. R. Allen. 1990. Sociodemographic and environmental correlates of racial socialization by black parents. *Child Development* 61:401–409.

U.S. Bureau of the Census. 1975. *1970 Census of Population and Housing: Evaluation and Research Program. Vol. 2, Accuracy of Data for Selected Population Characteristics as Measured by the 1970 CPS-Census Match.* Washington, D.C.: U.S. Government Printing Office.

Veroff, J., E. Douvan, and R. A. Kulka. 1981. *The Inner American: A Self-Portrait from 1957 to 1976.* New York: Basic Books.

Williams, D. R., D. B. Larson, R. E. Buckler, R. C. Heckmann, and C. M. Pyle. 1991. Religion and psychological distress in a community sample. *Social Science and Medicine* 32:1257–1262.

13 THE BENEFITS AND COSTS OF SOCIAL SUPPORT FOR AFRICAN AMERICAN WOMEN

Beverly A. Gray and Verna M. Keith

African American women play an essential role in the maintenance of complex systems of kin and non-kin networks in the
Black community. The provision of social support is a major
function of these network systems, and researchers have shown that support,
especially emotional support, contributes to the ability of African American
women to lead satisfying and emotionally healthy lives (Brown and Gary 1987;
Dressler 1991; McAdoo 1980). Social support appears to be especially salient
for maintaining good mental health during times of great stress and turmoil.
Indeed, studies of African Americans generally (Dressler 1991), and African
American women specifically (Brown and Gary 1987), show that ongoing life
problems and stressful life events are less detrimental to psychological well-
being when support levels are high. Voluntary organizations, especially the
church, are also an important part of social networks and are a major source
of social support (Taylor and Chatters 1988), especially among Black women.
It is well established that Black women tend to be more heavily involved in
church activities and other organizations than Black men are (Lincoln and
Mamiya 1990). Further, studies have linked religious involvement to feelings
of emotional well-being (e.g., Ellison and Gay 1990), although some variations by age and social class have been reported (Dressler 1991).

Social support, however, can be a double-edged sword, as Neighbors (1997)
points out. On the one hand, it can be positive and helpful. On the other hand,
it can be negative, harmful, or nonexistent. The negative, and conversely the
positive, aspects of social support are a function of the personal characteristics
and qualities of the persons who are members of individual social networks
(Suls 1982). The size and complexity of many network systems make it likely
that the individuals who provide support at any given time are the very same
individuals who are the source of stress at some later time. Consequently,
researchers increasingly recognize that social relationships have costs as well

as benefits for African American women (Boyd-Franklin 1987; Carrington 1980; Gray 1986; McCray 1980; Neighbors 1997). Our understanding of how and to what extent these costs affect African American women's mental health remains under-explored.

This investigation begins by reviewing findings about the African American woman's social networks of immediate and extended family, friendships, and community/social organizations and the support that they provide. A major goal is to evaluate empirically the effects of supportive and problematic aspects of social relationships on African American women's mental health. The consequences of participation in voluntary organizations for women's mental health are also examined. A second goal is to evaluate the degree to which supportive interactions with network members and social participation protect Black women from the detrimental psychological effects of life stress and the extent to which problematic interactions intensify the effects of stressors.

SOURCES OF SUPPORT FOR AFRICAN AMERICAN WOMEN

Traditionally, research on the support systems of African Americans placed much emphasis on the support provided by immediate and extended family (Myers 1980). Brown and Gary (1985) reported family and extended kin as the primary source of social support for both married and unmarried African American women, although less than a third of the married women cited their spouse as a source of support. Family members, often residing in separate households, share economic resources and information, assist one another with shopping and meal preparation, share services such as child care and transportation, and make members feel loved and cared for.

The importance of friends in the informal network systems of African Americans is also well documented (McAdoo 1980; Myers 1980; Stack 1974; Taylor, Chatters, and Jackson 1997). Friends are more likely to be a source of emotional support, while the family is more likely to provide financial assistance (Taylor, Chatters, and Jackson 1997). Allen and Britt (1983) report that an invaluable source of support for African American women is that which is derived from the friendships they share with other Black women. Similarly, hooks (1993), who developed supportive groups such as "sisters of the Yam," documents the positive impact of female friendships among African American women. Denton (1990) investigated how African American women's friendship networks contributed to personal growth, contrasting other-oriented (i.e., asymmetrical) and self-enhancing (i.e., reciprocal) relationships. Denton (1990:454) concluded that "quantitative data show that self-enhancing relationships provided higher levels of all types of benefits (social companionship, instrumental help, and supportiveness) to study participants."

Voluntary social organizations are an integral part of the African American community, having been born out of "collectivist" strategies for community and individual survival (Higginbotham and Weber 1996; Stack 1974). Historically, African American women have been active organizers and participants in numerous Black civic, social, and religious organizations (Hine 1993; Sterling 1988). Ralston (1997:276) states: "Black women's sociohistory also shows a collective industriousness and a desire for individual, family, and community development, as demonstrated by their progress in educational attainment and their work to enhance community well-being." Black churches, an integral part of this participatory tradition, are an especially important source of support (Taylor and Chatters 1988; Taylor, Chatters, and Jackson 1997). After family and friends, the church and clergy are important as support systems for women, and Black women tend to be more involved than Black men are (Myers 1980; Ralston 1997).

STRESS, SUPPORTIVE SOCIAL RELATIONSHIPS, AND MENTAL HEALTH

Numerous studies of the relationship between life stress and mental health have investigated the role that social support plays in protecting individuals from the detrimental effects of stressors (Turner and Marino 1994; Pearlin 1999). Social support may be particularly important for African American women, who are disproportionately exposed to both primary and secondary stressors (Pearlin 1999) because of higher rates of poverty, unemployment, underemployment, and a greater likelihood of residing in neighborhoods characterized by crime and other social problems. For example, job loss, a primary stressor, may lead to losing health insurance and the inability to access health care in a timely manner, a secondary stressor. Social support may protect individuals from the harmful effects of stressors in two ways (Cohen and Wills 1985). First, social support can have an effect on mental health that is independent of the number and chronicity of stressors to which an individual has been exposed. This direct relationship, or main effects model, suggests that people who perceive that they have high levels of emotional support are less likely to become depressed, while those with low levels of support are more likely to become depressed. Second, the effects of stressors on well-being may vary by level of support. According to this buffering hypothesis, stress has less impact when support levels are high.

Studies of stress, support, and mental health among African Americans have yielded mixed findings. Some show support for the main effects model, while others show a buffering effect. In a study of depressive symptoms, Brown and Gary (1987) found direct and buffering effects for perceived extended-family support, but only among African American females. Warren (1997) found a direct, inverse relationship between social support and depressive symptoms among middle-class African American women. Similarly, Sloan, Addlesperger, and Jason (1996) reported on the social networks of single Black and Hispanic inner-city women and found that social support from friends resulted in fewer psychological and physical health problems. Dressler (1991), reporting findings from his study of a Southern Black community, found that direct and buffering effects varied by age, socioeconomic status, stressor, and source of support under consideration.

Some research has also addressed the issue of whether affiliations with voluntary organizations and religious involvement moderate the stress-distress relationship. As with findings for social support, studies have yielded inconsistent findings. Dressler (1991) found that an index of cultural resources, which included religious involvement, buffered the effects of stressors for at least some subsets of his Southern African American sample. Neff and Husaini (1982) found that stressful life events had the strongest effects on depressive symptoms among those who were least religious. Brown and colleagues (1992) reported nonsignificant effects for affiliation with voluntary social organizations. In addition, higher religious involvement intensified depressive symptoms among those experiencing economic strain, suggesting that economic hardship may have motivated respondents to turn toward the church. Understanding of the moderating role of affiliation with voluntary organizations among African American women remains fairly limited.

PROBLEMATIC SOCIAL RELATIONSHIPS AND MENTAL HEALTH

Interactions with network members can be negative, problematic, and costly to psychological well-being (Gray 1986; Horwitz, McLaughlin, and White 1998; Okun and Keith 1998; Rook 2001). This is especially the case for Black women, who appear to be much more deeply embedded in social networks than males are. Based on data from the National Survey of Black Americans, Neighbors (1997) reported that family and friends were the most important source of social support, and that all types of problems are taken to the informal network of family and friends. Nevertheless, relationships with family and friends also were sources of stress when loved ones faced

246 KEEPING ON … KEEPING ON

stressful situations or when relationships with loved ones were conflictual or difficult. Neighbors also found that women were more likely than men to report an interpersonal problem as causing a great deal of stress. In addition, women reported more stress from family-related problems resulting from concern for family members' problems or conflictual relationships.

The negative aspects of social relations may stem from African American women's involvement in multiple roles and from the sense of obligation that results from being recipients of support. The family roles of the African American woman, like those of all women, are defined in terms of her relationship to others; she is the wife, mother, grandmother, daughter, sister, aunt, niece, cousin, daughter-in-law, and godparent who nurtures immediate-family and extended-family members. This is especially true if she is the oldest sibling, has the most education, or has the most financial resources. She often has the task of maintaining family ties and traditions. Thus, she often mediates disputes, allocates duties and responsibilities to other family members, and listens to the problems of others—all of which may be stressful for her. Boyd-Franklin (1987:398) observed, on the basis of three therapy support groups that consisted of a cross-section of African American women: "Many Black women feel so absorbed by duties and responsibilities in the nuclear and extended family they have little emotional energy for themselves. This pattern, once established within the family of origin, can be repeated within count-less new relationships unless it is checked and changed."

Carrington (1980) argues that this sense of obligation to the social network contributes to depression in Black women because it leads them to put energy into others and not to engage in any self-enhancement. Similarly, Ralston (1997) suggests that the cumulative effect of the multiple roles performed by Black women and their social environment contributes to their higher risk of chronic disease and other health problems as compared to White women and men of both races. Although often stereotyped as the strong, self-sufficient female who is responsible for the survival of the entire Black family (McCray 1980), African American women may be at high risk for both mental and physical health problems owing to these many demands.

In addition to family demands and conflicts, the African American professional/career or semiprofessional woman often expends more time and energy on professional and community activities than her White peers do. Previous and current professional discrimination, as well as de facto social segregation, has led to the development of parallel African American organizations within any given profession (e.g., the American Medical Association and the National Medical Association; the American Psychological Association and the Association of Black Psychologists). Black women participate in these parallel organizations as well as in majority organizations, an investment that entails many demands on their time. Thus, the gains in psychological well-being derived from participation in social organizations may be partially offset by being overcommitted.

SYMMETRY IN SOCIAL SUPPORT

The balance between supportive and problematic aspects of social support may be more important for mental health than either considered separately (Horwitz, McLaughlin, and White 1998). Information on the symmetrical nature of African American women's support systems is limited. In their study of Black and White professional managerial women from working- and middle-class backgrounds, Higginbotham and Weber (1996) found that almost half of Black women from stable middle-class backgrounds felt that there was equity or reciprocity in family relationships. Where imbalance existed, 48 percent felt they had received more than they had given. However, almost a third of the Black women from working-class backgrounds felt they had given their families more than they had received. Although these researchers found a general pattern of equity in the friendships of the women in their study, Black women were more likely than White women to feel that they gave more than they received in their friendships. Denton (1990) also documented "other-oriented" or asymmetrical relationships whereby Black women reported that their friend received more support than was returned. While Denton did evaluate symmetry in relationship to personal growth, neither study investigated more traditional mental health outcomes.

This study assesses the impact of symmetry in social relationships on African American women's mental health. The effects of symmetry are contrasted with the effects of social participation and supportive and problematic interactions with network members. Each dimension of social support is assessed for its potential to buffer chronic financial stress, a major problem among African American women owing to their higher poverty and near-poverty rates.

METHODS

SAMPLE

The data for this study were derived from the first wave of the Americans' Changing Lives Survey (House 1986). The survey consisted of face-to-face interviews with respondents drawn from a national probability sample. A total of 3,617 adults 18 and over residing in the United States were interviewed, for a response rate of 67 percent. This study included the 778 African American women who participated in the interviews and was weighted to account for the oversample of women over age 60.

MEASUREMENT

Depressive symptoms is the mental health outcome used in the study, and it is measured by using 11 of the 20 items that make up the Center for Epidemiologic Studies Depression (CES-D) Scale (Radloff 1977). These items are (1) felt depressed, (2) everything was an effort, (3) sleep restless, (4) happy (reverse coded) (5) people were unfriendly, (6) felt lonely, (7) enjoyed life (reverse coded), (8) appetite was poor, (9) felt sad, (10) felt people disliked me, and (11) could not get going. Responses were coded 1 for *hardly ever,* 2 for *some of the time,* and 3 *for most of the time.* The internal consistency reliability for the short CES-D was .84, with a mean of 16.94 and a standard deviation of 4.34.

Supportive and problematic aspects of social relations are assessed separately for five different network members—spouse, mother, father, children age 16 and older, and other friends and relatives. Supportive interactions with each network member are measured by asking respondents to indicate how much the specified network member (1) makes them feel loved and cared for and (2) is willing to listen when they need to talk about their worries or problems. Problematic social interactions with each source are measured using two items that ask respondents to indicate how often the referenced network member (1) makes too many demands and (2) is critical of them or what they do. Responses to both supportive and problematic items were coded on a five-point scale ranging from 1 = *not at all* to 5 = *a great deal.* For both supportive and problematic interactions, scores are summed across the five sources of support because 53 percent of respondents had no spouse, 31 percent had no mother, 54 percent had no father, and 39 percent had no children age 16 or older. Following Turner and Marino (1994), these scores were then adjusted by dividing them by the number of support sources available (supportive interactions mean = 8.21, SD = 1.39; problematic interactions mean = 3.83, SD = 1.49). The correlation between problematic and supportive relationships is −.27. Symmetry in supportive and problematic relationships is measured by subtracting problematic interactions from supportive interactions (mean = 4.38, SD = 2.28).

Social participation is measured using two items: (1) how often do you attend meetings of clubs and groups that you belong to? and (2) how often do you attend religious services? Responses ranged on a 6-point scale from 1 = *never,* to 6 = *more than once per week* (mean = 6.93, SD = 3.06). The correlation between the two items is .50.

Chronic financial strain is measured with three items assessing how difficult it is to pay monthly bills, with responses reversed-coded as 1 = *not difficult* to 5 = *extremely difficult;* satisfaction with financial situation, with responses ranging from 1 = *completely satisfied* to 5 = *not at all satisfied;* and money left over at the end of the month with responses coded as 1 = *some money left over*, 2 = *just enough money*, and 3 = *no money left*. The reliability coefficient for these items is .78. The sum of responses was averaged to account for the varying metrics of the scale items (mean = 7.38, SD = 2.64).

Control variables. Age is measured in years (mean = 47, SD = 16.10); marital status contrasts the married (44%) and unmarried (56%); and the employed (56%) are contrasted with those not working (44%). The number of respondents' children under 18 residing in the household is also included (mean = 1.47, SD = 1.45). Socioeconomic status (SES) is measured using a multiple-item index that is based on three components—occupation, income, and education (Nam and Powers 1983) (mean = 36.56, SD = 23.11). Current occupation is used for women currently employed, most recent occupation is used for those who are retired or are unemployed, and husband's occupation is used for women who have never worked. To tap into health problems, a Gutman-type scale was used to create four levels of (1) no disability (79%); (2) least severe disability, consisting of respondent's having experienced a lot of difficulty doing heavy housework or could not do it (6.7%); (3) moderately disabled, a category consisting of those who experienced a lot of difficulty climbing stairs or could not do it and/or had a lot of difficulty walking or could not do it (9.0%); and (4) most severe disability, consisting of those who were confined to bed or chair and/or who experienced a lot of difficulty bathing or could not bathe (5.4%). The mean for disability is 1.41 and the standard deviation is .86.

FINDINGS

DESCRIPTIVE RESULTS

Preliminary analyses (data not shown) indicate that just 4 percent of respondents report only one source in their social network, while 13 percent report all five sources—spouse, child, mother, father, and other friends and relatives. Only 25 percent of the women indicate that they have low participation in social and religious organizations, and depressive symptoms are significantly higher for those with low involvement. Consistent with past literature on social support among African American women, only 15 percent of respondents can be classified as having low levels of supportive interactions with network members, while 70 percent fall into the moderate range. Sixteen percent of the women indicate that their relationships are highly problematic. As expected, those with high levels of supportive interactions have the lowest level of depressive symptoms, while a clear incremental increase in symptoms results as interactions become more problematic. Women with low symmetry in supportive and problematic relationships have the highest risk of depression.

MULTIVARIATE RESULTS

Results from OLS regression analyses are presented in table 13.1, showing the net effects of financial strain, supportive and problematic relationships, social participation, and symmetry on depressive symptoms. In the interest of space, the data are organized by panels, with each panel presenting summary findings for financial strain and the support measures. However, the control variables are included in all equations. In each panel, main effects appear in Model 1, while statistical interaction effects appear in Model 2. Panel 1 presents the effects of financial strain and social participation net of all control variables. The results indicate that financial strain significantly increases depressive symptoms among African American women even when social participation is controlled. Yet symptoms are less severe for those who are active in civic and religious organizations. There is also a significant interaction effect between financial strain and social participation. The effect of financial strain on depressive symptoms is 2.03 when participation is low, 1.62 when average, and 1.20 when high (data not shown in Table 13.1). Although financial strain continues to exert a significant effect on depressive symptoms across all levels of participation, the effect is diminished, and stress buffering is supported.

Similar results are observed for the effects of supportive interactions in Panel 2. Women with higher levels of supportive interactions are less likely to be depressed (*beta* $= -.440$, $p \le .01$), and the interaction effect is significant and negative. The coefficients for low, average, and high levels of support are 1.81, 1.49, and 1.16, respectively. Each effect is significant, but the overall decrease across levels of support indicates that supportive relationships buffer the effects of financial strain. As expected, problematic interactions with network members are associated with increased symptoms (see Panel 3). The interaction effect, however, is not significant. Economic hardship has a detrimental effect on emotional well-being, but the effect does not vary by how demanding and critical network members are. When all three dimensions of support are considered in Panel 4, the results show that negative interactions (*beta* = .18, $p \le .01$) have a more robust effect on depressive symptoms than either social participation (*beta* = −.09, p ≤ .01) or supportive interactions (*beta* = −.08, $p \le .05$). Interaction effects are not significant when entered as a block (data not shown).

As symmetry in relationships becomes increasingly positive, the risk of depression decreases (Panel 5). Symmetry also moderates the relationship between financial strain and symptoms. The effect of financial strain on symptoms is 1.79 when symmetry is low, 1.43 when symmetry is average, and 1.07 when symmetry is high, evidence of a buffering effect (data not presented in table 13.1). Following Horwitz, McLaughlin, and White (1998), symmetry is assessed controlling for both supportive (Panel 6) and problematic (Panel 7) relations, respectively. Social participation is also included in both equations. Consistent with Horwitz et al. (1998), the results show that the symmetrical nature of social interactions has a greater impact on depressive symptoms than either supportive interactions or problematic interactions. In sum, what is most important for African American women's mental health is the overall balance in social relationships.

DISCUSSION AND CONCLUSIONS

This study sought to investigate the benefits and costs of social support for African American women's mental health. The findings reveal that participation in voluntary organizations and having family and friends who make one feel loved and nurtured are associated with lower levels of depressive symptoms. Moreover, these supportive resources offer protection against the potentially devastating effects of chronic economic problems. The effects of financial strain are increasingly attenuated as organizational involvement and supportive interaction increase. Thus, consistent with findings reported by Brown and Gary (1987) and Dressler (1991), these resources buffer the effects of stress and point to the beneficial aspect of social support. Problematic social relations have the opposite effect in that they are costly for African American women's mental health. Black women who feel that their network members are critical and demanding are more likely to report depressive symptoms. Contrary to expectations, however, problematic relationships with friends and relatives do not intensify the effects of

TABLE 13.1 Regression of Depressive Symptoms on Financial Strain and Support

PANEL 1—EFFECTS OF FINANCIAL STRAIN AND SOCIAL PARTICIPATION[a]

	MODEL 1—MAIN EFFECTS		MODEL 2—INTERACTION EFFECTS	
	BETA	B	BETA	B
Financial strain (FS)	.330	1.655***	.323	1.617***
Social participation (SP)	−.115	−.166***	−.117	−.168***
FS x SP			−.083	−.137*
R^2 adjusted	.195		.201	

PANEL 2—FINANCIAL STRAIN AND SUPPORTIVE INTERACTIONS[a]

	MODEL 1—MAIN EFFECTS		MODEL 2—INTERACTION EFFECTS	
	BETA	B	BETA	B
Financial strain (FS)	.303	1.520***	.298	.493***
Supportive interactions (SI)	−.440	−.137**	−.123	−.395**
FS x SI			−.074	−.242*
R^2 adjusted	.210		.215	

PANEL 3—FINANCIAL STRAIN AND PROBLEMATIC INTERACTIONS[a]

	MODEL 1—MAIN EFFECTS		MODEL 2—INTERACTION EFFECTS	
	BETA	B	BETA	B
Financial strain (FS)	.296	1.485***	.3061	.535***
Problematic interactions (PI)	.608	.205***	.194	.575***
FS x PI			.056	.197
R^2	.228		.231	

PANEL 4—FINANCIAL STRAIN, SOCIAL PARTICIPATION, AND SUPPORTIVE AND PROBLEMATIC INTERACTIONS[a]

	MODEL 1—MAIN EFFECTS		MODEL 2—INTERACTION EFFECTS	
	BETA	B	BETA	B
Financial strain (FS)	.285	.427***	na	na
Social participation (SP)	−.092	−.132**	na	na
Supportive interactions (SI)	−.075	−.240*	na	na
Problematic interactions (PI)	.180	.533**	na	na
R^2 adjusted	.243			

TABLE 13.1 *(continued)*

PANEL 5—FINANCIAL STRAIN AND INTERACTION SYMMETRY[a]

	MODEL 1—MAIN EFFECTS		MODEL 2—INTERACTION EFFECTS	
	BETA	B	BETA	B
Financial strain (FS)	.281	.408***	.286	.432***
Interaction symmetry (IS)	−.215	−.417***	−.199	−.358***
FS x IS			−.075	−.159*
R^2 Adjusted	.234		.239	

PANEL 6—FINANCIAL STRAIN, SOCIAL PARTICIPATION, SUPPORTIVE INTERACTIONS AND INTERACTION SYMMETRY[a]

	MODEL 1—MAIN EFFECTS		MODEL 2—INTERACTION EFFECTS	
	BETA	B	BETA	B
Financial strain	.285	.427***	na	na
Social participation	−.092	−.132**	na	na
Supportive interactions	.092	.294*	na	na
Interaction symmetry	.275	−.533***	na	na
R^2 adjusted	.232			

PANEL 7—FINANCIAL STRAIN, SOCIAL PARTICIPATION, PROBLEMATIC INTERACTIONS AND INTERACTION SYMMETRY[a]

	MODEL 1—MAIN EFFECTS		MODEL 2—INTERACTION EFFECTS	
	BETA	B	BETA	B
Financial strain	.285	1.427***	na	na
Social participation	.092	−.132**	na	na
Problematic interactions	−.099	.294	na	na
Interaction symmetry	−.124	−.240*	na	na
R^2 adjusted	.232			

[a]Age, marital status, number of children, SES, employment status, and disability controlled
*$p \leq .05$ **$p \leq .01$ ***$p \leq .001$

Source: Americans' Changing Lives, 1986

financial strain on symptoms. Thus, Black women who have both high levels of economic strain and problematic relationships are no more likely to be depressed than those who experience high economic strain but without problematic social relationships.

The balance or symmetry between supportive and problematic relationships with family and friends appears to be more important than either type of relationship alone. As African American women's social support relationships become more positively balanced or more symmetrical (i.e., the positives increasingly outweigh the negatives), the women are less likely to report depressive symptoms. Thus the combination of benefits and costs—how well demands and criticisms are offset by perceptions of being loved and cared for—best predicts depressive symptoms among Black women. Symmetry also buffers the effects of financial strain. As interactions with network members become more positively balanced, the effects of financial strain on symptoms are diminished.

The conclusions drawn from this study must be tempered by a discussion of several limitations. First, as with other cross-sectional research, we do not know whether social relationships with network members influence depression, as presumed in this study, or whether the causal process is reversed. Second, the benefits and costs of specific sources of support were not analyzed because the number of cases ($N = 778$) is insufficient for entering all five sources of support plus interaction terms in the regression models. Instead, respondents' assessments of supportive and problematic interactions are aggregated across the five sources—spouse, mother, father, adult children, and other friends and relatives. The effects of positive and negative relationships are likely to vary by source. For example, support or criticism from a spouse may affect well-being more than support or criticism that comes from parents or more distant relatives. A related issue is that problems in one relationship may be offset by a more positive relationship with another network member. Okun and Keith (1998), for example, found that older respondents' problems with spouses are associated with fewer depressive symptoms when relationships with adult children are positive, and problems with children are offset or buffered by positive relationships with other friends and relatives. An additional limitation is that this study focused on financial strain, only one of the many stressors that African American women encounter. Future research should examine how long-term problems in other areas affect well-being and whether positive and negative interactions alleviate or heighten symptoms.

Information on coworkers and work groups, an area where the balance between positive and negative relationships may be more heavily weighted toward the latter, was unavailable in this survey. African American women encounter a number of work-related stressors, including performance pressures, racial stereotyping, isolation, and tokenism, and they are often belittled as "affirmative action" hires (Boyd-Franklin 1987). Davidson (1997) also notes that minority women managers face unique stressors that result from living in a bicultural world. Yet while social support from family and coworkers has been found to reduce the effects of job stressors among Whites (Constable and Russell 1986), support is less effective for Black women (Bailey, Wolfe, and Wolfe 1996; Gray 1986). Coworker relationships are, therefore, more problematical for African American women. Future research should assess the costs and benefits of social support across all important life domains and determine the extent to which African American women differ from other women.

REFERENCES

Allen, L. and D. E. Britt. 1983. Black women in American society: A resource development perspective. *Issues in Mental Health Nursing* 5:61–70.

Bailey, D., D. Wolfe, and C. Wolfe. 1996. The contextual impact of social support across race and gender: Implications for African American women in the workplace. *Journal of Black Studies* 26 (3): 286–307.

Boyd-Franklin, N. 1987. Group therapy for Black women: A therapeutic support model. *American Journal of Orthopsychiatry* 57 (3): 394–401.

Brown, D. R. and L. E. Gary. 1985. Social support network differentials among married and nonmarried black females. *Psychology of Women Quarterly* 9 (2): 229–241.

——. 1987. Stressful life events, social support networks, and the physical and mental health of urban Black adults. *Journal of Human Stress* 13:165–174.

Brown, D. R., L. E. Gary, A. D. Greene, and N. G. Milburn. 1992. Patterns of social affiliation as predictors of depressive symptoms among urban Blacks. *Journal of Health and Social Behavior* 33:224–253.

Carrington, C. H. 1980. Depression in Black Women: A Theoretical Appraisal. In L. Rodgers-Rose, ed., *The Black Woman*, 265–271. Beverly Hills: Sage.

Cohen, S., and T. A. Wills. 1985. Stress, social support, and the buffering hypothesis. *Psychological Bulletin* 95:310–357.

Constable, J. F., and D. W. Russell. 1986. The effect of social support and the work environment upon burnout among nurses. *Journal of Human Stress* 12:20–26.

Davidson, M. J. 1997. *The Black and Ethnic Minority Manager.* London: Paul Chapman Publishing.

Denton, T. C. 1990. Bonding and supportive relationships among Black professional women: Rituals of restoration. *Journal of Organizational Behavior* 11 (6): 447–457.

Dressler, W. W. 1991. *Stress and Adaptation in the Context of Culture: Depression in a Southern Black Community.* Albany, N.Y.: SUNY Press.

Ellison, C. and D. A. Gay. 1990. Region, religious commitment, and life satisfaction among Black Americans. *Sociological Quarterly* 31:551–568.

Gray, B. 1986. "Self-esteem, Stress, and Support Systems of Black Female Professionals." Ph.D. diss., Fordham University, 1986. *Dissertation Abstracts International* 47 (4-B): 1788.

Higginbotham, E. and L. Weber. 1996. Moving Up with Kin and Community: Upward Social Mobility for Black and White Women. In E. N. Chow, D. Wilkinson, and M. B. Zinn, eds., *Race, Class, and Gender: Common Bonds, Different Voices*, 125–148. Thousand Oaks, Calif.: Sage.

Hine, D. C., ed. 1993. *Black Women in America: A Historical Encyclopedia*. New York: Carlson.

hooks, b. 1993. *Sisters of the Yam: Black Women and Self Recovery*. Boston: South End Press.

Horwitz, A. V., J. McLaughlin, and H. R. White. 1998. How the negative and positive aspects of partner relationships affect the mental health of young married people. *Journal of Health and Social Behavior* 39:124–136.

House, J. S. 1986. Americans' Changing Lives: Wave I [MRDF]. Ann Arbor: Survey Research Center [producer], Inter-University Consortium for Political and Social Research [distributor].

Lincoln, C. E. and L. Mamiya. 1990. *The Black Church in the African-American Experience*. Durham, N.C.: Duke University Press.

McAdoo, P. P. 1980. Black Mothers and the Extended Family Support Network. In L. Rodgers-Rose, ed., *The Black Woman*, 125–144. Beverly Hills: Sage.

McCray, C. A. 1980. The Black Woman and Family Roles. In L. Rodgers-Rose, ed., *The Black Woman*, 67–78. Beverly Hills: Sage.

Myers, L. W. 1980. *Black Women: Do They Cope Better?* Englewood Cliffs, N.J.: Prentice-Hall.

Nam, C. B. and M. G. Powers. 1983. *The Socioeconomic Approach to Status Measurement*. Houston: Cap and Gown.

Neff, J. A. and B. A. Husaini. 1982. Life events, drinking patterns, and depressive symptomatology: The stress-buffering role of alcohol consumption. *Journal of Studies of Alcohol* 43:301–317.

Neighbors, H. W. 1997. Husbands, Wives, Family, and Friends: Sources of Stress, Sources of Support. In R. J. Taylor, J. S. Jackson, and L. M. Chatters, eds., *Family Life in Black America*, 279–293. Thousand Oaks, Calif.: Sage.

Okun, M. A. and V. M. Keith. 1998. Effects of positive and negative social exchanges with various sources on depressive symptoms in younger and older adults. *Journal of Gerontology: Psychological Sciences* 53B:P4–P20.

Pearlin, L. I. 1999. The Stress Process Revisited: Reflections on Concepts and Their Interrelationships. In C. S. Aneshensel and J. C. Phelan, eds., *Handbook of Sociology of Mental Health*, 395–415. New York: Kulwer Academic/Plenum.

Radloff, L. S. 1977. The CES-D Scale: A self-report depression scale for research in the general population. *Journal of Applied Psychological Measurement* 1:385–401.

Ralston, P. 1997. Midlife and Older Black Women. In J. M. Coyle, ed., *Handbook on Women and Aging*, 273–289. Westport, Conn.: Greenwood.

Rook, K. 2001. Emotional health and positive versus negative social exchanges: A daily diary analysis. *Applied Developmental Science* 5:86–97.

Sloan, V. J., E. Addlesperger, and L. Jason. 1996. Social networks among inner-city minority women. *Education* 117 (2): 194–199.

Stack, C. B. 1974. *All Our Kin.* New York: Harper and Row.

Sterling, D., ed. 1988. *Black Foremothers.* 2d ed. New York: Feminist Press.

Suls, J. 1982. Social Support, Social Relations, and Health: Benefits and Liabilities. In G. Sanders and J. Suls, eds., *Social Psychology of Health and Illness*, 220–229. Hillsdale, N.J.: Erlbaum.

Taylor, R. J. and L. M. Chatters. 1988. Church members as a source of informal social support. *Review of Religious Research* 30 (2): 193–203.

Taylor, R. J., L. M. Chatters, and J. S. Jackson. 1997. Changes Over Time in Support Network Involvement Among Black Americans. In R. J. Taylor, J. S. Jackson, and L. M. Chatters, eds., *Family Life in Black America*, 295–318. Thousand Oaks, Calif.: Sage.

Turner, R. J. and F. Marino. 1994. Social support and social structure: A descriptive epidemiology. *Journal of Health and Social Behavior* 35:193–212.

Warren, B. J. 1997. Depression, stressful life events, social support, and self-esteem in middle class African American women. *Archives of Psychiatric Nursing* 11 (3): 107–117.

.

14 PATTERNS OF MENTAL HEALTH SERVICES UTILIZATION AMONG BLACK WOMEN
Cleopatra H. Caldwell

P revious research on the utilization of outpatient mental health services among minority populations concludes that significant progress has been made in providing greater access and in changing attitudes toward mental health services in general (Snowden, Ulvang, and Rezentes 1989), yet much remains to be done to achieve parity among the races in access and in use of mental health services. Although there has been increased interest in understanding barriers to the use of mental health services among minority populations, specific studies of Black women are few and often limited in scope (for review, see Gibbs and Fuery 1994; Padgett et al. 1994b). Of particular importance is the finding that Blacks are more likely than Whites and other ethnic groups to discontinue mental health services prematurely (Flaskerud and Hu 1992; Sue et al. 1991). Factors related to this interruption of services are rarely identified. A better understanding of Black women who use specific mental health services and why they do so is important if we are to achieve the nation's goal of providing adequate mental health services to the entire population (Hu et al. 1991).

This chapter addresses this concern by examining patterns of outpatient mental health services utilization in a sample of 450 Black women who participated in Wave 4 of the National Survey of Black Americans (Jackson 1991). It is a follow-up to a study of mental health symptoms and service utilization patterns among Black women that used Wave 1 data. The initial analysis identified demographic, sociocultural, and social support correlates of different patterns of mental health services used by Black women (Mays, Caldwell, and Jackson 1996). We found that when Black women perceived their problems to be severe, they sought professional mental health services. Black women in the 35–54 age range used mental health services more than other age groups, and women who lived in the South were less likely to use private therapists than were women in other parts of the country. In addition, Black women who viewed themselves as "not at all religious" reported the most severe problems, and they tended to use community mental health centers more than any other type of professional service. The current study extends this work by describing in more detail the characteristics of Black women who specifically sought assistance from ministers, private therapists, and/or community mental health centers for a variety of personal problems. We also predict which Black women are most likely to seek assistance from outpatient mental health resources, with emphasis on the influences of religious factors on utilization behaviors.

MENTAL HEALTH SERVICE UTILIZATION AND BLACK WOMEN

It is generally accepted that women are more likely to seek professional help for emotional problems than men are. Findings from community-based studies show, however, that this sex difference in emotional help-seeking may be limited to the use of physicians and not extend to the use of outpatient mental health services (Hoff and Rosenheck 1997). Neighbors and Howard (1987) found that Black women were 1.8 times more likely than Black men to use private physicians, even when problem severity and problem type were controlled. Further, Black women used social services for personal problems significantly more than Black men did; however, no gender differences were found in the use of community mental health centers, private therapists, or ministers. These findings suggest that despite an indication of emotional need, Black women's use of professional services is often limited to private physicians and social service agencies rather than mental health professionals. A number of barriers exist that can influence the use of outpatient mental health services by Black women.

The most consistent findings suggest that age, education, marital status, race, diagnoses, and duration of disorder are the best predictors of who will use outpatient mental health services (Capers 1991; Howard et al. 1996; Vessey and Howard 1993). Specifically, younger women, women with more education, married women, White women, and those with major depression are most likely to use such services. Practical issues such as a lack of information about services, location of the facility, transportation difficulties, and lack of recognition that there is a problem all have been found to influence a person's decision to seek professional mental health services (Gibbs and Fuery 1994; Howard et al. 1996). By far, most research on race and barriers to mental health services utilization has focused on financial access to services. Studies have found that race differences in use of outpatient mental health services exist even among insured populations (Padgett et al. 1994a, 1994b). Because of the persistent racial disparity found in utilization behavior, some researchers have suggested that factors other than lower socioeconomic status or insurance coverage may better explain observed differences in use of mental health services, especially for Black women (Padgett et al. 1994a). One such factor may be specific cultural orientations toward seeking help that may influence the use of professional mental health services.

In considering cultural factors as barriers to mental health services utilization, personal attributes and environmental conditions have implications for who will or will not use such services (Gibbs and Fuery 1994). Specifically, individual characteristics such as attitudes and beliefs about the service environment, as well as a person's sense of self-esteem and self-efficacy, are important for determining who will be able to accomplish the negotiations necessary to enter the mental health services arena (Howard et al. 1996). Interpersonal relationships, especially among Black women, can serve as barriers because members of a person's social network can either hinder or facilitate her access to mental health services (Caldwell 1996; Snowden 1998). In both situations, the stigma associated with entering the service arena and a basic mistrust of mental health professionals can be major barriers. This is especially true among ethnic minority populations who believe that many professionals lack commitment to and competence in working with different ethnic groups.

Sussman, Robbins, and Earls (1987) identified fear of treatment and fear of being hospitalized as important reasons that prevented Black people from seeking professional mental health services. Establishing a successful relationship between professional mental health workers and Black clients can be difficult when feelings of oppression and discrimination are considered (Nickerson, Helms, and Terrell 1994; Strakowski et al. 1995; Watkins-Duncan 1992). An alternative strategy for meeting mental health needs may be to rely on less formal resources, such as religious institutions. Gibbs and Fuery (1994) found that the utilization rates of formal mental health services by Black women were low because they often used alternative resources to cope with psychological distress. The Black church was identified as one of several community-based resources available to Black women for emotional and instrumental support. Many Black churches have developed extensive outreach programs to assist Black women (Caldwell 2000). Although counseling from the minister is a traditional benefit of church membership, the adequacy of the training that ministers have received to address serious mental health concerns has been called into question (Taylor et al. 2000). Nevertheless, Black women often rely on Black churches to provide emotional, economic, and social support in addition to religious and spiritual guidance (Caldwell 2000; Mattis and Jagers 2001; Thompson and McRae 2001; Taylor and Chatters 1988).

The Black church represents a strong community-based institution that has provided for the emotional needs of Black people when access to the mental health system was more limited (Baker 1995; Lincoln and Mamiya 1990). Thus, the role of subjective religious beliefs among Black women and the nature of religious institutional assistance received by Black women as they influence the use of mental health services are important cultural considerations, and ministers represent a viable option as mental health resources (Neighbors, Musick, and Williams 1998; Williams et al. 1999). In a comprehensive review of literature, Taylor et al. (2000) identified several studies that highlight the significance of ministers as mental health resources for the Black population. In comparing the level of severity of problems that were brought to ministers to that of those taken to mental health professionals, several studies indicated that both type and severity of psychiatric symptoms were similar. Regardless of their preparation or training for handling mental health problems, ministers are often faced with having to assist Blacks, especially Black women, with such problems (Neighbors, Musick, and Williams 1998). The effectiveness of ministerial assistance as a mental health resource is beyond the scope of this study, but because Black women often take mental health problems to ministers, they have been included as a mental health resource for this study.

The research questions of interest are (1) Is there a need for professional services among Black women? (2) What are the characteristics of Black women who seek assistance from ministers, private therapists, or community mental health centers? (3) Is financial access a major barrier to mental health services utilization among Black women? And (4) What demographic and personal factors (i.e., religious orientation, self-esteem, depressive symptoms) distinguish Black women who use specific mental health services from those who use other services?

METHODS

SAMPLE

This study is based on a subset of the 450 Black women who participated in Waves 1 and 4 of the National Survey of Black Americans (NSBA). NSBA is the first multistage area probability sample of the Black adult population in the United States (for a complete description of the sample, see

Jackson 1991). The average age of these women at Wave 4 was 53 years ($SD = 15$). Fifty-five percent were employed, with a median family income of $35,000 in 1991. Forty percent were married, 19 percent were divorced, 7 percent were separated, 22 percent were widowed, and 12 percent had never been married. Women from the South accounted for 55 percent of the sample, followed by 24 percent from the north central region of the country and 17 percent from the northeastern region. Only 4 percent of these Black women were from the western region of the country.

MEASURES

Respondents with a personal problem were asked whether or not they had sought help from a variety of professional services, including medical facilities, social services, and mental health resources. This chapter focuses on the use of three specific mental health resources: a community mental health center, a private therapist (e.g., a psychologist, psychiatrist, social worker, or counselor), or a minister. Because of our interest in developing a profile of Black women who used mental health resources, the dependent measure for the logistic regression analysis is a dichotomous variable that combines those women who sought professional help from any of the three mental health resources in one category coded as 1. The other category is coded as 0 and includes women who did not seek professional help or who sought help from other professionals (i.e., mostly private physicians or social service agencies).

Self-esteem was measured by a six-item scale based on Rosenberg's (1965) assessment of negative and positive perceptions of self. The response categories were on a four-point Likert scale ranging from 1 = *never true* to 4 = *almost always true*. The internal consistency for this summed index was .54. Depressive symptomatology at Wave 1 was measured by a twelve-item checklist based on Gurin, Veroff, and Feld's (1960) measure of distress. Questions asked included how often the respondent felt lonely, depressed, jumpy, had crying spells, poor appetite, trouble sleeping, illness, or anger. Response categories were on a five-point Likert scale that ranged from 1 = *never* to 5 = *very often*. The responses for each item were summed to form the index, and scores ranged from 12 to 60. High scores reflected higher levels of depressive symptoms. The internal consistency for this measure was .93.

Religious orientation was assessed using two single-item measures. The first assessed the frequency of church attendance. The specific question asked, How often do you usually attend religious services? Response categories were on a five-point Likert scale ranging from 1= *less than once a year* to 5 = *nearly every day*. The second question assessed the respondent's subjective religiosity or her view of how religious she is, using a response category of 1 = *not religious at all* to 4 = *very religious*. A series of single-item measures were also included to examine the level of insurance coverage of the sample to assess financial access. Standard demographic items were included to control for the influences of age and marital status in the multivariate analysis.

RESULTS

NEED FOR MENTAL HEALTH SERVICES

With regard to establishing a need to utilize mental health services, 76 percent of the 450 respondents in Wave 4 reported having had one or more problems within the past month that had caused them distress ($N = 344$); 24 percent reported having had no problem at all ($N = 106$). An assessment of the severity of problems indicated that slightly less than half (44%) of the total sample felt that they had a serious problem that they could not handle alone or they had recently experienced a serious emotional problem (e.g., depression, nervous breakdown). Of those who had a problem, 67 percent had talked with someone ($N = 230$). In most cases, problems were shared with family members and friends (65%), while professional services of any type were least often sought (35%). When professional assistance was sought, private physicians and social service agencies were consulted more frequently than mental health services. Eighty-six percent of the women felt that the person with whom they shared their problem had been helpful.

PROFILES OF BLACK WOMEN WHO USE DIFFERENT MENTAL HEALTH RESOURCES

In assessing the use of mental health services by Black women, one of the most striking findings is that even in this national sample of the Black population, very few women used outpatient mental health services. This is despite the fact that the majority of women recognized that they had at least one current serious problem. Only 15 percent of the 344 women with any type of problem sought specialty mental health services. Specifically, 34 women, or 10 percent, reported that they had sought assistance from a private therapist, and 17 women, or 5 percent, went to a community mental health center

TABLE 14.1 Characteristics of Black Women Who Use Specific Mental Health
Resources

CHARACTERISTIC	MINISTERS	PRIVATE THERAPISTS	CMHC
	(N = 69)	(N = 34)	(N = 17)
Median family income	$29,000	$49,500	$50,000
Average age	51.29	49.47	51.53
Region			
South	56%	53%	41%
Northeast	22%	29%	41%
North central	22%	9%	6%
West	2%	9%	12%
Marital status			
Married	33%	29%	18%
Not married	67%	71%	82%
Employment status			
Employed	45%	59%	41%
Not employed	55%	41%	59%
Average self-esteem	3.36	3.34	3.21
Average Wave 1 depressive symptoms	23.32	24.24	25.76
Weekly church attendance or more	78%	65%	56%
Very religious sense of self	57%	38%	35%

Source: National Survey of Black Americans.

(CMHC). An additional 20 percent, or 69 women, reported seeking help
from a minister. Interestingly, 17 out of the 34 women who went to a private
therapist and 7 out of 17 who went to a CMHC also sought assistance from a
minister.

In an effort to better understand the characteristics of Black women who
used specific types of mental health resources, separate analyses were conducted for each of the three types of mental health resources with selected
characteristics of the women. Table 14.1 provides a summary of these characteristics by type of mental health resource consulted.

USE OF MINISTERS. Although ministers have the least amount of mental health
training of the three types of mental health providers included in this study,
a greater number of Black women consulted ministers rather than other types

of mental health resources. Black women who sought help from ministers had a median income of $29,000 in 1991, and their average age was 51 ($SD = 14.32$). Most lived in the South (56%), 67 percent were not married, and 45 percent were employed. Self-esteem was moderately high, and most had moderate levels of depressive symptoms at Wave 1 ($M = 23.33$, $SD = 14.68$). In addition, more than three-fourths (78%) attended church at least once a week or more, and 57 percent described themselves as very religious.

USE OF PRIVATE THERAPISTS. For this sample, private therapists represented the largest category of trained mental health professionals from whom the respondents sought help. Black women who used private therapists had a median family income of $49,500 in 1991. They tended to be a little younger ($M = 49.47$, $SD = 16.50$) than those who used ministers, most lived in the South (53%), 71 percent were not married, and more were employed (59%) than among those who sought help from ministers. Self-esteem was moderately high, and most had moderate levels of depressive symptoms at Wave 1 ($M = 24.24$, $SD = 15.54$). Approximately two-thirds (65%) attended church once a week or more, and 38 percent perceived themselves as very religious.

USE OF COMMUNITY MENTAL HEALTH CENTERS. Community mental health centers were least often selected as a mental health resource. Women who did choose this option had a median family income of $50,000. They were about the same age ($M = 51.53$, $SD = 17.98$) as those who used ministers. They lived in both the southern (41%) and northeastern (41%) regions of the country. The majority (82%) were not married, and more than half (59%) were not employed. Self-esteem of users of CMHCs was slightly lower than that of women who used ministers and private therapists. However, most had moderate levels of depressive symptoms at Wave 1 ($M = 25.76$, $SD = 15.90$). More than half (56%) attended church once a week or more, and 35 percent stated that they were very religious.

In a comparison of the profiles of women across the mental health resources, the data indicate that Black women who sought assistance from ministers appear to have less income than those who used private therapists or CMHCs. Black women who went to CMHCs were less likely to be married or employed than those who sought help from ministers or private therapists. In addition, CMHC users were more regionally diverse than women who utilized ministers and private therapists. Black women who used private therapists also were more apt to be employed than those who sought help from ministers or CMHCs. However, women utilizing any type of mental health resource seemed to have similar levels of self-esteem and previous depressive symptoms. Table

14.1 also shows that a larger percentage of women who sought help from ministers attended church more frequently and considered themselves to be more religious than those who went to private therapists or CMHCs. In general, Black women who sought help from ministers appear to be more similar to than different from those who used private therapists with regard to most demographic and personal characteristics. Users of CMHCs, on the other hand, may be somewhat different from those who used the other two types of mental health resources.

FINANCIAL ACCESS ISSUES

A primary enabling factor for access to professional mental health services is having health insurance. Almost all of the women (87%) reported having some type of health insurance. Specifically, 57 percent reported having health insurance from their place of employment, 33 percent had Medicare, 20 percent had Medicaid, 29 percent purchased private health insurance, 9 percent had military insurance, and 7 percent had some other type of governmental health assistance. Some women had multiple forms of insurance to meet their health care needs. Although the adequacy of health insurance available for mental health services could not be evaluated, these findings do suggest that financial access to services may not have been a primary barrier to mental health services utilization for this sample.

CORRELATES OF MENTAL HEALTH SERVICE USE

Few differences were found in the profiles of Black women who used specific types of mental health resources. We therefore combined these groups in an effort to provide an overall profile of women who use mental health resources as compared to women who did not use a specific mental health resource. These analyses were restricted to the 344 women who reported that they had experienced one or more serious personal problems within the past month. As previously indicated, only 35 percent of the 344 women with a problem used a mental health resource. In addition, 34 percent used other professionals (mostly physicians and social workers), while 31 percent sought no professional help at all. A logistic regression analysis was conducted to identify the best predictors of who would use mental health resources for this sample. Table 14.2 presents the results of this analysis. Predictors were selected based on the literature review, which suggested that age, marital status, self-

TABLE 14.2 Logistic Regression Analysis of Use of Mental Health Resources by Selected Characteristics

CHARACTERISTIC	Bᵃ	ODDS RATIO
Age	−.021*	.979
Marital statusᵇ	−.722*	.486
Self-esteem	−.623*	.536
Church attendance	.561***	1.752
Subjective religiosity	.380⁺	1.463
Wave 1 depressive symptoms	.017⁺	1.017

X^2 = 30.04, degrees of freedom = 6, $p \leq$ .000   −2 Log Likelihood = 363.872
ᵃ Unstandardized regression coefficients
ᵇ 0 = not married, 1 = married
⁺$p \leq$ .10   *$p \leq$ .05   **$p \leq$ .01   ***$p \leq$ .001
N = 327
Source: National Survey of Black Americans

esteem, depressive symptoms, and sociocultural factors (i.e., church attendance and subjective religiosity) should influence who will or will not use mental health resources. For all variables except depressive symptoms, Wave 4 variables were included. The measure of Wave 1 depressive symptoms was used in an effort to determine the influences of a long-term condition on mental health services utilization among Black women.

The results of this analysis indicate that all variables in the model, with the exception of depressive symptoms at Wave 1 and subjective religiosity, are significant predictors of who will or will not use the identified mental health resources. Specifically, younger women as compared to older women, women who are not married rather than married women, women with lower self-esteem versus those with higher self-esteem, and women who frequently attend religious services rather than those who are less frequent church attendees are more likely to use mental health resources. Both depressive symptoms at Wave 1 ($p < .10$) and perceptions of religiosity ($p \leq .10$) only approached standard levels of significance for this sample.

DISCUSSION

The use of outpatient specialty mental health services among Black women at Wave 4 of the NSBA panel study is low compared to the level of need expressed in the sample. Among those who sought professional outpatient mental health services, private therapists (10%) were consulted most frequently. CMHCs were used with much less frequency (5%). Combined, only 15 percent of the Black women in this study sought help from outpatient mental health services. This overall figure is quite comparable to those found in the general population, as reported by the Epidemiologic Catchment Area Study (13%) and the National Comorbidity Study (12%) (Howard et al. 1996). On the basis of these figures, one could conclude that the mental health needs of the majority of Black women are not being met by the current mental health service delivery system. For the present study, the low utilization rate of outpatient mental health services does not appear to be a reflection of lack of access resulting from not having health insurance. Padgett et al. (1994a, 1994b) also found that Black women underutilized mental health services even though they had adequate health insurance. This result raises the issue of understanding other determinants of the utilization behavior of Black women.

The present study incorporated ministers as mental health resources for Black women, and the percentage of women who sought help from a mental health resource increased from 15 percent to 35 percent. Although we could not determine the effectiveness of the type of help received from ministers, we were able to identify characteristics of women who sought assistance from the three different mental health resources. Black women who used ministers appear to be similar in most characteristics as those who used private therapists. They may vary to some degree from those who used CMHCs, most notably with regard to income, marital status, and patterns of religious orientation. We found that Black women who sought assistance from ministers had less income, a larger percentage were married, they attended church more regularly, and they viewed themselves as religious more frequently than those who went to CMHCs. Because of the small numbers of women who used professional mental health services, however, it was difficult to determine if these differences were significant. Future studies should investigate these differences more fully to assess the specific groups of Black women who are likely to underutilize particular types of mental health resources. The similarities in characteristics of Black women who sought assistance from ministers and private therapists, except with regard to income and employment, might suggest that Black women with greater financial resources tend to use private therapists more than Black women with fewer resources. Those with fewer financial resources may rely on the free assistance available from ministers. However, because the overwhelming majority of women in this study had health insurance, the financial access argument does not seem to be the most plausible explanation for these different patterns of use. A more promising direction for future research is to further elaborate the role of trust in determining who will choose to go to a minister rather than to a private therapist when faced with a serious problem.

The overlap in the number of Black women who sought help from ministers in addition to private therapists or CMHCs raises the issue of whether or not ministers may serve as a barrier to use of mental health services. This proposition is supported by the work of Neighbors et al. (1998), which found that Blacks who initially sought help from ministers were less likely to contact other professionals than those who sought professional help first. Others have suggested that ministers often serve as gatekeepers to the mental health service delivery system, with few referring needy individuals for professional specialty mental health services (Chang et al. 1994; Taylor et al. 2000). Williams et al. (1999), on the other hand, found that 50 percent of the Black ministers in their study had actually referred people to a mental health agency or professional, while Snowden (1998) found that religious helpers served as complements to the mental health service system for Blacks. Future research should clarify the role of ministers as a barrier or a facilitator of the use of mental health services among Black women. If it is found that Black churches and secular service organizations tend to be more cooperative than conflictive, developing collaborative relationships would be a more useful service strategy than considering ministers to be an independent or alternative mental health resource for Black women. This approach would avoid the potential for ineffective treatment by ministers who have not been trained to address serious mental health problems.

Another important issue addressed in this study was whether religious involvement might serve as a barrier to outpatient mental health service utilization. By incorporating ministers in this category, one might assume that religious factors would easily predict utilization behavior. We found, however, that only church attendance was a strong predictor of use. In a related area, Hatch (1991) found that involvement in church activities was a significant predictor of the amount of help received from nonrelatives among Black women. Determining whether or not different aspects of religious orientation serve as facilitators or barriers to use of mental health services among Black women is an issue that must be addressed. It is clear that Black women who attend church regularly may be more receptive to discussing their serious problems with people who are outside their family support networks. The willingness of churchgoers to seek help from ministers and specialty mental health services is important information to have in targeting Black women who could benefit from a collaborative approach between ministers and mental health professionals.

In terms of predictors of mental health service utilization, the results of the logistic regression analyses indicated that younger Black women used mental health resources more than older women. Because the average age of the women in this study was 53 years old, however, those who used mental health resources were actually middle-aged women who remained as part of this panel study rather than young adult women. Even with the inclusion of ministers as mental health resources, this age finding is very similar to those from the study by Mays et al. (1996) that is based on Wave 1 data from NSBA. This suggests that middle-aged Black women may feel freer to use mental health services. Future research must determine why middle-aged rather than young adult or older Black women appear to be more receptive to the use of outpatient mental health services.

Unlike previous studies (Russo and Olmedo 1983), in this study unmarried rather than married women were more likely to use the identified mental health resources. Perhaps the inclusion of ministers increased the likelihood of unmarried women using these resources because personal problems frequently brought to ministers involve bereavement, grieving, and interpersonal relationships (Neighbors 1991). In this study, 22 percent of the women were widowed and 26 percent were divorced or separated; thus, bereavement and interpersonal relationships among unmarried women may have been contributing to their need for help from ministers. The independent assessment of mental health resources used, however, indicated that unmarried women used all resources at a much higher rate than married women did. An alternative explanation considers the role of husbands as potential barriers to mental health services utilization, specifically among Black women. From a social support perspective, husbands are often viewed as the primary source of both emotional and instrumental support for married women (Thoits 1995). Having a spouse who is a confidant is expected to significantly reduce the effects of stress on psychological well-being (Cohen and Wills 1985). Thus, married women may have less of a need for mental health services than unmarried women do. Brown and Gary (1985) found, however, that Black women often relied upon family members other than the spouse for assistance, regardless of marital status. On the other hand, Hatch (1991) found that unmarried Black women sought help from nonrelatives more frequently than married women did. This reliance on nonrelatives for assistance among unmarried Black women may influence their willingness to seek assistance from mental health resources, including specialty services as well as ministers. The present study does not directly test these ideas. Future research should consider how the nature of the relationships with a spouse, female family members, and people outside the family may either facilitate or hinder the mental health help-seeking behavior of Black women.

Interestingly, self-esteem was a significant predictor of mental health services use. Specifically, Black women with lower self-esteem had a greater probability of using mental health resources than did those with higher self-esteem. Previous research indicates that higher self-esteem may be necessary in order to negotiate the complicated mental health system (Gibbs and Fuery 1994). Our findings might be an indication that the use of ministers may require fewer negotiation skills so that access is easier than with other mental health resources. Further clarification of the role of personal resources in utilization behavior involving less formal resources than the mental health system is important when considering the help-seeking behaviors of Black women.

While previous studies report that people with major depression tend to seek assistance from mental health professionals more frequently than those who are not depressed (Howard et al. 1996), the findings in this study on depressive symptoms at Wave 1 only approached standard levels of significance. Perhaps the pattern of attrition in the data resulted in the more depressed respondents' dropping out of the study such that this relationship was not large enough to detect. A better assessment of the nature of depression and outpatient mental health services utilization among Black women is needed before conclusions can be made about the influence of diagnosis and long-term disorders on their utilization behavior.

The outpatient mental health service system must continue to focus on eliminating barriers to service use by Black women. This should include more consideration as to how ministers might serve as collaborators as well as referrals for informing more Black women about the benefits of mental health treatment. This does not mean that all Black women will be persuaded by ministers; however, women who attend church regularly provide a starting point for ministers to disseminate information and recruit them into more appropriate outpatient specialty mental health services when they are faced with a serious emotional problem.

REFERENCES

Baker, F. M. 1995. Mental health issues in elderly African Americans. *Clinics in Geriatric Medicine* 11:1–13.

Brown, D. R. and L. E. Gary. 1985. Social support network differentials among married and nonmarried Black females. *Psychology of Women Quarterly* 9:229–241.

Caldwell, C. H. 1996. Predisposing, Enabling, and Need Factors Related to Patterns of Help-Seeking Among African American Women. In H. W. Neighbors and J. S. Jackson, eds., *Mental Health in Black America*, 146–160. Thousand Oaks, Calif.: Sage.

———. 2000. Social Networks: Community-Based Institutional Supports for Black Women. In N. J. Burgess and E. Brown, eds., *African American Women: An Ecological Perspective*, 99–114. New York: Falmer.

Caldwell, C. H., A. D. Greene, and A. Billingsley. 1994. Family Support Programs in Black Churches: A New Look at Old Functions. In S. L. Kagan and B. Weissbourd, eds., *Putting Families First: America's Family Support Movement and the Challenge of Change*, 137–160. San Francisco: Jossey-Bass.

Capers, C. F. 1991. Nurses' and African Americans' views about behavior. *Western Journal of Nursing Research* 13:123–135.

Chang, P. M., D. R. Williams, E. Griffith, and J. Young. 1994. Church-agency relationships in the Black community. *Nonprofit and Voluntary Sector Quarterly* 23: 91–105.

Cohen, S. and T. A. Wills. 1985. Stress, social support, and the buffering hypothesis. *Psychological Bulletin* 98:310–357.

Flaskerud, J. H. and L. Hu. 1992. Racial/ethnic identity and amount and type of psychiatric treatment. *American Journal of Psychiatry* 149:379–384.

Gibbs, J. T. and D. Fuery. 1994. Mental health and well-being of Black women: Toward strategies of empowerment. *American Journal of Community Psychology* 22:559–582.

Gurin, G., J. Veroff, and S. Feld. 1960. *Americans View Their Mental Health*. New York: Basic Books.

Hatch, L. R. 1991. Informal support patterns of older African-American and White women. *Research on Aging* 13:144–170.

Hoff, R. A. and R. A. Rosenheck. 1997. Utilization of mental health services by women in a male-dominated environment: The VA experience. *Psychiatric Services* 48: 1408–1414.

Howard, K. I., T. A. Cornille, J. S. Lyons, J. T. Vessey, R. J. Lueger, and S. M. Saunders. 1996. Patterns of mental health service utilization. *Archives of General Psychiatry* 53:696–703.

Hu, T., L. R. Snowden, J. M. Jerrell, and T. D. Nguyen. 1991. Ethnic populations in public mental health: Services choice and level of use. *American Journal of Public Health* 81:1429–1434.

Jackson, J. S., ed. 1991. *Life in Black America*. Thousand Oaks, Calif.: Sage.

Lincoln, C. E. and L. Mamiya. 1990. *The Black Church in the African American Experience*. Durham, N.C.: Duke University Press.

Mattis, J. S. and R. J. Jagers. 2001. A relational framework for the study of religiosity and spirituality in the lives of African Americans. *Journal of Community Psychology* 29:519–539.

Mays, V. M., C. H. Caldwell, and J. S. Jackson. 1996. Mental Health Symptoms and Service Utilization Patterns of Help-Seeking Among African American Women. In

H. W. Neighbors and J. S. Jackson, eds., *Mental Health in Black America,* 161–176. Thousand Oaks, Calif.: Sage.

Neighbors, H. W. 1991. Mental Health. In J. S. Jackson, ed., *Life in Black America,* 221–237. Newbury Park, Calif.: Sage.

Neighbors, H. W. and C. S. Howard. 1987. Sex differences in professional help-seeking among adult Black Americans. *American Journal of Community Psychology* 15: 403–417.

Neighbors, H. W., M. A. Musick, and D. R. Williams. 1998. The African American minister as a source of help for serious personal crises: Bridge or barrier to mental health care? *Health Education and Behavior.* Special Issue. *Public Health and Health Education in Faith Communities* 25:759–777.

Nickerson, K. J., J. E. Helms, and F. Terrell. 1994. Cultural mistrust, opinions about mental illness, and Black students' attitudes toward seeking psychological help from White counselors. *Journal of Counseling Psychology* 41:378–385.

Padgett, D. K., C. Patrick, B. J. Burns, and H. J. Schlesinger. 1994a. Ethnicity and the use of outpatient mental health services in a national insured population. *American Journal of Public Health* 84:222–226.

———. 1994b. Women and outpatient mental health services: Use by Black, Hispanic, and White women in a national insured population. *Journal of Mental Health Administration* 21:347–360.

Rosenberg, M. 1965. *Society and the Adolescent Self-Image.* Princeton, N.J.: Princeton University Press.

Russo, N. and E. Olmedo. 1983. Women's utilization of outpatient psychiatric services: Some emerging priorities for rehabilitation psychologists. *Rehabilitation Psychology* 28:141–155.

Snowden, L. R. 1998. Racial differences in informal help-seeking for mental health problems. *Journal of Community Psychology* 26:303–313.

Snowden, L. R., R. Ulvang, and R. Rezentes. 1989. Low-income Blacks in community mental health: Forming a treatment relationship. *Community Mental Health Journal* 25:51–59.

Strakowski, S. M., H. S. Lonczak, K. W. Sax, S. A. West, A. Crist, R. Mehta, and O. J. Thienhaus. 1995. The effects of race on diagnosis and disposition from a psychiatric emergency service. *Journal of Clinical Psychiatry* 56:101–107.

Sue, S., D. C. Fujino, L. Hu, D. T. Takeuchi, and N. W. S. Zane. 1991. Community mental health services for ethnic minority groups: A test of the cultural responsiveness hypothesis. *Journal of Consulting and Clinical Psychology* 59:533–540.

Sussman, L. K., L. Robbins, and F. Earls. 1987. Treatment-seeking for depression by Black and White Americans. *Social Science and Medicine* 24 (3): 187–196.

Taylor, R. J. and L. M. Chatters. 1986. Church-based informal support among elderly Blacks. *Gerontologist* 26:637–642.

———. 1988. Church members as a source of informal social support. *Review of Religious Research* 30:193–203.

Taylor, R. J., C. G. Ellison, L. M. Chatters, J. S. Levin, and K. D. Lincoln. 2000. Mental health services in faith communities: The role of clergy in Black churches. *Social Work* 45:73–87.

Thoits, P. A. 1995. Stress, coping, and social support processes: Where are we? What next? *Journal of Health and Social Behavior* (Extra Issue): 53–79.

Thompson, D. A. and M. B. McRae. 2001. The need to belong: A theory of the therapeutic function of the Black church tradition. *Counseling and Values* 46:40–53.

Vessey, J. T. and K. I. Howard. 1993. Who seeks psychotherapy? *Psychotherapy* 30:546–553.

Watkins-Duncan, B. A. 1992. Principles for formulating treatment with Black patients. *Psychotherapy* 29:452–457.

Williams, D. R., E. H. Griffith, J. L. Young, C. Collins, and J. Dodson. 1999. Structure and provision of services in Black churches in New Haven, Connecticut. *Culture Diversity and Ethnic Minority Psychology* 5:118–133.

PART VI
CONCLUSION

I need
to check on my sanity,
ponder on my pain,
Straighten out my dress
consider my own mess.
I need
to sit down and drink from the cup of restoration
and extend my pinky
with the confidence of the "well-healed."

—Michele D. Balamani, "Dancing on Our Graves."

15 IN AND OUT OF OUR RIGHT MINDS: STRENGTHS, VULNERABILITIES, AND THE MENTAL WELL-BEING OF AFRICAN AMERICAN WOMEN

Verna M. Keith

This volume opened by noting that the social science literature and the media often present seemingly contradictory images of African American women and, by implication, contradictory images of their mental health. On the one hand, African American women are portrayed as resilient and enduring, with few mental health problems. On the other hand, this group experiences lower income, higher unemployment, less likelihood of being married, and poor physical health, which would suggest that African American women should be at higher risk for a wide range of emotional problems. In an effort to resolve this apparent contradiction between strength and vulnerability, this book documents the mental health status of African American women and evaluates, from an empirical perspective, the social, psychological, and cultural factors that are associated with their well-being.

In keeping with this general theme, the volume is organized around a conceptual framework that argues that the mental well-being of African American women is in large part determined by their position in the social structure as characterized by their race, gender, and class. In American society, being African American and female is less valued than being Caucasian and male. These two devalued statuses affect African American women's mental health by influencing how these women see themselves, how they are perceived by others, and how others respond to them. As Greene (1996) writes, African American women are often viewed by the larger society as socially inferior, unattractive, and unfeminine, and tend to be stereotyped as servants, mammies, and prostitutes. These negative images, often internalized by Black women themselves, are reflected in mistreatment and disrespect that undermine their self-concept in ways that make them vulnerable to psychological distress and mental illness. Equally important, both race and gender shape the socioeconomic status of African American women through racism and sexism.

Discriminatory treatment results in lower personal and household income, educational attainment, occupational status, and accumulated wealth. As a consequence of race- and gender-based inequality, Black women's opportunities for leading fulfilling and emotionally satisfying lives are not optimized. Black women, especially if they are poor and possess few resources, are disproportionately exposed to a series of acute and chronic stressors including ongoing financial problems, role overload and conflict from occupying multiple roles, domestic violence, and the strain of living in unsafe neighborhoods and in lower-quality housing. Even when African American women beat the odds and become economically successful, they still experience gendered racism in many life domains (St. Jean and Feagin 1998). Thus the triangulation of race, gender, and socioeconomic status plays a major role in the etiology of African American women's mental health.

Our model also recognizes that Black women have developed mechanisms for protecting their inner emotional selves by reaching out to sociocultural resources embedded in family, community, and spirituality. The strength and support derived from family and friends, the Black church, and voluntary groups have grown out of the historical need to cope with adversity (Greene 1996). Psychological resources such as self-esteem and feelings of mastery or control over one's life also protect Black women's emotional well-being. These social and psychological resources operate in many ways to assist African American women with overcoming the day-to-day consequences of occupying subordinate racial and gender status positions. It is these resources that in part explain why the vast majority of African American women are able to remain in their right minds.

The contributing authors elaborate on various aspects of the conceptual framework, with each addressing in some manner the seemingly contradictory images of Black women. This chapter draws on the various findings presented throughout this volume to explore what we know and what we still need to discover regarding the mental health status of African American women, factors that heighten or diminish risk for mental distress and illness, and their practices of help-seeking for emotional problems. In these concluding sections we discuss recommendations for prevention and treatment and note several specific subgroups of African American women who deserve more focused attention than this volume could provide.

STATE OF MIND: MENTAL HEALTH

In reviewing the epidemiological data on the mental health status of African American women, we consider the full continuum of mental states—

diagnosable mental disorders and subclinical psychiatric symptoms typically referred to as psychiatric distress or minor depression, as well as indicators of mental health such as life satisfaction and happiness. Each point across this broad spectrum provides unique insights into how African American women function emotionally, examines how they compare to other race-gender groups, and identifies key social, cultural, and environmental elements important for etiology.

DIAGNOSABLE MENTAL DISORDERS AND SUBSTANCE ABUSE

Data from the National Comorbidity Study (Brown and Keith, chapter 2) show that the most prevalent lifetime disorders among African American women are major depression (MDD) and anxiety disorders—simple phobia, agoraphobia, social phobia, and post-traumatic stress disorder (PTSD). Anxiety disorders also figure prominently in disparities between Black women and other race-gender groups. Compared to Whites and African American males, Black women have the highest twelve-month and lifetime prevalence of simple phobia, agoraphobia, and PTSD. African American women also have higher lifetime rates of MDD than males, but lower rates than their White female counterparts. The twelve-month rate of non-affective psychoses or schizophrenia, arguably the most serious mental disorder, is highest for Black women in both the Epidemiological Catchment Area Study and the National Comorbidity Study.

With the exception of age (i.e., being young), research has not clearly and systematically identified sociodemographic factors that delineate which African American women are at highest risk for phobic and other anxiety disorders. Neal-Barnett and Crowther (2000) suggested that victimization (e.g., sexual assault and domestic violence) is an underlying factor in the development of anxiety disorders, but they were unable to confirm this hypothesis in their study of Black middle-class women, perhaps because of their small sample size. The DSM diagnosis of PTSD is thought to capture the psychological consequence of exposure to violence and other traumatic events. Yet Neal-Barnett and Crowther (2000) argue that questions designed to elicit a PTSD diagnosis did not consistently yield reports of victimization in their sample, and they recommended the inclusion of a separate victimization screening section. With respect to PTSD, more research is also needed to identify traumatic events other than rape, the most likely event to result in PTSD in the general population, that pose major threats to African American women's emotional stability. For example, in the general population the trauma of seeing someone injured or killed is less common among women and has a fairly low probability of resulting in a diagnosis of PTSD (see Kessler and Zhao 1999), but this may not be the case for African American women living in inner-city neighborhoods where violence is more common. A useful avenue for future research is to investigate how neighborhood context affects the prevalence of these disorders among African American women. A growing body of literature finds that neighborhood characteristics such as economic disadvantage, perceptions of neighborhood quality (e.g., crime, drug use, and social cohesion), and degree of racial segregation affect mental health outcomes, either directly or indirectly, in both adolescents (Aneshensel and Sucoff 1996) or adults (Cutrona et al. 2000; Ross 2000; Schulz et al. 2000). Although these studies focus on distress rather than psychiatric disorders, the evidence to date warrants extending community/neighborhood context models to the study of anxiety disorders.

Slightly more is known about the risk for clinical depression among Black women. Brown and Keith (chapter 2) find that the risk for MDD includes being unmarried, experiencing high levels of psychosocial stressors, having one or more chronic medical conditions, and being under forty-five years of age, although their data are limited to respondents under age seventy-five. The findings for socioeconomic status are mixed. The data examined in chapter 2 indicate that African American women with higher education and personal income are at greater risk, but these results do not consider the joint impact of age and SES on MDD. Thus, the lower income and education of midlife women, who tend to have lower rates of MDD, are undoubtedly reflected in these findings.

The complex interplay between demographic and social variables in developing profiles of those at risk of MDD is but one of the many issues regarding depression in Black women that needs to be addressed more completely. Research is also needed on issues that pertain to the onset and trajectory of clinical depression among African American women, including the probability that a first episode will become chronic as well as issues pertaining to episode frequency and relapse, the speed of recovery, and the effects of traumatic childhood events on depression in adult life (Kessler and Magee 1994a, 1994b).

Beatty's chapter on substance use and abuse also points to several significant findings that are important for forming a more comprehensive picture of Black women's mental health. African American women do not use substances any more frequently than other groups of women do, but two issues emerge that highlight the salience of drugs in their lives. First, illicit drug use is concentrated among adolescent and young adult women, the ages most closely associated with educational achievement, career launching, marriage, and childbearing. A second issue is that substance use appears to have more serious consequences for African American women because it is more strongly linked to poverty, leaving substance-abusing Black women at higher risk for HIV/AIDS, pregnancy complications, emotional problems, and stigma.

Echoing the discussion of MDD, more research is needed on the onset and trajectory of substance use and abuse, as well as a more complete understanding of the impact of drug use on African American women's family and personal lives. Equally important is the need to understand the co-occurrence of substance use and abuse with other mental disorders. Many studies report comorbidity between substance use and clinical depression (Kessler and Zhao 1999). Some research also suggests that the causal order is gendered, with depression preceding substance abuse in women and substance abuse preceding depression in men (Kendler et al. 1993). Sorting out which disorder manifests first in African American women is important for prevention and treatment.

PSYCHOLOGICAL DISTRESS AND MENTAL HEALTH

Much of the mental health research on African American women has focused on psychological distress, which generally consists of subclinical depressive symptoms that do not meet the *DSM* diagnostic criteria for depression. A majority of studies show that African American women are more likely to be distressed than Whites and African American men. Being young, being unmarried, having lower socioeconomic status, experiencing racial discrimination and violence, and experiencing stressors that emanate from major social roles are key factors in identifying Black women who are at higher risk. Increasingly, researchers are recognizing that high scores on depressive symptom screening scales are associated with significant social and functional disability (Wells et al. 1989). Disability rates associated with subclinical depression, often labeled subthreshold or subsyndromal depression, equal or exceed those associated with *DSM*-defined depressive disorders. Subthreshold depression seems to be an especially productive direction for future research on African American women, given their higher distress levels, higher chronic disease rates, and higher disability rates.

On the opposite end of the continuum, happiness and life satisfaction are widely used indicators of the positive dimensions of mental health. African American women generally have reported lower levels of life satisfaction and happiness than Whites, although not necessarily lower than African American males. Lower levels of education and less positive financial situations play key roles in generating these subjective feelings that life is not as good as it should be. Despite being disadvantaged relative to Whites, African American women have surprisingly high levels of subjective well-being, a finding that is inconsistent with their high levels of depressive symptoms and that should be explored through further research. Needed also is research that incorporates the social and cultural context of Black women's lives into definitions and measures of mental health indicators, studies that seek to understand the evaluative process involved in defining oneself as happy or satisfied, and penetrating analyses of the role of agency (i.e., what do Black women do to make themselves happy?).

DATA AND METHODOLOGICAL ISSUES

Rigorous assessment of the mental health status of African American women continues to be plagued by problems with data availability and unanswered questions regarding the validity of mental health measures. Problems with data availability include failure to report prevalence by race and gender, inadequate numbers of African American respondents, and failure to include social and contextual factors pertinent for assessing how the triangulation of race, gender, and class jointly affect Black women's risk for mental illness. It is also not clear to what extent women subjects in psychiatric studies are representative of the social, demographic, and cultural diversity in the total population, given the challenge of recruiting minority respondents (Adebimpe 1994; Thompson et al. 1996). Methodological studies are needed to address issues of sample representativeness and problems of recruitment that specifically focus on African American women.

The extent to which current psychiatric assessment tools are valid for African Americans, women as well as men, remains an unresolved issue. Some researchers argue that structured instruments (e.g., the Diagnostic Interview Schedule) and symptom scales may not give sufficient attention to the role of culture in shaping the manifestation of mental disorders among African Americans, such as a possibly greater tendency for African Americans to express emotional problems in terms of somatic (physical) symptoms (Baker 2001; Gallo, Cooper-Patrick, and Lesikar 1998). Similarly, the overdiagnosis of schizophrenia and the underdiagnosis of depression have been attributed to lack of cultural awareness among clinicians and to the Eurocentric context in which symptoms are evaluated (Adebimpe 1994). Paranoid symptoms and suspiciousness, previously attributed to schizophrenia, may indeed be an appropriately rational response to the hostile and dangerous environment in which many African Americans find themselves (Blazer, Hays, and Salive 1996) or may reflect interpersonal vigilance that comes from living in a racist and class-based society. A related problem is a failure to recognize the greater prevalence of psychotic symptoms in depressed Black patients, which can also lead to a misdiagnosis of schizophrenia (Baker 2001; Trierweiler et al. 2000). The extent to which African American women are affected by misdiagnosis deserves attention.

OUT OF OUR RIGHT MINDS: STRAINS, STRESSORS, AND VULNERABILITIES

By virtue of their disadvantaged social and economic position in U.S. society, African American women are exposed to high levels of stressful life events and chronic strains that make them vulnerable to psychological distress and certain psychiatric disorders. Racial discrimination is a key stressor in their lives. Everyday exposure to verbal insults, discourteousness, and disrespect is prevalent, especially in the workplace, and is associated with elevated risk of depressive symptoms (Brown, Keith, and Jackson, chapter 4). Research on discrimination and mental health is still emerging, and much work remains to be done in this area. Studies are needed that identify those most likely to perceive and experience discrimination, that probe the context in which these perceptions of discrimination occur, and that examine coping responses to discrimination. Important for African American women is research that examines the joint effects of race- and gender-based discrimination. As discussed by Brown and colleagues, the pervasive nature of discriminatory experiences among African American women calls for serious consideration of the establishment of a psychiatric diagnostic category called "oppression-reaction disorder due to race and/or gender discrimination."

Discriminatory experiences may vary for subgroups of African American women. Historically, variations in skin tone or complexion have led to differential treatment of Black women in American society whereby dark-skinned women with more obviously African facial features and hair texture have fared less well socially and economically than lighter-skinned women with more-European facial features and hair texture (Keith and Herring 1991). This process of colorism or positive evaluation of light skin has implications for African American women's mental health. Keith and Thompson (chapter 6) found that, compared to lighter-complexioned Black women, those with darker complexions tend to have lower self-esteem, with esteem being lowest for those who are both dark and have low income. Many issues pertaining to colorism and discrimination need to be explored further, including the extent to which childhood socialization messages concerning skin tone and racial discrimination are valuable resources for coping with such experiences (Fischer and Shaw 1999); the relationship between skin tone, the development of racial identity, and mental health; and the links between skin tone, racial hetero-geneity of adult contexts (e.g., work), discrimination, and well-being.

Physical violence is a stressor implicated not only in anxiety disorders among Black women but also in other mental health problems, such as depression. Barbee (chapter 5) documents the low self-esteem and depression that result from domestic violence as well as reports of women self-medicating to the point that they become negligent of their children. Barbee also discusses other forms of violence, including childhood sexual abuse, verbal sexual abuse in public places, and the symbolic forms of violence found in hip-hop music. She argues that violence against African American women is rooted in stereo-typical myths about Black women's nature and the tendency to devalue them as victims. Violence against Black women is tacitly supported by institutional and cultural practices, and it poses its greatest threat to mental health because African American women are encouraged to keep silent. The internalization of stressful experiences is thought to explain, in part, why women have higher levels of depression than men do.

Several of the contributors to this volume touch upon how social statuses and their accompanying roles affect the mental health of African American women. A common theme resounding in several of the studies is that the relationship between mental health and role occupancy and/or role strains is conditioned by economic consideration. Tucker (chapter 7), for example, found that poverty had a much stronger effect on distress than relationship status (i.e., married, cohabiting, divorced/separated, never married) did, and that Black male unemployment had a significant impact on women's life satisfaction. Tucker argues that maintaining intimate relationships is a chal-lenge for African American women because they must cope with compromised male provider roles that stem from racism and because they are often expected to sacrifice their own emotional needs to the egos of Black men. A. P. Jackson's (chapter 8) findings may reflect the kind of emotional sacrifices to which Tucker alludes. Unemployed single mothers were more likely to be depressed when the father could not provide financial support and had limited contact with the child, even when the mother's own relationship with the father was satisfactory. P. B. Jackson (chapter 9) provides some additional insights on the importance of financial status to intimate relationships with her finding that family income is important to the well-being of both Black and White wives, but for different reasons. For African American wives, money affects psychological well-being by reducing marital conflict, while money affects the well-being of White wives by increasing self-esteem.

Two chapters in this volume shed light on work and mental health among African American women. Riley and Keith (chapter 10) find that employed Black women have higher levels of life satisfaction, mainly attributable to poorer health among those not in the labor force. Work, they note, is not without problems. African American women who are employed in jobs over which they exert little control and those with low job satisfaction are less satisfied with their lives. Echoing Tucker and P. B. Jackson, these researchers find that financial satisfaction plays the most influential role in determining global life satisfaction among Black women. A. P. Jackson (chapter 8) further supports the significance of employment for African American women. In her study of the impact of nonresident fathers on the well-being of low-income mothers, she finds that employment offers psychological advantages, even when the jobs offer low wages.

A major research question in the mental health literature is the extent to which multiple social roles enhance mental health or have detrimental effects on it. Brown and Cochran (chapter 11) find that midlife African American women who engage in more than one social role tend to experience fewer depressive symptoms, perhaps because the demands of one role are offset by those of another. Being employed and being a volunteer are emotionally rewarding roles in this group of women, but the authors note that midlife and older African American women often have less opportunity to be employed because poor physical health compels them to withdraw from the labor force. As Brown and Cochran acknowledge, role quality is just as important as role occupancy in understanding African American women's mental health. Greater exploration of role quality and mental health among African American women is needed, along with a comprehensive investigation of how stressful social roles interact to affect well-being. Fruitful investigations might assess the impact of parental strains in the context of problematic versus non-problematic romantic relationships or evaluate the impact of parental strains if Black women are unemployed or employed in jobs with little autonomy.

IN OUR RIGHT MINDS:
SPIRITUALITY AND HELPING HANDS

Several chapters in this volume explore how religious involvement and support from family and friends help Black women cope with problems and get on with life, a process often referred to in African American communities as "making it." Lincoln and Chatters (chapter 12) find that nonorganizational religious involvement (e.g., reading religious books, watching and listening to religious programs, praying frequently) has a positive effect on well-being. They also find a positive relationship between stress and religious involvement, suggesting that women use private religious practices to cope with stressors. As Lincoln and Chatters point out, it is not clear whether these religious practices benefit Black women because they provide a framework for interpreting and making sense of events or because they instill a positive sense of self. It is clear, however, that this coping strategy is effective. Black women who pray and read religious material have a psychological advantage over those who do not.

Historically, family and friend networks have been critical to the survival of the African American community, providing emotional comfort, financial assistance, and a mutual exchange of services. In this volume, Gray and Keith (chapter 13) report that African American women who have loving and caring family and friends (i.e., emotional support) have fewer depressive symptoms. Supplementing the results from the Lincoln and Chatters study, the authors also report that church attendance and participation in other organizations reduce depressive symptoms. Both emotional support and social participation are especially protective of mental health among women who are experiencing chronic financial strain, having a stress-buffering effect. Gray and Keith, however, also find that problematic relationships with family and friends are detrimental to mental health, although the effects of financial strain are not intensified by such relationships. Exploring further the double-edged sword of social networks, these authors conclude that balance or symmetry between supportive and problematic relationships with family and friends is more important than either is alone. As relationships move toward a more positive balance, depressive symptoms decline. This topic needs further consideration given that African American women are often embedded in complex networks consisting of both immediate and extended family; it would also be most enlightening to extend this line of research to work settings. Friendships with other African American women are of special significance (Denton 1990). The friendship networks and supportive relationships of African American women vary by socioeconomic status, marital status, parental status, and over the life course. Research is needed to fully explicate how these variations heighten or diminish risk for mental illness and psychological distress. Do these relationships become more or less operative as women enter and exit social roles?

Traditionally, African American women have been reluctant to seek help when they are experiencing emotional problems, and Caldwell (chapter 14) finds that this remains the case. In her study, slightly more than a third of Black women who report a distressing problem in the past month say that they sought assistance. Consistent with past research, Caldwell also finds that African American women most frequently seek out ministers, followed by private therapists and community mental health centers. She also finds that the overwhelming majority of women in her study have health insurance, so financial access to mental health services is not a major barrier, although her study did not examine the institutional obstacles and provider limitations placed on the use of mental health services. Instead, she hypothesizes that "trust" may explain why African American women turn to ministers more often than to private therapists or other mental health specialists. Caldwell raises two weighty issues: Are ministers and the Black church in general equipped to handle emotional problems? Are ministers a barrier to or a facilitator of the entry of African American women into the mental health specialty sector? Caldwell discusses some of the many unanswered questions regarding help-seeking by Black women, including the extent to which it is possible for ministers and the specialty mental health service sector to work together to meet the mental health needs of this group. This would be an interesting question to explore in a demonstration project, accompanied by a stringent evaluation of effectiveness. Additional research is also needed on pathways to care that may incorporate ministers, network members, and community norms as well as allowing for the probability that these factors are likely to vary by illness episode (Pescosolido and Boyer 1999).

PREVENTION AND TREATMENT FOR AFRICAN AMERICAN WOMEN

The most effective strategy for preventing mental health problems among African American women is to address the larger structural forces that affect their lives—sexism, racism, and economic position. Since this kind of societal-level restructuring is not on the horizon, mental health prevention must focus on approaches that help women to overcome or cope with the consequences of these structural forces. Gibbs and Fuery (1994) advocate an empowerment model that focuses on developing Black women's social competencies, which are often thwarted because of structural barriers and lack of resources. They suggest that competency can be strengthened through the Black church and through Black women's community and voluntary organizations, which can be called upon to assist women with such tasks as parenting, resolving relationship disputes, negotiating work-related problems, and reducing overall stress.

Many researchers and mental health service providers contend that the treatment of African American women, and minority group members generally, must be culturally sensitive to the experiences of these consumer groups. To achieve this end, Takeuchi, Uehara, and Maramba (1999) note that one recommendation is to increase the cultural competence of mental health service agencies either through staff training or by employing ethnic minorities. Another recommendation is to develop culturally sensitive programs. Sue and colleagues (1991) demonstrated the efficacy of ethnic and language matching in a large multicultural study. Matching decreased dropout and increased the number of sessions attended. Some preliminary data also indicate that ethnic-specific programs increase utilization (Takeuchi, Uehara, and Maramba 1999). Yet, as these researchers note, biological models of mental disorders that make the unwarranted assumption that psychiatric symptoms are universally distributed mitigate against such an approach. Assuming uniformity in cultural values and beliefs without allowing for within-group diversity is also problematic.

As both women and members of a racial minority group, African American women need programs that are both gender and culturally sensitive and that are attentive to the continuum of mental health problems outlined in chapter 2. Further, these programs should be stringently evaluated to determine a set of best practices. Greene (1996), commenting on psychotherapy, observes that African American women often enter treatment unaware that they have internalized racist and gender stereotypes and believing that coming to therapy is an expression of weakness. Green also argues that therapists must be willing to discuss the issue of race openly when it is appropriate to do so and that therapists must be able to acknowledge and validate the client's perception of discrimination and oppression. For African American women, the freedom to explore such issues, whether or not the therapist is of the same race, is vital for the therapeutic process.

CASTING A WIDER NET

Noting at the outset that an exhaustive treatment of the mental health experiences of African American women could not be presented in a single volume, we end this project by briefly discussing several groups that are deserving of more attention. First, adolescent Black girls are an important group because many of the mental health issues covered in this book begin in the preteen and teen years. In adolescence, African American girls become concerned with body image and issues of attractiveness (Rierdan and Koff

1997), which can be sources of stress. Emotional problems in teens have been linked to other stressors, including parental alcoholism (Rodney and Mupier 1999), perceived family economic hardship (McLoyd et al. 1994), and exposure to violence and victimization (Moses 1999). Because African American adolescents are more likely to be poor, their exposure to such stressors is greater. Documenting the various types of coping skills used by adolescents and how these skills are developed is salient for understanding how stress is managed across the life course.

Midlife and older African American women also face age-related problems that may have a strong bearing on their mental well-being. Many researchers agree that menopausal symptoms such as mood swings, hot flashes, and weight gain are distressing for some women. Recent findings of racial differences in attitudes toward menopause has led to speculation that this life transition is experienced differently by African American women, perhaps because of unique cultural beliefs and practices (Rousseau and McCool 1997). If this is the case, it is likely that the prevalence and nature of menopausal-related mental problems differ for African American and White women, a possibility that should be investigated more extensively. A recurring finding in the literature is the association between physical health and depressive symptoms. Chronic conditions such as hypertension, diabetes, arthritis, and cardiovascular disease are significantly more common among African American women than among their White counterparts, as is obesity, a major risk factor for cardiovascular disease that has also been linked to depressed mood (Siegel, Yancy, and McCarthy 2000). An important question to be asked is, Do physical health problems and poor health behaviors such as overeating affect mood, or is the causal order reversed?

African American mothers, childless women, lesbians, and immigrant women may experience unique stressors and risk factors. A disproportionate number of African American mothers find themselves and their children trapped in violent neighborhoods, and many of them see their children gunned down, assaulted, or succumbing to violent behavior or drug abuse. The strong link between femininity and motherhood may influence some women to question their adequacy as women, which may in turn lead to feelings of low self-esteem and worthlessness. Childlessness, whether involuntary or voluntary, may have implications for relationships with intimate partners, parents, and extended kin. Spouses/partners may abandon the relationship, parents may constantly express longing for grandchildren, and women may be compared to the sister or cousin who appears to have the "perfect" family. With so much pressure, many women without children perceive that they are being judged and somehow do not measure up. Moreover, African American women who experience involuntary childlessness may not have the financial resources to seek treatment for infertility. Lesbian women remain a stigmatized group over- all, and African American lesbians experience not only negative mental health consequences associated with the triangulation of race, gender, and class but also the additional consequences associated with sexual identity. Black les- bians, therefore, face many unique stressors. Rejection by family, friends, and coworkers may leave them without the social support needed to buffer these stressors. Traditional institutional supports such as church and other social organizations may also be unavailable to them. Clearly, many other subgroups of African American women merit special consideration. Migrant women must cope with the stressors associated with acculturation, such as language diffi- culties and a clash of values between their countries of origin and U.S. culture (e.g., traditional versus modern gender roles). Many of them may experience racial discrimination for the first time upon migrating to this country.

   This volume brings together data culled from a variety of sources to elaborate on African American women's mental health, but it presents one overarching theme. A simple dichotomy of strength versus vulnerability is counterpro- ductive for capturing the diversity and complexities of Black women's lives as they affect emotional well-being. Collectively, the analyses in this volume point to the heterogeneity found among African American women and instruct us that this heterogeneity produces an amalgamation of strengths and vulner- abilities that culminate in differential risk profiles for mental health problems. We urge researchers, policymakers, and advocates to continue to be mindful of these complexities.

REFERENCES

Adebimpe, V. 1994. Race, racism, and epidemiological surveys. *Hospital and Com- munity Psychiatry* 45:27–31.

Aneshensel, C. S. and C. A. Sucoff. 1996. The neighborhood context of adolescent mental health. *Journal of Health and Social Behavior* 37:293–310.

Baker, F. M. 2001. Diagnosing depression in African Americans. *Community Mental Health Journal* 37:31–38.

Blazer, D. G., J. C. Hays, and M. E. Salive. 1996. Factors associated with paranoid symptoms in a community sample of older adults. *Gerontologist* 36 (1): 70–75.

Cutrona, C., D. Russell, R. Hessling, P. A. Brown, and V. Murry. 2000. Direct and moderating effects of community context on the psychological well-being of African American women. *Journal of Personality and Social Psychology* 79:1088–1011.

Denton, T. C. 1990. Bonding and supportive relationships among Black professional women: Rituals of restoration. *Journal of Organizational Behavior* 11:447–457.

Fischer, A. R. and C. M. Shaw. 1999. African Americans' mental health and perceptions of racist discrimination: The moderating effects of racial socialization experiences and self-esteem. *Journal of Counseling Psychology* 46:395–407.

Gallo, J. J., L. Cooper-Patrick, and S. Lesikar. 1998. Depressive symptoms of Whites and African Americans aged 60 and older. *Journal of Gerontology: Psychological Sciences* 53B:P277–P286.

Gibbs, J. T. and D. Fuery. 1994. Mental health and well-being of Black women: Towards strategies of empowerment. *American Journal of Community Psychology* 22:559–582.

Greene, B.. 1996. African-American Women: Considering Diverse Identities and Societal Barriers in Psychotherapy. In Sechzer, J. A., S. M. Pfafflin, F. L. Denmark, A. Griffin, and S. J. Blumenthal, eds., *Annals of the New York Academy of Sciences* 789:191–209. New York: New York Academy of Sciences.

Keith, V. M. and C. Herring. 1991. Skin tone and stratification in the Black community. *American Journal of Sociology* 97:760–778.

Kendler, K. S., A. C. Heath, M. C. Neal, R. C. Kessler, and L. J. Eaves. 1993. Alcoholism and major depression in women: A twin study of the causes of comorbidity. *Archives of General Psychiatry* 50:690–698.

Kessler, R. and W. J. Magee. 1994a. Childhood family violence and adult recurrent depression. *Journal of Health and Social Behavior* 35:13–27.

———. 1994b. The Disaggregation of Vulnerability to Depression as a Function of the Determinants of Onset and Recurrence. In W. Avison and I. H. Gotlib, eds., *Stress and Mental Health: Contemporary Issues and Prospects for the Future*, 239–258. New York: Plenum.

Kessler, R. and S. Zhao. 1999. The Prevalence of Mental Illness. In Allan V. Horwitz and Teresa L. Scheid, eds., *A Handbook for the Study of Mental Health: Social Contexts, Theories, and Systems*, 58–78. New York: Cambridge University Press.

McLoyd, V. C., T. E. Jayaratne, R. Ceballo, and J. Borquez. 1994. Unemployment and work interruption among African American single mothers: Effects on parenting and adolescent socioemotional functioning. *Child Development* 65:562–589.

Moses, A.. 1999. Exposure to violence, depression, and hostility in a sample of inner city high school youth. *Journal of Adolescence* 22:21–32.

Neal-Barnett, A. and J. Crowther. 2000. To be female, middle class, anxious, and Black. *Psychology of Women Quarterly* 24:129–136.

Pescosolido, B. A. and C. A. Boyer. 1999. How Do People Come to Use Mental Health Services? Current Knowledge and Changing Perspectives. In A. V. Horwitz and T. L. Scheid, eds., *A Handbook for the Study of Mental Health: Social Contexts, Theories, and Systems*, 392–411. New York: Cambridge University Press.

Rierdan, J. and E. Koff. 1997. Weight, weight-related aspects of body image, and depression in early adolescent girls. *Adolescence* 32:615–624.

Rodney, H. E. and R. Mupier. 1999. The impact of parental alcoholism on self-esteem and depression among African-American adolescents. *Journal of Child and Adolescent Substance Abuse* 83:55–71.

Ross, C. 2000. Neighborhood disadvantage and adult depression. *Journal of Health and Social Behavior* 41:177–187.

Rousseau, M. E. and W. McCool. 1997. The menopausal experience of African American women: Overview and suggestions for research. *Health Care for Women International* 18:233–250.

St. Jean, Y. and J. R. Feagin. 1998. *Double Burden: Black Women and Everyday Racism.* Armonk, N.Y.: M. E. Sharp.

Schulz, A., D. Williams, B. Israel, A. Becker, E. Parker, S. A. James, and J. Jackson. 2000. Unfair treatment, neighborhood effects, and mental health in the Detroit metropolitan area. *Journal of Health and Social Behavior* 41:314–332.

Siegel, J., A. Yancy, and W. McCarthy. 2000. Overweight and depressive symptoms among African-American women. *Preventive Medicine* 31:232–240.

Sue, S., D. Fujino, L.-T. Hu, D. Takeuchi, and N. Zaone. 1991. Community mental health services for ethnic minority groups: A test of the cultural responsiveness hypothesis. *Journal of Consulting and Clinical Psychology* 59:533–540.

Takeuchi, D., E. Uehara, and G. Maramba. 1999. Cultural Diversity and Mental Health Treatment. In A. V. Horwitz and T. L. Scheid, eds., *A Handbook for the Study of Mental Health: Social Contexts, Theories, and Systems,* 550–565. New York: Cambridge University Press.

Thompson, E. E., H. Neighbors, C. Munday, and J. S. Jackson. 1996. Recruitment and retention of African American patients for clinical research: An exploration of response rates in an urban psychiatric hospital. *Journal of Consulting and Clinical Psychology* 64:861–867.

Trierweiler, S. J., H. Neighbors, C. Munday, E. E. Thompson, V. J. Binion, and J. P. Gomez. 2000. Clinician attributions associated with the diagnosis of schizophrenia in African American and non–African American patients. *Journal of Consulting and Clinical Psychology* 68:171–175.

Wells, K., A. Stewart, R. Hays, M. A. Burnam, W. Rogers, M. Daniels, S. Berry, S. Greenfield, and J. Ware. 1989. The functioning and well-being of depressed patients: Results from the medical outcomes study. *Journal of the American Medical Association* 263:914–919.

INDEX

Gates, Henry L., 102

Gelles, R. J., 105, 145

gender: depression and, 34; myths about women, 100–101; sex ratios, 142–143; as social construct, 1–2; stereotypes, 2; violence and, 99–115

gender differences: attractiveness and, 121–123; in marriage, 6; mental health services utilization and, 259; in religious participation, 223–224

genetic factors, 11–12; in depression, 33; depression and, 37; in mental disorders, 29

Gilkes, Cheryl, 9

Giovanni, Nikki, xix

Gottfredson, D. C., 68

grade school environment, 126–128, 131–132

graffiti, 101–102

grandmother role, 209, 210; role overload/conflict and, 212, 213, 214, 216–217

Gray, Beverly, 14, 242–257

Greene, B., 146, 277

Grier, W. H., 24, 139

Hampton, R. L., 105, 145

Hatchett, S, 144

heads of household, 6

health: behaviors, 12–13; depression and, 35, 36–37; depressive symptoms and, 45; employment and, 199; self-efficacy and, 126–128

social class and, 181; in well-being, 10–12

Health and Retirement Study (HRS), 210–211

health care: access to, 12–13; residential status and, 8; substance abuse and, 64, 69–70; underutilization of, 46–47; utilization patterns, 258–274; violence and, 108–110

health insurance, 266, 268

heart disease, 37–38

Herbert, B., 104–105, 106

heroin, 60

Higginbotham, E., 247

hip hop music, 101–102

HIV, 11; depressive symptoms and, 45; sexual assault and, 104; substance abuse and, 64

homicide, 105; substance abuse and, 63

hooks, b., 10, 243

Hopkins Symptom Checklist, 85–86

housework, 144, 204

Hughes, Langston, 192

Hurston, Zora Neale, 191, 192

hypertension, 11, 86

identity: culture and, 8; skin color and, 122–123

immune system, 37–38

imprisonment, 143

income: depression and, 35, 36; depressive symptoms and, 44; effects of racism and sexism on, 4; gap between male and female, 141–142; life satisfaction and, 154, 198–199; marital conflict and, 183, 187–188; marriage and, 141–142, 149, 150–152; mental health services utilization and, 259–260, 268–269; role of men in, 141–142, 143; role overload/conflict and, 211; self-efficacy and, 133; self-esteem and, 185; skin color and, 118, 121, 126–128, 130–131, 132; social class and, 173–174, 176–177, 180; social support and, 249, 250, 252–253. *See also* employment

individual difference approach, 161–162

in-groups, 83

interracial relationships, 146–147

Jackson, Aurora P., 14, 160–172

Jackson, J. S., 14, 83–98

Jackson, Pamela B., 173–190, 284

Jerry McGuire, 177